Baby Milestone

(With 100+ Fun Activities to ~~strate Them)

[12-24 Months]

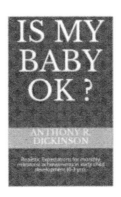

Copyright © 2023, Anthony R, Dickinson.
All rights reserved.

Professional & Educational

Softback Edition - Amazon.com

Also available in Hardback print & Kindle eBook Editions, from Amazon.com

Praise for Dr. Dickinson's "*Baby Milestones" (0-3 Years)*' Book Series:

Fun activities to explore together with your baby, and to demonstrate monthly Expected Milestone Achievements of development, for ages 0-36 Months

"A very well researched and comprehensive guide to participating in the early development of your baby. A hands-on approach that allows you to spend meaningful time with your child and stimulate their mind and body".
Me First ! Design

"The milestones are well laid out, with all the activities and games clearly explained in a consistent easy-to-follow format. My baby loves to play the games with me, especially those involving mirrors, or walking on different surfaces".
Parenting 2.0

"A fun and fascinating read! I love reading up on the activities, [and] the premise of the book that acceptance leads to baby's sense of self efficacy as a teenager. The comparison of baby with baby's previous self is a point well emphasized throughout".
Early Childhood Directors (ECE)

"I am blown away by the volume of work and sheer number of activities that have gone into each volume. Very useful for those looking for a comprehensive guide and lots of ideas for how to test and develop certain skills [in your developing baby]".
ChildLed Play Activities

ψ
Baby Milestones of Development
(With 100+ Fun Activities to Help Demonstrate Them)

[12-24 Months]

Preface

Ideal for use by any parent with an infant baby in the home, exploring activities with friends over coffee, or within a semi-structured playgroup/centre, the original Expected Milestone Achievement (EMA) sets of the *"Is My Baby OK ?"* (IMBO) early child education series presented some of the most distinctive human developmental hallmarks of normally developing babies and growing infants. For each monthly age range (covering a total range from 0-3 years), the full milestone set is comprised of 29 unique 30-item Expected Milestone Achievement lists (with no repeated items across age sets, giving a total of 870 milestones). Each EMA set contains readily observable child developing behaviours which can be determined as easily by baby's parents in the home, as they can by baby playgroups, pre-clinical primary care-givers, professional child trainers and/or educators. The full milestone set covers all the critical early development periods from birth to 3 years (0-36 months), and applies irrespective of whether any given baby-child be attending any structured playgroups or training classes. The complete milestone ability indicator set is divided into 5 domains of easily recordable physical, intellectual, psychological, personal and social achievement baby-infant milestones. Details of the rational, history, design, and the full IMBO-EMA assessment set itself (together with scoring comparisons), has been presented in earlier volumes of the series *"Is My Baby OK ?": Realistic Expectations for monthly milestone achievements in early child development (0-3 years).*

The book that you are currently reading combines the earlier series' reach, and by popular request, each now presents milestone sets covering an extended period of time, together with the most highly commended fun activities specifically designed to afford simple home-demonstrations of the key milestone achievements listed in each. In order to prevent a 1200+ page book experience, this new series comprises 3 volumes, each covering a different 12 month period for parents with babies aged 0-3 years, With a unique milestone set for each month of baby's development (0-12 months for this volume), each listing is then accompanied by a set of unique fun games and activity suggestions for you to enjoy at home alone with your baby(ies), or to enjoy together with friends. Little or no special equipment is needed in setting up most of the games/activities as designed and listed here, most items readily available within modern households and nurseries/learning centres serving parents with young infants. Additional pictorial illustrations (in colour plate for the Kindle edition !) show exemplar items that have been previously created for some of the games/activity suggestions presented, as have been put together in parent's private homes, small baby-toddler groups, and commercial centres, respectively, from around the world.

Anthony R. Dickinson (Dorset, UK, 2023).

Baby Milestones of Development

Contents

Introduction

    Preface   3
    Introduction   5

1. On Having Realistic Expectations   7
2. Individual Baby Variation Across the Age Ranges   10
3. Example Game/Activities Description & Instruction Format   13
4. Developmental Milestones & Fun Games (12 Months)   16
5. 13 Months (Milestones & Fun Games/Activities)   44
6. 14 Months (Milestones & Fun Games/Activities)   73
7. 15 Months (Milestones & Fun Games/Activities)   100
8. 16 Months (Milestones & Fun Games/Activities)   126
9. 17 Months (Milestones & Fun Games/Activities)   153
10. 18 Months (Milestones & Fun Games/Activities)   179
11. 19 Months (Milestones & Fun Games/Activities)   206
12. 20 Months (Milestones & Fun Games/Activities)   233
13. 21 Months (Milestones & Fun Games/Activities)   260
14. 22 Months (Milestones & Fun Games/Activities)   289
15. 23 Months (Milestones & Fun Games/Activities)   316
16. 24 Months (Milestones & Fun Games/Activities)   343
17. Complete Milestone Set Listings (12 - 24 Mths, 1-2 Yrs)   370
18. Author's Afterword   384
19. Tips for the Most Useful Baby Milestone Assessments   385
20. Use of Milestone Observations in Consultancy   388
21. Disclaimer & Appendix (Baby/Infant Psychometrics)   389

Introduction

During the time of my talking with parents at the day nursery of the Psychology Department at the University of Edinburgh 30 years ago, and ever since then when visiting baby-care centres in various countries all over the world, the question most often asked of me has always been, "Is my baby OK ?". My initial response was to encourage the asking parent to simply observe the behaviour of their developing infant child, and to then assess their observations in the light of their *expectations* for their developing child's achievements, given a quick calculation of their child's current age. In so doing, I was forgetting that most parents were not attending my taught courses, nor reading the latest child development journals in their local library, and it wasn't too long before I began to realise why I was so persistently and repeatedly being asked that same question, "Is my baby OK ?". I quickly learned that the parents of newly born babies had begun to pass on their previously used piles of mother & baby pregnancy magazines and books, which had guided them with regular month-by-month pre-natal baby development stages, maternal monitoring information, and other practical advice.

Having finally passed through their average nine-months of conception-to-delivery stages, these same parents were now searching for future monthly signs of their developing baby's *continuing milestone achievement(s)*. Indeed, it was not enough for the parents to now sit back and await the emergence of the classic milestones of their baby's starting to crawl, walk, wean and talk, all of which at first seem to be so far away into the future. What the parents wished to know, and were really *seeking* to learn when asking me "Is my baby OK ?", was rather, "Now our baby is 4 months old [or 2, 6, 10, 14 or 24 months old], how can we be sure that s/he is developing OK ?". *This* was the key information that I was really being asked to provide, whilst also informing them as to some of the key developmental behavioural milestones they might be *looking for* in the weeks immediately before and after each and every month of their baby's ongoing development. As the years have passed, and as my own experience grew in answering the many parents I have since met, from a variety of countries across the world, my list of observable monthly milestones became both longer, and increasingly detailed, at their request. Furthermore, parents' feedback and their many letters have revealed that this same information had frequently helped them to resolve some of their parental anxieties with regards their now knowing *which* of their baby's behaviours were 'normal' at any given age (or not), and thus what exactly they might now realistically *expect* their own developing baby to be capable of demonstrating, and now expect to attain, within any particular age range.

Over the years, I have continued to develop what became known as the "TD-lists" of behavioural-developmental milestones into what are now more formally called the '*Expected Milestone Achievement*' lists (EMAs), having spent 1000s of hours behind two-way mirrors, observing individual baby video-recordings, sharing activities with care-giver/parent-baby dyads, and/or groups of young baby infants playing happily together. My developmental research has now extended far beyond the single nursery, to include data that I have generate whilst working within several countries, and across a wide range of academic university research labs, clinical, and private educational teaching institutions, with whom I have been associated as either academic consultant or professorial teaching faculty.

Presented here in the second of this latest 3-volume set of the 'Is My Baby OK ?" series*, is the 12-monthly period milestone sets for baby's 2nd year of development (0-12, 12-24, & 24-36 months in each, respectively), together with fun ways to help baby demonstrate them. These milestones and activity sets are the result of my many observations of developing children, from birth to age 3+ years, pooled together to provide a single listing of the most easily observable and key developmental behaviour milestones that anyone can see for themselves. Listings of the 30 most commonly visible month-by-month milestones of behavioural development (EMAs) for babies aged 0-2 years are included for *each and every month*, and thereafter for ages 2-3 years for less-frequently spaced monthly intervals [25-26, 27-28, 29-30, 31-32, & 33-36 mths]). This same milestone list has taken the form of a standardised psychometric assessment tool (commonly known as the 'IMBO-EMA' test**), which has also been presented and included in the earlier (especially the 1st) volumes of the East-Asia series*, and thus the scoring sections are omitted here for brevity. Anyone purchasing these books may freely use both the milestone sets and/or activity suggestions for their own purposes without my specific permission (though acknowledgement would be preferred when used commercially), whether used as a parent alone with baby at home, grandparent, care-giver, nanny, pre-clinical practitioner, playgroup organiser, or early child education (ECE) centre professional.

It is my sincere hope that this new 3-vol series format has seen my adequately responding to some of the requests and comments received from parents and users of previous volumes of the series, Please let me know, whether you are using such with your baby(ies) at home alone, with friends, or in a community setting. Photo images of activity materials (with or without baby) are also welcome, and may be considered for inclusion in future updated editions (following your permission to do so). I particularly enjoy reading your feedback with stories which tell of your baby's enjoying the great variety of simple, yet fun activity suggestions which you have found to be of most value in helping you to facilitate baby's demonstration of the target EMA behaviours that you may wish to exercise and explore together.

---

*NB: Referenced parts extracted from: AR. Dickinson, 1st Edition, (2019)
"*Is My Baby OK ?*": *Realistic Expectations for monthly milestone achievements in early child development (0-3 years)*: "Short History of the Milestone Development Set (IMBO-EMA)"

**Comparison of the INBO-EMA with other professional baby/infant psychemetric tests may be found in Appendix A, at the end of this book.

Ψ

- 1 -

Baby Milestones of Development

On Having Realistic Expectations

To love and enjoy one's own baby for who she is, and for what he looks like, for what they DO, and for what they can share, is in my view of critical importance. Indeed, I actively encourage all parents to avoid the temptation to think about what their baby does *not have*, or *cannot yet do*. In my experience, the child who is appreciated for how s/he is, whether they be bright and bouncy, fretful, clumsy, or seemingly slow, can nonetheless continue to grow up with every happiness and with full confidence in themselves. Given a nurturing environment, most babies can develop an optimistic spirit that makes the best of all the abilities that they might possess at any given time, and thus venture forth to approach the many challenges which may come their way, even in the face of possibly severe shortcomings. Alternatively, the baby-infant that has *not* been fully accepted by her/his parents, one who has grown up feeling that s/he "is not quite right", will likely become a toddler-teenager lacking in adequate self-esteem and confidence. Indeed, it is with the development of such self-efficacy and inner-strength with independence for her/himself that, once exploring kindergarten or pre-school, that your 'baby' will then be able to make the most use of their body and brains. This will include all of their still-developing sensory and motor skill integrations, cognitive, intellectual, and social skill sets. But what exactly are the individual developing traits and behaviours one might look *for*, given your baby's particular age, rather than simply looking *at* your baby's behaviour as s/he is developing over time ? …. This is the question that the *"Is My Baby OK ?"* (IMBO) series of books answered.

Some people like to keep a notebook besides their bed, in order to record any dream recall/memory scenarios they may have experienced upon waking, and before they are so quickly lost in the process of beginning to plan and operationalise the day's coming events. Similarly, I strongly advise that every parent of a developing infant keep a pen and notebook/diary in an easily accessible place, for recording as many events occurring as might interest you during this unique and special time. I further suggest that such records include not only baby's sleeping/feeding times and their durations, crying bouts and intensities, or changing facial expressions (for some reason these are the things most of us seem to remember best, or at least choose to talk about !). Be sure to also include your own observations of any/all developments and changes of body and/or behaviour that you may notice, and to do so at the time at which you have noticed such a change (whether real or suspected), before it is forgotten. Even the smallest of details may prove to be of critical importance to have noted down (and dated), for future reference. Include by all means the most visible markers (skin rashes, nappy soiling consistencies relative to feed changes, and ongoing teething developments), but try to also include everyday novel (especially first) achievements that you might have noticed, such as baby's imitation of your/other's postures and vocal expressions, as well as new fine and gross motor skill developments. The monthly milestones listed in this new 3-volume book set, together with the accompanying fun games and activities, afford you the ability to demonstrate most of the target milestones listed for babies aged from birth to 3 months. In contrast to the relatively more homework-like 'recommended activity suggestions' to be found in the original "*Is My Baby OK ? (0-3 yrs)*" book of the series, this (and the other subsequent age-range specific volumes), provide a more structured and formalised step-by-step presentation of some of the most popular fun milestone-focused baby-games and activities, as designed by TD (this author), and ETDZ (the author in collaboration with Elaine Zheng Song-li, one of the world's leading parent-baby activity Master Trainer and training consultants). All of the games and activities included here were specifically designed to facilitate parents being able to demonstrate for themselves, their associated behaviour milestone achievements.

Designed to identify and demonstrate the progressive achievements and abilities of normally-developing children, our latest complete milestone listing has become known as the *Expected Milestone Achievement* (EMA) set, which include behavioural milestones of achievement for babies aged 1 Month, 2 Mths, 3, 4, 5, 6, 7, 8, 9, 10, 11, 12, 13, 14, 15, 16, 17, 18, 19, 20, 21, 22, 23, 24, 25-26, 27-28, 29-30, 31-32, & 33-36 months, inclusively. Each of the 390 (13 x 30) milestones listed in this book have been extracted from the earliest volume of this series *"Is My Baby OK ?": Realistic Expectations for monthly milestone achievements in early child development (0-3 years)*. They have been grouped here, 30 milestones for each of the thirteen monthly-itemised lists, each divided into five major developmental ability-activity areas, with six milestone items listed under each of the 5 different behavioural development domains for each month. For each monthly age range, the final set of expected baby achievement behaviours (total = 1 x 30-item milestone set) has been listed, *without* repeated use of any milestone items across/between the adjacent monthly age sets presented. Not every baby will actually achieve every milestone at exactly the time indicated, *but on average, most babies will do so* (see the next section below for more about realistic expectations regarding individual baby development variations). The milestones are presented in one of five developmental behaviour domains, with 6 milestones listed for each of the five domains, for each month (i.e.,12 months inclusive, giving a total of 390 behaviour developmental milestones for the age range covered by this book). The 5 domains are as follows:

1. *Gross Motor*: Exploring baby-infant's ability to hold posture and control of either their whole body or individual limb movement(s) through space.
2. *Fine Motor:* Enhanced coordination and controlled use of the hands, feet, fingers, eye and facial muscles.
3. *Cognitive Ability*: Developments of purposeful movement, problem solving, planning and creativity.
4. *Communication:* Verbal and non-verbal interaction, language understanding and speech developments.
5. *Socio-personal*: Emotional management, play/sharing, hygiene awareness, and the development of social skills.

Such facilitated observations of baby's behaviours as described in this book will allow parents to become increasingly aware of their child's ability levels' across a wider spectrum of behavioural development than would normally be considered within the home, both according to their baby's current age, and in contrast to similar others (babies of friends & associates). Furthermore, and perhaps more importantly, parents will find themselves to be increasing their observations and interactions with their own baby through regular use of the various milestone-specific games and fun activity ideas suggested in this book. Furthermost, many parents will enjoy learning how to realise that their child is developing according to comparison with their *baby's own earlier self* (instead of simply comparing them to other babies of a similar age). All of this may be easily recorded, and enjoyed, whilst observing the changes in your baby's developing abilities according to their relative domain strengths and weaknesses, as they continue to grow and mature over time.

ψ

Baby Milestones of Development

Individual Baby Variations Across the Age Ranges

Most parents will have learned from a variety of sources, that the average ('normal') time for a baby's independent walking could reasonably be expected to occur at around 12 months of age. However, it does not happen that *every* baby suddenly gets up and starts wandering around the room simply because it is their first birthday !... Indeed, as with any other emerging developmental behaviour, there is a *range of ages* across which any particular baby may be expected to be up and about. For example, the typical range of ages for stable, independent walking behaviour is somewhere between 9 months and 16 months (hence the average ['norm'] given = 12 months). However, whereas about 50% of babies will indeed be up and about on their feet at 12 months, there will be a few who showed stable walking by their 8th month (advanced), and others showing such as late as 1.5 years of age (18 mths = "delayed", but still within long-term 'normal' ability ranges).

One of the most valuable uses that you can make of the milestone set evaluations with your baby, is for you to learn exactly what it is s/he *is* currently capable of, at any given age. In particular, it will always be reassuring for you to know what exactly your baby CAN do, and/or DID do before reaching any given age, rather than persistently worrying about what it is they *cannot yet do*, or *are not currently doing* (according to the milestone listing provided for any given age). Collating such information over time will also provide a valuable record of baby's ongoing achievements with development, and at the very least will help you to know whether, and *what*, to worry about, if anything. Most babies will simply 'catch up' just fine, or show either advanced or delayed development in one domain in any given month, and then perhaps display a quite different profile in another few month's time. *As a general rule of thumb, however, there is little to worry about your baby's not demonstrating one or two of the particular milestone behaviours described for any one of a particular month's five domains each time.*

Comparing the abilities listed in the previous month's milestone set(s) will also help you to determine whether any lack of achievement might be representing simply a 'delay' (e.g., at 1 yrs old: "He's currently 12 months old, but only showing the abilities typical of a 10-month old baby); or is indicating a more significant lack of behaviour suggesting the need for a doctor's visit or other professional's attention (e.g., 3-4 months consistent milestone missing, [or if EMA scoring, achieving results below 2 Standard Deviations of the norm levels, as indicated in the IMBO Scoring tables for any given 3-month age-related EMA sets]).

On the other hand, parents suspecting their more precocious baby to be showing early signs of giftedness, may wish to check their baby's behaviours against milestone demonstrations for later lists beyond the actual age of their child: "She's only 12 months old, but is already showing some of the behaviours expected of a child aged closer to 18-months of age",...... remembering that some 'advanced' developers might also come to demonstrate more 'normal' levels of development in future months, after a series of early growth spurts !

Nonetheless, having now studied 1000s of babies over the course of more than a quarter century, the author's current IMBO-EMA milestone set clearly codifies what most normal babies are capable of, and suggests what the majority of babies *will most probably* DO at any given early age in their development (0-3 years). Such information serves to inform parents' best *expectations* as to which behaviours their baby-infant might normally demonstrate at any of the various ages and stages of their development. Understanding 'what your baby is up to' is the first step in learning how to best get along with them [NB: Indeed, you will quickly learn that you do not need to "keep telling your baby what to do"; ... in fact, you probably would not know 'what instructions to give', say, in order to guide your baby in being able to digest their food, or grow longer arms and legs !]. And although any given baby may develop a particular skill/ability within a range of +/- 1-2 months of any average age-specified milestone, for an otherwise normal baby, only rarely will "delayed" or "slow development" have anything to do with inadequate care or inherited defects, or neglectful parenting (real or imagined).

The *Gross Motor* development domain as used here covers such skills as 'holding the head erect unsupported', and alludes to baby's control of various whole-body movements through space, such as sitting and standing postures, crawling, walking and running. Average ages for attaining these are well documented, and the variations are often greatest amongst babies who are otherwise entirely normal, healthy infants. This is also true of *Fine Motor* developments, including the increasingly controlled use of the fingers, and facial musculature. Indeed, the overwhelming majority (>90%) of babies show some level of relatively slow motor development at some early age, which simply reflects a degree of normal variation seen in this skill type.

A similar situation is seen with much of baby's *Cognitive* and mental skill developments. Indeed, it is particularly important for the parents of a child who seems to be slow in their motor development to know that there is usually very little/no correlation between this observation and developing intelligence. More than 90% of babies showing slow development in their motor development turn out to show normal intelligence levels as measured in later life when attending school.

Variations in different babies' *Socio-personal* and *Communication* skill developments are somewhat more complex in comparison to the other three developmental domains covered by this milestone/activity series. These latter two are further influenced to a greater extent by each individual baby's temperament (e.g., quiet, active, fractious), and their personal interaction experiences (including their history of *opportunities* for socialisation, their variation, frequency and enjoyment of such exposures, etc.). You may remember that, during their first months of life (0-3 months), your baby experienced relatively little contact with the 'outside world', and when 'all was well' (fed, clean, comfortable), baby was perhaps alone, peaceful and quiet, most of the time. As baby moved beyond this period, s/he began to take more (active) notice of the world around them, and when handled with plenty of affection and sensitive firmness, continued to explore the world with a friendly smile and an acceptably placid nature. It is now at these 12-24 month stages that parents be well advised to present themselves as 'role models' for their babies, at all times, remembering that, *although your baby is not always going to 'do as they are told', they certainly ARE going to 'do what you DO' !*

For example, if a mother or father feeling nervous tension is frequently silent when doing something for baby, then it is likely that baby will learn/feel that 'lack of communication', and remain likewise 'within their own shell' [*NB: to avoid this, quietly share with baby what it is you are doing all the while, and why,.. in a soft, loving tone of voice*]. At the other extreme, if the adults of baby's family are forever 'going at each other' (or at baby) too hard or too frequently (e.g., constantly telling one another what to do, giving instructions, making complaints and demands of each other), baby will inevitably feel uncomfortable, and will themselves become *less* responsive or anxious when certain other people are around. [*NB: Instead, demonstrate comfortable affection, trying not to boss or fuss too much*]. If possible, try to encourage socialisation by providing opportunities for baby to be around other babies/children,....but in any event, I strongly suggest that you try to avoid making angry demands, that your baby "Do as I say" (not as I do !), or 'perform' for others, including that they "Say something" to an otherwise expectant listener nearby !

As with the wide range of variations in different baby's temperaments, growth and development rates, remember that there will always be great variation in the responses and attitudes of ourselves as parents, and between other adults, also. These variations fluctuate according to y/our own personal life history, parenting expectations, family circumstances, educational opportunities, and choice of personal study or learning experience(s).

ψ

- 3 -

Baby Milestones of Development

Fun Games/Activity Structure

Activity Description Format

Number = Baby Month -12 (Age). Game/Activity No - "Activity Name"

E.g., for Age = 12 Months: G/A 12.9   "My Favourite Baby Game"

Task description:
- A concise verbal description of game, or type of activity focus. May also include suggestions for your planning one (or as many as five) levels of difficulty, with clues to some of the key approaches/measures which you wish to engage in with your baby/other babies/infants/parents during activity-task play.

Focal Expected Milestone Achievements (EMAs):
- A listing of some target key EMAs (mostly for the current month only) which are relevant to the particular game/activity being described. These behaviours are to be noted for both the individual baby's performance during play and for the monthly formal IMBO-EMA Assessment (if appropriate), but can also prove critical for later review/debriefing/discussion with a relevant professional. The primary target EMAs being born in mind for any particular game/activity are normally written in this section, but subsequent items from the complete listing of EMAs for the current month (or possibly the last or next ?), might also be made visible and noteworthy. For example, you may wish to develop game play adaptations/variations according to the needs of an individual baby's past and current ability and performance level(s). Such additional EMAs and related behaviours as observed during the play session may also be helpful to take note of as incidental (opportunistic) observations of your baby's increasing skill set development as can, and will, be seen to be now occurring, at the same time as those of items included in the target task EMA set for that month.

    For example, the following EMAs might be listed for a game/activity at *end month 12 (say, Game/Activity number 12.9):*

- Turns whole body (rather than just head) to see things behind self   (G6)
- Enjoys exploring object properties (e.g., sinking/floating them in water (Cog2)
- Invites other(s) to engage in shared creative/play activity   (SP6)

[*Where "G6" = use of target EMA 6 (Gross Motor domain), 12rd month, e.g., G/A 12.9]

NB: EMA results will always be useful for facilitating parent/caregiver discussions of task/game/challenge material and experiences – but please do NOT view these as test or exam questions !!... Instead, the EMA results are designed to be used within the natural dialogue of the discussions of baby's development, throughout time, whilst also informing of task level appropriacy, with the purpose of comparing baby's performance/ability growth in contrast to *his/her own earlier self*. The more professional analysis of the full monthly 30-item EMA set (as presented in the 1st volume of the original "Is My Baby OK ?" book series), for each month, is for norm-comparative purposes with a view to determining the same individual baby's performance/abilities relative to others showing normative (and delayed/advanced = +/- 2SD) ages and stages of growth and development.

Materials:
A list of recommended (and/or other optional) materials and sources to be made available in order to carry out the specific game/activity being prepared for play.

- *E.g.,* Sand and/or water bath.

- Different material quality and sizes of small toys (e.g., rubber ducks, building blocks, ping pong balls, spoons/ladles, cups, bowls, and so forth).

Procedure:
Suggested step-by-step procedure for conducting the specific game/task/challenge – this will be especially helpful if preparing a structured delivery to a small class, or having fun with a group of friends gathered with their babies at home. [NB: If preparing games for a small class of parents, consider to demonstrate several of the different level activities, including materials usage, before inviting other parents or guardians/care-givers to begin playing their own game with their babies each time].

- Illustrations of reproducible/printable example materials as appropriate to each game/activity will be shown under 'Materials', and immediately above this section.
- May also include indicants of available pre-made materials for construction.
- May include between 1-5 levels according to level of baby's ability/competence.
- May also include extra tips and activities for consideration whilst preparing play.

Variations:
- A bullet-pointed list of alternative ideas and ways to vary the described games/tasks/activities according to different parent's and baby's individual learning/teaching styles. And/or, more importantly, an individual baby/infant, parent-caregiver/class' learning-style *preferences* or ability levels.

- Activity planners should in no way feel themselves to be restricted to presenting each game/task/activity exactly as TD/ETDZ has designed or presented it in each of the game play suggestion sections included (nor should you feel restricted to only using them for the purpose, and in the way(s), being suggested here !). E.g., modifications to the choice of materials (texture, quality and variety) might also be necessary on order to accommodate the different lifestyle choices and possessions made available within your particular households, and/or to those of different parents-friends/organisations.
- The modified or extendable options included in this section should likewise NOT be considered to be in any way exhaustive, and are only limited by the imagination. It is easy for me to imagine that any one of the age-specific TD' "*Is My Baby OK ?*" game/activity archives would otherwise become a book of several thousand pages long !!
- The true number and extent of variations conductable are likewise limited only by the parent/teacher/clinician/caregiver's imagination, so allowing baby an infinite repetition of individual skill learning without boredom or tiredness !

Additional thoughts/Game-Activity Preparation/Planning Tips:
- This final section of each game/task/activity listing for the parent's planning and preparation, provides a by no means exhaustive listing of some critical ideas and issues to be aware of when planning a particular activity, as part of your baby's overall home or centre-based 'lesson plan'. It is ALWAYS necessary to bear in mind the individual baby's age and stage(s) of development already attained (i.e., their personal history of achievement, but also some general facts about normal baby development), each and every time, but also be sure to allow baby adequate time to 'dine-out' on their success awhile, instead of swiftly moving on to a higher level of difficulty !
- Whether preparing only for yourself and baby at home, or preparing a 'class' for others to enjoy, try to know about the attending baby's learning and developmental history, bearing in mind the particular EMA focus of the game(s) being planned.
- This section also presents some reminders with respect to some key health and safety issues which may arise during the activity play/focus. Independent of the current learning objectives (both short-term and long-term session goals), it is of vital importance to remain fully aware of the condition and dangers of the equipment being used, and the associated putative health risks that might need be warned of/prepared for in the course of their use [e.g., sharp edges/water play/object swallowing].

- 4 -

Baby Milestones of Development

(With 100+ Fun Activities to Help Demonstrate Them)

[Age 12 Months]

ψ

Baby Milestones of Development (0-3 Yrs)

Expected Milestone Achievements
Age = 12 Months (52 Wks)

[Key: e.g., 3 = Game No. 12.3]

Gross Motor

• Makes independent stepping experiments (even short walking)	8
• Shows increasing confidence with balance, and wishing to be mobile	2, 5, 10
• Moves around the room holding onto a variety of objects	8, 11
• Climbs stairs and on to low furniture independently (though not always climbing down again successfully !)	5
• Attempts pushing along/riding on wheeled toys, without help	2, 6, 10
• Turns whole body (rather than just head) to see things behind self	8, 12

Fine Motor

• Maintains grip whilst rotating wrist (e.g., as when attempting to bring a spoon to the mouth)	[M10.4], 9
• More skilled/selective in manipulating shape sorter, buttons or rotary knobs	1
• Stacks objects to form low towers (to then knock down !)	7
• Assembles large, simple insertion puzzle pieces together	1
• Twists/turns small objects and their parts	3, 9
• Draws continuous lines with crayon/pencil (not just scribbling)	4

Cognitive

• Shows simple groupings of classes/categories of objects, puts together in one place	1, 6, 7
• Enjoys exploring object properties (e.g., sinking/floating them in water)	10, 12
• Shows increasingly selective hand use (left or right, though still quite ambidextrous)	4
• Appears to 'read' and turn pages of books, especially if designed with interactive features (e.g., opens/closes flaps, raises pop-ups)	
• Willing and able to reassemble simple objects when taken apart	1, 7
• Produces discrete lines and scribbles with drawing materials	4

Communication

• Changes behaviour in appropriate ways according to sounds and spoken language heard from others (independent of vision)	2, 3
• Points to images of objects/events being described	3
• Showing more appropriate use/imitation of adult language in context (though maybe still without any clear understanding of its meaning ?)	5
• Vocabulary sensitivity significantly increasing (though generates no fluent speech)	8, 11
• Beginning to name objects pointed to by others ("What is x ?","Where is your/my nose ?")	3, 6
• Increasing length of utterances (especially if not interrupted)	

Socio-Personal

• Leads adults (by the hand) towards objects/events of interest	5
• Willing and interested to create and act in fictional 'plays'	11
• Imitates adults, possibly with toy tools, *as they are occurring* (e.g., cleaning, cooking)	9
• Enjoys swinging, and attempts to self-propel using feet when on wheeled toy	2, 6
• Handles/explores objects inside containers, to discover what is inside them	7
• Invites other(s) to engage in shared creative/play activity	4, 12

G/A 12.1 - Fix It In Place !

Task description:
- Exploring the manipulation of like pairs of matched shapes and colours.

Focal Expected Milestones for Month:
- More skilled/selective in manipulating shape sorter, buttons or rotary knobs. (F2)
- Assembles large, simple insertion puzzle pieces, together (Vars 2-3) (F4)
- Shows simple groupings of classes/categories of objects, puts together in one place. (Cog1)
- Willing and able to reassemble objects when taken apart (Cog5)

Materials:
- Mosaic shape boards, Shape sorter.

Procedure:
Level 1
1. Demonstrate three different kinds of shapes from a mosaic shape board, e.g., one with a circular insert, one equilateral triangular, and one of a square.
2. Slowly and gently take out the different insert pieces from the boards, and place them on to the floor/table, naming the different pieces for baby each time.
3. Next, slowly using your middle finger and opposing thumb to pinch the 'handle/knob'/sides of a first piece, gently lift it towards its matching/paired space on its board, then continuing to separately complete each board, one piece at a time (maybe inviting baby to help you to do this each time (if reaching forward ?).
4. Present now the same/similar mosaic shape board to baby, together with the accompanying, separated pieces, inviting baby to pair each piece with its matching insert space.
5. As/when baby succeeds in pairing each space with insert piece 'correctly', provide prompt praise and encouragement as they do so.

Level 2

1-5 Repeat the level 1 steps 1-5, now presenting to baby other boards and/or shape sorters of different sizes (possibly offering pieces to choose from that are of the correct shape, but the *wrong* size for the sorter/board being used !).

Level 3

1-5 Repeat the level 2 steps 1-5, this time presenting baby with boards and/or shape sorters of different colours (possibly offering pieces to choose from that are *of the correct shape, but of both the wrong size and colour* in matching your instruction/request being used each time !).

Variations:

- Provide for baby sets with three different kinds of mosaic shape boards, each with different kind of shapes and sizes of insert pieces, inviting baby to select the most appropriate sizes and shapes to insert. E.g., if circular, the baby must choose the biggest circle, if the triangle, the baby must choose biggest first,..etc,….
- Consider creating very large piece, simple jigsaw puzzles for baby to complete (maybe 3-4 pieces only) which when reconstructed show/form a coloured shape, or familiar picture (even a picture of baby ?, prepare by simply sticking image to cardboard, and cut to puzzle-piece placement shapes with scissors).
- Offer baby the pieces of different shape parts (e.g., inviting baby to form a red circle, when offered the (3-4) pieces of a red circle, but also some of a blue square as distractors).

Additional thoughts/Game-Activity Preparation/Lesson Planning Tips:

- Do not provide all of the mosaic shape boards and pieces to baby at one time, (at least not at first) instead, as baby pairs each piece successfully, provide another set for them to explore each time.
- Try to avoid the temptation to interrupt baby's explorations and/or engagement with pieces (unless trying to eat them !). Instead, *allow baby to pair pieces with sorter/board spaces independently, as far as is possible. Even if "wrong"; Realise that baby needs to experientially discover which they can/cannot put together, then continue to adjust his/her choices, and thus learn from their 'mistakes', an important part of baby's study at this time (rather than simply being 'told what to do' every time !).*
- When preparing the activity materials, be sure to inspect both the mosaic shape board(s), shape sorter(s) and ALL pieces for cleanliness, safety and defective or dangerously edged parts, so helping avoid the scratching/infection of baby's skin.
- Likewise, pay careful attention to avoiding baby taking the triangle or square shape, and with the corner poking themselves (or others) in/near the eyes or surface skin, and cause injury.

G/A 12.2 - Round and About

Task description:
- Exploring the maintenance of self-balance when upset by an external force.

Focal Expected Milestones for Month:
- Shows increasing confidence with balance, and wishing to be mobile   (G2)
- Attempts pushing along/riding on wheeled toys, without help   (G5)
- Changes behaviour in appropriate ways according to sounds   (Comms1)
  and spoken language heard from others (independent of vision).
- Enjoys swinging, and attempts to self-propel using feet when on wheels   (SP4)

Materials:
- Stroller, small roller board/cart, rideable wheeled toy.

Procedure:
Level 1
1. Demonstrate a small board/cart/rideable wheeled toy, showing how to sit on its upper surface whilst using each hand to hold the handle(s)/steering wheel. Then draw baby's attention to using your feet upon the floor to cause the board/cart (and yourself upon it) to slowly rotate full circle, until facing baby once more.
2. Present now the board/cart to baby, situating baby to sit centrally on the board/cart (without legs touching the ground), each hand holding onto some part of the vehicle with firm grip (not just resting the hands/arms upon it).
3. Once comfortable, invite/help baby to revolve (as per your previous demonstration), allowing the baby to feel the need to remain balanced as they do so [NB: *whether or not doing this for the first time, be sure to provide support, noting that baby will 'feel' some discomfort and surprise at the initial loss of balance as the vehicle moves (and passively so, remember, as far as baby is concerned !).*
4. As/when baby gently revolves, each time 'coming back to face you once more', offer encouragement via a pleasantly surprised (or other special facial expression) in attracting baby's attention with reassurance in supporting with continued comfort.

Level 2
1. Following success with the level 1 activity, invite baby to now sit facing centrally on the board/cart/vehicle, this time with their legs touching the ground (if they are long enough !), with each hand holding onto a handle/steering/bar as available.
2. Sit/stand separately nearby them yourself, as you now help baby to revolve/move along (if somewhat jerkily !), letting baby explore/feel how to do so, whilst also remaining upright/balanced [NB: *baby may simply try to move themselves and the vehicle by simply thrusting their body forward at the trunk/upper body, without using their legs/lower body as a lever at all !, at least initially*].
3. Be sure to offer continuous encouragement as appropriate, never scolding if falling or failing to self-propel at this time.

Variations:
- If already competent with self-propelled vehicle use, set up a mini-goal for baby to reach – such as 'parking' their cart under an umbrella, or a small area built by arranging cushions or boxes in a "U-shape" somewhere in the room/on the floor.
- Ditto, organizing a small road/pathway with left and right turns as space allows.
- If conducting the task outdoors, be sure to elaborate/arrange the space with baby's safety from falling/collision in mind at all times (e.g., remaining close enough to be prepared to 'catch' and so break baby's falling to the ground).

Additional thoughts/Game-Activity Preparation/Lesson Planning Tips:
- As/when you are helping baby to rotate or turn, pay attention to the speed of movement being attained by baby+cart/vehicle, *accelerating only gradually according to baby's ability to adapt to their changing stability situation (rebalancing skill); whilst also finally decelerating at a relatively slow rate, so avoiding head injury as baby's cerebrum and cranial development will still remain incomplete at this time.*
- Likewise, pay careful attention to providing suitable cues/smoothness when changing the direction of motion, so helping avoid baby's movement adaptations to one direction then requiring some sudden re-adaptation to another. *Baby needs time to continually adjust and maintain their balance with some necessary delay (which may seem quite a long time to an adult, that's why we enjoy the faster-changng roller-coaster ride !); else baby may become continuously 'dizzy' and/or confused (mainly due to their experiencing visual and kinaesthetic sensory information conflict in real time).*

G/A 12.3 - Finding What I Hear ?

Task description:
- Exploring options for structural change, following verbal instruction.

Focal Expected Milestones for Month:
- Twists and turns (small) objects and their parts   (F2)
- Changes behaviour in appropriate ways according to sounds and   (Comms1)
  spoken language heard from others (independent of vision).
- Points to images of objects/events being described   (Comms2)
- Beginning to name objects pointed to by others ("What is x ?",   (Comms5)
  "Where is your/my nose ?")

Materials:
- Boxes, animal picture cards (e.g., cat, dog, rabbit, duck)
- Object picture cards (e.g., sock, ball, hat, banana, dog, automobile).

Procedure:
Level 1
1. Demonstrate a large (empty) box, to each of its large outer four surfaces (excluding the top & bottom) attaching a different animal picture card (e.g., pre made, or A4 sized printed/magazine pictures: panda, dog, tiger & duck).
2. Slowly rotate the box, presenting each of its four large outer surfaces in turn for baby to see, clearly showing each of the animal pictures in turn.
3. Present now the same prepared box, ask baby now, and at different times, e.g., "Where is the panda ?", inviting baby to change the orientation of the box, so as to be able to show the picture of the panda forwards, for you both to see.
4. As/when baby succeeds hearing/finding/showing the 'correct' animal image as requested each time, provide much praise and encouragement.
5. Continue promptly then to ask a similar question with reference to the next animal image in turn, repeating steps 4-5 as interest and motivation allows (occasionally changing the picture images as necessary).

Level 2

1. Demonstrate a new box, to each of its large outer five (of 6) surfaces attached this time a different object picture card (e.g., sock, ball, hat, banana, automobile).
2. Slowly rotate the box, presenting each of its five pictured outer surfaces in turn, clearly showing each of the object pictures for baby to clearly see.
3. Present now the same box for baby to hold.
4. Ask baby now, at different times, e.g., "Where is the hat ?", inviting baby to change the orientation of their box, so as to be able to show you the picture of the hat forwards. Repeat steps 3-4, as per level 1, providing praise as continuing.

Variations:

- Consider to use any cube-shaped object's surfaces upon which to place each of its six faces a different fruit picture, or pictures of different family members, for baby to search for and /or identify each time.
- Consider also to use the '6' sides of the box for Level 2 (or even more, using the inner surface of the 'bottom', lid flaps etc., !) to offer additional surfaces for image display and baby's search/exploration.
- Ditto, using any variety of objects as card mounts (pegging to furniture/walls, hanging from strings/curtains/coat hangers), at different locations about the room.
- Consider changing the person offering/asking the instructions/questions to baby on different rounds (if such another be present in home/room at the time – or can even try using a telephone from the next room ?).
- For either/both Levels 1-2, consider requesting baby (verbally) to not only show a particular face/object, but also to place their box, showing that face/object forward, in a particular location for all to see (and in a different location each round).

Additional thoughts/Game-Activity Preparation/Lesson Planning Tips:

- The card adhesive chosen for use on the box' surfaces must be both non-toxic and reliable, so avoiding them falling off as the baby rotates them each time.
- However, given that cardboard boxes may not be easily cleaned without damaging if impregnated with adhesive, pay attention to avoiding attaching the picture with any absorbable fluid (unless unlikely to reuse them in the future) – using plastic containers and Blu-tack may help get around this situation arising.
- Remember that *the emphasis for this activity/task's 'behavioural observation/demonstration does* not *target the 'successful' manipulation of the picture box per se, but instead focuses upon baby's ability with listening to someone else's instructions, and baby then demonstrably changing the environment in some way, according to the instruction(s) given to them by that person.*

G/A 12.4 - Mystery Figures !

Task description:
- Exploring the controlled use of drawing materials to deliberate produce increasingly recognisable images.

Focal Expected Milestones for Month:
- Draws continuous lines with crayon/pencil (not just scribbling)   (F6)
- Shows increasingly selective hand use (left or right, though still quite ambidextrous).   (Cog3)
- Produces discrete lines and scribbles with drawing materials   (Cog6)
- Invites other(s) to engage in shared creative/play activity   (SP6)

Materials:
- Water-drawing sheet, water pen/small brush, cup, warm water.
- or,….wax crayon & paper, ……or chalk & small chalk board.

Procedure:
Level 1 [If Water-drawing sheet available]
1. Demonstrate the water-drawing sheet, and a small cup half filled with water.
2. Slowly and clearly show baby the use of one of your index fingers, dipping it first into the cup of water, then taking it out to place it upon the water-drawing sheet, so producing 'magically' a line picture as your finger moves across the sheet, for baby to clearly see.
3. Present next the water-drawing sheet, and a small cup half filled with water for baby to explore, inviting baby to first gently dip their finger(s) into the water in order to use it to then 'paint' pictures as per your demonstration (your holding the cup steady as necessary !).
4. Finally, invite baby to demonstrate/introduce their own picture to you (and/or anyone else present), describing their 'drawing' content, as you then lead/provide baby with much applause and praise as they do so.

Level 2 [If Water-drawing sheet available]

1. Demonstrate now the water-drawing sheet and a waterpen (a plastic tube with felt tip, inside of which has been placed some water only).
2. Slowly and clearly show baby how you hold the water pen (as an adult would any other pen/pencil used for writing); place it next upon the water-drawing sheet, again producing outline pictured drawings (though now with even greater control, in comparison with level 1 above), as you move the pen firmly across the sheet, for baby to clearly see.
3. Present the same water-drawing sheet, and water pen for baby to explore, inviting baby to now 'draw' new pictures of their choice, in the manner just demonstrated.
4. Upon completion, again request baby to introduce his/her work, as you prepare to provide feedback, whilst also expressing praise, admiration and affirmation of their efforts.

Variations: [Especially if no water-drawing sheet be available]
- If the weather is warm outside, consider to use a finger or brush to 'draw' with water outdoors, on a light surface, concrete slabs, paving stones, etc.,.. (though you'll need to be quick with presentations due to fast evaporation of the water into the air (possibly also of great mystery and fascination to baby ? !).
- Present to baby a drawing board (clamped to which is some plain white drawing paper), and a water paint brush or wax pencil. Invite baby to use the pencil/brush on the drawing paper to produce drawings of particular objects.
- Ditto, providing pre-prepared papers with feint line drawings for baby to trace over with crayons.
- Present to baby a mini-sized chalkboard (slate), and a piece of chalk (white would be best for maximum line contrast), inviting baby to then use the chalk on the drawing slate to produce drawings of particular objects.
- Use multiple boards (or the same board) for baby to make copy(ies) of your own simply lines/drawings, taking it in turns to reproduce each other's efforts.

Additional thoughts/Game-Activity Preparation/Lesson Planning Tips:
- If using one of the Water-based drawing schemes proposed, be sure to hold baby's water cup at all times (especially working indoors with the Level 1 activity), so helping avoid spillage of fluids to the room floor or clothing at any time.
- As/when baby is painting pictures, provide encouragement by exhibiting surprise as baby's 'lines' appear on the water sheet/paper/board each time, so increasing baby's interest and enthusiasm for continuing with the activity.
- Be sure to also pay careful attention to preventing baby holding any writing/drawing tools in such a way as to poke themselves (or others) in/close to the eyes or facial areas.

G/A 12.5 - O'er the Hills We Go !

Task description:
- Exploring and manoeuvring about steps and ascending/descending paths.

Focal Expected Milestones for Month:
- Climbing stairs and on to low furniture independently (though not always climbing down again successfully !) (G4)
- Increasing confidence with balance, and wishing to be mobile (G2)
- Showing more appropriate use/imitation of adult language in context (though maybe still without understanding of its meaning ?). (Comms3)
- Leads adults (by the hand) towards objects/events of interest (SP1)

Materials:
- Plastic boxes of increasing size (firm enough to hold baby's weight), or furniture cushions (firm), boxes/cases.

- Large round balls, or Peanut Ball, Baby stroller/cart

Procedure:

Level 1 [construct a stable 'staircase' in the home from boxes/cushions if no stairs]

1. Create within the room a series of 3-4 step climbs/descents using a set of container boxes of increasing size (according to baby's current average weight), either very close to, or against the wall; or use two such sets abreast, one forming a staircase upward, another downwards.
2. Invite/lead baby to stand on the lowest step of one side, and then move to the side, baby to then come towards you, up and over the staircase (or turning at the top if ascending facing the wall) and down again to the lowest level(s) once more.
3. If baby appears reluctance/resistant to climb/descend alone, encourage baby by holding a preferred toy, 'following' in front, as you gently coax baby forwards, guiding baby to climb over the step array in order to gain access to the toy. [*Note, however, that although encouraging movement forward, be sure to hold the toy low to baby's eye level, as they now be looking at thee target toy, and will likely stop looking down at the surface along which they are trying to travel* !].
4. As/when baby succeeds with both ascending and descending the steps, provide baby with much praise and encouragement, allowing them to receive and play with the toy as a reward for their efforts (increasing the number and height of steps in later rounds as appropriate to baby's strength, confidence and abilities with balance control).

Level 2

1. Build now a new and relatively uneven road by placing several cushions, large balls, and/or similar objects next to each other, to create a 'crawling pathway', close/tight up against the wall, with some support at either end to prevent the balls rolling away !! [using either large cushioning (or any other persons who may be present in the room), one standing at each side like supportive book ends !].
2. Invite/lead baby from one side, to crawl from the first cushion/ball across the other 2-3 in order to reach the other side, perhaps again standing at the end point in order to attract baby to come forwards (NB: *again, a conflict here will ensue between baby looking at their hands/surface over which they are moving, whilst also looking at you, distracting but attractively coaxing them forwards*).
3. As/when baby succeeds with crawling along the uneven surface, provide baby with much praise and encouragement, allowing them to receive and play with the toy as a reward for their efforts (increasing the number of balls/cushions to traverse in later rounds, again, as appropriate to baby's strength, confidence and abilities with balance control).

Variations:

- Consider also to use a large-piece of cushioning or a bedding mattress to build uneven sloping pathways, with the beginning and end points using separate cushioning pieces (possibly allowing for changes in direction also); Invite baby to then traverse from their 'beginning point' and to then crawl towards their assigned end point, along a path with varying details over time;

- Increase the number and range of obstacles, heights, slope levels, etc., according to baby's increasing ability level(s) and confidence with maintaining their balance without external support.
- Consider to conduct the exercise out of doors, if suitable equipment be available very close to home.
- If baby is not sufficiently competent with stair ascent/descent at this time, continue to lead baby along 'walk-through' pathways and 'roads' built in the room, using a stroller or cart for baby to hold on to whilst walking along (non-adult supported body).

Additional thoughts/Game-Activity Preparation/Lesson Planning Tips:
- If no stairs be available in the home (or close by, outside the door of the home ?), consider to construct a 3-5 step ascent using smallish, stable, boxes or containers/cases, and/or firm cushioning stacks – sufficiently stable enough to hold baby's weight without crushing/collapsing.
- When establishing the uneven slopes/steps, be sure to construct the materials such as to allow baby to pass along/over/through their (your) chosen pathway as a relatively stable surface. This will help avoid so much increase in effort required by baby to simply maintain their balance, and to thus crawl forwards *without* so much risk of falling over or otherwise injuring themselves. *Remember that, the key learning demonstration objective here is the development with controlled movement over an uneven surface, and not necessarily negotiating a moving surface [i.e., not necessarily walking independently] as such at this time).*
- In the level 1 activity, you may need to encourage/coax baby to go forward quite frequently, or even to face/lean against the wall to provide baby with safekeeping or security (but *do try to resist the temptation to physically hold/support/pull baby along – again, the goal is for baby to learn HOW to do this, and not merely to reach the bottom again safely !!).*
- According to baby's developing skill level(s), increase the number of sloping and uneven pathway segments established about the room, so allowing baby to become familiar (and expert !) with an increasing range of challenges and accomplishments to enjoy overcoming.
- Ditto, making the various uneven roads to be both spacious and relatively far apart from each other; if too narrow, baby will want/tend to place one leg upon the floor, so arriving at their destination without really having gone up or down the slopes/steps of the uneven road at all (!), but instead keep one foot firmly on the floor (the other high on the path's edge contour only, or will even try to crawl along the more open, spacious floor, in order to gain the toy), so ignoring the uneven roadways altogether !).
- After each round of crawling, and if still needing the different toys to attract baby's attention (and/or increase their motivation to move), be sure to provide ample time for baby to enjoy playing with the toy reward once attained (i.e., don't simply take it away from baby once attained,... and then have him/her start again).

G/A 12.6 - BB Delivery for You !

Task description:
- Exploring independent operation of a tethered, wheeled vehicle to deliver items to a new location.

Focal Expected Milestones for Month:
- Attempts pushing along/riding on wheeled toys, without help   (G5)
- Shows simple groupings of classes/categories of objects, puts together   (Cog1) in one place.
- May begin to name objects pointed to by others ("Where is x ?")   (Comms5)
- Enjoys swinging, and attempts to self-propel using feet when on wheeled toy (SP4)

Materials:
- Small roller board, or similar wheeled vehicle

- Boxes, toy fruits and vegetables, baby doll/soft toy.

Procedure:
Level 1
1. Place a baby doll/soft toy along one side/end of the room (target location), and an array of many toy fruits and vegetables in a different location ('pick-up point').
2. Demonstrate the use of a large wheeled vehicle, as you now kneel down to crawl along as you push the vehicle towards the location of the toy fruits and vegetables, and gather some of them to ship for delivery to the baby doll located elsewhere in the room.

3. Present now the same/similar wheeled vehicle, inviting baby to kneel down and crawl along with you in collecting more toy fruits and vegetables, and to then transport them also to the baby doll, as per your previous demonstration.
4. Each time baby succeeds in shipping food to the baby doll, be sure to express "Thank you's" promptly, adding appropriate praise for any additional efforts made by baby each time.

Level 2
1. Demonstrate next a vehicle/roller board, upon which is placed an empty box.
2. Slowly and gently stand up to place the toy fruits and vegetables into the box, using your hands, then deliver the 'box + food' for the baby doll/soft toy to receive.
3. Present the same vehicle/roller board + empty box, inviting baby to kneel down and crawl along with you to collect more toy fruits and vegetables (or bricks), first placing some into their box on the vehicle, and to then 'drive' both box and contents to the baby doll/soft toy as before.
4. Each time baby succeeds in shipping the food to their destination, *and without spillage of any contents from the box*, be sure to express thanks promptly, adding appropriate praise for their deliveries each time.

Variations:
- Consider providing a larger variety of items to transport/deliver each time (e.g., animals to a vet/zoo park, bricks to a construction site).
- Ditto, but selecting only a subset of items (from one category, to be picked out from amongst an array of other distractor objects), to then collect together and deliver only, each time.
- Ditto, plus changing the destination/location/receiving person(s) each time.
- If appropriate to ability/attention level of baby, consider to set up a 'relay' delivery chain – taking the delivery for different legs of a much longer journey, with baby taking care of many smaller parts along a further path, one delivery at each leg.
- Ditto, arranging less 'open' pathways for baby to negotiate/travel along (using large cushions or similar barriers/detours, as pathway direction indicators.

Additional thoughts/Game-Activity Preparation/Lesson Planning Tips:
- As/when the baby is attempting to propel their stroller/trolley/vehicle forward in transporting and delivering their items, baby must maintain a certain balance. This is not only quite difficult for many a baby at this age: *as they are required to also manipulate the wheeled vehicle in a particular direction, baby may easily fall down or even prefer on occasion to travel in the reverse direction ! Be sure to provide encouragement, whilst remaining patient, and, being careful to resist the temptation to physically help baby overcoming any delays/deviations from their targets as they may encounter during each round.*
- During the level 2 explorations, present a box large enough to cover much of the vehicle's upper surface, so allowing baby to grab the box' top edge/border as a handle. Providing its impetus and advancing this way will help baby avoid kneeling, and grasping the wheeled vehicle by the base directly (as it is most likely baby may choose to still crawl to their delivery stations each time).

G/A 12.7 - Sizing Up the Stack

Task description
- Exploring and demonstrating knowledge of relational size differences.

Focal Expected Milestones for Month:
- Stacks objects to form (short) towers (to then knock down !)   (F3)
- Shows simple groupings of classes/categories of objects, to put together (Cog1) in one place.
- Willing and able to reassemble objects when taken apart   (Cog5)
- Handle/explore objects inside containers, to discover what is inside them (SP5)

Materials:
- Plastic stacking/nesting cups, stackable bricks.

Procedure:
Level 1
1. Demonstrate three stacking cups (one large, one medium, and one small), letting baby know (*and letting* you *know whether* they *know*) which is the 'biggest' and 'smallest' of the three.
2. Slowly show now in turn, choosing the biggest first, then choosing the next biggest to place inside the larger one, the latter also placing nested inside the 2nd again, so combining them inside the original (biggest) one to form a 3-level nested set, for baby to clearly see.
3. Present together to baby the same three-sized set of stacking/nesting cups.
4. Invite/guide baby to now assemble the nested cup configuration as per your demonstration.
5. As/when baby succeeds in nesting the three cups in this way, provide prompt praise and encouragement as you ask baby to show their results (including to whomever else may be present at the time).

Level 2
1. Following the level 1 success, present now four-six differently sized, but distinctly nestable cups.
2. Invite baby to next also combine these stackable cups, as before.
3. As/when baby succeeds in achieving their new multiple-nested cups of increasing number, provide baby praise and appropriate applause without delay.

Level 3
1-3. Following success with the level 1-2 procedures only, present now with increasing numbers of differently sized, but distinctly nestable cups each time.

Variations:
- With increasing success with nesting, present similar materials or the same materials to be stacked in different way(s). Demonstrate, then invite baby to use the same/different size orderings to pile up the cups one on top of another in order to forms 1-2 single towers (rather than placing one inside the other, but with the 'largest' cup always being on the bottom/base of the tower each time).
- Present to baby a variety of small nesting/stackable cups, inviting baby to then combine then in any way they wish.
- Ditto, presenting to baby a stackable brick and/or ring set(s), inviting baby to build as higher stacks as possible each time !

Additional thoughts/Activity Preparation/Lesson Planning Tips:
- Before providing/presenting the various plastic stacking/nesting cup sets to baby each time, pay careful attention to your inspection of each and every cup's surface structure, and especially the aperture borders/edges, to ensure that they are smooth, so helping avoid scratching of the baby's delicate skin and lips (NB: cup edges may become jagged/sharp following baby's repeated 'biting' of their rims over time).
- Ditto, ensuring that ALL cups are thoroughly cleaned, sterilised and dried – both before and after use.

G/A 12.8 - Little Houdini Boxes !!

Task description:
- Exploring and planning escape, and routes towards attaining a distant goal.

Focal Expected Milestones for Month:
- Makes independent stepping experiments (even short walking) (G1)
- Moves around the room holding onto a variety objects (G3)
- Turns whole body (rather than just head) to see things behind self (G6)
- Vocabulary sensitivity significantly increasing (though generating no (Comms4) fluent speech).

Materials:
- Various boxes, cushioning, baby's preferred toys (or otherwise attractive object).

Procedure:
Level 1
1. Demonstrate and present to baby an empty box, inviting baby to then be put into standing position *in their box,* possibly requiring you to also hold the box top steady in support, as baby settles in to balancing comfortably in their new position a while.
2. Present now some cushioning pieces, placing them around baby's box in order to to protect them, or at least reduce the probability of the box tipping/falling over.
3. Demonstrate now a preferred/attractive toy, placed at a certain distance on the floor (outside the box) in such a way as to attract baby's attention.
4. Invite baby to now attempt coming out from their box in order to gain their toy.
5. Carefully observe how baby achieves 'escaping' from their 'Little Houdini Box', and the way(s) in which they move themselves around in order to do this.
6. As/when baby succeeds in escaping their box, and then accesses their target toy, without taking help from another, provide prompt praise and some play time for baby to enjoy their success, and newly found freedom !

Level 2
1. Demonstrate and present to baby now another empty, but this time larger box, inviting baby once more into a standing position *in their box,* possibly requiring you to again hold the box top steady in support, as baby settles in to balancing comfortably in their new position a while.

2-6 Repeat steps 2-6 as above, carefully observing how baby achieves 'escaping' from increasingly, and then significantly larger boxes, as they move themselves around in order to do this.

Variations:
- Demonstrate a small box 'camp', spreading around about it some cushioning, both inside and outside the upper edges. Place baby inside the 'camp' area, scattering several different kinds of toy outside the 'camp', all around at a certain visible distance, so attracting baby to come out from the camp interior to collect them. Observe *how* baby selects to then come out to gain the toys for themselves.

Additional thoughts/Game-Activity Preparation/Lesson Planning Tips:
- Be sure to spread out the cushioning about the crawling areas, for baby's increased protection and security, so helping with building confidence.
- When egressing the box, ensure that you are always on hand/close by in order to hold baby's box steady, so helping prevent baby from falling out/over from their box. *As baby's whole body movement will cause their centre of gravity to shift, this will often result in the inclining of the box, even reverse tipping, and thus baby may become thrown down (as their legs will unlikely be long enough to reach the floor when astride the edge – especially when trying to 'escape' from a larger box in this way).*
- If not wishing to reuse any relatively large box(es) being used – consider to also cut away an openable 'doorway' that baby may be able to 'find' and escape by (also later usable as a baby hideout, or doll's house when turned upside-down !).
- When baby gains their toy each time, allow baby sufficient time to enjoy their success before taking it from them to begin a next round.
- Ditto, considering to replace the motivation toy with time, so keeping baby's attention, and desire to 'escape' their Little Houdini Box before 'time is up' !.

G/A 12.9 - Scooping It Up !

Task description:
- Exploring controlled use of manual tool use, with some purpose.

Focal Expected Milestones for Month:
- Maintains grip whilst rotating wrist (e.g., as when attempting to   (F1)
    bring a spoon to the mouth).
- Twists and turns small objects and their parts   (F5)
- Imitates adults, possibly with toy tools, *as they are occurring*   (SP3)
    (e.g., cleaning, cooking, eating).

Materials:
- Soup spoon/ladle, boxes, small plastic handled bucket/pan (light in wt)
- Ping pong balls, bells or ball, bowl.

Procedure:
Level 1
1. Demonstrate two boxes, one empty, the other containing 6-8 ping pong balls.
2. Slowly and carefully show how to use a soup spoon/ladle to scoop up a ping pong ball, then holding it up for baby to clearly see, then placing it into the empty box.
3. Presenting the spoon, invite now baby to attempt scooping up a ping pong ball for themselves.
4. As/when baby succeeds to scoop up a ping pong ball using their spoon/ladle, *and* then places it into the empty box without dropping it first to the floor, provide prompt praise and encouragement.
5. Repeat step 4 adding additional ping pong balls with success, counting off the number of balls in baby's box from time to time.

Level 2
1. Demonstrate next two plastic bowls to baby, one empty, the other containing some small bells, showing how to use this time a small long-handled bucket/pan (or simply the same spoon/ladle as before) to transfer the bell(s) between the two bowls.

2. Present to baby the small long-handled bucket/pan, inviting baby to 'scoop' up the bell from the bowl, and transfer it into their bucket.
3. As/when baby succeeds to scoop up the bell(s) using their pan/spoon/ladle, and then places it into their bucket, without dropping it first to the floor, provide prompt praise and encouragement for their efforts.

Variations:
- Present to baby a bowl of Wheet Cheerios (or similar cereal prepared solely for this purpose), or small fresh fruit pieces; Invite baby to then feed themselves (or to feed you ?) with the spoon/ladle, and to then eat together.
- Adjust the distance/height between the two vessels in order to either increase or reduce the level of difficulty at this stage.
- Ditto, adjusting the distance/height between the two bowls, and/or between the bowls and baby, respectively.

Additional thoughts/Game-Activity Preparation/Lesson Planning Tips:
- When providing for baby the small items to be transferred, be sure to pay attention to preventing baby from placing any of the tools/objects into their mouth (unless foodstuffs are provided for the purpose of eating), so helping avoid any choking or swallowing danger.
- If using plastic products, take the time to inspect all materials for signs of damage or breakability, signs of slight defects etc, so lessening the risk of scratching baby's skin.
- Ditto, ensuring that ALL bowls/spoons/ladles are thoroughly cleaned, sterilised and dried - both before and after use.

G/A 12.10 - Play in Motion !

Task description:
- Exploring the interactive movements of mobile objects for learning and fun.

Focal Expected Milestones for Month:
- Shows increasing confidence with balance, and wishing to be mobile (G2)
- Attempts pushing along/riding on wheeled toys, without help (G5)
- Enjoys exploring object properties (sinking/floating them in water) [Var2] (Cog2)

Materials:
- Variously shaped and sized balls, baby trolley, stroller.

Procedure:
Level 1
1. Demonstrate a baby trolley or stroller.
2. Gently push against the trolley/stroller, causing it to move forward, for baby to see,
3. Invite/lead baby to now stand at one side of the room, then presenting baby full charge of the stroller/trolley's movement.
4. At all times under your protection, encourage/guide baby to push the stroller/trolley, causing it to move slowly forwards along the floor.
5. As/when baby continues to succeed in providing a sufficient impetus to cause the vehicle to advance, provide continuous and prompt praise, so motivating baby to continue moving along for a greater distance.

Level 2
1. Invite baby to next stand on one side of the room, as you present a large ball.
2. Invite/guide baby to push/roll the large ball forwards, towards the centre of the room.
3. As/when baby can supply a steady impetus to cause the large ball to advance, provide appropriate encouragement and prompt praise with controlled success.

Variations:
- Provide baby with a peanut ball or large teddy bear, inviting baby to walk it forwards.
- Consider to set up a small warm water bath for baby to 'push along' the surface a light plastic ball or duck.
- Provide baby with a small trolley, inviting baby to use the vehicle to collect and/or deliver objects, to various stated locations each time.

Additional thoughts/Game-Activity Preparation/Lesson Planning Tips:
- When baby is working to provide sufficient impetus to an object in order to cause its advancing movement (hopefully with increasing amounts of control !), provide a certain amount of protection, remaining by baby's side at all times, but WITHOUT maintaining physical contact unless necessary in preventing/softening a fall.
- Especially when walking supported unsteadily, you may need to help impel the mobile objects together with baby, possibly even letting baby follow you to go forward together at the early stages of learning this level of controlled movement of such moving objects.

Baby Milestones of Development (0-3 Yrs)

G/A 12.11 - Rhythm and Speech Together

Task description:
- Exploring rhythmic and proto-speech during interactions with others.

Focal Expected Milestones for Month:
- Moves around the room holding onto a variety of objects   (G3)
- Vocabulary sensitivity significantly increasing (though generates   (Comms4)
  no fluent speech).
- Willing and interested to create and act in fictional 'plays'   (SP2)

Materials:
- Large ball, small ball, baby doll/soft toy, cushions.

Procedure:
Level 1
1. Demonstrate a cushion and a baby doll/soft toy, positioning the baby doll/toy to be sat upon a cushion, both legs straight out in front, on your lap/legs, as you use both hands to hold the doll/toys' armpits/forelegs to provide it support.
1. Situate baby to now sit as just shown, upon your two legs/lap, as was the doll/toy in your demonstration (maybe having baby now hold the doll/toy also ?).
3. Once settled in this way, begin to narrate a rhythmic nursery song, whilst simultaneously bouncing up and down a springing knee, baby now moving along with the same springing movements of the rhythm. At the end of the last phrase, gently opening both legs, baby now sitting directly on the cushion floor beneath: e.g., "The/black/hen/is/under/the/egg, the/black/hen/is/under/the/egg, cluck/cluck, cluck/cluck, cluck/cluck", (opening both legs for still held baby to gently fall !).
4. As/when you begin to follow your rhythm together, with high and low springing knees, finally rest with baby sat suddenly on the cushion/floor, (and maybe after repeating a few times) baby will be very happy and smiling once able to predict the coming 'fall' time. [consider slowing down/pause just prior to the fall, to test].
5. Continue to start the rhyme again, narrating out loud the nursery song. Lead making of the movements, the baby also studying the variations in the same

nursery song's delivery, so coming to better predict, anticipate (and thus enjoy) the falling time to the floor with increasing experience.

Level 2
1. Demonstrate and present next to baby a large ball, inviting/hugging baby to sit down upon it.
2. Encourage comfort and stability by using both your hands to hold baby's armpit in supporting their balance as baby sits upon the large ball, gently bouncing them up and down according to the rhythm of the song/rhyme you wish to use.
3. Upon reaching the concluding phrase of the rhythm, again pick up baby, and place them suddenly, but gently on to the floor, wherever you are at the time.

Variations:
- Present to baby a peanut ball (other largish ball, or baby bouncer/rocking horse as may be available), inviting/positioning baby seated across it (with one leg either side of it), both you and baby face-to-face, hands in hands, swing side to side according to the "swing of a rhythmic song", each time inclining to one side or the other, letting baby's foot make contact with the floor each time.

- Ditto, letting baby sit facing you on the floor, kneeling on your own legs/knees, whilst singing out a rhythmic rhyming song.
- Ditto, using a gentle (and secure) swing apparatus.

Additional thoughts/Game-Activity Preparation/Lesson Planning Tips:
- As/when you have only just started to lead baby to make the rhythm, be sure to have them only 'slowly' open their legs for the first few times, baby falling onto soft cushions, their otherwise receiving too sudden a shock/fright. After treating baby in this way safely, and with resettled comfort a few times, their becoming able to anticipate/predict the (by then) familiar postural change, you may begin to behave more 'normally', as you would with an older child.
- Likewise in the case of disembarking from a relatively large peanut or other ball, gently lift baby from the ball up high into the air (still in rhythm to the song) before coming fully down to the ground to rest, only once baby becomes more able to anticipate/predict the familiar postural changes to be experienced, only slowly over time, behaving in a less exaggerated manner.

G/A 12.12 - Gone Fishin' !

Task description:
- Exploring shared water play, floating, sinking and fishing for different objects.

Focal Expected Milestones for Month:
- Turns whole body (rather than just head) to see things behind self (G6)
- Enjoys exploring object properties (e.g., sinking/floating them in water (Cog2)
- Invites other(s) to engage in shared creative/play activity (SP6)

Materials:
- Sand and/or water bath.

- Different material quality and sizes of small toys (e.g., rubber ducks, building blocks, ping pong balls, spoons/ladles, cups, bowls, and so forth).

Procedure:
Level 1
1. Demonstrate a water bath, inside of which is installed some warm water (less than half full).
2. Clearly and slowly now show baby how to insert separately the different toys into/onto the water, letting baby observe the different toy's behaviour/motion once introduced into the water (then removing each of them once more).
3. Invite baby to now come forward and, taking up a different kind toy each time, to place it into the water bath themselves.
4. Encourage baby to be able to observe each toy's state of motion after each placing of the different toys into the water.
5. Once all of the toys are again in the water, provide a summary description of each, e.g., "The duck swims happily in the water", "The ladle/spoon falls/swims slowly to the bottom of the water to rest", and so forth.

Level 2
1. Demonstrate again the water bath, once more partly filled with water, and several different kinds of toys (some floating on the surface, some partly submerged, some sinking to the bottom [small screw-top plastic jars with different amounts of water in them can also be interesting for baby to explore !]).
2. Invite baby to come forward and to this time 'fish out' a pair of assigned objects, encouraging baby to then fish 'for' at least one floating, and one underwater toy each time.
3. As/when baby successfully fishes according to the request for toys made, provide prompt praise and thanks for their 'fishing trophies' collected from the water bath.

Variations:
- Present baby with a transparent plastic box, half-filled with water, and several different kinds of (waterproof) toys, inviting baby first to place each toy in turn into the water, observing those toy's 'different' states of motion, then asking baby to 'fish' for them again as per the level 2 activity.
- As an alternative to water play, provide the same table/tray/box containing a baby-friendly non-toxic modelling clay, sponge, sand, or similar malleable substrate, inviting the baby to play with it freely; Be sure to also pay special attention to preventing baby making contact with their materials and their mouth, eyes or nose, so avoiding any breathing or skin surface danger. Provide also wet wipes and or similar materials sufficient to keep baby's hand promptly clean as necessary.

Additional thoughts/Game-Activity Preparation/Lesson Planning Tips:
- When using the bath (or a water table), be sure to place directly beneath it a large bath towel, so helping mop up any spillage to the floor, and thus help prevent baby's slipping, and/or from falling over (unless you are *in* the bath playing together already !).
- Provide bib and towel for baby to use, after using both their hands to retrieve the toys each time – also drying off the toys promptly each time after getting wet.
- Pay also keen attention to preventing baby from pulling/pushing, or otherwise colliding suddenly with, the water bath, so helping prevent unnecessary spillage.
- Take the time to supervise baby at all times when engaged in water play, especially managing them when baby is enjoying/making an effort to pat/splash the water outside the bath.
- If exploring whilst seated, situate the water source and baby's seat (if not standing) a certain distance apart, so helping avoid accidental collisions between baby and yourself/furnishings when playing with the water objects (or getting them wet).

Baby Milestones of Development (0-3 Yrs)

- If being conducted in the winter months, pay attention to the choice water installation, assuring an anti-drip bath is in use (and/or the leak-proof quality remaining high for any vessels used). Ensure also that the bath has been dried and covered when not in use (so reducing infection transmission risk), whilst also considering to use luke-warm water.
- Ditto, considering instead to use children's modelling clay, or sand.

- 5 -

Baby Milestones of Development

(With 100+ Fun Activities to Help Demonstrate Them)

[Age 13 Months]

ψ

Baby Milestones of Development (0-3 Yrs)

Expected Milestone Achievements
Age = 13 Months

[Key: e.g., 8 = Game No. 13.8]

Gross Motor	
• Bearing own weight unsupported, feet flat on ground most of time	6
• Attempts bending down to pick up dropped items, whilst standing	6, 7, 8
• Attempts walking with less dragging and/or tripping over own toes	8
• If walking, will try walking self-supported with only one hand	7, 8
• Retrieves and returns a ball rolled towards them	
• Successfully negotiates small obstacle courses set up on the floor	
Fine Motor	
• Uses pincer grip to hold objects, even if not looking at them	1, 5, 6
• Picks up, holds, and repositions toys/other objects without dropping them	2, 4, [M14-13.5]
• Uses opposing finger/thumb to pick up (1cm) object on flat surface	11
• Perseveres/continues trying to pick up string/paper after failing to do	10
• Explores page-turning of books and magazines/paper	12
• Points to wanted objects beyond immediate reach	3, 8, 9, 12
Cognitive	
• Retrieves items from small containers by shaking or poking at them	7, 9, [M14-13.5]
• Retrieves visibly-hidden objects without prompting	2, 7
• Recognises self and familiar others in photo/video images	6
• Enjoys generating sound by banging a variety of different objects together	
• Deliberately places multiple objects *into* the same container	3, 5
• Imitates the efforts of others to write, scribble or draw lines	
Communication	
• Follows simple verbal requests, without accompanying gestures	2, 9, 11
• Tries to join in 'singing' simple nursery rhyme actions without imitation (following a verbal request/suggestion to do so)	
• Uses the same double syllable sounds to refer to fewer objects (e.g., bottles, teddy bears and father are no longer *all* referred to as being "dada")	9, 12
• Acquires attention and/or objects in ways other than by simply crying	5, 7, 8
• Shows appropriately controlled head nodding (e.g., to indicate yes/no responses)	4
• Recognises a wider variety of faces and facial expressions	1, 10, 11
Socio-Personal	
• Attentive to distant objects which are being pointed at/to, by others	
• Helps with dressing once clothing is in contact with the body	
• Predicts participation in an increasing number of daily routines	11
• Cleanly releases held objects being passed/handed to another person	1, 11
• Enjoys experimenting with own image in mirror (and with others, if present)	6, 10
• Looks at objects (if present) that are being referred to by others	2, 3, 10

G/A 13.1   Savour Flavours !

Task description:
- Exploring different liquid taste sensations.

Expected Milestone Achievements (EMAs):
- Screws face when not liking novel taste of something   [cf Mth4-F6]
- Associates simple words with particular smells and tastes   [cf Mth10-Comms2]
- Uses pincer grip to hold objects, even if not looking at them   (F1)
- Recognises a wider variety of faces and facial expressions   (Comms6)
- Cleanly releases held objects being passed/handed to another person   (SP4)

Materials:
- Cotton buds (unused), transparent cup, bib
- Clean water (i.e., H2O without flavour), vinegar, soy sauce, brown sugar.

Procedure:
[NB: to prevent taste preference/adaptation, consider 'cleaning' baby's lips/palate after each sample has been tried, and before 'applying' the next].

Level 1 (Sweet Vs Salty)
1. Present two transparent cups, placed in different locations on the floor/table.
2. Dilute clean water in each cup, with soy sauce and brown sugar, respectively, without filling or spilling any fluid from either cup.
3. Demonstrate the use of a clean cotton bud, gently dipping it into the diluted water-sugar mixture to gently wipe a small liquid residue onto you own lip.
4. Continue to next stretch out your tongue and to lick your pursed lips in order to taste the sweet flavour, whilst smiling agreeably for baby to clearly see.
5. Next take the diluted water-sugar mixture, again doping the lip until tasting its flavour as you then place a little gently onto baby's lip (or now guide baby to dip with the cotton bud themselves, and to then taste it).
6 Carefully pay attention to observing baby's facial expression(s), as well as any request s/he may make to continue tasting it (if any).
7 Repeat steps 2-6, using a fresh cotton bud and water to this time demonstrate and test baby's reactions to a weak water+soy sauce mixture. Especially noting any differences in facial response to that shown following the sugar-water sampling.

Level 2 (Salty Vs Sour)
1. Now demonstrate/present clean waters diluted with vinegar, and then soy sauce.
2. Repeat steps 2-7 as per level 1, using the two new flavouring materials.

Level 3 (Salty Vs Neutral)
1. Lastly demonstrate/present one pure water diluted with salt, the other undiluted (i.e., clean water only).
2. Repeat steps 2-7 as per levels 1-2, using the new flavouring material.

Baby Milestones of Development (0-3 Yrs)

Variations:
- If no clean cotton buds are available, try providing baby with a spoon, familiar sucker/dummy or small ladle, inviting baby to 'feed' to taste (with only a very small quantity) each time.
- An alternative taste set could include use of differently coloured fresh fruit juices (orange, lemon, watermelon, etc,..) for baby's sweet, bitter and sour taste response comparison testings.
- NB: *It is quite likely that the smell/appearance of each liquid may well influence your baby's decision to taste (especially if unfamiliar to them). Well before truly 'tasting' each fluid, be sure to pay keen attention to your observing baby's response before, during, and after the presentation of each (having smelled it 1st).*
- Likewise, and to add interest to the experience/experiment, consider adding (non-flavoured) food colouring so as to make sure that baby is NOT simply responding to the liquid's colour each time *[it is TD's view that many of our supposed 'food preferences', are actually visually-associated learned responses to past pleasant/unpleasant experiences !]*.

Additional thoughts/Activity Preparation/Lesson Planning Tips:
- Because babies' organic developmental age is still relatively sensitive, and to avoid kidney burden, the soy sauce and the salt used need only be introduced in very small quantities (e.g., an adult minimal detection [just noticeable] difference limit is probably level sufficient).
- When presenting the liquids and tastings (especially if encouraging self-feeding), provide baby with a small towel, avoiding any liquid overflow or spillage resulting onto baby's clothing or skin becoming wet/stained.
- When using the cotton buds, pay special attention to preventing baby admitting it fully into their mouth, between the lips and thus attempting to eat it !
- Before commencing this activity, be sure to select known safe foods for sampling, such that there be no need for baby to abstain from participation if known to possess any allergenic response to any of the materials being considered for use (say, a variety of different herbs or spices ?).
- To help prevent taste preference/adaptation, consider to 'clean' baby's lips/palate after each sample has been tried, before 'applying' the next one.

G/A 13.2 Mysterious Movements !

Task description:
- Watching/tracking the hiding places of visually mobile objects.

Expected Milestone Achievements (EMAs):
- Picks up, holds, and repositions toys/other objects without dropping them (F2)
- Retrieves visibly-hidden objects without prompting (Cog2)
- Follows simple verbal requests, without accompanying gestures (Comms1)
- Looks at objects (if present) that are being referred to by others (SP6)

Materials:
- Four identical size/shaped bowls (three of which are the same colour)

- Squeaky toys (turtle/duck)

Procedure:

Level 1
1. Show two same coloured bowls, placed upside-down on the floor/table.
2. Demonstrate the sound made by squeezing a small rubber turtle/duck.
3. Move the small turtle/duck slowly, towards, next to, then covered by, the bowl, such that baby can no longer directly see the turtle/duck.
4. Next *slowly* change the bowls' positions (*without lifting them from the surface, and ensuring that baby is watching what it is that you are doing*), one at a time, inviting baby to then look *for* and reveal its (the turtle/duck's) new location.
5. Once 'found' again, offer praise/encouragement, allowing baby ample free time to play with their newly re-found small turtle/duck 'friend'.

Level 2
1. Show three bowls, with one of a dissimilar colour to the other two, again upside-down on the floor/table.
2. Demonstrate the sound made by squeezing the small rubber turtle/duck.
3. Move the small turtle/duck slowly, towards, next to, then covered by the dissimilarly-coloured bowl such that baby can no longer see the turtle/duck.
4. Again now *slowly* change the bowls' positions, one at a time, inviting baby to look *for* and reveal its new location.
5. Once 'found' again, offer praise/encouragement, allowing baby free time to play with their newly re-found small turtle/duck 'friend' once more.

Level 3
1. This time show three bowls of the *same* colour, again upside-down on the floor.
2. Move a new small toy animal slowly, towards, next to, then covered by one of the coloured bowls such that baby can no longer see it
3. *Slowly* change the bowls' positions once more, one at a time, inviting baby to look for its new location.
4. Once 'found' again, offer praise/encouragement, allowing baby free time to play with their newly refound animal 'friend'.

Variations:
- With increasing success, consider to up the difficulty level by moving the bowls around a greater number if times, or at a slightly faster pace.
- Ditto, moving two bowls at the same time, rather than only one at a time; or even to cross your arms over/under when doing so (if baby is getting really good at tracking the target bowl's movements !).

Additional thoughts/Game-Activity Preparation/Lesson Planning Tips:
- Move the bowls around with a timing and speed guaranteed to capture baby's eye (and attentive movement 'action watching' – not simply gaze direction).
- Ensure that the bowls are moved around without being obscured by the (your) arms – from baby's point of view (especially at first, as they develop their tracking skills).
- Change the choice of 'hiding' toy occasionally, in order to maintain baby's interest and curiosity as task repetitions continue.
- When repeating the task (especially in level 3), be sure to *not* place the duck/turtle/toy under the same bowl/location each time – else baby will develop a left/right/centre choice reveal strategy, or use some other cue based upon slight differences in colour/size/staining of the bowls that s/he might be able to detect !!].

G/A 13.3   The Colour Red

Task description:
- Exploring baby's knowledge of different 'red'-coloured objects.

Expected Milestone Achievements (EMAs):
- Points to required wanted objects beyond immediate reach   (F6)
- Shows simple groupings of classes/categories of objects, puts   [M12-Cog1]
  together in one place.
- Deliberately places multiple objects *into* the same container   (Cog5)
- Looks at objects (if present) that are being referred to by others   (SP8)

Materials:
- A variety of red-coloured, but differently shape material objects (e.g., red building blocks, red ribbon, a red circle, red baby-safe modelling clay, a red apple, soft toy, etc).
- Black building block, Green building block; basket/box.

Procedure:
Level 1
1. Demonstrate a basket/box containing a number of small 'red-coloured' toys
2. Select a red building block, clearly demonstrating its appearance to baby, saying, "This is red".
3. Continue to select other red toys in turn, again saying, "This is red" each time, and then placing them on the floor/table in a line, saying each time, "These are all red".
5. Now returning all of the toys to the basket, each time baby receives/sees any of the same toys again, reinforce the association by saying, "This is red".
6. Present now a basket containing red toys for baby to become familiar with.
7. Continue to say, when baby takes up any of the (red) toys from the basket, "This is red", without exception.

Level 2
1. Prepare/show again that your basket/box contains a number of small 'red coloured' and other-coloured toys.
2. Select a red building block, clearly demonstrating its appearance to baby, saying, "This is red" (repeat a few times as for step 3 above).
3. Now select a NON-red building block, shaking your head towards the baby, placing it nearby, but NOT together with the other red objects previously selected.
4. Continue to select other toys in turn, if 'red' say to baby, "This is red", placing them with all the other red objects in a line; placing other *Non-red-coloured* objects in a separate place nearby.
5. Finally, with all of the red toys now placed in a line together, point at them saying, "All of these are red", then reload the basket with all the red objects only.
6. Finally, present the basket now containing both red and non-red toys for baby to explore.

Baby Milestones of Development (0-3 Yrs)

7. Again, each time baby takes up any of the red toys from the basket, say, "This is red" (but only if it truly is !), and do so without exception.
8. Encourage/guide baby to now pass each red toy to their your hand (*but NOT so the non-red items*), promptly praising each 'correct' action.

Variations:
- For baby successfully selecting each kind of colour for the *same* type toy (e.g. building blocks only), provide only one that is red, guiding baby to then select the red one from amongst all the other non-red ones; Next, provide for baby again a similar selection, each of the same kind but different colourations of the same toy (e.g. coloured balls or beads), for further discrimination and practice.

Additional thoughts/Game-Activity Preparation/Lesson Planning Tips:
- The use of red toys (mainly, only) for this session is quite deliberate, and so doing will deepen baby's conceptual understanding of 'redness', and we thus avoid using too many different colours at this stage to prevent baby becoming confused [NB: The issue here is, to facilitate baby to learn that "RED" is a possible, *particular* 'property' *of an object* being referred to, and NOT the name of the object or its objective category, per se].
- If baby repeatedly fails to correctly identify the 'redness' of red objects, frequently encourage baby to identify such target objects in this way, repeatedly.
- Ditto, considering a possible 'red-green' or other possible colour-blindness pairing condition to warrant further investigation.

G/A 13.4   Little Tower Builders

Task description:
- Exploring block stacking, with five-to-seven piece high towers.

Expected Milestone Achievements (EMAs):
- Picks up, holds, and repositions toys/other objects without dropping   (F2)
- Shows simple groupings of classes/categories of objects, together   [M12-Cog1]
- Enjoys seeing effects of own actions (e.g., knocking down brick towers)   [M8-SP1]
- Appropriately controlled head nodding (to indicate yes/no response)   (Comms5)

Materials:
- Variously shaped building blocks (circular, cylindrical, cubes, rectangular, etc.,).

Procedure:
Level 1
1. Demonstrate 5-7 level (same-shaped) building block towers, arranged on the floor.
2. Next, demonstrate building together, creating several tall towers.
3. Present a large enough building block set for baby to build towers to levels and heights below those that you had previously demonstrated (used in step 1).
4. Invite/guide baby now to build (2-5) multi-layer towers, providing baby with frequent encouragement and praise as they do so.
    NB: even at this age – many babies will often enjoy knocking down their towers, more than they enjoy to build them, and may knock them down very quickly after building them, or not build them so high as you may be encouraging them to do !

Level 2
1. Present additional materials sufficient for baby to now build towers of 5-7 piece height levels, as previously demonstrated (level 1, step1), before baby began their own tower building explorations.
2. Invite/guide baby in building increasingly taller towers, providing baby with frequent encouragement and praise as they succeed each time.

Level 3
1. Again present additional materials, so allowing baby to build towers of 5-7 piece height levels, *but this time using bricks of different shapes, and base areas.*
2. Invite/guide baby in building new designs of tall towers, continuing to offer baby frequent encouragement and praise with success.

Level 4
1. Present sufficient materials for baby to again build 5-7 block height towers – this time using blocks with the smallest widths (i.e., tall, but also thin, towers).
2. Invite/guide baby to build such taller buildings, providing baby with frequent encouragement and praise as/when they succeed each time.

Variations:
- For different rounds, consider providing baby with many of the same shaped building blocks only (for example, all are rectangular, or cylinders only), for baby to explore and build with.
- Ditto, considering to use a single block colour (but different shapes) as the defining variable for tower type.
- Encourage cuboid block building rounds for building vertical towers; and other shaped block building rounds for flat, horizontal structures (rather than only 'towers'), guiding baby according to the different instructions given each time.
- Consider providing baby with a variety of safe, non-breakable materials other than building blocks with which to build towers (sandwich boxes, small unopened tins, boxes, shoes, etc).

Additional thoughts/Game-Activity Preparation/Lesson Planning Tips:
- Building blocks chosen for this task/activity would ideally include the use of coloured blocks (*for some*, if not all levels).
- When attempting each first time to build increasingly higher towers, you may need to help baby to straighten their growing building block tower, so aiding baby to realise their progress towards success (otherwise their frustration can result in a loss of task motivation, and/or tendency to keep knocking-down their already growing towers too early !).
- You may also help with assembling/moving the building blocks (ideally by only passing pieces to baby), as doing so this can attract/increase baby's interest to operationally continuing to build towers of increasing heights.
- However, even at this age – *note that many babies will often enjoy knocking down their towers, more than they enjoy to build them, and thus may knock them down very quickly after building them, or not build them so high as you may be encouraging them to do !*

G/A 13.5   Little Water Pumps !

Task description:
- Exploring the transmission of fluids, using a sponge as water holder/carrier.

Expected Milestone Achievements (EMAs):
- Uses pincer grip to hold objects, even if not looking at them (F1)
- Manipulates/explores objects with some purpose (using tools) [M11-Cog]
- Enjoys exploring toy with material transfer [M9-Comms6]
  (e.g., pouring water/sand from cups/buckets).
- Deliberately places multiple objects *into* the same container (Cog5)
- Acquires attention and/or objects in ways other than by simply crying (Comms4)

Materials:
- Small transparent vessels, water, towel, sponge.

Procedure:
Level 1
1. Show a transparent vessel, partially filled with water, and the other materials.
2. Demonstrate how a sponge may be squeezed to change its shape, then loosened in the hand slowly, to resume its original appearance – allowing baby to try same.
3. Next demonstrate water absorption: place the sponge in the vessel with water, allowing the sponge time to absorb water, showing that the sponge can absorb water and release it upon squeezing now, such that the water can be seen to clearly fall back into the vessel (maybe also making a 'drip-drip' sound), so also arousing baby's interest and curiosity.
4. Presenting sufficient material to explore, invite/guide baby to now try the water absorption and release operations for themselves.

Level 2
1. Show next two transparent vessels, only one of which is partially filled with water, the other remaining empty.
2. Demonstrate how the sponge may now be used to both absorb and transfer some water: place the sponge in the vessel with water, allowing the sponge time to absorb water, showing that it can then be gently lifted away from the first vessel and released into the second by squeezing the sponge over/in it, in such a way that the water can be seen to clearly fall into the second (previously empty) vessel.
3   Presenting sufficient materials for baby to explore, invite/guide baby to try the water absorption, transfer and release operations for themselves.

Variations:
- Consider to mix some pale coloured pigments with the water (using vegetable of food colouring, or non-toxic water paint), enabling the water to take on a light colour, showing baby the observable water colour change, *as it happens.*
- Present baby with two transparent vessels, one loaded with a dry sponge, the other with a wet sponge, guiding baby to make contact with the dry sponge first; encouraging baby to then contact/soak up liquid from the wet sponge, thereafter transferring the newly absorbed water to the empty vessel; Finally use both of the dry sponges to absorb water, transferring water with one sponge in each hand, between each vessel in turn.

Additional thoughts/Game-Activity Preparation/Lesson Planning Tips:
- Before allowing baby to play with/near water, ensure that baby is adequately protected re your furnishings, their clothing and exposed body parts, so avoiding the water getting (and keeping !) themselves wet. [Unless already *in* the bath !].
- Clean/dry baby and other surfaces promptly with a dry towel, also cleaning the outside of the vessels each time they are used, so keeping them dry; remember also to dry baby's palms, wrists and forearms after each transfer attempt.
- Choose vessels of adequate diameter and depth for your purpose(s), so also helping to avoid water from easily splashing out, or being too easily overturned.
- Monitor/alter the distance between the two vessel's, in accordance with baby's attention to their own sensorimotor coordination, and increasing manual dexterity skills.
- Be constantly vigilant throughout the task activity, especially in preventing baby from lifting the filled vessels, so pouring water onto their own (or your) clothes, or on to the floor !
- Ditto re preventing baby from drinking any of the likely unboiled, or otherwise contaminated water, as it is being used throughout the activity.

G/A 13.6   Bigger Steps

Task description:
- Exploring walking, with adult and baby footsteps being taken together.

Expected Milestone Achievements (EMAs):
- Bearing own weight unsupported, feet flat on ground most of time   (G1)
- Attempts bending down to pick up dropped items, whilst standing   (G2)
- Picks up, holds, and replaces toys/other objects without dropping them   (F2)
- Recognises self and familiar others in photo/video images   (Cog3)
- Enjoys experimenting with own image in mirror (and with others, if present)(SP5)

Materials:
- Large mirror, hand puppet.

Procedure:

Level 1
1. Invite baby to come to you as you demonstrate the task/activity to follow.
2. Standing together with baby facing you, place baby's insteps and toes on top of your own.
3. Hold baby's two hands in supporting their balance, gently moving one foot, then the other in a backwards direction, as you slowly walk whilst stating that the walking command password is, "1, 2, 3, ..forward" (as baby is now 'walked' passively forward, as you (actively) step backwards, baby standing on your feet).
4. With success (and hopefully smiling & pleasure), next lead baby to 'walk' together with you in both backwards and forwards directions in this way.

Level 2
1. Take up the same positions as per level 1 once more.
2. Now hold baby whilst stepping forwards, and stating that the backward walking command password is, "1, 2, 3, ..back", (as you now lead baby to 'walk' passively backwards, as you slowly and gently step forwards), smiling at baby all the while.

Level 3
1. Place a large mirror against the room wall (if you do not already have one installed there), in front of the mirror laying a hand puppet (or soft toy).
2. Invite baby to 'walk with' you, again placing baby's two insteps toes upon yours, you both now standing together, faced forward towards the mirror.
3. Moving forward together (approaching mirror), walk forward whilst saying that the password is, "123, forward" once more.
4. Arriving at the front of the mirror, encourage/guide baby to pick up the puppet on the floor, allowing then baby to spend time to relax and play with the puppet/soft toy a while.

Level 4
1. Set up the materials, again, as per level 3.
2. Invite baby to 'walk with' you, again placing baby's two insteps toes upon yours, but this time standing faced with their back to the mirror.
3. Moving together (approaching mirror), walks towards the mirror whilst saying that the password is, "123, back" once more.
4. Arriving at the front of the mirror, encourage/guide baby to once again pick up the puppet on the floor, and to let baby spend time to relax and play with the puppet/soft toy a while (repeat level 3 & 4 activities according to baby's interest).

Variations:
- Consider to use two mirrors, one at either end/sides of the room, standing separately but nearby to each other; Walking the slowly between the two mirrors, exchange your hand puppet/toys with others from a pile/box in the centre, when you cross in the centre of the room each time.
- With good control and adequate balance/comfort, you may begin to feel comfortable/willing to also lead baby in making more complex stepping movements; for example, separating their two feet a little, swaying from side to side at the knees, eagerly anticipating dancing, and so forth.

Additional thoughts/Activity-Game Preparation/Lesson Planning Tips:
- Be sure to check/secure the nature of the chosen 'walking' paths each time, so helping to avoid injury or any danger of collision (concerning either baby with furnishings/objects, or collisions with other persons who may be present !).
- *If walking for the first time in this way (or at early exploratory stages of walking), your steps must be very small, and the raising of each foot above the ground not made too high each time (as baby's legs are so short, and may encounter muscle strain (even breakage) if their little legs be extended out too far apart).*

G/A 13.7   Hidden Harvest Hunters

Task description:
- Searching together for hidden objects.

Expected Milestone Achievements (EMAs):
- Retrieves items from small containers by shaking or poking at them   (Cog1)
- Retrieves visibly-hidden objects without prompting   (Cog2)
- If walking, will try walking self-supported with only one hand   (G4)
- Attempts bending down to pick up dropped items, whilst standing   (G2)
- Acquires attention and/or objects without simply crying   (Comms4)

Materials:
- Large box, toy fruits & vegetables.

Procedure :
Level 1
1. Prepare 5-6 large boxes around the room floor, each opened at one face.
2. Inside some (but not all) of the boxes place a different toy vegetable or fruit.
3. Demonstrate exploring the different boxes, making sure that baby had observed your surprise and pleasure at discovering that some of them contain hidden fruits and vegetables 'ready for harvesting'.
4. Invite baby to now crawl/walk over to hold/explore a box for themselves, in search of the potential harvest of vegetables or fruit to be gained from them.
5. Encourage baby's finding the toy foods to then share their harvest with you in pretend picnic eating (and/or to show their finds to any other person present).
6. Repeat steps 4-5 several times, until baby has explored all of the boxes, and 'harvested' all the produce hidden.

Level 2
1. Prepare 5-6 large boxes around the room floor, each again open at one face.
2. Inside *only one* of the boxes this time, place *all* of the different toy vegetables or fruit.

3. Demonstrate exploring the different boxes, making sure that baby has observed your surprise and pleasure at discovering that one of them contained hidden fruit or vegetable ready for harvesting.
4. Invite baby to now crawl over to hold/explore a box for themselves, in search of the potential harvest of vegetable or fruit from them.
5. Encourage baby's finding of the toy food, and to then share their harvest with you in pretend eating, and/or to show to their finds to any others present.
6. Repeat steps 4-5 several times, until baby has explored and harvested the available fruit or other hidden treasure.

Level 3
1. Prepare 5-6 large boxes around the room floor, this time placed upside-down.
2. Inside some (but not all) of the boxes place a different toy vegetable or fruit.
3. Demonstrate exploring the different boxes, making sure that baby has observed your surprise and pleasure at discovering that *some* of them contain hidden fruits and vegetables ready for harvesting, after turning each box to see what is inside.
4. Invite baby to now crawl over to explore the boxes for themselves, in search of the potential harvest of vegetables or fruit from them.
5. Encourage baby's finding the toy foods to then again share their harvest with you in pretend eating.
6. Repeat steps 4-5 several times, until baby has explored and harvested all.

Variations:
- Consider to also use colour cues to indicate 'which' boxes may contain the fruit.
- Ditto, using a variety of different containers/cases/bags/packaging/labels to enhance baby's interest and curiosity.
- Consider to change the box orientations, stacking, height, locations, etc, so increasing both interest and difficulty levels between rounds.
- If baby appears to be little motivated to search and harvest the toy foods, try soft toys or known preferred toys.

Additional thoughts/Game-Activity Preparation/Lesson Planning Tips:
- After baby attains the toy vegetables or fruit each time, they will likely attempt to place them between their lips to eat, be sure therefore to have had the toys thoroughly disinfected/cleaned before using them for this activity.
- The vegetable or fruit toys to be used here must be lifelike models, otherwise baby's interest will be much reduced.

G/A 13.8   Pick Your Own

Task description:
- Selecting objects (from amongst distractors) according to given criteria.

Expected Milestone Achievements (EMAs):
- Attempts bending down to pick up dropped items, whilst standing   (G2)
- If walking, will try walking self-supported with only one hand   (G4)
- Attempts step walking with less dragging and/or tripping over own toes   (G3)
- Points to wanted objects beyond immediate reach   (F6)
- Acquires attention and/or objects in ways other than simply crying   (Comms4)

Materials:
- Basket, toy vegetables and fruits, toy balls, reaching tool.

Procedure:
Level 1
1. Demonstrate a basket loaded with various kinds of vegetables, fruit and/or balls
2. Clearly show that similar vegetables/fruit/balls have also been placed around the walls (or even suspended from the ceiling/coat hangers or room furnishings ?), and are now ripe for 'picking'.
3. Invite baby to now handle the samples, and then to 'pick' the vegetables/fruit/balls, whilst you hold baby up high and close to them within reach (their arms free).
4. Be sure to praise baby as they do so, encouraging them promptly as they pick each item one at a time.

Level 2
1. Select one vegetable/fruit/ball from your basket (one at a time), and which matches one of those also placed around the walls (or hanging somewhere in the room ?), and point it out to baby.

2. Invite baby to thereafter search *for*, then point to, the various matching items as placed around the room, and to then move to where it is located, and to stand beside/beneath it.
3. Offer baby prompt praise as they do so, encouraging them to 'pick' each item from the different 'trees'.

Level 3
1. Select one vegetable/fruit/ball from your basket (one at a time) which matches one of those also placed around various surfaces, walls (or suspended from the ceiling), and again show it to baby.
2. Invite baby to now search for the matching item as placed around the room, and to then move themselves close to where it is located, and to 'pick' them from the surface/walls/ceiling string all by themselves (i.e. having placed the fruits/target objects at a height/location where baby can this time retrieve them without being picked up by you, or otherwise helped in any way).
3. Praise baby as they do so, encouraging them promptly as they pick up each item.

Level 4
1. Again selecting one vegetable/fruit/ball from your basket (one at a time) which again matches one of those also placed around the walls (or suspended from a string), and showing it to baby, point out that they are this time slightly beyond their natural reach.
2. Demonstrate the use of various tools which may be used in order to reach them (some cushioning/steps, and/or a short stick/rake/spoon be used to acquire them).
3. Be sure to carefully observe whether baby appears to understand either how to pick up/move and use the different tools in order to 'pick' the various vegetables, fruit, or balls from the wall/ceiling strings.
3. Offer praise to baby as they do so, encouraging them promptly as they successfully 'pick' each item, each time.

Variations:
- Consider inviting baby to 'pick' a specific vegetable/fruit/ball each time (i.e., baby needing to match name to target object without being shown a 3D model/example of what they are to search *for*).
- Be creative with placing/securing your items on a variety of home-made 'trees', walls and/or other locations.

Additional thoughts/Game-Activity Preparation/Lesson Planning Tips:
- When awaiting baby's discovery of matching items about the room, be sure to realise whether (or not) baby is indeed able see it from their current location !
- If/when engaged in climbing attempts, be sure to monitor baby's balance and posture stability as being within baby's safety limits, whilst remaining at baby's side at all times (if not actually being held), so providing additional protection.

Baby Milestones of Development (0-3 Yrs)

- *If baby requests that you hold on to them as they acquire the item, this is also to be regarded as a successful solution to their problem/method; so be sure to also praise this request being made, whilst also encouraging baby to attempt other methods which do not require your direct support as they move towards their target object each time.*
- Once the reaching/'picking' activity has ended for each round, encourage not only by baby's praise, but be sure to also allow sufficient time for baby to explore/play with their new item each time (rather than simply taking them away after all their effort/hard work spent in gaining them !).

G/A 13.9   Bigger or Smaller ?

Task description:
- Exploring, identifying, and naming the differences in size of different object sets.

Expected Milestone Achievements (EMAs):
- Points to required wanted objects beyond immediate reach   (F6)
- Retrieves items from small containers by shaking or poking at them   (Cog1)
- Follow simple verbal requests, without accompanying gestures   (Comms1)
- Uses the same double syllable sounds to refer to fewer objects   (Comms3)
  (e.g., bottles, teddy bears & father are no longer *all* referred to as "dada").
- Stacks multiple objects with larger items below smaller ones   [M14-Cog2]

Materials:
- Large and small buttons, large and small building blocks.

- Stacking cups and/or ring combination sets.

Procedure:
Level 1
1. Demonstrate (for example) two differently sized buttons/blocks, placing them afterwards on the floor for baby to clearly see.
2. Inform baby which is big (bigger), and which is small (smaller), of the two.
3. Taking up the button/blocks again in the hand to compare them, ask baby, "Which is big/small ?".

4. Encourage/guide baby in identifying/choosing the size, then allowing baby to pick/take the big/small button and give it to you (or place in a small box).
5. Encourage baby with praise when 'correctly' choosing each time.
6. Next, present set(s) of differently sized combinations of toys (e.g., large and small building blocks, large and small buttons, and so forth).
7. Invite/guide baby to distinguish their relative sizes, increasing the number of choices with success.

Level 2
1. Demonstrate the stacking/nesting of a group of cups or combination rings (at most using 5 cups/rings of obviously different sizes).
2. Refer especially to the ordering, as you turn the cup/rings and then arrange them flat on the floor, in a straight line, for baby to clearly see.
3. Next demonstrate their combination as a pile of cups/rings, as you explain what you are doing in a clear, unambiguous way.
4. Reverse now the procedure, again explaining clearly what you are doing, until only two of the components remain.
5. Holding up the two left over cups, carrying on with the size discernment as before, Selecting, "The biggest one" for baby to see/guess.
7. Lastly, point now to the last cup/ring, as being, "The smallest", then set it back with the previous one.
8. Demonstrate the last two cup/rings again giving them to baby, so allowing baby to explore/observe how they may be 'fitted'/stacked/nested together.
9. Finally, present baby with different sizes of cups/rings.
10. Invite/guide baby to then nest/stack them, whilst also distinguishing their relative sizes.

Variations:
- With success, reduce the size differential to let baby distinguish between any two rings/blocks/objects with increasingly fine acuity.
- Increase the variety of differently sized toys used, so again encouraging baby to generalise different object size relations (and not other distinguishing features !).
- Increase size classification, by using 'big toys' which may be placed into other 'bigger vessel's, small ones into smaller (but larger) vessels, etc,…
- Build high pagodas, stacking with cup discrimination sizes (i.e., "On top of each other", rather than "Nested within").

Additional thoughts/Game-Activity Preparation/Lesson Planning Tips:
- Consider to increase the quantity of toys offered according to baby's ability to gradually differentiate them by size (though do not provide too many from the very beginning).
- As baby succeeds with each new sorting-challenge set successfully, be sure to ascertain prompt encouragement is offered as reward, so increasing/maintaining baby's attention and interest over time.

Baby Milestones of Development (0-3 Yrs)

G/A 13.10   Five Facial Features

Task description:
- Exploring and recognising five structural features of the human face.

Expected Milestone Achievements (EMAs):
- Perseveres/continues trying to pick up string/paper after failing to do   (F4)
- Recognises a wider variety of faces and facial expressions   (Comms6)
- Enjoys experimenting with own image in mirror (and with   (SP5)
  others, if present).
- Looks at objects (if present) that are being referred to by others   (SP6)

Materials:
- Doll, large paper images of human face (with & without the five facial features).

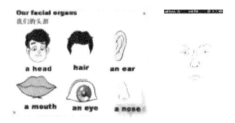

- Scaled pictures of the five facial features (nose, ears, eyes, mouth & eye-brows)

- Disinfection fluid, small mirror

Procedure:
Level 1
1. Demonstrate 'peek-a-boo' by facing baby, and blocking sight of your whole face with both hands, whilst also attracting baby to pay attention to your face.
2. Following a "meow " (or similar attractive) sound, slowly open both hands, to reveal your face and make a "peek-a-boo".
3. Smile and look at baby, asking, "Where are your eyes" (observe baby's responses)
4. Self-answer, "In here !" (simultaneously using both hands to point at your own eyes).
5. Continue to self-refer, as you guide baby through the identification of each of the human body's most visible 'five senses' about the head/face being explored here.
6. Showing now a human image doll, ask baby about the location of the different five sense organs which are visible, and as previously explored, encouraging baby to indicate and confirm their new knowledge, in their own way.
7. To indicate and confirm each baby's 'correct' answer, use the doll to 'kiss' baby's cheek as a reward.
   NB: Although technically inaccurate, use the visible external 'ear' as the hearing sense organ for your purposes here, likewise the 'nose' for smell, etc,.. tho' neither are true !!}.

Level 2
1. Demonstrate how learning about these five facial features can now lead baby to know more about the structure of the human face (and indirectly, the senses ?).
2. Next present the blank face and feature pictures for baby to explore, placing the five facial feature images for baby to handle, initially faced down on the floor.
3. Encourage baby to now select each of the five facial features in turn.
4. As each of the features is 'correctly' selected, place/paste the different features onto their normal facial positions, onto the blank face image.
5. Each and every time baby is seen to help create the completing face (in order to possess its five features), encourage/express thanks to baby for their help.

Variations :
- For level 1, consider presenting a human doll/plush toy, inviting baby to indicate and confirm the location of the five features on the doll's body.
- Ditto, using a hand-held mirror, inviting baby to show/indicate their own facial and sensory body parts.
- Invite/directly interact with baby, asking baby to indicate and confirm the location of *your* five facial features; encouraging/providing feedback each time.
- For level 2, consider allowing baby to choose the locations (corresponding to the selected five features) to be pasted onto the *featureless face* picture provided.

Additional thoughts/Game-Activity Preparation/Lesson Planning Tips:
- Ensure the cleanliness of any doll and/or paper faces presented for use, maintaining them to be both clean and neat throughout the activity whenever possible. [NB: Simple black felt/marker outlines drawn on white paper will suffice].

Baby Milestones of Development (0-3 Yrs)

- When indicating and confirming the locations of the five facial features on your own/other's faces, be sure to maintain clean hands and thus observing healthy physical interactions, paying special attention to not letting baby touch/rub their eyes after making contact with body fluids and/or recently changed nappy waste.
- In coming to an understanding the five facial features activity, inform baby of the functions associated with the five features being explored (e.g., the ears being involved in our ability to listen to sounds, the mouth being use when speaking, or eating, etc).

G/A 13.11   Eating Together

Task description:
- Encouraging baby to share edible foods with different persons.

Expected Milestone Achievements (EMAs):
- Uses opposing finger/thumb to pick up (1cm) object on flat surface   (F3)
- May follow simple verbal requests, without accompanying gestures   (Comms1)
- Recognises a wider variety of faces and facial expressions   (Comms6)
- Predicts participation in an increasing number of daily routines   (SP3)
- Cleanly releases held objects being passed/handed to another person (SP4)

Materials:
- Small biscuits, paper cup, disinfection fluid.

Procedure:
Level 1
1. Show the paper cup, inside of which is a small biscuit (or piece of).
2. Demonstrate the disinfection of the hand(s) using the visible cleaning materials.
3. Remove a biscuit from the cup and place it between your lips to eat, saying, "Mmmm, yummy,.. this really delicious".
4. Invite baby to now receive a biscuit to eat, guiding baby to saying "Thank you", after receiving it.
5. Present next a paper cup with biscuit to baby.
6. Invite baby to now offer the cup (with biscuit inside) to you, as you respond to baby by saying "Thank you".

Level 2
1-x. Invite/guide baby to offer their cup/biscuit to anyone else who may be present (or to a doll/plush toy), remembering also to ensure that baby hears a, "Thank you" from whomever baby may be offering the foodstuffs to, each and every time.

Variations:
- Change the approach procedure, with the recipient moving towards baby, who then offers a biscuit to them (e.g., if no one else be present, consider acting the part of different 'customers': by wearing different hats !, or repositioning yourself to be standing in different locations in the room (then signalling, "I am ready to receive a biscuit").
- Ditto, using a variety of dolls and/or soft toys.

Additional thoughts/Game-Activity Preparation/Lesson Planning Tips:
- Before distributing any biscuits for eating, ensure that both your own, and baby's, hands have been treated with hand disinfection and dried.
- As baby offers/shares food to eat, be sure to provide encouragement with politeness, both in accepting the offer *and* also in express your thanks each time, [otherwise baby will likely experience feelings of confusion and frustration with the 'play' each time – *remember that, your courtesies provide good politeness role-models for baby to follow, as well as provide for clear end-markers for social interactions !].*
- If/when baby is *not* willing to share food with others (including yourself, other familiar persons, or even *any* other person), encourage baby to do such by yourself taking the opportunity to demonstrate the exchange with other persons themselves, and *thus not forcing baby to 'perform' against their will some actions that they never observe you to perform either,....*
  .... (i.e., be wise to teach by example, and NOT simply by decree alone).
- When the activity has ended, be sure to feed baby with clean water, so helping prevent any dehydration caused by the consumption of so many dry biscuits !
- The biscuit choice must be carefully considered (rusks or whole wheat cheerios are often a good choice, if available), checking also to control for the use of ingredients which may be known cause allergic reactions with baby (or others to be involved) in exploring this activity.

G/A 13.12   Small Animal Sounds

Task description:
- Associating different animal images, with their associated sound(s).

Expected Milestone Achievements (EMAs):
- Uses the same double syllable sounds to refer to fewer objects   (Comms3)
  (e.g., bottles, teddy bears and father are no longer *all* referred to as "dada").
- Explores page-turning of books and magazines/paper   (F5)
- Points to wanted objects beyond immediate reach   (F6)

Materials:
- Individual animal pictures/images (e.g., Cat, dog, chicken, duck, frog, etc.,..).

- For sound sources, can use 'real' animal sounds if preferred, though these are harder for baby to imitate, in comparison to those made by yourself !
  [compare activity for Mth9: G/A 9.2].
    NB: Such sound sources may be obtained from online websites, library-based

recording media, or audio extracts from video/TV/radio action. Consider also recording your own baby's sounds at different times, or those of other babies you might encounter when attending the clinic or a play group.

Procedure:
Level 1
1. Demonstrate several animal pictures, e.g., dog, asking baby, "What is this ?".
2. Wait for baby to provide feedback, then informing baby that, "This is a dog".
3. Lead baby to then imitate the dog's cry together, "Puppy Bozo is happy,... woof !".
4. Take the dog's picture closer for baby to view, inviting baby to then imitate the dog's sound.
5. Present the picture to baby, encouraging continued sound making with praise.
6. Promptly continue to demonstrate other pictures (e.g., a cat, or a chicken), repeating steps 4-5 with the appropriate sound and name changes, each time.

Level 2
1. Demonstrate next the animal pictures of the duck, and the frog.
2. Invite baby to now imitate the duck and frog's calls, providing examples of each.
3. Next place the pictures on the floor, assigning random locations to each animal.
4. Invite baby to again imitate each assigned animal's call, in turn.
5. Offer baby prompt praise as/when 'correct' each time.
6. If baby appears confused, guide baby to follow your lead to continue imitation of the two animal's cries, as appropriate, and/or until clearly understood.

Level 3
1. Demonstrate an animal picture - e.g., a dog, asking, "Who is this ?".
2. Invite baby to this time say the animal *name* (with guidance/clues if needed), rather than to simply make/utter its cry (sound).
3. Continue to demonstrate other animal pictures, encouraging baby to say the animal's name each time.

Variations:
- Imitating each kind of animal's sound at the same time as introducing its name, will increase the corresponding image-sound association formations, whilst welcoming baby's sound imitations.
- Following successful imitation of each animal's sound, encourage baby to seek/find the corresponding image from different locations on the floor/walls.
- Consider replacing the animal pictures with puppets or soft toys to continue with the sound generation and speech training (i.e., a 2D => 3D material shift).

Baby Milestones of Development (0-3 Yrs)

Additional thoughts/Game-Activity Preparation/Lesson Planning Tips:
- With baby's increasingly 'correct" pronunciation of names/words, be sure to offer prompt praise and positive reinforcement, so stimulating baby's motivation to continue to attend and study the world of objects and events with you.
- Be sure to enable distinctions to be made between the 'actual sound' of any given animal (e.g., a barking dog, or mewing cat) from its human language reference to such 'sounds' (e.g., onomatopoeic "woof-woof", or "Meow-meow" !!).

- 6 -

Baby Milestones of Development

(With 100+ Fun Activities to Help Demonstrate Them)

[Age 14 Months]

Expected Milestone Achievements
Age = 14 Months

[Key: e.g., 9 = Game No. 14.9]

Gross Motor

• If standing unsupported, will try walking with only one hand held by another person	3, 4, 11
• Tries to stand up independently and take steps without support	2, 4
• Pro-actively walking rather than crawling across distances	2, 3, 11
• Walks many consecutive steps before stumbling, or sitting	3, 10
• Attempts to climb up onto furniture unaided	10
• Squats down in order to pick up an object from standing position	4

Fine Motor

• Successfully stacks 2 stable blocks on top of each other	8
• Touches, grasps and/or reaches towards unfamiliar objects	9
• Attempts to imitate action of throwing a ball (though may not release it at all !)	5
• Pincer grip used to hold/control a cup, crayon or pencil	6, [Mth14.5]
• Makes marks on paper unaided, as if attempting to draw	6, [Mth14.5]
• Tries to 'appropriately' turn the pages of a book	1

Cognitive

• Successfully avoids large object collisions when walking	
• Stacks multiple objects, placing larger items below smaller ones	[M12.9], 8
• Removes visible objects from bottles by turning them over	7
• Obtains distant objects by grasping parts, or uses tools to do so	
• Imitates simple object representations drawn by others	
• Focuses upon more details, including parts/components of images in pictures/books	1

Communication

• Imitates multi-word statements	10
• Begins simple nursery rhyme/game/actions without imitation (following a verbal request/suggestion to do so)	
• Utterances include four or more sounds in addition to intentional use of "Mama" or "Baba"	12
• Produces multiple syllable sound sequences (e.g., "da-ba-boo-ba-ma")	11
• Generates and imitates a variety of noises (both vocally and instrumentally) for oneself, and orients towards novel sounds	2, 12
• Spontaneously waves hand(s) to indicate "Hello" and/or "Bye-bye" unprompted	12

Socio-Personal

• Brings cup directly to mouth in order to self-feed or drink	6
• Enjoys exploring nesting and/or stacking toy interactions (alone or with others)	8
• Enjoys a variety of sounds and/or 'playing' simple musical instrument opportunities	7, 9, 11
• Excited to play on swings and watch others (though may be passive)	10
• Assists with dressing by pushing arms and legs through presented clothing	
• Begins to undo buttons of own clothing/undress once returned home	

G/A 14.1   Reading Together

Task description:
- Exploring picture-book imagery and identifying their associated features.

Expected Milestone Achievements (EMAs):
- Focuses more upon details, including parts/components of images in   (Cog6)
  pictures/books.
- Tries to 'appropriately' turn the pages of a book   (F6)

Materials:
- Picture-book.

- Coloured and/or shaped paper stickers/'post-it' labels.

Procedure:
Level 1
1. Demonstrate a baby picture-book, to each page of which you have attached a sticker somewhere for baby to peel off.
2. Continue to demonstrate opening/turning each page of the book, and when discovering the attached sticker/paper label, rip down the sticker/label with your hand, to reveal what is below it (e.g., some feature of the object in the picture).
3. Show the now detached sticker/label with both hands, for baby to look at.
4. Invite/guide baby to 'read' with you together, and as/when baby discovers the sticker/label each time, encourage baby to remove it from the page, and to then place it onto your hand/arm.

Level 2
1. Present now a new baby picture-book (on each page of which you have attached a coloured sticker) – this time showing the same colour as the object below it, e.g., a yellow coloured paper placed over a picture of a banana.
2. Invite/guide baby to 'read' along with you together, and as/when baby discovers the sticker/label each time, to make a guess as to what may be beneath it.
3. After encouraging with praise at guessing, invite baby to again remove it from the page, and to place it into your hand (or other assigned place).

Variations:
- To increase the level of difficulty, choose a variety of different objects to cover, possibly covering more than one object on some pages (and others with none ?).
- Attach a label/sticker onto a small rubber ball, placing the ball into a basket/box provided for the purpose. Invite baby to then inspect each ball, pulling off the label/stickers once found, as before.
- Consider to create some kind of paper/box template, onto which baby is to place each of the stickers as they are removed from the book pages, so forming a new pattern/display once stuck transferred to the new paper/box template.

Additional thoughts/Game-Activity Preparation/Lesson Planning Tips:
- Be sure to use only such stickers/post-it labels, etc., which are relatively easy for baby to remove, have no toxic adhesive, nor will leave marks on the book pages/objects surfaces, or otherwise require scrub-cleaning to remove adhesive.
- Provide 'baby's picture-books' with sufficient thickness and page numbers (i.e., do not use a magazine), for baby to easily have interest in, and to glance through.
- Ditto, using picture-books with content and colours which are relatively rich, and thus easy to affix "hideaway" stickers/labels.
- As/when baby 'reads" the picture-book, be sure to "look" with baby to the same places, as far as is possible, so not accidentally guiding baby to pay special attention (focus) towards the stickers/labels, before they can detect them.
- Once baby has discovered the label/sticker each time, and has removed it, encourage/guide baby to 'read' on/more (rather than to stop for too long to explore the sticker and ignore the remaining page's information).

G/A 14.2   Sound & Seek !

Task description:
- Searching *for* the location of target sounds heard in the environment.

Expected Milestone Achievements (EMAs):
- Tries to stand up independently and take steps without support   (G2)
- Pro-actively walking rather than crawling across distances   (G3)
- Generates and imitates a variety of noises (both vocally and   (Comms5)
  instrumentally) for oneself, and orients towards novel sounds.

Materials:
- Cushions, room furnitures/fittings.

Procedure:
Level 1
1. Present a large cushion (or other room feature, door) for you to hide behind.
2. Situate baby to sit in a safe place in the room (preferably on a soft mat/surface).
3. Hide yourself from direct view of your baby (e.g., behind the cushion/door).
4. Next, call baby's name from behind the cushion/door.
5. As baby then responds, and succeeds in finding you, encourage/greet them warmly with a big hug in celebrating their achievement, as they arrive/reveal you.

Level 2
1. Repeat level1, this time calling the name of a soft toy that baby would recognise.
2. As baby again responds, and succeeds in finding the 'correct' toy being named, pay close attention to observing baby's response(s), and in attempting to hug the 'correct' toy as baby arrives with it (i.e., brings the soft toy who's name you actually called).

Level 3 [if a 3rd person be present with you at the time]
1. Repeat level 2, this time calling yourself, from a hiding place (or requesting of a third person, if present), calling the name of baby.
2. As baby again responds, and succeeds in finding the name caller, ensure that all present pay attention to observing baby's response(s), and greeting baby with a large hug upon their arrival.

Variations:
- Consider changing the way (pitch or tone of voice) in which you most usually speak in calling baby's name. Observe any differences in baby's response in seeking you out ! (e.g., maybe baby shows novel facial expressions, movement speeds, changes in direction, etc., ?).
- If the members of more than one family is present in the home during the game-activity, consider inviting some other (besides the other parent/guardian) to hide behind differently positioned cushions (in different locations), and to then simultaneously call baby's name, observing to whom baby chooses to seek out from amongst the multiple sound locations heard from [e.g., location vs person ?].

Additional thoughts/Game-Activity Preparation/Lesson Planning Tips:
- When calling baby's name, *try to avoid continuously calling, instead resting awhile, so giving baby the opportunity to both hear and process the sounds that they hear. This will allow for better attempts in baby's determining/distinguishing the sound source' location, and thus to successfully seek for the person actually producing the sound each time (tho' it is especially apt to note when baby has previously moved only half way to call-sound source, and then stops/hesitates).*
- As/when baby succeeds in finding you (or whomever has called), try to always display pleasant surprise in receiving them once finding you, so fuelling encouragement for baby, whilst also boosting their interest and 'feelings' of success; *However, too sudden and intense feedback provided immediately may frighten baby, who though pleasantly surprised to find you, may be disturbed from concentration (especially if only just begun independent walking).*
- Throughout the activity, be sure to keep the room clean and safe, and clear of object clutter in the area(s) across which baby will be moving towards your (callers') locations each time (so helping avoid unsupervised collisions/injury).
- Be sure to call baby's name using their family name (not just "baby"/"baba") as far as possible (also checking for 'similar named' persons also attending in the home), thus avoiding naming ambiguities for baby to discriminate between).
- When receiving baby (having 'found' you), be sure to pay due regard to appreciating baby's situation/personality/ability level(s), in providing the most suitable feedback (e.g., some babies will be uncomfortable with those they regard as 'strangers', or otherwise react strongly to being hugged if 'out of breath' following exertive movements), so as to not frighten/unduly concern them.

G/A 14.3   I Wanna Hold Your Hand !

Task description:
- Exploring walking skill and upright posture, with immediate adult hand contact.

Expected Milestone Achievements (EMAs):
- If standing unsupported, will try walking with only one hand held (G1)
  by another person.
- Pro-actively walking rather than crawling across distances (G3)
- Walks many consecutive steps before stumbling, or sitting (G4)

Materials:
- Cushions, hula hoop.

Procedure:

Level 1
1. Arrange a group of cushions about the room built about a small 'runway'/path.
2. Situate baby standing at one end of the runway, with some (target) toys at the other end.
3. Provide one hand for baby to grab/hold on to, so helping them to maintain their balance, in order to safely arrive at the other end of the runway, without falling.
4. As baby exits from the runway's end, enable their steady arrival at the end point in order to gain a toy still using your supporting hand, whilst providing prompt encouragement and praise.

Level 2
1-4. Repeat level 1, this time instead using a hula hoop (small rod, or similar shorter 'connecting' object between you at first ?) to help baby maintain their balance.

Level 3
1. As per level 1, this time 'letting go' of baby's hand each time s/he stops still.
2. Try to occasionally loosen both hands straight, to let baby stand alone a while

if/when appearing to be stable.
3. Next, move in front of baby a short distance, opening both your hands/arms to form a receptive hug shape, so guiding baby to move forward into your hug.
4. Arriving at their new 'end point' (i.e., into your hug), present baby with the toy in recognition of their new achievement with excitable praise and encouragement (and perhaps renewed stable relief for baby !!).

Variations:
- Consider instead (and especially for a baby still unwilling to stand/walk at this stage), inviting baby who is standing up leaning against the room wall, as you squat down in front of baby at a short distance, encourage baby to then move forward as they approach you (within a few steps) to receive their hug. Slowly increase the distance between the relative starting positions of yourself and baby, allowing progressively more independent movement initiation by baby, as s/he attempts to step/walk several steps towards their target 'hug' and praise.

Additional thoughts/Game-Activity Preparation/Lesson Planning Tips:
- If no hula hoop be available in the home, consider using a short stick/long handled spoon, or similar short 'connecting' object to encourage distancing baby from simple hand-to-hand-holding for immediate balance support and dependence.
- When balancing baby along the runway with the hula hoop (or similar connecting item), allow baby to control their balance by themselves as far as possible, thereby making little/no effort to instead 'tow'/pull along your baby (which will actually perturb, not help them to develop their independent balancing skills).
- When walking along holding the hula hoop (or similar connecting item), consider lessening your grip with time (when baby is looking well coordinated), so letting baby attempt to walk more independently.
  NB: because some babies' ability to walk alone may only be hindered by the psychological pressure (or fear) that they will fall down if 'letting go' – the hula hoop thus serves only as one kind of psychological comfort - the 'tool' giving the baby a useful, but actually 'false' sense of security.
- After baby has successfully attempted to walk independently towards target hugs, *adjust/increase the distance little by little; some babies may become fractious (upset) if the 'goalposts' (the rewarding hug) are continually moved each and every time success was achieved – so do allow sufficient time for baby to enjoy their success before increasing the level of difficulty, else they may not be able to obtain sufficient confidence and increasing satisfaction with their efforts, and may choose to give up (even if rewarded with loving hugs each time !).*

G/A 14.4   Squat & Reach It !

Task description:
- Exploring changing postures in order to reach objects beyond arm's length.

Expected Milestone Achievements (EMAs):
- Squats down in order to pick up an object from standing   (G6)
- Tries to stand up independently and take steps without support   (G2)
- If standing unsupported, will try walking with only one hand held (G1)
    by another person.

Materials:
- Toy car, small ball, various small toys.

- Clear plastic tape, Boxes.

Procedure:
Level 1
1. Present a *relatively* large box in the centre of the room, with several smaller toys strewn nearby about the floor.
2. Place a toy car on the box, guiding your standing baby to reach out onto the box and to take the toy into their hand(s).
3. Next, place the same toy on the floor (with baby still standing), inviting baby to now either bend at the waist or to squat down (may or may not sit on floor), in order to pick up the toy from the floor/ground.

4. As baby succeeds in picking up the toy successfully from the ground according to the request made, provide prompt encouragement, whilst also allowing sufficient time for baby to enjoy playing with their newly attained toy, before the next round.

Level 2
1. Demonstrate the use of a wall/plastic surface-mounted sticky tape (adhesive tape curled-back to make a two-sided sticky surface), and its ability to hold a small, light toy in place (when placed upon it).
2. Demonstrate also the posture of standing with one hand holding the wall, then bending at the waist or to squat down in order to pick up other small toys or balls to stick then onto the adhesive tape.
3. Invite/lead baby to stand by the wall, and hold/leaning towards the wall with one hand.
4. Guide baby in now squatting down in order to pick up the toys/balls (one at a time), each to be then stuck onto the adhesive tape on the wall.
5. Carefully observe whether baby bends at the waist, or squats down in order to pick up the ball/toy each time, providing baby with continuous encouragement and praise as they do so.

Variations:
- If not willing to use adhesive tape as supportive equipment, consider instead to provide a magnetic attachment mechanism (though being cautious with standard letter and number sets, which may end up in baby's mouth !).
- Provide baby with two large boxes, the distance between each box far enough for baby to put out a hand and to be able to reach either one. Place various toys about the floor, close to the two boxes, inviting baby to then shuttle back and forth between the two boxes, as they reach down to the ground to pick up a toy to place in each box, alternately.
- Using multiple boxes, placing different toy items in different places, inviting baby to 'sort' them such that each box only contains one type of toy.
- Ditto, arranging different items to be already in each box at the start of the task (However, remember that the EMA focus here is upon gross movement control, not the cognitive sorting abilities per se).

Additional thoughts/Game-Activity Preparations/Lesson Planning Tips:
- Be sure to employ boxes of sufficient depth such that bending is really necessary in order for baby to view/place items each time – though not so large that baby solves the problem by tipping the box over !
- You may need to assist baby to stand by/in boxes in a stable way, taking care also to avoid baby's effort leading to the tipping of the box over on to its side, and thus baby also falling down and hurting themselves.

Baby Milestones of Development (0-3 Yrs)

- When preparing/using the wall or door/board/mirror with the adhesive tape strip, pay good attention to prevent baby from tearing down the whole strip, instead initially guiding baby by showing them the best way to 'stick' the ball/toys to the tape.
- Prepare adequate cleaning fluids for use as necessary during/after the task – including the cleaning of hands/fingers, toys, and other sticky surfaces.
- *As baby will hold the wall when picking up the ball/toys they will experience the interesting phenomenon of having to pay attention to their not hitting their head on the wall, whilst also learning to attempt bending at their waist/squatting,… each technique having different consequences for their being able to continually see what it is that they are reaching down for !!*

G/A 14.5   Throw Them Balls !

Task description:
- Exploring held object release, and ball throwing.

Expected Milestone Achievements (EMAs):
- Attempts to imitate action of throwing a ball (though may not release it at all !) (F3)
- Picks up, holds, and repositions toys/other objects without dropping them [M13-F2]
- Retrieves items from small containers by shaking or poking at them   [M13-Cog1]

Materials:
- Small balls, inflated balloon, boxes.

Procedure:
Level 1
1. Demonstrate a medium-sized box, inside of which are placed several small balls.
2. Standing inside a box, demonstrate, facing the room wall, picking up one of the box's balls, and gently throw them towards the wall (or into another box nearby).
3. Present the same (or a different) box for baby, inviting/helping baby to stand inside the box.
4. Pour several small balls into the box (around baby's feet).
5. Insuring the stability of baby (and box), invite/guide baby to pick up a ball to throw.
6. Encourage baby to move their shoulder position prior to finger release of the ball, and to have thrown it a certain distance and altitude, providing prompt encouragement (whatever baby actually achieves at this time, even if simply dropping it behind their shoulder !)

Level 2
1. Demonstrate now a (larger) ball or inflated balloon, also showing the coordinated throwing of it, using both hands to throw it upwards for you (to then catch).
2. Present the balloon to baby, sitting opposite you on the floor.

Baby Milestones of Development (0-3 Yrs)

3. Throw the balloon towards baby, encouraging her/him to then loosen their hands/fingers in throwing the balloon back to you, ensuring that the most appropriate praise and encouragement be given.
4. Repeat steps 2-3 back-and-forth for as long as interest and ability allow.

Variations:
- For the lower level ability baby at this time, consider to conduct the same 'passing' a ball or balloon to-and-fro along the ground, whilst seated on the floor with your outstretched legs touching baby's, in order to better guide it towards them as it rolls away after releasing it each time.
- For the equatically-excitable baby, consider arranging the task/activity using small floatable toys and a warm bath of water !

Additional thoughts/Game-Activity Preparation/Lesson Planning Tips:
- As/when baby stands in the box, be sure to remain close to the box in order to provide baby additional stability and/or protection as needed, so avoiding baby's falling from the box to the ground, especially protecting their forehead or face from injury should they become unbalanced.
- Encourage/guide baby to throw the ball as far as s/he possibly can, timing the ball release attempts, and allowing practice with loosening the hand/finger grips in order to release the ball appropriately (without forcibly holding/manipulating their fingers as they attempt to do so each time !).

G/A 14.6   Installations

Task description:
- Exploring the selection and placing of assorted objects into containers by hand.

Expected Milestone Achievements (EMAs):
- Pincer grip used to hold/control a cup, crayon or pencil   (F4)
- Makes marks on paper unaided, as if attempting to draw   (F5)
- Brings cup directly to mouth in order to self-feed or drink   (SP1)

Materials:
- Wax crayons (non-toxic), non-leaded pencils, plastic cup (with & without handle).

Procedure:
Level 1
1. Demonstrate a pile of wax crayons/pencils scattered upon the floor/table, and a handled plastic cup.
2. Taking the handled plastic cup in one hand, load the wax crayons/pencils into the cup, slowly, one at a time for baby to clearly see.
3. Present the handled plastic cup to baby, together with a pile of wax crayons.
4. Invite/guide baby to now place the wax crayon/pencil collection into their cup.
5. Upon completion, encourage baby to then pick up their cup (together with its crayons/pencils still inside of it, and to return them together to you, being sure to provide praise and encouragement as they do so.

Level 2
1. Repeat level 1 steps 3-5, this time using a second plastic cup, one with no handle.

Level 3
1. Once successfully completing levels 1 & 2, present baby with two cups (one with a handle, the other without), and a mixed pile of waxed crayons and/or pencils.

2. Invite/guide baby to now place the wax crayons and/or pencils each into only the handled or the non-handled plastic cups, respectively.
3. As/when baby succeeds in their sorting-and-installation task, encourage her/him to then alone take their two cups (one now containing wax crayons, the other containing pencils) and to return it to you, being sure to provide praise and, "Thank you" in encouragement, as they do so.

Variations:
- Consider using any variety of objects to be placed in a variety of vessels (remembering that *the target EMA here involves baby's object handling and finger grip choice(s) – be sure to be looking out for that detail, and helping build those skills here – and not to become distracted by any writing or drawing abilities this time !*).

Additional thoughts/Activity Preparation/Lesson Planning Tips:
- Be sure to use relatively high quality component cups, so allowing for a firmer grippage by baby's small hands.
- Ditto, selecting with an intention to reuse, rather than choosing those of brittle quality material; else cups will/can easily break and need discarding after use.
- Ensure the use of certified *non-toxic crayons/pencil* contents, as baby may place them in their mouths if unsupervised – preferably new, or at least non-sharpened, at this time.
- As baby gathers their load(s) for placing into the plastic cups, try to avoid the temptation to help baby in holding the cup steady. Instead, allow baby to discover (for themselves) the best method(s) of installing the crayons/pencils, using their own initiative and trial-and-error experiential learning.
- Likewise, when baby returns their loaded cup(s) to you, allow baby to take full control of both their body movement, and that of the cup that they are carrying (even if it spills).
- Be sure to pay full attention to the plastic cup's edges, so avoiding any of the cup's surfaces scratching against baby's skin (which can cause a rash or abrasion if rough/jagged).
- As baby attains the wax crayons/pencil, they may wish to draw or doodle. Be sure to have white paper available for baby to attempt drawing should they wish to, but to do so only after AFTER they have gathered the crayons/pencils into the cup and returned them together to you. (*Again, remember that the target EMA here involves baby's object handling and finger grip choice(s) – not the skills of writing or drawing per se*).

G/A 14.7   Pouring to Order !

Task description:
- Exploring the filling and emptying of vessels, transferring small objects.

Expected Milestone Achievements (EMAs):
- Removes visible objects from bottles by turning them over   (Cog3)
- Explores the emptying and refilling of containers with objects   [M17-Cog1]
- Enjoys a variety of sounds and/or 'playing' simple musical   (SP3)
  instrument opportunities.

Materials:
- Handled and non-handled plastic cups, glass marbles.

- Ping-pong ball, bells, plastic bottle, plastic box/tray.

Procedure:
Level 1
1. Demonstrate the handled plastic cup, and two plastic boxes/trays (one of which contains ping-pong balls, the other empty.
2. Using the handled plastic cup scoop several ping-pong balls, and then pour them into the empty box/tray.
3. Present to baby the same materials just demonstrated.
4. Invite/guide baby to now use the cup to pour the ping-pong balls into the empty box/tray.
5. As baby succeeds with the task, provide prompt praise and expressions of excitement.

Level 2
1. Demonstrate next the non-handled plastic cup, and two plastic boxes/trays (one of which contains glass marbles, the other empty.

2. Using the non-handled plastic cup scoop several glass marbles, and then pour them into the empty box/tray.
3. Present to baby the same materials, inviting/guiding baby to use the cup to pour the glass marbles back into the empty box/tray (from whence they came).
4 As baby succeeds with the task, encourage with prompt praise and excitement.

Level 3
1. Demonstrate now the plastic bottle, two-thirds full of bells (or something similar), and one empty plastic box/tray.
2. Gently pour bells into the empty box/tray, for baby to clearly see (and hear).
3. Present to baby the same materials, inviting/guiding baby to hold the plastic bottle in the same way as just demonstrated, and in order to gently pour the bells into the empty box/tray.
4 As baby succeeds with the task, provide prompt praise and expressions of excitement.

Variations:
- Provide baby with two plastic cups, one of which is loaded with ping-pong balls (or bells/glass marbles), the other one empty. Encourage/guide baby to then pour the ping-pong balls (or bells/glass marbles) into the empty cup, alternately using their left hand and then their right hand, each time.
- For those wishing to engage in water play, consider transferring ice cubes, or water-coloured ice shapes between vessels (maybe a fun bath-time activity ?).

Additional thoughts/Game-Activity Preparation/Lesson Planning Tips:
- Be sure to remain ever vigilant to ensure that the small bells and glass marbles are NOT picked up and placed into baby's mouth – so helping to avoid any accidental choking or swallowing risks.
- If baby is not careful to pour the ping-pong ball/bells/glass marbles only onto the receiving tray/box, promptly collect/retrieve any spillage yourself before they scatter too widely about the floor, so helping avoid any one else present from treading and slipping on them (or yourself/baby doing so at a later time).
- Pay attention to adjusting the distance between the filled and empty boxes/trays, so as to minimise the/any spillage/scattering space (tho' not so close as to make the task too easy !), depending upon baby's sensorimotor integration ability level.
- Allow baby to use both their two hands if preferring to do so at this time, but do encourage/guide baby to attempt using only a single hand to pick up the cup (both left and right hands can be used to practice this developing skill).
- The cups and plastic bottles used must ALL be cleaned and disinfected before and after use with bells; dried, and void of all water, else the bells will rust.
- Consider placing a soft towel under the region within which each baby is working, so lessening the distance that any dropped/spilt balls/marbles/bells will travel before coming to rest.

G/A14.8   Stacking 'em High !

Task description:
- Exploring the building of higher towers, by using large(r) foundations.

Expected Milestone Achievements (EMAs):
- Stacks multiple objects with larger items below smaller ones   (Cog2)
- Successfully stacks 2 stable blocks on top of each other   (F1)
- Enjoys exploring nesting and/or stacking toy interactions (alone or   (SP2)
  with others).

Materials:
- Non-interlocking stackable building blocks (cylinders, cubes), rings.

Procedure:
Level 1
1. Demonstrate a set of 2-3 circular/cylindrical building blocks of different sizes, arranged on the floor/table for baby to clearly see.
2. Clearly compare the 2-3 building blocks' sizes, then attempt to build a high tower according to their size (placing the smaller ones towards the top).
3. Present the same/similar 3-block sets to baby.
4. Invite/guide baby to now compare the building blocks' sizes each time, selecting the largest to stack next, as they build their tower with the smallest piece at the top.
5. As baby successfully compares the sizes and continues to build higher, according to decreasing block size(s), provide appropriate and prompt encouragement.

Level 2
1. Repeat level 1 steps 4-5, this time having presented 5 blocks of different sizes.

Variations:
- Consider providing tower/stacking materials which are either small (will fit in one of baby's hands), and/or which are relatively large (cushions/washing bowls), requiring two hands to manipulate each time.
- Provide differently shaped building block (big and small), guiding baby to construct their tower(s) according to the size and/or shape of the building blocks, comparing the result each time, then combining the two sets to make a single VERY tall tower *(NB: Reducing the size contrast gradient will also increase the difficulty level).*

Additional thoughts/Game-Activity Preparation/Lesson Planning Tips:
- When choosing baby's building block set, using the same colour for each shape may assist with discrimination based upon the 'correct' block feature at first (e.g., red circles/cylinders, green cubes, blue triangles, etc).
- Before successfully building their block towers, be sure to attempt clearly guiding baby to distinguish 'bigger' and 'smaller' (possibly including the language names for those words ?), so ensuring that they truly understand this basis of block size discrimination.

G/A 14.9   Full of Beans !

Task description:
- Exploring material object manipulation, and construction of a musical instrument.

Expected Milestone Achievements (EMAs):
- Independently fills containers with small (< 1cm objects) [M16-Cog5]
- Touching, grasping and reaching towards unfamiliar objects (F2)
- Enjoys a variety of sounds and/or 'playing' simple instrument opportunities (SP3)

Materials:
- Plastic bottles, bowls of dried rice, soybeans (or similar), glass marbles.

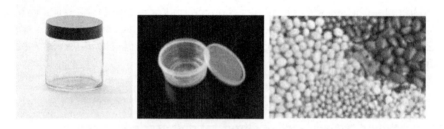

- Small plastic bottle (bottle mouth = baby palm size).

Procedure:

Level 1
1. Demonstrate the bowl (containing rice) and a plastic bottle, placing some grains of the dried rice inside of the plastic bottle.
2. Demonstrate next placing the rice grains into the smaller plastic bottle, place the lid on, then gently sway it in order to make it (the moving dried rice) sound.
3. Emptying the small vessel once more, next guide baby to place the dry contents into the small bottle, helping thereafter to secure the bottle cap once more.
4. Once all done, lead baby to then sway/shake their bottle, to 'sound' and play it.

Level 2
1. Demonstrate the bowl, this time filled with dry soybeans/marbles and a larger plastic bottle.
2. Demonstrate next placing the soybeans/marbles into the large plastic bottle, placing on the lid, then gently sway/shake it in order to make its *quite different* sound.

Baby Milestones of Development (0-3 Yrs)

3   Emptying the smaller vessel once more (or using a different one), guide baby to next place the new and different dry contents into the small bottle, your helping thereafter to secure the bottle cap once more.
4   Once all done, lead baby to then sway/shake their bottle, to hear its new sound. and to 'play' it. (If using two bottles, allow baby to shake both at the same time).

Variations:
- Provide baby with alternative materials, such as raisins/building bricks/sand/paperclips, etc.., exploring the different sound effects of each when shaken.
- Ditto, changing the bottle (but not the contents) which may be replaced by any variety of different types of container readily found about the house (esp., the kitchen), such as tins, storage boxes, bottles, and cups.

Additional thoughts/Game-Activity Preparation/Lesson Planning Tips:
- Be careful to choose bottles which are sturdy and not made of brittle materials as far as possible, and avoiding their being dropped and breaking, so potentially causing any wound to baby's skin surfaces.
- Ditto, rejecting use of/exposing baby to 'play' with medicine or tablet bottles/jars.
- Be sure to prevent baby taking small items into the mouth to eat, even if appearing to be edible foods, so preventing choking or swallowing of the dry foods.
- Ensure all materials are clean, sterilised and thoroughly dried, both before and after use (also advising the frequent washing of baby's hands).
- Consider placing a soft towel under the region within which baby is working each time, so lessening the distance that any dropped rice/marbles/beans will travel before coming to rest.

G/A 14.10   Hold 'em Balance

Task description:
- Exploring balance control whilst swinging supported on a moving surface.

Expected Milestone Achievements (EMAs):
- Walks many consecutive steps before stumbling, or sitting   (C4)
- Attempts to climb up onto furniture unaided   (G5)
- Imitates multi-word statements   (Comms1)
- Excited to play on swings and watch others (though may be passive) (SP4)

Materials:
- Large ball, baby doll or large soft toy
  [NB: If no large ball be available in the home, see variation 2 below, large bath towel].

Procedure:
Level 1
1. Demonstrate a large ball and a baby doll/plush toy.
2. Using the baby doll/soft toy placed face-down on the upper surface of the ball, hold the doll/soft toy at the 'waist', and gently begin to push slowly forward. As the ball rolls a little with doll/toy laying prone on the ball, bring the ball slowly back to its original position (before letting the doll/soft toy approach too close the ground).
3. Invite baby to be now laid gently on the top surface of the large ball (holding them initially in a stable position between their legs/knees/feet), then pushing slowly forwards as previously demonstrated, whilst all the while talking to baby and providing frequent encouragement (as they begin to shift their centre of gravity (and limb muscle tensions) in maintaining their balance whilst moving in this way.

Baby Milestones of Development (0-3 Yrs)

95

Level 2
1. Positioned initially as per level 1, demonstrate to baby the positioning with a doll or large soft toy.
2. This time holding the doll/soft toy at the 'waist' a little more firmly, and with more outstretched thumbs, gently begin to push slowly to one side (say, to the left). As the now ball rolls a little with doll/toy still laying prone on the ball, bring the ball slowly back to the starting original position (before letting the doll/soft toy approach too close the ground).
3. Repeat the same action, this time rolling slowly to the right.
4. Invite baby to now be gently laid upon the top surface of the large ball (again holding it initially in a stable position between their legs/knees/feet), then, pushing slowly to one side as just demonstrated, whilst all the while talking to baby and providing frequent encouragement (as they begin to shift their centre of gravity (and limb muscle tensions) in maintaining their balance whilst moving gently side to side.

Variations:
- If baby is obviously uncomfortable being rocked (in any way) whilst laying in prone positions, consider instead to try this activity when seated (supported) on the ball.
- If two adult persons be available consider having baby lay down on a bath towel. Invite the second person to hold one end of the towel (whilst you hold the other end), and to then lift/carry baby in their own 'human hammock'. You may now gently sway/swing the baby side to side(passively), with slow focused control of the hammock's motion. [NB: *When alone, please do NOT take the temptation to try this by affixing one end of a towel/sheet to a door knob or similar fitting*].

Additional thoughts/Game-Activity Preparation/Lesson Planning Tips:
- As you start to roll the large ball gently to and fro (in either direction), encourage adaptation to small and slow movements at first, so allowing baby sufficient time to slowly adapt to the motion being experienced. *This will help avoid baby becoming excessively frightened, and stiffening their four limbs, before they can realise the 'cause' of their kinaesthetic motion experience.*
- Once moving more comfortably and more rhythmically, be sure to continue to monitor and guarantee baby's safety, keeping their speed of motion relatively slow, or at least as far as baby's comfort (not yours) allows !
- *To help allay baby showing any initial discomfort/pressure, as you initiate/control the rocking of the massage ball, offer baby additional encouragement by continuing to interact with baby vocally, positioned in front of you, so quickly adjusting the immediate atmosphere and holding baby's mood/feelings of security.*
- *If (for any reason) you yourself should begin to feel tired during this activity (DO NOT WAIT for exhaustion !), you should immediately stop and rest awhile, simultaneously providing baby with additional kinaesthetic relaxation time also.*
- If baby makes a tearful scene or begins to cry, indicating that they are not willing to comfortably engage in this activity *at this time*, change to using alternative methods to carry on with your observational training skills with baby.

G/A 14.11   Sound Strings

Task description:
- Building and exploring sound producing 'instruments' using suspended motion.

Expected Milestone Achievements (EMAs):
- If standing unsupported, will try walking with only one hand held by another (G1) person.
- Pro-actively walking rather than crawling across distances   (G3)
- Producing multiple syllable sound sequences (e.g., da-ba-boo-ba-ma)(Comms4)
- Enjoys a variety of sounds and/or 'playing' simple musical instrument   (SP3) Opportunities.

Materials:
- Coloured ribbon, large bell, small bell, wind chimes (or similarly effective toys).
- Medium sized boxes

Procedure:
Level 1
1. Prepare the room by hanging differently coloured ribbons from the ceiling, furnishings/coat-hangers, upon each of which is also tied a kind of sound producing object, when touched.
2. Demonstrate (for example) 'shaking' a coloured ribbon holding a small bell to make a "tinkling/jingling" sound, or gently knocking/hitting it to make instead a relatively shorter "ding-ding" sound.
3. Prepare now boxes beneath each coloured ribbon hanging from the ceiling, for baby to grasp/manipulate once adequately balanced, standing on a box.
4. Next, guide baby to voluntarily approach (or crawl towards) a coloured ribbon, and to stand and grasp/manipulate it, in order to produce the sound(s) as previously demonstrated.

Baby Milestones of Development (0-3 Yrs)

5. As/when baby succeeds to catch the coloured ribbon and then sway/manipulate it in order to make the sound(s), provide immediate encouragement and praise in stimulating baby's continued interest and motivation.

Level 2
1. Demonstrate a large bell (or similar object), its sound produced by moving the string/ribbon to which it is attached; and/or wind chimes connected to a long coloured ribbon.
2. Attach the coloured ribbon this time across the sides (between two points) of the room (rather than being suspended from a single ceiling point as per level 1).
3. Encourage baby to then reach/grab the bell and to sound it as before – or now creating the sound and listening to the 'dingding, dingdong' sounds made as they walk along touching each bell/chime with an outstretched hand as baby moves from one end of the suspended ribbon to the other (accompanied by yourself, as necessary).
4. Once baby has successfully arrived at the other end of the two-point suspended ribbon, consider taking down the bells/chimes for baby to play with, in celebrating their new musical play achievements !

Variations:
- Consider also using string/ribbon/Velcro to attach the bells (etc) onto baby's arms and/or legs, encouraging baby to then wave their hands and feet about in order to further explore their sound(s), and how to make them.
- Ditto, doing such to both baby and yourself (body parts and/or clothing) – making additional music as you now both dance about the floor together !

Additional thoughts/Game-Activity Preparation/Lesson Planning Tips:
- Situate the hanging coloured ribbons at a suitable height for baby to be able to reach with their outstretched hand(s) (though at least higher than baby's forehead), but not hung from the ceiling so low such that baby may easily pull it down.
- When required to manipulate the ribbon, consider to tie the terminal end about the little finger, so making it more convenient for baby to grasp. If using inferior quality coloured ribbon material, such can also help avoid any finger slippage injury to baby's skin if partially letting go of the ribbon whilst still being held.
- Also of concern, should be your determination of the ribbon's 'breaking strain'– i.e., the weight above which any given suspended object may be too heavy for sustained suspension, and thus possibly subject to possibly falling down onto baby's head when being manipulated from below.

G/A 14.12 Be My Friend ?

Task description:
- Exploring friendship through language play and doll/soft toy interaction(s).

Expected Milestone Achievements (EMAs):
- Utterances include four or more sounds in addition to intentional use of "Mama" or "Baba". (Comms3)
- Generates and imitates a variety of noises (both vocally and instrumentally) for oneself, and orients towards novel sounds. (Comms5)
- Spontaneously waves to indicate "Hello" and "Bye-bye" unprompted (Comms6)

Materials:
- Baby doll, plush animal toys, small toys, toy container (box).

Procedure:
Level 1
1. Demonstrate the baby doll to baby, using the most suitable, normal of baby greetings (with respect to your own language/style/culture for age/experience).
2. Encourage/guide baby to now come forward and to politely greet the baby doll (as if meeting the for the first time/or otherwise returning after not seeing them for a while).
3. As baby achieves this, let the baby doll show cherishing/appreciation of the baby's greetings by 'air-kissing' their cheek in offering praise and encouragement.
4. Repeat the same greeting behaviours with baby her/himself, then present a baby doll to baby, together with some small toys in a box (or similar container).
5. Invite/guide baby to next choose a toy, with which to share/play together with the baby doll.
6. Simultaneously invite both baby and the baby doll to make a handshake, hug, spoken greeting, then to hold the baby doll by your side, and to play with both together.
7. After some appropriate time, inform both baby and the baby doll together that it is now finally time for the baby doll to return home, inviting baby to return the baby doll, having first said, 'Goodbye' and, "Thank you for playing with us today".

Level 2
1. Demonstrate in turn, several different plush animal toys for baby to greet.
2. Invite/guide baby to greet the different plush animal toys in turn.

3. Informing baby that each animal now wants a toy to play with, invite baby to choose a toy to be give to each of the animals.
4. Baby must then be prepared to next actually present each animal with the chosen toy, followed by much additional encouragement from you, (possibly also causing the 'receiving' animal to promptly 'air-kiss' or hug with baby, each time).
5. Once the animal has attained the toy, encourage baby to say, "Goodbye", yourself also saying, "Goodbye: to each animal in turn.
6. Continue to demonstrate with other animals, repeating as appropriate.
7. Once baby has completed the activity, invite baby to then/later return all the toys to the box from which they were taken, offering, "Thank you", as each arrives.

Variations:
- Consider requesting baby to identify and present an assigned toy for the baby doll to 'play' with, observing whether baby chooses the 'correct' one, and/or delivers the toy to the baby doll/animal on his/her own initiative. Either way, provide significant encouragement (simulating baby doll/plush animal hugs and kisses promptly).

Additional thoughts/Game-Activity Preparation/Lesson Planning Tips:
- Be sure to try preventing baby from using their lips/mouth to directly 'kiss' the baby doll (or the plush animal) on the mouth (instead encouraging 'air-kissing' or the bumping gently of baby's cheeks with those of the baby doll/animal, so reducing risks of dirt and/or infection transmission.
- Each time baby demonstrates greeting/play with the plush animal, encourage baby to say out loud the plush animal's name (or in some way imitate its call sound, or movement behaviour).

ψ

– 7 –

Baby Milestones of Development

(With 100+ Fun Activities to Help Demonstrate Them)

[Age 15 Months]

Ψ

Expected Milestone Achievements
Age = 15 Months

[Key: e.g., 7 = Game No. 15.7]

Gross Motor	
• Walks many steps without stumbling, or sitting down	4, 6, 7, 10
• Chooses to walk rather than crawl between rooms	
• Stands up independently and take steps without support from either another person, or furniture	2, 4
• Successfully climbs up onto low furniture items unaided	12
• Squats down to pick up an object, then resumes standing	1, 2
• Smoothly stops walking, and stoops down to pick up a dropped object, arises and walks again, all in a single action	1, 2

Fine Motor	
• Appropriately alters/prepares grip according to different object's size and shape	2, 5, 8
• Keen to try (but often still unable) to pick up very small, flat objects	7, 8
• Successfully stacks 2-3 blocks/toys on top of one another	
• Imitates action of throwing a ball (with/without release)	6
• Independently turns a few pages of a book at one time	
• Makes multiple marks on paper in an attempt to draw lines	5

Cognitive	
• Keen to explore moving fluids in/out of containers (especially in bath)	3
• Reaches for dropped/distant items using a retrieving tool	9
• Recognises specific sounds as being the name of an object, person or event	1, 8
• Developing fine control with selective grasping of one object from amongst a pile/collection	1, 7, 9
• Enjoys interacting with mobile objects, trolleys and/or rolling balls	6, 10
• Attempts to imitate multiple drawn object representations	

Communication	
• Shows interest in body parts, and pointing to them when named	11
• Responds to non-visible (including deliberately hidden) sound sources	
• Appears to recognise significance of facial expressions as they change	3
• Utterances include 6-8 or more sounds in addition to "Mama"	
• Makes vocal sounds which resemble particular 'words'	4, 7, 11
• Increased production of multiple syllable sounds ('doo-doo-wah')	5, 12

Socio-Personal	
• Deliberately grasps food objects and raises them to the mouth using a tool (such as a cup, spork, or spoon)	3
• Selectively/accurately points towards desired/referenced objects	1, 7, 10
• Enjoys exploring singing and other musical games with others	
• Attempts to 'look *for*' an object located in a different place (possibly outside the immediate room) when asked "Where is x ?"	8, 12
• Enjoys to produce sounds and play percussive toys with others	
• Holds and manipulates a spoon or fork in order to self-feed	3

Baby Milestones of Development (0-3 Yrs)

G/A 15.1 Searching for You

Task description:
- Exploring object selections according to spoken requests.

Expected Milestone Achievements (EMAs):
- Squats down to pick up an object, then resumes standing (G5)
- Smoothly stops walking, and stoops down to pick up a dropped object, (G6) arises and walks again, all in a single action.
- Recognises specific sounds as being the name of an object, person (Cog3) or event.
- Developing fine control with selective grasping of one object from (Cog4) amongst a pile/collection.
- Selectively/accurately points towards desired/referenced objects (SP2)

Materials:
- Variety of small toys (musical instruments, fruits, vegetables, animals, small balls.

Procedure:
Level 1
1. Demonstrate one musical instrument for baby to identify (NB: it is important for you to 'know' that baby can/will selectively respond to it by name).
2. Now place the same musical instrument on the floor/table, in front of seated baby.
3. Pour out the contents of a basket of small balls (or other objects), such that they surround the musical instrument already placed on the floor/table.
4. Invite baby to now seek out the location of the musical instrument from amongst all of the other distractor objects now scattered about the floor/table.
5. Provide continuous praise and motivation as baby scrambles about to find/reach the target instrument each time.

Level 2
1. Demonstrate several coloured toy fruits and vegetables, again checking to discover that baby 'knows' each by name (*before* you continue to use them).
2. Place now the various fruits and vegetables about the floor/table, in different positions, in front of baby.
3. Again pour out the contents of the basket of small balls, pouring them about the target objects (now fruits and vegetables) previously placed on the floor/table.
4. Invite baby to then seek out the location of each fruit or vegetable as you name them one at a time, for baby to now search 'for', as they choose the 'correct' target from amongst all the other distractor objects scattered about.

Level 3
1. Demonstrate several toy animals, again checking to make sure that baby can identify each of the objects by their animal name (*before* continuing to use them).
2. Place now the various animal toys about the floor/table, in different positions, in front of baby, as before.
3. Repeat the level 2 steps 3-4, as you call out the various animal names for baby to search for each time.

Variations:
- Instead of using a flat surface, arrange for the target and distractor sets to be placed together in an open box (all objects still remaining visible to baby ?).
- If you do not have access to many small balls, consider instead to use rolled up socks (or paper) to hide the target objects amongst.
- Consider instead to place exemplar targets in various locations about the floor/room (e.g., toy fruits and vegetables, animals), encouraging baby to then attempt to roll/throw a ball towards each target object, as you invite baby to do so, naming each, one at a time.
- With increasing identification and discrimination of the target objects chosen, up the level of difficulty by adding more distractors (rather than simply using balls), and/or more similar looking targets from which to choose.
- Consider to run this activity as a birthday party game, with invited babies of similar age – running the task as a race/competition, perhaps one baby at a time, and/or as a group(s), depending upon individual performance ability and motor skills suggest.

Additional thoughts/Game-Activity Preparation/Lesson Planning Tips:
- As/when baby is engaged in their search process, *try to avoid the temptation to tell baby what to do/where to go, impatiently,...* instead allowing baby to freely roam, explore and actively seek out/retrieve their target object each time.
- Once baby has successfully found the same toy several times, provide increasing motivation and praise by occasionally changing the attractive target toy, thereby increasing baby's search/retrieval behaviour with engaged interest.
- Be sure to carefully and continuously observe ALL baby's movements, in order to help prevent head/furniture collisions when bending over/crouching to pick up objects from the floor/table.

G/A 15.2   Pick-'em-Up Stable !

Task description:
- Exploring and handling/manipulating target objects whilst standing.

Expected Milestone Achievements (EMAs):
- Stands up independently and take steps without support from either   (G3)
  another person, or furniture.
- Squats down to pick up an object, then resumes standing   (G5)
- Smoothly stops walking, and stoops down to pick up a dropped object,   (G6)
  arises and walks again, all in a single action.
- Appropriately alters/prepares grip according to different object's size   (F1)
  and shape.

Materials:
- Bean bags/cushions, stepping stones (boxes, tiles, marked floor),
- Basket or plastic bucket, building blocks.

Procedure:
Level 1
1. Having scattered several bean bags/cushions about the room floor/furnishings, demonstrate a bean bag/cushion, then present to baby either a basket or plastic bucket (vessel large enough to contain one/them !).
2. Invite baby to now seek *for*, and gather into their basket, any/some/all bean bags that they may be able to find scattered about the room.
3. If/when baby is able to bend at the waist, or to squat down to pick up any of the bean bags that they find (without falling over, or taking multiple steps to do so), provide prompt praise and encouragement.

Level 2
1. Scatter this time several large(-ish) building blocks about the room, demonstrating one of the blocks (as a model target), this time to be stacked upon a growing wall (as they find each new one), thus placing them all together in one place.
2. Invite baby to now seek *for*, and gather into their basket, any and all of the large building blocks that they may be able to find scattered about the room, and add it to their building 'wall'.
3. As/when baby is able to bend at the waist, or to squat down to pick up any of the building blocks that they find (without falling over, or taking multiple steps to do so), AND then travels towards (and places each block upon) the growing wall, provide praise and encouragement promptly.

Level 3
1. Lay at random about the room (or mark) a number of single stepping-stones (which maybe simply made from paper, cardboard, tiles, or old shoe box lids).
2. Invite baby to then gather and move the individual stepping-stones (one at a time), and to help build up a true 'stepping stone bridge' across a marked 'river' elsewhere in the room, using the 'stepping-stone' material so gathered.
3. As/when baby successfully gathers and moves the stepping-stones without dropping them, AND helps to build the bridge, be sure to provide prompt encouragement praise with each success.

Variations:
- Following success with levels 1-2, guide baby to now use both their hands to pick up a toy, each time delivering *two* toys from the place which you have assigned each time, remembering to express your, "Thank you" to baby upon receiving your delivery(ies) each time !
- Establish a concave-convex fluctuating (wavy path) pathway on the room floor, inviting baby to walk along a more uneven/sinuous path surface, again requiring them to pick up various toys to be found along the way.

Additional thoughts/Game-Activity Preparation/Lesson Planning Tips:
- Situate the target toys to be laid aside the pathway some suitable distance appropriate for baby (i.e., not too far away, but also not so close as to be too easy for them to reach), whilst *also avoiding baby needing to be put off balance by transporting too heavy or too large a toy – as their walking unsteadily may cause them to fall down, crash, or otherwise sustain injury.*
- Likewise, if baby is choosing to move (what is for them) a relatively large-scale or heavy toy, be sure to provide guidance and protection (though not assistance, with carrying).
- Encourage baby to use both hands (or either their left or right hands at different times) in collecting and carrying their target toys as often as possible, when walking to their assigned locations with hands/arms full.

G/A 15.3   Sporking it up !

Task description:
- Vessel filling and material delivery according to 'ordered' requests.

Expected Milestone Achievements (EMAs):
- Keen to explore moving fluids in/out of containers (especially in bath)   (Cog1)
- Appears to recognise significance of facial expressions as they change (Comms3)
- Deliberately grasps food objects and raises them to the mouth using   (SP1)
  a tool (such as a cup, spork, or spoon).
- Holds and manipulates a spoon or fork in order to self-feed   (SP6)

Materials:
- Spork/spoon, cup, dried peas/beans, small bells, sealable jars
- Bowl/bowl lid/cover (flat)

- Real baby food(s): Pre-prepared high quality Internationally certified safe baby food in jars "off the shelf" [or pre-prepared baby food made in the home].

Procedure:
Level 1
1. Demonstrate a bowl that contains some small bells, with a sealable cover.
2. Removing the lid/cover, show now the spork/spoon, demonstrating how to use the spork/spoon to scoop up the bell(s) from the bowl (and/or transfer them to another sealable jar) using the spork/spoon. Finally covering the vessel containing the bells, gently shake it up and down in order to sound the bell(s) now inside of it.
3. Present next the same/similar materials to baby, inviting/guiding baby to scoop up the bell(s) using their spork/spoon.
4. Upon completion, invite baby to return all of the materials to you, offering encouragement and expressing, "Thank you", as they do so.

Level 2

1. Demonstrate a bowl that contains some dried peas/beans, with sealable cover.
2. Removing the lid/cover, show now the spork/spoon, demonstrating how to use the spork/spoon to scoop up the dried peas/beans from the bowl (and/or transfer them to another sealable jar) as before. Finally cover the vessel and gently shake it up and down in order to sound the dried peas/beans as they are being shaken inside of it.
3. Present next the same/similar materials to baby, inviting/guiding baby to scoop up the dried peas/beans using their spork/spoon, transferring them as before.
4. Upon completion, invite baby to explore the now quite different sound to be heard when gently shaken, then to return all of their materials to you, (your remembering to offer encouragement and, "Thank you", as they do so).

Level 3
1. Present next some paper napkins (bibbing baby if/as necessary), as you now use your own regular feeding materials as used during home/outings, inviting/guiding baby to scoop up the real food-stuffs using their spork/spoon, and then self-feed.
2. Upon completion, invite baby to again return all of their materials, with a big smile and expression of "thanks" as they do so.

Variations:
- Note that you may need to guide baby in coordinating vessel balance when using one hand to scoop inside their bowls, their other hand being used to keep the bowl steady in place (especially if light in weight).
- With success, consider providing for baby two (or more) different kinds of spork/spoons to explore using (of different shapes and sizes, handle lengths, and so forth).

Additional thoughts/Activity Preparation/Lesson Planning Tips:
- If/when choosing to engage baby with the level 3 activity here, be sure that you are planning for baby a *self-feeding* exercise, and to prepare and make available certain materials (preferred, familiar foodstuffs and personal utensils) that you may wish baby to use for this purpose (to be prepared *prior* to the session).
- After all activities have ended, promptly clean up the working area/floor/table, so also decreasing the chances of baby ingesting any spilled pieces which may be on the floor/surrounding area(s).
- As far as is possible, use familiar sporks and spoons, also avoiding those which may be easily broken and/or damaged.
- Be certain that all items (dry peas/beans, bells and all utensils) used are thoroughly cleaned and sterilised (not merely 'wiped') before using them.
- *If/when using 'real' foods, this is not a good time to be introducing novel tasting/smelling foods, which may likely be rejected by baby.*
- *Ditto any novel foods which may result in baby's sickness or vomiting. It would be a shame to have baby associate self-feeding and spoon-use with their becoming/feeling unwell !*

G/A 15.4   Home Hiking Trails !

Baby Milestones of Development (0-3 Yrs)

Task description:
- Exploring balanced walking in the face of obstacles and load burdens.

Expected Milestone Achievements (EMAs):
- Walks many steps without stumbling, or sitting down   (G1)
- Stands up independently and take steps without support from (G3)
  either another person, or furniture.
- Makes vocal sounds which resemble particular 'words'   (Comms5)

Materials:
- Coloured ribbon, small ball. Large and smaller cushions (as obstacles).

Procedure:
Level 1
1. Demonstrate two coloured ribbons, each ribbon attached at one end to a small ball.
2. Invite baby to make the following action demonstration together with you: Ask baby to use both hands to grasp (and hold on to) the ball at the end of the ribbon, as you hold the other end as drooped over the back of your shoulders, standing forward to draws the ribbon tighter, then slowly walk forwards, leading both you and baby to gently walk forwards together (baby following you).
3. With good balance, continue to slowly lead baby around in a circle within the room, as you walk together as a pair.
4. With increasing stability, and at a walking pace most comfortable according to baby's ability and comfort level, consider to either speed up, or to slow down, your pace, as you continue to play together in this way, whilst also providing frequent praise and sharing of reassuring/comforting communication(s).

NB: if baby is still unstable without more support, consider to replace the use of a ribbon with something more solid, such as a hiking pole, broom handle, or short stick.

Level 2
1. Establish now a series of obstacles about the 'circle' path previously walked in level 1, by placing several large and/or small cushions about the room floor.
2. Now starting from different locations about the room each time, gently pull/coax baby along using the same coloured ribbon as per level 1, to this time move along, and around the obstacle(s), as you now walk together in a path that frequently changes direction.
3. As/when baby may hit these cushioning obstacles (possibly knocking them over when colliding with the cushioning at high speed !), ensure that you stop moving forward, though continuing to hold your pairing together, whilst baby regains their steady balance,.... then continuing forwards as before.
4. With increasing stability, and at a walking pace most comfortable according to baby's ability, consider to either speed up, or to slow down, and to change direction more often, as you continue to play together in this way, whilst also providing frequent praise and sharing comforting communications.

Level 3
1. Extending the level of difficulty with level 2 further (and with increasing success), establish now some uneven surfaces (with cushioning support if needed) for baby to travel along.
2. Again crossing the room floor, now invite/lead baby (as per levels 1-2 above) to walk along together, this time over the new and uneven, unsteady cushioned surfaces (relatively slowly at first !).

Variations:
- Consider also to invite baby to pull *you* along, also using the same coloured ribbon to practice walking about with purpose, the *baby now also experiencing leadership success as the young driver of others !*
- If not able to successfully secure the ball to the ribbon without coming apart when tethered and moving with baby, consider replacing the ball with some other 'handle', or even a second 'soft' ribbon loop, more easily held by baby's small hands.

Additional thoughts/Game-Activity Preparation/Lesson Planning Tips:
- Before conducting this activity, be sure to have cleaned up the room with regards any potentially dangerous collision objects, especially removing (relocating) some/any of the harder objects which baby may otherwise collide with, and possibly injure themselves if contacting.
- Be sure also to check that you are always able to adequately monitor (and adjust) baby's speed and direction(s) of movement, according to their developing strength and balance/coordination abilities, so avoiding baby's overexerting, and/or becoming frustrated in their attempts to achieve their goals.

G/A 15.5   Drawing Up and Down !

Task description:
- Exploring muscle organisation (shifting to/from whole arm, to wrist control) when drawing independent lines.

Expected Milestone Achievements (EMAs):
- Appropriately alters/prepares grip according to different object's size   (F1) and shape.
- Makes multiple marks on paper in an attempt to draw lines   (F6)
- Pincer grip used to hold/control a cup, crayon or pencil   [M14-F4]
- Makes marks on paper unaided, when attempting to draw   [M14-F5]
- Increased production of multiple syllable sounds ('doo-doo-wah')   (Comms6)

Materials:
- Coloured (non-toxic, child-safe) wax crayon/pencil, white drawing paper.

Procedure:
Level 1
1. Demonstrate white drawing paper, and a few coloured wax pencil(s).
2. Clearly show how to use the wax crayon/pencil to draw a single horizontal line on the paper.
3. Present the sheet of paper and wax crayon/pencil to baby, now guiding baby to draw a horizontal line, as long (continuous) a line as possible.
4 Ensure appropriate praise and encouragement for baby with success in so doing.

Level 2
1-3. Repeat level 1, steps 2-4, this time demonstrating, then inviting baby to draw, vertical lines.

Variations:
- Provide baby with a long handled paint brush, guiding baby to grasp the stylus and to paint/stroke the line as per you instructions (can also use water, if no paint be available – even adding vegetable/food colouring).
- Consider introducing novel straight line patterns ((e.g., checking, hatched lines) or different angles with success, diagonals, arcs, circles with increasing success.

Additional thoughts/Activity Preparation/Lesson Planning Tips:
- Allow for your demonstration time to be long enough, with additional language usage and movement exaggeration, in order to create sufficient interest and motivation for baby to draw picture lines, (e.g., drawing lightening strikes with a "crash-bang crash-bang !"...
- Be sure to carefully observe baby's ability to grasp (or not !) the pen/stylus posture, so helping you better understand which of baby's fine and gross motor skills, and thus which coordinated muscle developments are involved in doing the holding and manipulating of the crayon/brush each time.
- Encourage the drawing of increasingly longer lines as far as possible, so exercising baby's developing skills in controlling the force of different muscle actions when engaged in a task such as this. [though also *consider to place sheet(s) of unwanted newspaper under baby's 'drawing sheet' so as to protect any surface that you would not like to be colour waxed also !*].
- As/when completing this activity, be sure to share baby's work and achievement, possibly by building 'Baby's Art Gallery' at home (with additional photography).
- Take care to monitor the need, and action, to keep clean baby's clothing (bib needed ?) and hands as/when appropriate, whilst also keeping ALL materials away from baby's eyes and mouth.
- When drawing/painting their picture(s), be sure to remind baby to draw ONLY on the drawing paper surface, and not spread out their crayons/paints on the supporting lower surface/ground mat (difficult to clean), using a plastic tray and or protective film below them as protection for the floor, walls and other equipment/furnishings. [NB: *Purpose made drawing easels may also help (but may also encourage baby to draw on the walls, at this age !)*].

G/A 15.6   BB Bowls !

Task description:
- Exploring throwing, with increased underarm and hand release control.

Expected Milestone Achievements (EMAs):
- Walks many steps without stumbling, or sitting down   (G1)
- Imitates action of throwing a ball (with/without release)   (F4)
- Enjoys interacting with mobile objects, trolleys and/or rolling balls   (Cog5)

Materials:
- Toy bowling set (or own made version of same using clean plastic bottles/large bricks and small balls).

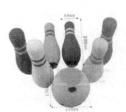  

Procedure:
Level 1
1. Demonstrate a bowling set, gently showing how to release the ball with an underarm 'throw' each time.
2. Demonstrate next the ball/bottle arrangement on the floor, releasing the ball using the same technique as above, aimed now ultimately towards the arranged bottles' location in order to knock down the bottles with the ball.
3. Assigning a region of the room clear for the activity, locate the bottles now in the centre of a marked out floor-space.
4. Arrange the bottles as a bowling set together, and then guide baby to 'throw' the ball in order to strike (knock down) the bottles, as previously demonstrated.
5. As/when baby succeeds in hitting/knocking down the bottles with the ball, ensure that you provide prompt encouragement and appropriate praise (*whatever baby achieves - remembering that the focus here is upon controlled ball release timing, and NOT bottle hitting per se !*).

Variations:
- Adjust both the bottle's quantity, spacing, and distance from 'throwing' position, in order to decrease or increase the level of difficulty, as appropriate, with increasing accuracy and release timing.
- Ditto re the task itself (or if no 'skittle/bottles' be available/buildable in the home), using larger and smaller boxes/baskets as targets for baby to 'throw' their balls into.
- Another alternative to bowling, it to have baby match throw differently coloured balls/rolled socks with/into differently coloured boxes, each colour placed at a different distance (maybe inviting baby to try doing this all at the same time you do, or throwing alternately, but from different throwing locations !).

Additional thoughts/Game-Activity Preparation/Lesson Planning Tips:
- After baby has hit/knocked down the bottles each time, ensure that you promptly return to the target bottle area to 'reset' the bottle arrangement into their vertical standing positions, so allowing baby to continue 'bowling' without losing interest and motivation to try again.
- As/when baby does hit any bottle(s) with their thrown ball, be sure to quickly provide warm encouragement and excitable praise (i.e., baby has not 'broken' them, and is now in trouble !).
- *Encourage/guide baby in making forward motions of the upper and lower arm joints (especially if their controlled 'ball release' action has improved), their effort thence supplying extra impetus to making the ball travel further forwards (rather than just 'letting' go, and it dropping to the floor in front of them !), the ball thus becoming more likely to roll away from them and towards the direction of the bottles*
- Pay careful attention to preventing baby facing towards any other persons who may be in the room as they practice their ball throwing (some will naturally attempt an overarm or sidewise sweep throw of the ball at first !), so helping avoid wounding those other persons with baby's ball hitting their head or face.

G/A 15.7   I Can Pick it up Myself !

Task description:
- Exploring the fine, controlled manipulation of small objects.

Expected Milestone Achievements (EMAs):
- Walks many steps without stumbling, or sitting down   (G1)
- Keen to try (but often still unable) to pick up very small, flat objects   (F2)
- Developing fine control with selective grasping of one object   (Cog4)
  from amongst a pile/collection.
- Makes vocal sounds which resemble particular 'words'   (Comms5)
- Selectively/accurately points towards desired/referenced objects   (SP2)

Materials:
- Wishing-tree card (ideally laminated, so reusable)

- Small fruit image cards/stickers (max 1cm width, laminated)
- Individual candy picture/image cards (max 3cm width, laminated), tray.

Procedure:
Level 1
1. Demonstrate a wishing-tree card, upon which has been attached different candy image cards (each with a picture of a different candy on it).
2. Slowly remove the candy-cards from the tree, one at a time, and place them into the tray, as you also pretend to taste and enjoy them.
3. Present the same full candy fruit tree card now to baby, inviting/guiding baby to carefully remove the candy from their trees, one piece at a time.
4. As/when each baby completes their task, have them then share their 'candies' with you (and/or their soft-toys, or other babies/persons who may be present), finally giving all the remainder to you, as you indicate your appreciation with much encouragement and, "Thank you", as they do so.

Level 2
1-4. Repeat level 1 steps 1-4, this time building trees (if able), as well as 'harvesting' the fruit from the different cards, according to baby's individual ability level(s).
5. Consider inviting baby to move between several tree-cards, collecting the 'same' kind of fruit (placing then only that fruit as requested onto their building tree), else to then deliver the non-target types for you to eat [or to some other assigned person, or soft toy to receive each time].

Variations:
- Consider running further rounds using, e.g., animal image-cards showing different birds {penguin, magpie, owl), butterflies, insects, or small mammals which may be found in/around trees (squirrel, mouse, red panda).
- Alternatively, place differently sized image-cards about the room/walls/furnitures, inviting baby to try finding the solution as to how take them down.
- Ditto, placing differently sized image-cards about the floor (or on different low-height surfaces), inviting baby to then pick up each (as many) of the image-cards that they can find.

Additional thoughts/Game-Activity Preparations/Lesson Planning Tips:
- Ensure that all of the image-cards which you use are both clean and safe for baby to handle (or have been laminated if wishing to reuse them), and trimmed of any sharp or pointed edges, in order to help prevent scratching of baby's skin, eyes, or mouth parts.
- As/when baby takes up any of the fruit image-cards into their hand(s), encourage/guide baby to also say the name of the fruit shown on the card image, so also enabling demonstration of their increasingly rich cognitive and language developments.
- Rather than using glue or blu-tak (to help prevent toxicity effects and swallowing, respectively), make use of two-sided tape to attach the image-cards to the trees each time.

G/A 15.8 Pick and Place

Task description:
- Exploring the acquisition of small objects, and their placement, to request.

Expected Milestone Achievements (EMAs):
- Appropriately alters/prepares grip according to different object's size (F1)
  and shape.
- Keen to try (but often still unable) to pick up very small, flat objects (F2)
- Recognises specific sounds as being the name of an object, person (Cog3)
  or event names.
- Attempts to 'look *for*' an object in a different place (possible outside the (SP4)
  immediate room) when asked "Where is x ?".

Materials:
- Play mat square, transparent tape, bells, large dried seeds/beans.

- Bowls, small-mouthed plastic bottles.

Procedure:
Level 1
1. Demonstrate a square shaped ground mat, upon which has been placed two rows of wide, transparent tape strips together, with their adhesive tape attaching many bells.
2. Slowly and gently now show baby how to use a pincer grip to remove the bells, and to then take them away and place them into a bowl, one at a time.

3. Present the remaining set of materials closer to baby.
4. Invite/guide baby to remove the bells from the tape as just demonstrated, placing them (one at a time) into the bowl that you are now holding.
5. Once completely removing all bells, and placing them all into the bowl, provide baby with the appropriate encouragement and prompt praise as they do so.

Level 2
1. Demonstrate now the same square shaped ground mat, again with its two rows of tape width, but this time with their adhesive tapes attaching dried seeds/beans.
2. Slowly and gently now show how to use a pincer grip to remove the seeds/beans, from the tape, and to then take them away and place them into a small-mouthed bottle, one at a time.
3. Present the remaining materials to baby.
4. Invite/guide baby to next remove the seeds/beans from the tape as per your demonstration, placing them (one at a time) into the bottle that you hold for them.
5. Once completely removing/relocating all of the beans, and placing them all into their bottle(s), provide prompt encouragement and praise as baby does so.

Variations:
- Provide for baby a transparent, but sealed vessel, into which has been inserted a thick straw (i.e., with an internal diameter wide enough to contain/transport the item to be transferred); inviting baby to then bring the seeds/beans from a bowl, one at a time, and to place them into the lip of the straw, so facilitating their entry into the otherwise sealed vessel ! (keeping it away from the mouth ar all times).
- If providing a mix of different dried beans/rice/peas, consider encouraging baby to place only one type of object into each of several vessels as they remove them from the tape.

Additional thoughts/Game-Activity Preparation/Lesson Planning Tips:
- Be sure to pay close attention at all times to preventing baby placing any of the small objects (seeds/beans/bells) into their mouth, so helping avoid swallowing or choking risk.
- Use adhesive tape which is sturdy, non-toxic, and reliable, and not likely to release much tacky residue on baby's hands (and faces) – make wet-wipes available for immediate cleaning throughout/after the task.

G/A 15.9   Sticky Sticks

Task description:
- Exploring use of an extended reach tool to acquire objects (without directly using the hands to pick them up).

Expected Milestone Achievements (EMAs):
- Reaches for dropped/distant items using a retrieving tool   (Cog2)
- Developing fine control with selective grasping of one object   (Cog4)
  from amongst a pile/collection.

Materials:
- Smooth stick (with two-sided/or outward-facing sticky tape strip at one end)
- Small gloves/socks, and a wooden stick/long spoon (each prepared with an outward-facing sticky surface, using adhesive tape).

- Small balls, boxes.

Procedure:
Level 1
1. Prepare for the activity by pouring many differently coloured small balls (rolled socks, or similarly sized objects) about the room floor/table for baby to see.
2. Demonstrate now a prepared glove/sock (with outward-facing sticky tape), showing how it may be used to 'pick up' a small ball using the strange 'glove' placed over the hand, and then to raise it (the ball now stuck to the 'glove'), carry it over to an empty box, and placing the ball (stroke/shake it off) into that box.
3. Present to baby their own 'mysterious glove/sock', inviting baby to then collect/stick a small ball to it, and to then place it into the box as per your demonstration.
4. As/when baby succeeds with collecting and placing each ball in this way, be sure to lead in providing prompt praise and encouragement for baby's efforts.

Level 2
1. Present this time a prepared smooth stick, with a sticky end-surface (at the non-held end), again also pouring many differently coloured small balls about the room floor/table.
2. Demonstrate now the use of the prepared stick (with outward-facing sticky tape), showing how to 'pick up' a small ball using the stick held in the hand (by the non-sticky end !), and then to lower it towards the bowl on the floor/table (the ball now sticking to the 'sticky-stick'), carrying it to the empty box for baby to clearly see.
3. Present now to baby the prepared 'sticky stick', inviting baby to then collect a small ball as before, this time using their new tool, and to then place the ball into the box each time.
4 As/when baby succeeds with collecting and placing each ball in this way, lead in providing prompt praise and encouragement for baby's newly developing skills.

Variations:
- Increase the level of difficulty by requesting baby to collect/place the differently coloured balls into boxes of the same corresponding colours (or at least so marked/coded), once retrieved using the tools of levels 1 & 2 described above.
- Ditto, placing the balls upon different cushions of different heights about the room for collection.
- With increasing ability(ies), consider placing the small balls about the room, each at different heights/altitudes, providing baby with folded-paper sticks, in order for them, e.g., to get them down from the wall (by jumping/hitting them down).
- Ditto, placing the balls behind a raised barrier, so that baby can 'see' them when laying on the ground, but not reach them with their outstretched arms alone, and thus MUST the tool in order to reach them !

Additional thoughts/Game-Activity Preparation/Lesson Planning Tips:
- Build the smooth sticks out like a spatula with paper-card sticky-stick ends if the rounded surfaces are not large enough to easily attach/transport the balls you are using, (so it instead now looks something like a flyswatter !).
- Watch baby carefully when s/he is using their long-handled tool(s), whilst helping to prevent baby from wounding others should they be tempted to wave them about and accidentally hit you or someone else (or indeed themselves !).
- Be sure to supervise adequate cleaning of all balls, sticks (and baby !), after the activity, to clear all sticky residues derived from the tape, from all equipment and contact surfaces.

G/A 15.10   Push or Pull BB Delivery !

Task description:
- Exploring the wheeled transportation of select items to an assigned destination.

Expected Milestone Achievements (EMAs):
- Walks many steps without stumbling, or sitting down   (O1)
- Enjoys interacting with mobile objects, trolleys and/or rolling balls   (Cog5)
- Selectively/accurately points towards desired/referenced objects   (SP2)

Materials:
- Small roller board/stroller/buggy, boxes

- Toy fruits and vegetables, plush animal toys, etc., coloured ribbon.

Procedure:
Level 1
1. Establish a 'delivery pathway' with an obvious beginning and end point; at the 'beginning' place a box loaded with toys, at the 'end' a series of empty boxes.
2. Demonstrate now the placing of a particular toy (which you name), onto the small baby trolley (or similar wheeled vehicle), kneeling down to slowly pull along the trolley (together with its new 'load' [toy item]), to then deliver it to one of the empty boxes (which you also name, before leaving for that destination).

3. Present now the small trolley to baby, inviting baby to now deliver a/the 'specified -by-name' toy to a/the 'specified-by-colour-name' box at the other end of the 'delivery pathway'.
4. As/when baby succeeds with transporting their load (target toy), and places it then into the specified box (without falling down, or dropping their 'load' to the floor en route), provide prompt praise and appropriate encouragement.

Level 2
1. Present baby with a coloured ribbon.
2. Demonstrate attaching the coloured ribbon to each of both sides of baby's trolley (or similar wheeled vehicle), showing baby how to then take up/draw the coloured ribbon by its middle, so forming a 'lead rope'.
3. Encourage baby to now slowly walk forwards and to draw their trolley along by pulling it along holding the ribbon, in order to transport the toy load to its stated destination each time.
4. As/when baby succeeds with transporting their load (target toy) in this way, *and* then also places it into the specified box (without falling down, or dropping their 'load' to the floor en route, provide prompt praise and appropriate encouragement.

Variations:
- If preferring not to use a wheeled vehicle indoors just now, consider presenting baby with a simple cushion or a tray, inviting baby to then slowly walk with their toy loads, in order to transport them to their assigned destinations.
- Ditto, baby dragging a large towel or pillow case with its parcels place on/inside it.
- For the aquatically excitable – arrange for the task to be conducted in a bath or large bowl of water – with suitably identifiable 'docking' areas for executing the loading/unloading.

Additional thoughts/Game-Activity Preparation/Lesson Planning Tips:
- When baby is/may be moving to 'deliver' the respective toys, be sure to adequately separate their 'pathway' from overhanging or obstructive room furnishing, so avoiding (or at least reducing) the likelihood of any head-bumping or painful limb collisions, and especially during Level 1, so also preventing their fingers getting squished between their stroller [as baby may be holding on to it at the edge(s)], and any other object/person contact.

G/A 15.11   Different Bits of Me !

Task description:
- Exploring and naming the locations of body parts, and some senses.

Expected Milestone Achievements (EMAs):
- Becoming interested in body parts, and pointing to them when named (Comms1)
- Makes vocal sounds which resemble particular 'words'   (Comms5)

Materials:
- Small balls, large human character picture (and/or animal pictures, if preferred). *NB: Compare materials as used for Facial and sensory body parts [G/A 13.10].*

 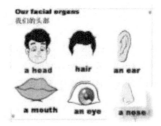

Procedure:
Level 1
1. Invite baby to consider and respond to the following type of question, for example, "Where are your [baby's] eyes"; invite baby to then refer to either the display picture or their own face, to show to you where indeed they [baby] believe their eyes to be (and not to indicate instead what they are looking at !).
2. Clearly indicate to baby whether their response/performance is "correct" or not, providing prompt encouragement and praise as appropriate.

Level 2
1. Demonstrate now a large human character picture (naming/asking baby to name) the various visible body parts on that picture (referring/pointing to the [A3] picture parts each time).
2. Present now a collection of small balls, inviting baby to take it turns with you to come forward, and according to your instruction each time, place/stick one of the small balls on to the character picture's body – in a location corresponding to the position of the body parts mentioned in your instruction (e.g., "Would you please place one of the blue balls onto the picture character's nose/leg").

3. As/when baby places such a ball 'correctly' onto the body position stated (as per your request, although picking the 'correct" ball is less important here than its subsequent placement), provide prompt praise and encouragement for baby to enjoy.
4. Continue to call out requests concerning identification and placements upon the different limbs, hands, and other currently nameable parts of the body known.

Variations:
- Consider to arrange a human character picture with small balls already placed upon the various body parts that baby can name (or at least know the names of); inviting baby to then come forward and *remove* balls according to an assigned body part each time.
- Run variations of this activity using a variety of non-human animal pictures.
- Ditto, using robots, or even bodies with identifiable body parts placed in unusual locations !!

Additional thoughts/Game-Activity Preparation/Lesson Planning Tips:
- Pay attention to observing how baby refers to his/her own five senses, especially with respect to the degree of position accuracy as they may indicate each time, so gauging a better understands of baby's own (versus others') body perceptions.
- If placing the large character picture on the wall, consider asking baby to show you the corresponding different body parts (of it), *and* themselves, with comparison pointing.
- … If able to do this with several persons in the room at the same time, supress baby's desire to start poking other's bodies too hard/sharply (especially around the face and eyes).

G/A 15.12   Lost and Found !

Task description:
- Exploring and seeking out the location of recently visible objects, when suddenly lost from view.

Expected Milestone Achievements (EMAs):
- Successfully climbs up onto low furniture items unaided (G4)
- Attempts to 'look for' an object in a different place (possibly outside (SP4) the immediate room) when asked "Where is x ?".
- Increased production of multiple syllable sounds ('doo-doo-wah') (Comms6)

Materials:
- Adult bed sheet sheet/blanket, plush animal toys, baby doll.

Procedure:

Level 1
1. Demonstrate a large adult bed sheet/blanket, showing baby what the open sheet looks like when unfolded.
2. Singing and dancing with baby together, manipulate the sheet's movement to be alternately high and low, fluctuating its motion together, as you cause the sheet or blanket to flutter.
3. Upon calling out a signal password 'NOW', allow the sheet/blanket to gently float above the floor/bed (wherever you happen to be), somehow managing to leave baby outside of the sheet-covered area, then pulling it down towards the bed or floor, as you alone remain now hidden beneath it !!
3. Guide the baby (by calling ?) to then come and seek out where you are (under the sheet/blanket).

Level 2
1. Place now various plush animal toys or dolls (and possibly other objects according to baby's particular interests ?) at various locations for baby to clearly see.
2. Covering the toy array with the sheet/blanket, evenly spread out its edges, flat against the floor/bed surface.
3. Invite now baby to sneak under the sheet, and to seek for, and collect, a specified toy (noting whether they rely upon memory to guide their search direction, or may move about at random until they find it).

Baby Milestones of Development (0-3 Yrs)

4. As/when baby returns from their search with a toy (whether or not they retrieve the specified toy), facilitate the most appropriate and comforting 'welcome back' and, "Thank you" for collecting/delivering any toy item they may present you with.

Variations:
- Consider establishing a multi-shelf structure with many hideaway spots (using a variety of boxes and other large-scale cushioning and/or climbing equipment, placing the different toys in the different hideaway spots for baby to seek and find.
- Ditto, placing 'new' pieces of equipment (stools/boxes) in front of and around previously visible 'toy shelf' arrays, which baby then watches you hide/obscure/cover with a variety of other equipment/cushions/cloths etc/.; then invite baby to seek out/recover a particular item according to you specification request (by name).

Additional thoughts/Game-Activity Preparation/Lesson Planning Tips:
- When raising the sheet up and down above baby, be sure to 'know' that s/he is standing/jumping about in "the safe region" (away from the edges, which may catch their heads/faces/eyes), whilst also avoiding baby's potentially colliding with furnishings or banging their head against anything/anyone else !
- If baby is too uncertain/insecure in travelling alone beneath the sheet to retrieve their target toys, travel beneath the sheet/blanket to go 'eduventuring' together.
- As/when baby is invited to sneak under the sheet to retrieve their target toys, be sure to pay attention not only to baby's travel direction relative to the remembered target, but also to the possible collisions likely with any objects located in a direction *outside* the sheet that baby may be crawling towards (but cannot now see !), thus helping baby avoid any head-on collision with that/those objects also.
- Ditto any bed edges (top/bottom/or side falling), if not conducting the task/activity on the floor, but instead on an adult-sized family bed.
- Consider to run this activity at a birthday party with invited baby's of similar age – running the task as a simultaneous 'all-in' under the sheet raising and lowering fun time; perhaps one baby at a time as they move through the space when raised; or as baby-parent group(s), depending upon individual performance abilities and motor skills.

ψ

– 8 –

Baby Milestones of Development

(With 100+ Fun Activities to Help Demonstrate Them)

[Age 16 Months]

ψ

Expected Milestone Achievements
Age = 16 Months

[Key: e.g., 8 = Game No. 16.8]

Gross Motor	
• Walks many steps without stumbling, whist carrying object(s)	1, 4, 5
• Prefers walking rather than crawling across large distances	4, 6
• Kicks a ball with more flexible and coordinated limb joints	
• Throws a ball (with release), though with little/no directional control	11
• Reaches down in order to pick up an object whilst moving	5
• Shows increased co-ordination of different body parts when climbing	11, 12
Fine Motor	
• Successfully stacks 3 or more blocks/toys in a stable pile	4
• Pulls strings and presses buttons in order to produce object movement/sounds	2, 6
• Uses controlled finger grips when climbing up onto, and off of, furniture	5, 12
• Scribbled patterns becoming more stable/stereotyped	3
• Makes longer, and increasing numbers of marks when drawing on paper	3
• Attempts multiple strokes/lines in order to draw a single image	3
Cognitive	
• Spontaneously changes seating/kneeling position on a chair (in order to see/reach more distant objects)	3, 7
• Remembers to pull strings and press buttons in order to produce object movement and/or sounds	2, 6
• Reaches for distant items using a retrieval tool (without prompting)	7
• Shows more differential responses to (or curiosity about) unfamiliar objects	7, 9
• Independently fills containers with small (< 1cm) objects	8
• Explores tearing and crumpling actions with paper, tissues and similar objects	8
Communication	
• Looks for' and retrieves an object from a different place (even from outside room) when asked "Where is x ?"	1, 10
• Becoming more attentive to adults' use of books as 'reading' and story content source (rather than being simply an object to tear/chew)	
• Utterances now including the use of 3-6 reliably understandable words	1
• Appears to begin questioning ('What dat ?", at least in gesture, if not verbally)	9
• Enjoys repetitive and 'favourite' story telling/singing time	
• Points and requests more accurately in order to acquire distant objects	5
Socio-Personal	
• Shows teeth brushing attempts with increased coordination	
• Responding to, and experimenting with, images in mirror	10
• Invites others to 'join' *their* activity by calling out loud	
• Keen to invent/discover creative climbing adventures !	12
• Shows fear responses to particular sound sources (e.g., dog barks, loud machines)	2
• Show overt 'suspicion' or fear of strangers	2

G/A 16.1 Looking For It !

Task description:
- Exploring and searching object locations according to verbal request.

Expected Milestone Achievements (EMAs):
- Walks many steps without stumbling, whist carrying object(s)　　(G1)
- 'Looks *for*' and retrieves an object from a different place (even from　(Comms1) outside room) when asked, "Where is x ?".
- Utterances now including the use of 3-6 understandable words　　(Comms3)

Materials:
- Mats, cushions, boxes, Toy fruits and vegetables, plush animal toys

Procedure:
Level 1
1. Arrange mats and cushioning about the room to create different areas with various coloured fruits and vegetables hidden between cushioning of the same colour(s).
2. Invite baby to now go search for the different toy fruits and vegetables.
3. As/when baby successfully finds any fruit and/or vegetable, provide prompt praise and encouragement.

Level 2
1. Arrange now, more complex cushioning buildings (within harder to hide/find spaces).
2. Use as a barrier a sheet/blanket, to separate baby from your construction(s) (suspended, say, across a string between two chairs).
3. Demonstrate and classify the different toys, 'plush animal toys', 'fruits and vegetables', each toy *type* to be placed in a separate box, after being found.
4. Hide now the various toys within the cushion-building system constructed (still keeping the sheet/blanket as a visual boundary as you do this.

5   Once 'hidden', invite baby to now go and search for the plush animal toys, or the fruits and vegetables, allowing baby to shuttle back and forth beyond the sheet/blanket barrier, and to find the assigned toy (that you have specified each time).
6   As/when baby successfully achieves this, be sure to provide prompt praise and appropriate encouragement.

Variations:
- With success, and according to baby's comfort level, consider to switch off /lower the room lighting, and/or draw the window blinds, adjusting to a dark room. Present now a flashlight for baby, inviting baby to then use the flashlight in order to search for the target fruits and vegetables/plush animal toy hidden in the room.
- Hide larger and/or smaller sized toys within the different cushion obstacle spaces, placing the same coloured toys and obstacles in the same locations with increasing success, [thus becoming relatively harder to find/neglect (see)].
- Consider showing baby your whole display, then cover it, to see whether baby can remember the toy classifications, and/or specific item locations, thereafter sending them to go to the places suggested, in order to check their claims !

Additional Thoughts/Game-Activity Preparation/Lesson Planning Tips:
- As/when baby successfully finds their target toy(s) each time, facilitate the provision of appropriate praise, and *take back the toy only after allowing some exploration time if wanted, only then inviting baby to continue to search for their next item (so allowing baby to enjoy their efforts awhile, else simply taking it away to soon might de-motivate their making further attempts to find new ones).*
- When using the sheet/blanket barrier, be sure to carefully observe baby's movements and progress, so helping prevent collisions, falling or accidental bumping into any nearby furnitures/objects.

Baby Milestones of Development (0-3 Yrs)

G/A 16.2   Brave Baby Now !

Task description:
- Exploring reactions and responses to identifiable sound sources.

Expected Milestone Achievements (EMAs):
- Pulls strings and presses buttons in order to produce object movement/sound. (F2)
- Remembers to pull strings and press buttons in order to produce object movement and/or sounds. (Cog2)
- Shows fear responses to particular sound sources (e.g., dog barks, machines). (SP5)
- May show overt 'suspicion' or fear of strangers (SP6)

Materials:
- Play mat or similar soft surface, cushions, coloured ribbons.

- Sound bites (e.g., mp3 animal calls, transport/vehicles), plush animal toys/puppets/pictures.
  NB: Such sound sources may be obtained from online websites, library-based recording media, or audio extracts from video/TV/radio action. Consider also recording your own such sounds at different times when out and about !

Procedure:
Level 1
1. Demonstrate and assign differently coloured ribbons as being associated with different animals (e.g., red = tiger, yellow = dog, blue colour = cat, green = duck and so forth).
2. Arrange these different animal-associated coloured ribbons on the floor/table, and flare-out the coloured ribbon extensions towards baby's direction, covered by/or lying over cushions, the other ends attached to the appropriate animal model/plush toy/puppet/picture (which baby cannot yet see), only the coloured ribbons being visible to them at this time.

3. Having established the detailed "association list", as/when baby then touches/pulls at one of the coloured ribbons, simultaneously broadcast the corresponding animal sound bite to the room for baby to clearly hear (or if no 'real' sound recording, make instead your own sounds accordingly each time). At the same time, baby should 'see' the soft toy/finger puppet/picture likeness.
4. Next, switch off the room lighting and draws the window blinds, causing the room to darken.
5. Invite baby to now pull a coloured ribbon (one at a time), as you again then simultaneously present the corresponding animal sound bite as before.
6. Carefully observe baby when drawing towards each coloured ribbon, and especially so as they begin to hear the animal's sound, noting what response(s) (if any) they may show (e.g., stop/change their movements, look about/cuddle into your body, curiously wait and sees what may happen next, etc.,).
7. Continue to invite baby to come forward and attempt touching each ribbon in turn, as you simultaneously play/utter appropriate colour-matched animal sound bites each time.

Level 2
1. Following the level 1 task as foundation, attach/associate this time the differently coloured ribbons with different transport vehicles(e.g., red = fire engine, green = train, blue = aeroplane, yellow = bus, and so forth), as per level 1 (steps1-3).
2. As/when baby draws each coloured ribbon, simultaneously broadcast the corresponding/associated transport vehicle sound bite, observing baby's response(s) as before.

Variations:
- Increase the stimulus set to include other sound fragments, e.g., weather indicants such as thunder & lightening, rainstorm, strong wind and so forth, associating each with corresponding picture scenes.
- Ditto using various identifiable musical instrument pictures and sounds.
- Ditto, using various mechanical and electrical machine sounds (e.g., doors closing, clocks, food mixers, radio, door bell, telephone, toilet flushing).
- Consider to try baby having the opportunity to operate the sound source(s) on/off broadcast switches/controls directly, if interested to do so, at appropriate times.

Additional Thoughts/Game-Activity Preparation/Lesson Planning Tips:
- Before broadcasting the sound bites, be sure to have tested the effects, and adjusted each timing for suitable volume first, so avoiding the frightening of baby by the sudden onset of an otherwise disruptive loud noise per se !!
- As far as possible, try to play/produce the sound bites *at the same time baby is drawing/touching the coloured ribbons.*
- If attaching the coloured ribbons to the 'real' associated object toy, be sure to have hidden the objects from clear view, otherwise baby will be distracted from 'listening', by the object that they can instead already 'see'.
- Be sure to enable distinction to be made between the 'actual sound' of any given animal (e.g., a barking dog, or mewing cat) from its human language reference to such 'sounds' (e.g., "woof-woof", or "Meow-meow" !!).

G/A 16.3   Little BB-Me Artist !

Task description:
- Exploring free-hand picture painting.

Expected Milestone Achievements (EMAs):
- Scribbled patterns becoming more stable/stereotyped   (F4)
- Makes longer, and increasing numbers of marks when drawing on paper   (F5)
- Attempts multiple strokes/lines in order to draw a single image   (F6)
- Spontaneously changes seating/kneeling position on chair (in order to (Cog1)
  see/reach more distant objects).

Materials:
- Painting bib, water sheet, water-pen/small brush, Cup, warm water.

- Real water paints & brush, white handkerchief, drawing board, protective cover.

Procedure:
Level 1
1. Placing a protective dry sheet on the floor/table, demonstrate use of the water pen and sheet for baby to clearly see. [NB: compare Month 12, G/A 12.4].
2. Present the same sheet and water pen to baby, and a bib, inviting the baby to be dressed/prepared for water drawing.
3. Encourage/guide now baby to 'paint'/draw the water directly onto the water paint sheet, in any way they wish (whilst monitoring their fine motor manipulation and gripping of the water pen as they move it about the sheet).
4. Finally, invite baby to demonstrate their work, as you/any 'audience' carefully observes the features of baby's new art work style and content.

Level 2 [Especially if no Water-drawing sheet available]
1. Demonstrate and present to baby a bib, once again inviting baby to be helped with putting it on.
2. Present baby now with a small protective ground/table cover, a drawing board and a white handkerchief, as you fix the white kerchief to the drawing board.
3. Demonstrate the water paints, clearly showing baby the application of the paint using your index finger (as 'brush').
4. Encourage/guide baby to now dip into the water paint pigment with their index finger in order to 'doodle' on the kerchief surface.
5. Invite baby to 'paint' directly ONLY onto the white handkerchief supplied (and NOT to extend their expressive 'artwork' onto any of the surrounding furnishings, surfaces, or themselves/others !).
6. Finally, organise a *Home Baby Art Show* during which baby presents his/her work for all to see (either one at a time, or all pieces together if completing more than one), also considering to capture the event via movie film and/or still photography for the baby's own 'gallery collection'.

Level 3
1. Repeat level 2, this time demonstrating/presenting a small paint brush for baby to use.

Variations:
- If the weather is warm outside, consider to use a finger or brush to 'draw' with water outdoors, on a light surface, concrete slabs, paving stones, etc.,.. (tho' you'll need to be quick with presentations due to fast evaporation of the water into the air (possibly also of great mystery and fascination to baby ? !).
- According to baby's individual abilities/skills, consider providing larger sizes of painting pigment brushes for baby to explore, possibly inviting them to self-dip with the brush in order to take up the pigment and then doodle with it.
- Present to baby a mini-sized chalkboard (slate), and a piece of chalk (white would be best for maximum line contrast), inviting baby to then use the chalk on the drawing slate to produce drawings of particular objects.
- Use multiple boards (or the same board) for baby to make copy(ies) of your own simply lines/drawings, taking it in turns to reproduce each other's efforts.
- If uncomfortable, or inappropriately dressed for 'wet' drawing/painting, consider supplying wax crayons instead (tho' still wearing/using a protective bib].

Additional Thoughts/Game-Activity Preparation/Lesson Planning Tips:
- In order not to waste an entire bottle's contents, place only a small portion of any paint pigment onto a paper plate/food container lid, allowing baby only to dip from the pigment plate, each different colour in a different 'pallette' location of the same plate/lid.

- We recommend that painting/drawing bibs used are able to *protect baby's entire body,* so avoiding the spoiling of baby's clothing (but then also beware of baby tripping and falling over if TOO long, when also trying to walk about with it on !).
- Select only paint pigment which are certified child-safe, non-toxic & water-based, whenever possible.
- As/when baby is advised to sit in a chair to paint, be sure to guide his/her body awareness in approaching the table to paint their pictures, so avoid any painting pigment spillage/collision, or spreading it about their own (or another's) body.
- Regardless of what paint doodles baby may produce, be sure to continue close monitoring of baby's behaviour – not only of their hand/finger motor skills – but to also ensure that baby does not attempt to eat the paint, or raise a 'paint-laden' hand to their mouth or eyes (or yours).
- Choose paint brushes carefully for baby's use, only selecting those which are both relatively thick and easy to clean after use.

G/A 16.4 Little Tower Builders II

Task description:
- Exploring tower building (and different blocks' handling) to new heights.

Expected Milestone Achievements (EMAs):
- Successfully stacks 3 or more blocks/toys in a stable pile (F1)
- Walks many steps without stumbling, whist carrying object(s) (G1)
- Prefers walking rather than crawling across large distances (G2)

Materials:
- Boxes, sound blocks (or self-made versions of same), building blocks.

 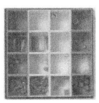 

- Stepping stones (either real 3D real objects, or floor-drawn/marked footprints).

Procedure:

Level 1
1. Demonstrate five sound blocks/containers, clearly showing how to stack them in a single pile, one on top of another.
2. Present baby with (at least) 5 such blocks, inviting baby to pile/stack them up one upon the other as previously demonstrated.
3. As/when baby succeeds to complete 5-level towers, provide prompt encouragement.

Level 2
1. Demonstrate now 5+ assorted sound blocks, again clearly showing how to stack them to form a single pile, one on top of another.
2. Present baby with (again, at least) 5 such blocks, inviting baby to then pile/stack them up one upon the other as per your demonstration.
3. As/when baby succeeds to complete 5-level+ towers, provide prompt praise and encouragement.

Level 3
1. Demonstrate now a variety of differently sized/shaped building blocks, again clearly showing how to possibly stack them (of same or different types !) to form a single tower, one on top another.
2. Invite baby to now collect (at least) 10 such blocks from some distant point, inviting baby to collect and carry them to a flat surface were they can begin piling/stacking them up one upon the other, either as just demonstrated, or in some different way.
3 As/when baby succeeds to carry them to their building site, and complete 5-level+ towers, provide prompt praise and encouragement as they do so.

Variations:
- Provide baby with a set of nesting boxes (of which some may be placed inside of the larger ones), inviting baby to then stack their boxes to form a single tower rising from the floor, (and later according to their size order if not spontaneously already doing so at first).
- Ditto, this time presenting each baby with sets of 5-6 boxes of the same size and colour only.

Additional Thoughts/Game-Activity Preparation/Lesson Planning Tips:
- If no sound blocks be available, simply construct a variety of same by placing clean, dried beans, rice, or paperclips into small sealable tins or small food storage containers for baby to hold and 'shake'/move in stacking them. *Be sure to seal them well, so preventing baby gaining access to the contents spilling out, and/or then placing the contents into their mouth.*
- As/when baby begins to build a relatively high tower each time, try to remain 'hands-off' as far as possible, instead allowing baby to continue their stacking even if building "crookedly" and likely to fall down, so allowing baby the opportunity to learn from their defeat each time. Only guide baby to adjust the building block positions as they continue upwards to build again (and thus become more self-aware of their changing strategy and developing sense of self-achievement).
- Be ever patient, and pursue careful monitoring so as to better 'scaffold' baby's growing building block and stacking ability, whilst increasing the tower's quantity of building blocks being used each time, as baby succeeds in building further upwards over time.

G/A 16.5   Busying About !

Task description:
- Exploring object interaction and manipulation whilst moving through space.

Expected Milestone Achievements (EMAs):
- Reaches down in order to pick up an object whilst moving   (G5)
- Walks many steps without stumbling, whist carrying object(s)   (G1)
- Uses controlled finger grips when climbing up onto, and off of, furniture (F3)
- Points and requests more accurately in order to acquire distant objects (Comms6)

Materials:
- Bean Bags, various small toy items and/or stacking bricks, hand-basket.

Procedure:
Level 1
1. Scatter and demonstrate several bean bags about the room floor/furnishings for baby to clearly see (replacing 'beanbags' with 'various small toys' as necessary).
2. Present to baby now a portable hand-basket (bag or case/bucket of some sort).
3. Invite baby to now move about and to collect the various beanbags, and to then collect, and place into their basket.
4. As/when baby has successfully picked up all the beanbags, invite them to then present their 'full' baskets to you, indicating your, "Thank you" and prompt praise when doing so.

Level 2
1. Demonstrate and distribute now various building block items about the room floor/furnishings.
2. Invite baby to now move about the room once more, and to collect the various pieces, and to place them into their basket as before.
3. As/when baby has successfully picked up all their target pieces, invite them to again then present their 'full' basket to you, saying, "Thanks", while also offering prompt praise and encouragement having done so.
4. Allow additional time for baby to then play with these toys (if they wish to do so).

Variations:
- Consider arranging toys/objects of different types, sizes and weight, inviting baby to raise their basket (not to drag it), then pick up the toy(s) to place into their basket, carefully observing which items baby then selects to pick up (given the choice), as well as whether their baskets are in motion, or are motionless, at the time the baby is loading them.
- Ditto, requesting baby to 'stop and pick up', or to 'pick up without stopping', on different rounds (consider also placing the items at different heights for baby to reach and manipulate each time).
- Ditto, affording baby the possibility of using a wheeled trolley or vehicle with which to collect their toys each time.

Additional Thoughts/Game-Activity Preparation/Lesson Planning Tips:
- Carefully place the items in locations about the floor/surface areas, so as to be separated by a sufficient distance to prevent frequent collisions with any furniture abutting baby's search path.
- Pay close attention to observing the way(s) in which baby raises their basket (bucket or bag) in order to walk along with it; …. and any changes in baby's gait/posture which may occur *as their basket's weight increases* with additional items, as well as any walking posture adaptations made as they continue along with their task of collecting the various toys together.
- According to baby's growing balance offset ability, consider to introduce some slightly heavier toys/items for baby to collect (but only with increasing task success, to avoid demotivation !).
- When baby is interested to gather building bricks by hand, and to then carry them to their 'building site', do NOT expect them to be able to walk about with too many of them at one time !! (hard to carry so many in their little hands, though many a baby will indeed try to move more than they can handle at once !).
- When providing the choice of baby's basket/bucket/bag, be sure to pay attention to inspecting the handle/grasping part(s), avoiding low quality plastic products with hinges that may easily detach, or otherwise cause wounding to baby's hand(s).

Baby Milestones of Development (0-3 Yrs)

G/A 16.6   BB-Delivery for You !

Task description:
- Exploring use of string, cords and/or rope as a tool to 'drive' a wheeled trolley.

Expected Milestone Achievements (EMAs):
- Prefers walking rather than crawling across large distances   (G2)
- Pulls strings and presses buttons in order to produce object   (F2)
  movement/sounds.
- Remembers to pull strings and press buttons in order to produce   (Cog2)
  object movement and/or sounds.

Materials:
- Thick string, coloured ribbon, basket/bag, plush animal toy

- Toy fruits and vegetables, boxes, baby trolley, stroller.

Procedure:
Level 1
1. Situate many toy fruits and vegetables toys about one side of room floor; on the other side separately arranged a set of independent (empty) boxes.
2. Demonstrate now a basket, to the handle of which is attached a coloured ribbon to form a connected loop.
3. Ensuring that baby is watching you, place next some toy fruits and vegetables into the basket, then grasping the loop (in either one or two hands), draw the basket along the floor towards the empty boxes, and place the toy into it/them, then towing the now empty basket back to its starting position.

4. Present now to baby the basket with ribbon attached, inviting baby to begin collecting toys and to place them into an empty box (either the same or a different one, depending upon the number of materials you are making available for the game), as just demonstrated.
5. As/when baby achieves success with this (multi-level) task, be sure to provide prompt praise and encouragement (consider also asking baby to later deliver 'their' newly full box [together with its new contents] to some specified location).

Level 2
1. Situate this time many plush animal toys about one side of room floor, the other side separately arranged with a set of independent (larger) boxes.
2. Demonstrate now a small baby walker/stroller, to the handle(s)/holes of which is/are attached a coloured ribbon (to again form a connected loop).
3. With baby surely watching you, place next a/some plush animal toy(s) onto the walker/stroller, then grasping the loop (in either one or two hands), drawing the stroller/walker along the floor towards the empty boxes, and place the toys into it/them, then towing the now empty stroller/walker back to its starting position.
4. Present to baby the same vehicle with ribbon still attached, inviting baby to now collect the toys and place them into their own empty box, as per your demonstration.
5. As/when baby achieves this, provide prompt praise and encouragement (considering also to ask baby to deliver their box (now with its new passengers) to some specified destination.

Variations:
- Sitting face-to-face opposite baby at a comfortable distance, place in front of you the basket or wheeled vehicle, as well as the different toys. In front of baby, place a long string/rope (which may be pulled continually, bit by bit, to pull/retrieve the basket or wheeled vehicle from in front of you), as well as a box. Place now a toy into/onto the basket or wheeled object, and then encourage baby to draw the string towards them, in order to draw the toy within their grasp (without getting up), and to then put the toy into their box. [NB: The string length may need be between 1-2 meters in length at first ?].

Additional Thoughts/Game-Activity Preparation/Lesson Planning Tips:
- If conducting the level 1 activity without a mat on the floor, select a basket for baby which has a smooth, non-scratching under surface.
- When baby is drawing their vehicles/vessels forward, they may often back up or be looking only at their 'goals' as they march forward, neglecting their peripheral visual field. As a result, be careful to help baby prevent the possibility of collisions (their own legs with the vehicle they are moving, with furnishings, or other persons), so better avoiding bumps and/or injury.
- For both the basket and/or wheeled vehicle's coloured ribbon design, if baby is not too careless, and reasonably controlled, consider flaring-out the string length further in order for baby to exercise increasing skill and more integrated motor organisation.

G/A 16.7   I Can use a Helping Hand !

Task description:
- Exploring tool use to acquire objects beyond immediate arm reach.

Expected Milestone Achievements (EMAs):
- Reaches for distant items using a retrieval tool (unprompted)   (Cog3)
- Spontaneously changes seating/kneeling position on chair (in order   (Cog1)
  to see/reach more distant objects).
- Shows more differential responses to (or curiosity about) unfamiliar objects (Cog4)

Materials:
- Cushions, Boxes, Bean bags , attractive toys, Rake (or kitchen spoon)

Procedure:

Level 1
1. Present a medium sized box, inviting baby to stand inside it, with your assistance (if/as needed).
2. Demonstrate next some bean bags, placing one each in front of baby (set at a location outside of their box on the floor surface), and at a distance just *too far* away/insufficient to allow them to reach it, without leaving their box.
3. Demonstrate and present to baby now a toothed rake, inviting baby now to attempt reaching the beanbag (using the rake), *without leaving their box.*
4. As/when baby is able to successfully use the toothed rake to gather the beanbag, without leaving their box, ensure that you provide appropriate praise and prompt encouragement.

Level 2
1. Construct now a cushion frame (to form a closed circle), inviting baby to stand inside it, on the floor, again with your assistance (if/as needed).
2. Demonstrate next some bean bags (or other attractive toys), placing them at locations outside of the circular cushion area on the floor surface), and at a distance again just too far/insufficient to allow baby to reach it with their outstretched arms, or without leaving circle frame.

3. Present again to baby the toothed rake, inviting baby now to attempt to reach (and acquire) the beanbag (using the rake), and without leaving the circle.
4. As/when baby is able to successfully use the toothed rake to gather the beanbag, without leaving the circular frame, provide praise and prompt encouragement.
5. Repeat steps 2-3 several times, adjusting the distance according to baby's increasing skills and abilities (encouraging high and low reaching, either over the cushion tops, or even between them, as appropriate).

Variations:
- Consider providing baby with different lengths/styles of tool with different handles/end parts (especially if no 'rake' be available, e.g., wooden spoons/kitchen implements, rods, brushes, cleaning attachments), allowing baby to choose 'appropriately' with respect to the target toy's distance to be reached each time.
- Ditto, using different types of toy at different distances each time (allowing baby a choice of both tool-type, AND target type for their problem solving activity !).

Additional Thoughts/Game-Activity Preparation/Lesson Planning Tips:
- As/when you are helping baby to stand inside the box, be sure to remain close-by throughout baby's time in the box, in order to provide baby with protection and support (if needed), so helping avoid baby from reversing and falling backwards within/from their box [unless a thick wooden box, baby may become quite unstable when attempting distance reaching in an uncoordinated way, ar least at first ?].
- Consider placing baby seated in a small bowl/bath if preferring not to have baby standing unsteadily in a relatively flexible cardboard box.
- If running the activity with more than one baby present, ensure the separation of a safe distance between babies in their different boxes, so helping avoid the lifting and waving of each baby's toothed rakes, and possibly wounding others nearby (including you).
- Ditto, carefully selecting the distance of targets around the circumference of each of the cushioned circle areas, when baby is 'fishing' outwards, from inside of it (especially if more than one is doing this at the same time !).

G/A 16.8   Show Case Display !

Task description:
- Exploring how and why certain objects come to be where they are.

Expected Milestone Achievements (EMAs):
- Independently fills containers with small (< 1cm objects)   (Cog5)
- Explores tearing and crumpling actions with paper, tissues and   (Cog6) similar objects.

Materials:
- Small coloured sponge (cut into small pieces), cotton wool, label/stickers

- Transparent small mouthed bottle (e.g., empty salt container/bottle).

Procedure:
Level 1
1. Demonstrate a salt cellar-sized glass/clear plastic jar and a pile of small coloured sponge pieces.
2. Slowly and clearly show baby how to turn the bottle cap in order to remove it, then taking up the sponges, loading each into the jar/bottle, one at a time, filling it to the top, before then replacing the bottle cap on top; finally saying, "Wow, the 'old' empty jar is now changed to have become a most attractive thing !".
3. Demonstrate, and then present, a selection of different empty transparent jars/bottles/vessels, informing baby, "I now invite you (baby) to also change your 'separate' materials to form a new, and more attractive display".
4. Present next for baby, a pile of small coloured sponges, as you guide baby in loading the sponges into the jars/vessels and to then close their lids/caps.
5 Finally, invite baby to present/demonstrate their work to you, facilitating appropriate praise after baby's new artwork piece can be shown to be really attractive, and mounted in baby's home gallery display !

Level 2-3
1. Repeat level 1, this time using assorted sizes (and colours ?) of cotton wool or tissue pieces, and/or other interesting, attractive (but flexibly-shaped) objects.

Variations:

- Provide large(-ish) balls of young children's modelling clay, for baby to pinch and mould into smaller pieces, and to then load into their jars.
- Ditto, using other small objects of interest to baby (buttons, dried beans, herbs).

Additional Thoughts/Game-Activity Preparation/Lesson Planning Tips:

- Be sure to select glass jars/bottles/vessels which are not made of a too brittle material quality, so helping avoid breakage and damage to skin if dropped.
- Pay close attention to baby's activity at all times, preventing baby from placing the small material pieces into their mouths, and avoiding the risk of choking or other breathing difficulty.
- If/when baby is trying to 'stuff' only large cotton wool pieces into their jars, encourage/guide baby to tear apart the cotton wool into smaller pieces, and to then place each piece into their bottle, rolled tighter, one piece at a time.
- Once baby has completed their new decorative display jar (possibly with disappointment, either having no more material, or being unable to get more into their bottle ?!), provide your completed artist' baby with a second (or even 3rd) jar + materials, so allowing continuation of the activity according to baby's interest and motivation level, each time.

G/A 16.9   Here to There, and Back !

Task description:
- Exploring the deliberate, visually-guided movement of fluids between vessels.

Expected Milestone Achievements (EMAs):
- Shows more differential responses to (or curiosity about) unfamiliar objects (Cog4)
- Keen to explore transfer of fluids between containers (especially in   [M17-Cog4] bath play).
- Appears to begin questioning ("What dat ?", at least in gesture,   (Comms4) if not verbally).

Materials:
- Water-paints/food colouring, transparent plastic bottle (in the bottom of which is some coloured pigment/powder), bottle cap(s)

- Plastic box/tray, teeth cleaning cup (or similar), water, bath towel.

Procedure:
Level 1
1. Demonstrate, then situate a bath towel on the floor, placing upon it a plastic box (no more than) half-filled with warm water.
2. Clearly now show baby a tooth-cleaning cup/glass and transparent plastic bottle (in the bottom of which you have placed a coloured pigment/powder).
3. Slowly demonstrate how to safely hold/grasp the transparent plastic bottle in one hand, and in the other a cup; working *inside/over* the plastic box only, gently ladle the water using the cup, and pour the water then into the transparent plastic bottle, exclaiming surprise and delight as you (and hopefully still observing baby) discover that the poured water then takes on a new (e.g., green, yellow) colour !
4. Once the transparent plastic bottle is approx. ½ - ¾ full, slowly and gently secure the bottle's cap/lid, then again show the 'final product' for baby to see and admire with interest.
5. Present to baby the same/similar materials, inviting/guiding baby to (as independently as possible) demonstrate the water colour 'magic trick' working for themselves.

6. Once completed to step 4, assist baby with placing the bottle lid on (at least stabilising the half-filled bottle, to help prevent spillage/dropping).
7. As baby then sways their sealed jar/bottle, and the water completely changes in coloured appearance, encourage with prompt praise and verbal expressions of delight such as, "Wow, such magic and skill, how did my clever baby do that ? !!".
8. Repeat steps 5-7 using different bottles, jars and pigments/colourings according to baby's ongoing interest and ability level.

Level 2
1. Using the level 1 activity as foundation ability, provide baby next with clean empty bottles/jars.
2. Invite baby to next change the water to become coloured, but this time using two kinds of colouring – pouring as before (L1), then on in turn into a third bottle (with a second pigmentation content) - e.g.,, if yellow and blue colour mixes, will change to provide green coloured water,.. etc... [remember your physics tho': pigments will mix differently from those seen when adding colours of light !!].

Variations:
- Provide baby with 'prepared' vessels, the 'pouring' bottle's body having a tiny hole in it (above the water fill level !), inviting baby to then transfer the water using a spoon/ladle, into a second vessel.

Additional Thoughts/Game-Activity Preparation/Lesson Planning Tips:
- Be sure to use only dry and/or non-toxic pigments/colourings, which will drop directly to the jar/bottle's base, and not stick to the sides before adding the water (NB: some food colourings may be better/easier to use than powdered-pigment, if available).
- Even if the pigment is certified non-toxic and infant-safe, be sure to prevent baby from attempting to drink the pigmented water, constantly remaining vigilant in this regard. Likewise, even if using vegetable-based food-colourings.
- Consider also to arrange for cleaning materials to be at hand throughout the activity - though not so visibly placed as to prove distracting to baby, or otherwise in the way during normal conduction of the activity).
- Consider preparing over-sleeves and/or a bib for baby to wear, whilst also facilitating baby to each carry out their 'pouring experiments' as far as possible either inside of over the plastic box/tray provided for the purpose.

G/A 16.10   I Can See What You See !

Task description:
- Exploring mirror reflection images with curiosity and purpose.

Expected Milestone Achievements (EMAs):
- Responding to, and experimenting with, images in mirror   (SP2)
- 'Looks for' and retrieves an object from a different place (even from   (Comms1)
  outside room) when, "Where is x ?".

Materials:
- Small labels/stickers, small reflective mirror.

Procedure:

Level 1
1. Demonstrate and present to baby several small labels/stickers and a mirror surface, inviting interaction with baby in gently placing the labels onto both your own and baby's faces.
2. Encourage/invite baby to then help to remove the labels from your face, Saying, "Thank you", as they do so.
3. Next demonstrate a mirror, inviting baby to then look at their own image in the mirror.
4. As/when baby looks into the mirror, encourage/guide baby to next look into the mirror with a view to their locating and removing all the labels they can see placed upon *their own* faces (whilst continuing to look into the mirror).
5. Once baby has succeeded in peeling off their face labels/stickers each time, provide baby with prompt praise, inviting baby to place the removed label/sticker instead onto their clothing (or other place that you have designated) each time.

Level 2
1. Again place small labels/stickers on baby's face, whilst also this time simultaneously placing more stickers onto the mirror' surface.

2. Show now the prepared mirror, guiding baby to look into the mirror and to notice that/how the mirror's labels (possibly also 'matching' their locations with those on their face), are show besides their own in the reflection of their own image.
3. Carefully observe how, whether, and which labels/stickers baby selects/attempts to remove (and in which order they do so), whilst also providing praise, and finally inviting baby to give the removed labels/stickers to you (or other person present) to wear.

Variations:
- Provide baby a fun-house (distorting image) mirror, inviting baby to observe their own and your images in the fun-house mirror, possibly whilst also making a range of different funny/ugly facial expressions.
- Ditto, placing labels/stickers onto baby's face - then illuminating the fun-house mirror, in order to observe how baby responds to the reflections seen.

Additional Thoughts/Game-Activity Preparation/Lesson Planning Tips:
- Be sure to gently place the labels/stickers onto baby's face, without pressure, and in different positions (e.g., on their nose, eyebrow, ear, chin, and so forth).
- Be sure to use only such stickers/post-it labels, etc., which are relatively easy for baby to remove, have no toxic adhesive, nor will leave marks on the mirror/object surfaces, or otherwise require scrub-cleaning to remove adhesive residue.
- Initially guide baby's hand towards their own face (not the mirror image of it !), as baby may otherwise look into the mirror but find it difficult to find/locate their target label/sticker to be removed each time.
- Be sure to provide adequate cleaning materials (simple soap/water, or wet wipes), to prevent sticker adhesive attracting dirt from the fingers/air, and or moving such into baby's mouth.

G/A 16.11   Bubble Busy BB !

Task description:
- Exploring and predicting the rhythm and motion of soap bubbles.

Expected Milestone Achievements (EMAs):
- 'Talks' and laughs when exploring bath toys (and especially bubbles). [M19-Comms6]
- Shows more co-ordination of different body parts when climbing (G6)
- Throws a ball (with release), tho' maybe still little/no direction control (G4)

Materials:
- Soft cushioning, bathtub, small balls, bubble-making jar/bottle and ring(s).

Procedure:
Level 1
1. Demonstrate and present a dry bathtub, inviting baby to sit (or lay down) inside of it [remaining clothed].
2. Present next a basket of small balls, slowly pouring the small balls/socks into the bathtub, so covering baby's body, saying, "Hey, it's time to take a funny ball--bath !" (using rolled up socks if insufficient balls be available for the purpose).
3. Facilitate encouragement of baby's moving their hands and feet up and down in order to create 'waves', which will then cause the balls to rise and fall as they do so (both of you laughing and praising the shared enjoyment at these actions).
4. Present now a bubble-making bottle, gently blowing many small bubbles above and over baby's head, encouraging baby to remain seated in their bathtub, whilst feeling and attempting to catch the bubbles as they float over/in front of them.
5. Tightly cover the bubble jar, and place it into the bathtub, and carefully observe whether baby begins to search for the jar immediately. Thereafter retrieving the jar (either receiving with, "Thank you" from baby, or by taking it back directly if ignored), continue with your bubble blowing (in interesting/attractive ways), or otherwise encourage baby to attempt blowing such themselves.

Level 2
1. Situate now several cushions to form the edges of a 'pool' in the room (arranged in circle form), inside of which is placed some cushioning with a 'hole' in the centre to form a small 'pool' of balls (or rolled socks).
2. Extend the structure to include additional cushioning all around the circular area to make a sloping road leading up to the circular frame's rim, encouraging baby to enter the 'pool' by climb up the ramp/steps, arriving at 'balance arch', then stepping in and down to the 'pool' at its centre.
3. Empty now the basket of balls into the 'pool', filling the space to half its volume.
4. Invite/guide baby to climb up the cushioned 'entrance' (the built sloping/stepped road to the circle rim), and to enter the pool of balls (now looking somewhat like a home-made baby doughnut Jaccuzi !).
5. Producing once more the bubble-making bottle, blow many small bubbles across/about baby from various directions.
6. Allow/encourage baby to now explore, watch, and dance with joy within their 'ball pool', whilst attempting to 'pop' the bubbles coming their way by throwing balls/socks at them.
7. After some time, tightly cover the bubble jar, and place it into the baby Jaccuzi, and carefully observe whether baby begins to search for the jar; thereafter retrieving the jar as before (either receiving with a, "Thank you" as baby gives it to you, or taking it back directly if ignored),.... then continuing to blow bubbles (in an interesting and attractive way), and/or encouraging baby to now attempt the blowing of bubbles by themselves.

Additional Thoughts/Game-Activity Preparation/Lesson Planning Tips:
- When 'pouring' the balls/socks over and around baby, be sure to do so slowly, as a sudden and unexpected appearance of ball's covering their body, may startle them or otherwise elicit a fear response.
- If no balls (or an insufficient number) be available to form the 'pool', consider instead to "fill' the specified area with rolled socks, smaller cushions, bean bags or soft toys, etc.,
- If/when baby does attempt to blow bubbles, be sure to prevent baby attempting to drink (or otherwise eat/taste) the soapy fluid.
- Ditto, paying careful attention to not soaking the bubble solution/bubbles too richly onto baby's face, and in particular taking care to avoid the frothing fluid from stimulating baby's eyes and or delicate skin areas.
- Be sure to also make sure that adequate cleaning materials be ready to 'mop up/remove' (not just wipe !) all residual bubble mixture from all of the room furnishings/materials and surfaces after activity use [NB: *bubbles do NOT really just 'disappear' (despite appearances) – the bubble residue still exists in the form of a thin sticky film which needs to be found and cleaned each time !!*

G/A 16.12   Finding My Way Up the Mountain !

Task description:
- Exploring ways to ascend even/uneven surfaces using steps and slopes.

Expected Milestone Achievements (EMAs):
- Shows increased co-ordination of different body parts when climbing   (G6)
- Keen to invent/discover creative climbing adventures !   (F3)
- Uses controlled finger grips when climbing up onto, and off of, furniture   (SP4)

Materials:
- Large cushioning, Boxes.

Procedure:
Level 1
1. Situate a set of boxes and cushions to build 35 degree angle ascents to form a (or a variety of) trapezoidal [flat topped] climbing structures within the room's floor and furnishings.
2. Invite baby to then attempt climbing up the trapezoidal structure via (one of ?) the side(s) with a ramped/stepped ascent pathway, and to then climb down from the top again, via the same (if only one) or a different ramped/stepped descent to the floor, as may be available to them each time - providing continuous encouragement/motivation and praise as necessary/appropriate each time.
3. As/when baby can succeed with climbing up to the 'table-top peak', and then back down the same/other side again, facilitate additional praise promptly, further rewarding their efforts with a toy to play with, after their various attempts at solo mountaineering !

Level 2
1. Repeat the level 1 steps, increasing the levels of complexity according to baby's success each time, their ability level, confidence, and physical coordination or strength – adjusting such variables as the available climbing height option (peak altitude !), approach ramp/stepping angles of elevation, number of different levels (up and down) to the 'peak', size and quantity/distance available to traverse in order to reach the 'peak'.

Variations:
- Allowing for baby's weight and body muscle strength, consider to also explore any safe and relatively clean play park area facility(ies) close to home.
- If uncomfortable with your baby climbing about furnishings in the home, consider visiting a supervised centre to make use facilities with open frame/ceiling suspended ropes connectable to baby's harness (quality contro will have such), as baby then begins to explore being/playing the 'little mountaineer' !
- Ditto, using small stone pathways, low walls or raised walking surfaces *wide enough for baby's feet to comfortably stand two feet astride.*
- … and in any/either case (Variations 1-3) ensure that you are walking alongside them (undistracted and without physical contact as far/as long as is possible), so ensure baby's comfort, reassurance, and safety from falling.

Additional Thoughts/Game-Activity Preparation/Lesson Planning Tips:
- Whether using boxes, steps, or slope-shaped cushions to build your sloping ascent paths each time, it may prove relatively 'slippery' to the (baby's) foot touch. Consider therefore to request that baby removes their socks (or have you remove them), in order to increase the frictional contact with the surfaces that they are crossing – or even allowing baby to crawl if not so confident when moving whilst standing at increasing heights as yet.
- When moving about the 'mountainous terrain' materials during the activity, be sure to remain close-by baby as they both ascend and descend, so being able to provide immediate safekeeping and a sense of security, when needed, (and without holding onto them, or otherwise directing their direction/speed of motion, unless absolutely necessary !).

ψ

– 9 –

Baby Milestones of Development

(With 100+ Fun Activities to Help Demonstrate Them)

[Age 17 Months]

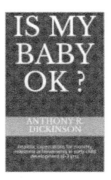

ψ

Expected Milestone Achievements
Age = 17 Months

[Key: e.g., 9 = Game No. 17.9]

Gross Motor

• Will attempt *descent* of stairs if held by the hand	3
• Spontaneously stands up in order to move to a new location, (without support, and without being asked to do so)	1
• Prefers to walk rather than to crawl, even short distances	4
• Seeks holding hands of others in order to secure balance	1, 6
• Climbs onto furniture in order to obtain object out of reach	12
• Successfully throws objects (such as a ball), though with poor control of direction/distance	2

Fine Motor

• Freely grasps and drinks from cup without being given it	4
• Makes appropriate grasping and release of objects, to/from others	4, 5, 7
• Attempts two-handed ball catching (albeit unsuccessfully !)	
• Attempts bent overarm ball throwing (or similarly of other objects)	2
• Removes whole articles of (most) own clothing, without help	5
• Plays with percussion toys more deliberately, and with more refined movements	9

Cognitive

• Explores the emptying and refilling of containers with various objects	4, 8, 10
• Identifies (some) familiar picture contents without prompting	7
• Opens and explores contents of cupboards (including refridgerator !)	
• Keen to explore transfer of fluids between containers (especially in bath play)	[[M16.9] 8
• Associates simple words, sounds and smells with particular actions	3, 10
• Shows consistency in use of drawing tools	

Communication

• Points correctly to specific book images when asked, "Where is the x ?"	7, 12
• Initiates activities (rather than passively waiting for adult prompting)	3, 9
• Makes simple two word utterances (e.g., "Baba eat", "Mama have")	11
• Shows increased turn-taking during speech patterns, and increasingly with intonation	4, 11
• 10-20 or more words now in common, daily usage	12
• Proto-speech concerning familiar objects/events clearly understandable by others	8, 11

Socio-Personal

• Increasingly willing to explore surroundings with other infants	
• Very likely to repeat behaviours which make others (especially adults) laugh	6
• Increasingly attentive to details of the activities of others' (especially other babies/infants)	
• Increasingly attentive to the causes and effects of the different behaviours of others (especially siblings/other babies)	12
• Utters proto-speech concerning shared perceptions, objects & events understandable to significant others (e.g., close family)	7
• Assists with self-dressing (and almost ALL *un*dressing !)	5

G/A 17.1   I Can Steer the Ball

Task description:
- Exploring the tactile-guided manipulation of a large movable object.

Expected Milestone Achievements (EMAs):
- Spontaneously stands up in order to move to a new location, (without support, and without being asked to do so).   (G2)
- Seeks holding hands of others in order to secure balance   (G4)

Materials:
- Play mat, large cushions, boxes, large ball.

Procedure:

Level 1
1. Establish a runway/path in the centre of the room using a variety of large cushions and other large item pieces (boxes, containers), inviting baby to stand at one end of the 'runway'.
2. Demonstrate next a large ball, slowly and clearly showing how to move from one end of the runway to the other, whilst pushing/rolling the large ball along the pathway/track.
3. Present the large ball now to baby, inviting baby to move along the built cushion track, rolling the ball from one side of the room to the other, along the same runway/path/track.
4. As/when baby succeeds to ship their large ball to the other end of the track, and does so WITHOUT rolling outside the runway/track, provide prompt, enthusiastic praise and encouragement.

Level 2
1. Using the same runway as per the level 1 activity, this time add a specific 'footpath' *within* the runway track (using 3-D 'stepping stones', or otherwise marking the floor), invite baby to stand along one side of the runway on the newly marked footpath.

2. Demonstrate once more a large ball, slowly and clearly showing how to move from one end of the runway to the other, whilst pushing/rolling the ball along the pathway (i.e., from one end), AND moving only along the footpath track within.
3. Present now the large ball to baby again, inviting baby to move along the footpath track, whilst rolling the ball by their side, along the length of the pathway.
4. As/when baby succeeds to ship their ball to the other end of the track, and WITHOUT rolling outside the pathway/track, providing prompt, enthusiastic praise and encouragement.

Variations:
- To increase the level of difficulty even further, establish the pathway(s) to have a curved section(s) (or a longer, less predictable path), inviting baby to otherwise move large balls along the track as before.
- For the more coordinated baby, consider to introduce small inclines or changes in height above the floor of the steppingstones/path with increasing success over time.
- Ditto, inviting baby to also carry a small object in their hand(s) as they do so.

Additional Thoughts/Game-Activity Preparation/Lesson Planning Tips:
- With increasing stability and balance control, try to avoid the temptation to help 'steer' your baby's actions and coordination as they move along the path each time,….However,…
- … do ensure that you remain 'close-by' at all times, to assist and offer necessary support should baby appear to becoming increasingly unstable whilst ball-rolling when their own weight is placed *upon* the ball's surface.

G/A 17.2   Hidden Treasures !

Task description:
- Exploring/discovering the hiding and retrieval of buried/submersed objects.

Expected Milestone Achievements (EMAs):
- Successfully throws objects (such as a ball), tho' with poor control of (G6) direction/distance.
- Attempts bent overarm ball throwing (and similarly of other objects)   (F4)
- Explores the emptying and refilling of containers with various objects (Cog1)
- Makes simple two word utterances (e.g., "Baba eat", "Mumma have") (Comms3)

Materials:
- Bath/Bowl, sand and/or warm water, ping pong balls, box.

Procedure:
Level 1 [NB: If no sand, socks, or other search substrate be available, consider using warm water to float the ping pong balls, possibly using bubbles/foam to make their finding a little more difficult].
1. Set up a sand bath in the room (or outdoors if clement, and preferred), inside of which has been packed some sand to a level sufficient to bury ping pong balls (i.e., such that they cannot be easily seen).
2. Hide now several ping pong balls in the smoothed-surface sand, in many shallow holes (hidden not so easily for baby to remove them directly without searching).
3. Invite baby to next carry out their discovery/treasure hunting (either individually or with you together), and to find/remove the ping pong balls, placing/throwing them into a small bucket box once found, each time.
4. As/when baby succeeds to find/remove the ping pong balls, provide prompt praise and encouragement as they do so.

Level 2
1. Set up the sand bowl/bath as before, also arranging this time for the surface to be presented at several different height/depth levels. [or increasing bubble density].
2. Hide now 5-8 ping pong balls in the smoothed (but uneven) sand, in many deep holes (again hidden not so easily for baby not to remove them directly without searching).

Baby Milestones of Development (0-3 Yrs)

3. Invite baby to next carry out their discovery/treasure hunting (either alone, or with yourself together), and to find/remove the ping pong balls, placing/throwing them into a small bucket box nearby, once found, each time.
4. As/when baby succeeds to find/remove the ping pong balls, *and* then throws them at/into the box, provide prompt praise and encouragement.
   [If using warm water to float the ping pong balls, make baby's searching and transferring a little more difficult by increasing the bubbles/foam density, and using a cup (handled or not ?) to scoop up the balls from the water each time].

Variations:
- Consider to hide plastic animal toys (or other similar objects not spoiled by sand/or otherwise easily cleaned) as you might request to be found by toy 'name', as hidden in the sand, inviting baby to then refer to these animal (or other) objects occasionally as they search *for*, and take them out each time.
- Consider to install water in the vessel table/bowl, placing different toys into the water, inviting baby to 'fish' for the toys from the water (using their hands).
- Ditto, using dried leaves, grass cuttings (depending upon season/time of year) ….

Additional Thoughts/Game-Activity Preparation/Lesson Planning Tips:
- Pay close attention to baby's hand postures and grasping posture changes, according to whether their reaching/grasping be visually (can see object to be grasped) or when only found tactile sense-driven discovery each time.
- When baby is exploring/playing in/with the sand (there is no need for baby to be actually *in* the bath at the time of exploring it !!), ensure that you pay careful attention to helping prevent baby pushing/spilling out the sand from the vessel/table, and onto the floor.
- If uncomfortable with natural or commercial sand material, be sure to provide cleaned (if not certified baby-safe) non-toxic special 'play sand' (the quality and consistency of which is a material without impurities), is soft, and so forth.
- Likewise with close attention to baby's safety, preventing baby from placing any of the sand into their (or your) mouth, or otherwise using their sandy hands to rub their (or others') eyes.

G/A 17.3   Alpine Explorations !

Task description:
- Exploring coordinated ascent and descent, with support.

Expected Milestone Achievements (EMAs):
- Will attempt *descent* of stairs if held by the hand   (G1)
- Associates simple words, sounds and smells with particular actions (Cog5)
- Initiates activities (rather than passively waiting for adult prompting) (Comms2)

Materials:
- Real staircase (as home environment allows), ...OR...

- … use large cushions, cases/boxes (to build one !)….

Procedure:
Level 1 [Use a real staircase if available in/close to/immediately outside the home]
1. Situate yourself and baby close to large-scale cushioning with ascending and descending ramps/steps.
2. Supporting baby by the arm(s) only, encourage baby to attempt making both the uphill and downhill portions of a few stairs (or your setup), paying special attention to working towards increasing baby's independence (or at least increasing comfort and confidence) with the descending parts.
3. With increasing success, invite baby to alone attempt both the uphill and downhill sections, providing only the minimum protection and support as baby's confidence and balanced coordination increases with more controlled movement each time.
4. As/when baby is able to climb alone, or especially descends alone, provide prompt praise and encouragement.

Level 2 [Again, use a real staircase if available in/close to/immediately outside the home].
1. Demonstrate a sets of cases/boxes/large containers, placed together as a group according to their height, and arranged to produce an ordered upward and downward staircase - i.e., solid surfaces, so allowing baby a more sure footing and easier balance.
2. Invite baby to join you in a coordinated demonstration of step climbing *and* descent together, all the while holding (at least one of) baby's hands, starting from the lowest level above the floor, leading baby to step/climb towards arriving at the first higher-level.
3. With increasing confidence and success, add additional cases/boxes to form higher-level (or multi-level staircases), for both upward and downward stepping explorations and practice.
4. Invite/lead baby to now carry out this same exercise alone, paying special attention to their quitenatural 'backing-downstairs' movement practice.
5. If baby will only descend the stairs with your hand's supporting them by their arm, with increasing confidence, be sure to provide baby with much praise and encouragement for this achievement also *(doing so independently is not necessarily to be expected from all/many babies at this age/stage)*.

Variations:
- Consider to add a third-level stair using the same model cushioning by arranging the pieces to be at their greatest height at the centre (as per the illustration – flat-topped tetrahedron shown above ?), again supporting baby by the arm, especially when *descending* the stairs.
- An alternative to the use of the boxes/containers (if not available in the home), might be to use wrapped bundles of old clothes/linens, newspaper, or books (with the risk of teaching baby some 'bad' climbing habits, unwanted if unsupervised in the home ? !!).

Additional Thoughts/Game-Activity Preparation/Lesson Planning Tips:
- As/when you are providing continuous physical support to baby, be sure to be *providing support only*, and not instead 'driving' baby's own balance control or forward motion. *Otherwise baby will take much longer to learn self-coordinated balancing when in motion, (or possibly even lose certain related motor coordination skills that they have already successfully learned !).*
- As baby succeeds in climbing and/or descending the stairs, provide baby with continuous encouragement. And even if/when baby may achieve this independently, you will need to remain close by in order to readily provide protection if baby should become unsteady or fatigued.

G/A 17.4   Fuel Stops !

Task description:
- Exploring self-grasping to pick up a drinking vessel from flat surfaces.

Expected Milestone Achievements (EMAs):
- Prefers to walk rather than to crawl, even short distances   (G3)
- Freely grasps and drinks from cup without being given it   (F1)
- Makes appropriate grasp/release of objects, to/from others   (F2)
- Explores the emptying and refilling of containers with various objects (Cog1)
- Shows increased turn-taking during speech patterns, and increasingly (Comms4) with intonation

Materials:
- Paper cups, plastic cups (with handle), warm water.

Procedure:

Level 1
1. Situate a firm cushion/low table in the centre of the room, sitting face-to-face with baby nearby the cushion/low table.
2. Present now two paper cups, each containing a little fresh drinking water, placing both on the stable surface. Invite/encourage baby to pick up one of the cups from the firm cushion/low table.
3. Guide baby to hold onto their paper cup, and to carry it towards you, clink your cups together ("Cheers"), and then to, "Empty your cups", as you then each drink your cup of water.
4. As/when you and baby 'empty your cups', continue (with additional supplied water) to 'empty your cups', as motivation and skill levels allow.

Level 2
1-4. Repeat the level 1 procedure, this time using handled cups, encouraging baby to travel a further distance to reach you and, "Cheers" your drinks together (allowing baby to refill the cups with increasing care with vessel handling).

Variations:
- To add variety and interest (as well as additional motor coordination skill practice), invite baby to 'feed' their water to you (as they would a doll/toy), to then drink.
- Ditto, inviting/encouraging any other person's present to also 'clink' cups with each other before drinking their own held water cups.
- To continuously enhance baby's need to use increasingly complex coordination, arrange for them to move in different ways (and across different distances) in order to collect, pick up, and/or interact with their cup of water prior to drinking it.

Additional Thoughts/Activity Preparation/Lesson Planning Tips:
- Be sure to pour for baby only a very small portion of water each time into their cup, so helping avoid baby's sprinkling it wet to the floor, and/or clothing.
- For the same reason, consider to provide/request baby wear a bib throughout the activity.
- Likewise be prepared with cleaning/mopping materials, standing by with the necessary equipment to remove any spillage from the area/furnishings (or other materials nearby !).

Baby Milestones of Development (0-3 Yrs)

G/A 17.5   I Can Undress Myself !

Task description:
- Exploring self-removal of outer clothing.

Expected Milestone Achievements (EMAs):
- Makes appropriate grasp/release of objects, to/from others   (F2)
- Removes whole articles of (most) own clothing (without help)   (F5)
- Willing and able to remove clothing at appropriate times   [M19-G6]
- Assists with self-dressing (and almost ALL *un*dressing !)   (SP6)

Materials:
- Baby vest, long sleeve coat/cardigan, bib (optional), protective clothing (long sleeved, with rear buckles/poppers).
- Dressing mirror (allowing baby to see their full body reflection).

Procedure:
Level 1
1. Without necessarily undressing baby, present a vest, inviting/guiding baby to put on the clothing item being presented.
2. Provide next a long sleeved coat/cardigan, inviting baby to put this on also.
3. Move together with baby to a place where you can now together look at their reflection in a mirror, to look at baby in their 'new' clothes, and to praise baby for looking so very attractive.
4. Facilitate baby to now make several movements, so causing the baby to become warm.
5. Guide baby to wish to take off their long sleeved coat/cardigan, as you provide instruction(s) to do such.
6. Continue to lead baby to make many movements (exactly how much depending upon the seasonal weather and indoor temperature/humidity), so letting baby to again become excited and warm.
7. Guide baby to next take off their vest, again under your provided instruction
8. Finally lead baby to lie down and relax comfortably on the floor/matting/in your arms.

Level 2
1. Repeat the level 1 activity, using this time a series of over-clothing protective garments (full body painting bib, shawl, jumpsuit, etc,...).

Baby Milestones of Development (0-3 Yrs)

Variations:
- Consider using a full set of baby's clothes, leading baby to put them on, thereafter guiding them to remove them once more, according to the order of clothing (by name) being described. [NB: best not to interrupt regular bath-time]
- Ditto dressing/undressing a baby doll of soft animal toy.

Additional Thoughts/Game-Activity Preparation/Lesson Planning Tips:
- If not conducting this activity within your own home, you may wish to take along a full 2nd set of baby's clothing, including a hat, coat, trousers/shorts or skirt, socks and so forth. It is better to use baby's own extant clothing collection for the purpose of this task/activity, even if familiar and known to be difficult for baby to self dress/undress with items containing buttons/zips etc.
- Make sure that any provided clothing is cleanly presented, is in good repair, freshly washed/smelling, and neatly folded before/after use.
- Be also careful to prevent baby from becoming overheated when wearing additional clothing for this activity, remaining sensitive in your preparations to the current climate and indoor/outdoor conditions at the time.

G/A 17.6   Hold that Balance !

Task description:
- Exploring more coordinated balance using own arms (rather than those of others) for support.

Expected Milestone Achievements (EMAs):
- Seeks holding hands of others in order to secure balance   (G4)
- Very likely to repeat behaviours which make others (adults) laugh   (SP2)

Materials:
- Large ball.

Procedure:

Level 1
1. Demonstrate a large ball, and then sit astride it with one leg either side, lean forwards to become supported by your unbent arms, and gently sway your body from side to side, using your legs as additional anchors to the floor for baby to clearly see.
2. Present now the same/large ball to baby, inviting baby to follow your example demonstration, and to gently rock side-to-side, yourself standing nearby them to provide any additional support if/as needed (maybe using a smaller ball).
3. If baby reaches for/pulls your two hands in order to carry on their swaying, provide prompt praise and encouragement.
4. With increasing success, encourage baby to promptly attempt their letting loose of your support, continuing to carry out the swaying action by themselves (even if only holding one of their hands to the large ball).

Level 2
1. Demonstrate the large ball again, this time laying upon it with your belly on the ball and both legs out the same side/back end, leant forwards with your outstretched arms forwards or below/around the centre of the ball, and gently sway your body from side to side to swing the ball about, using your legs as additional anchors to the floor for baby to clearly see (*as pictured above*).

2 Present next the same/similar large ball (or smaller as necessary) to baby, inviting baby to follow your example demonstration and to gently swing the ball about, as you again stand nearby to provide any additional support, if needed.
3. If baby reaches for/pulls your two hands in order to carry on their swaying on the ball, provide prompt praise and encouragement as they do so.
4. With increasing success, encourage baby to promptly attempt their letting loose of your support, continuing then to carry out the swaying action by themselves.

Variations:
- If no large ball be available, consider inviting baby to lie prone on a 'side-turned bucket or sturdy small bin sufficient to support baby's weight without distortion), as you then use both hands to support/protect baby at the waist, and to then carry out their swinging/rolling motion; once baby is able to maintain balance, holding only their arm lightly so as to not fall down
- Ditto, with baby situated on top of the ball, whilst you gently move them about to-and-fro, left/right, up/down, and so forth
- Consider providing/building for baby a rocking seesaw (e.g., using a short plank of wood and a brick), inviting baby to stand on the seesaw as it rocks to and fro, yourself standing in front of baby (facing) with both outstretched arms; baby will likely try to pull/grip your two hands in order to gain their physical support in order to carry on rocking !

Additional Thoughts/Game-Activity Preparation/Lesson Planning Tips:
- When baby is standing with both legs astride the large ball, sitting, their feet may well not be able to reach the floor at the same time. It is critical therefore that you help adjust baby's position on the ball (or use a smaller one), *thus enabling the adoption of a more stable posture which will allow baby to shift their centre of gravity by themselves, more steadily, and thus be less likely to fall/roll to the ground.*
- As/when you are providing baby with physical support, try to avoid the temptation to make any effort to also push/pull their baby into rocking motions, instead letting baby make the effort to find their centre of gravity and resistance limits, in order to maintain their balance whilst driving their own motion.

G/A 17.7   Animals Sillhouettes !

Task description:
- Exploring the use of simple black and white (only) contrasting picture outlines, profiles/fills to recognise animals by their shape alone (without differential colour feature cues).

Expected Milestone Achievements (EMAs):
- Makes appropriate grasp/release of objects, to/from others   (F2)
- Identifies (some) familiar picture contents without prompting   (Cog2)
- Points correctly to specific book images when asked,   (Comms1)
   "Where is the x ?".
- Utters proto-speech concerning shared perceptions, objects & events   (SP5)
   understandable to significant others (e.g., close family).

Materials:
- Card-mounted animal picture designs I (white paper, black images)
- Card-mounted animal picture designs II (non-white paper, white images).

Procedure:

Level 1
1. Demonstrate in turn, each of a set of animal picture card designs (I), allowing baby to observe/comment upon them (showing, e.g., a cat, dog, penguin, and so forth, one animal per card).
2. Now place the same card set arranged on the floor/table, inviting baby to explore them, and to point out/discover/identify the different animals each time.
3. As/when baby 'correctly' describes/discovers/identifies a given animal card image, be sure to provide prompt praise and encouragement upon their success.

Level 2
1. Demonstrate now the animal card animal picture designs (set II, with inverted black and white parts this time), again allowing baby to observe/comment upon them (showing, e.g., a cat, fish, elephant, and so forth).
2-3. Repeat as per level 1, steps 2-3.

Baby Milestones of Development (0-3 Yrs)

Level 3
1. Demonstrate now items from BOTH sets I & II of the animal card picture design collections (as used for levels 1-2 above, respectively), again allowing baby to observe/comment upon them (showing e.g., a cat, fish, bear, etc.,).
2. Place now the same mixed card sets I & II arranged at random about the floor, inviting baby to point out/identify a different animal MATCHING PAIR each time, either from the same, or one from each, image set.
3. As/when baby 'correctly' identifies/pairs up any two matching animal picture images, be sure to provide prompt praise and encouragement for their success.

Variations:
- If unable to present contrasting black-on-white Vs white-on-dark coloured paper silhouettes, simply use instead contrastive black & white Vs colour image sets.
- If requiring additional stimulation, demonstrate/use of black and white contrasting images of transport/vehicle item designs, or daily household objects, clothing, and so forth, for baby to distinguish/identify.
- Ditto, using black and white only building bricks/construction items placed in different configurations in order to increase perspective change and challenge.
- With increasing individual success, consider inviting baby to match different pairs of objects (e.g., to 'match' with each other, their own image cards with others that *you* may be holding up).

Additional Thoughts/Game-Activity Preparation/Lesson Planning Tips:
- For this particular task/activity (at this age/stage) be sure to use pictorial designs which offer only the maximum black and the white contrast outlines as far as is possible, which do not provide for any detail for baby to otherwise describe (e.g., if the cat, then only provide the cat's shape outline, without shading/accessory details).

G/A 17.8   Pouring Them Out

Task description:
- Exploring the transfer of objects and fluids between different vessels.

Expected Milestone Achievements (EMAs):
- Walks many steps without stumbling, whist carrying object(s)   [M16-G1]
- Explores the emptying and refilling of containers with various objects   (Cog1)
- Keen to explore transferring of fluids between containers (especially   (Cog4)
  in bath play).
- Proto-speech concerning familiar objects/events understandable to   (Comms6)
  others.

Materials:
- Cups, marbles, glass jars (small diameter), plastic mineral water bottle, dried black/soy beans, small balls, plastic trough/bucket, basket.

Procedure:
Level 1
1. Demonstrate two cups, one of which is 2/3 filled with marbles.
2. Slowly show how, using both hands to grasp the cups (one in each hand), to gently pour the marbles into a third, empty cup (or shallow bowl).
3. Present to baby two cups: one empty, the other containing a few marbles.
4. Invite/guide baby to now attempt transferring the marbles between vessels according to your demonstration, as just provided.
5. As/when baby succeeds with pouring the marbles into the empty cup, and does so without spilling any to the floor, be prompt to provide baby with adequate praise and encouragement.

Level 2
1. Demonstrate this time a small glass jar (with a relatively narrow diameter), and an empty plastic water bottle, the former partially filled with dried black beans.
2. Slowly show how, using both hands to grasp the two vessels (one in each hand), to then gently pour the beans from the jar into the empty bottle.

3. Present to baby now the two vessels: one empty, the other containing dried beans.
4. Invite/guide baby to attempt the item transfer between vessels according to your demonstration, being prompt with appropriate encouragement and praise.

Level 3
1. Present next to baby a bucket/trough, having also established a suitable room setup and arrangement to facilitate the following task/activity:
2. Seated in some fixed position within the room, hold a collection of small balls to supply baby with, upon their request (as baby presents their empty trough/bucket to you for ball-filling).
3. Once baby has completed having their trough/bucket filled with small balls, invite baby to then carry their bucket/trough towards the (larger) basket nearby, and to then pour their collection of small balls into the basket.
4. As/when baby succeeds to transfer all of their small balls into the basket, and neither falls over, nor drops any of the small balls to the floor, provide prompt praise and encouragement for their efforts each time.

Variations:
- Demonstrate a baby bathtub, partially filled with clean water, presenting to baby a small cup and a larger transfer vessel. Invite baby to then 'scoop up' bathtub' water with the cup, and to then transfer that water several times to begin filling up the larger vessel.
- If preparing for a birthday party, or for other reasons multiple babies be present, consider to run this activity (especially level 3 ?) as a timed race over several rounds (possibly using a countdown timer or hourglass, with different bonus or penalty conditions according to the different baby's ability levels and motivations.
- Ditto, using paired baby Vs parent/guardian as two team race set ups !

Additional Thoughts/Game-Activity Preparation/Lesson Planning Tips:
- As/when baby is transferring/handling the different items for transfer between the different vessels, be sure to pay close attention to observing baby's use of preparatory hand and wrist joint angles, as well as their finer finger movements and eye-hand coordination.
- Be sure to also keep careful watch of baby's safekeeping and security at all times, especially when operating transfers with small items, helping to prevent baby from putting these pieces between their lips to eat by mistake (so avoiding any risk of choking or swallowing).
- Be sure to provide thoroughly cleaned (but also well dried) materials as bottle/jar transfer tools/objects.

G/A 17.9 Buckets of Fun Together !

Task description:
- Exploring rhythmic sound making, with and without coordinated others.

Expected Milestone Achievements (EMAs):
- Plays with percussion toys more deliberately, and with more refined movement. (F6)
- Initiates activities (rather than passively waiting for adult prompting) (Comms2)

Materials:
- Spoon/ladle, plastic trough/bucket.

Procedure:
Level 1
1. Demonstrate a spoon/ladle and barrel/bucket, clearly showing how to use the spoon/ladle to knock against the surface of the barrel/bucket to sound a rhythm.
2. Present to baby the same spoon/ladle and bucket, inviting baby to use their right hand to grasp the bucket, and to follow your rhythm to knock on the bucket.
3. Knocking the bucket in time to your rhythm, request the baby to also "Stop" (upon your saying so), the baby stopping their knocking on the bucket when you say this (thus also encouraging them to listen whilst also deliberately making noise themselves); baby stopping to create rhythm sounds to affirm that they are indeed also listening.
4. Invite baby to next take up the bucket in their left hand, repeating steps 3-2-3-2.... as their continued interest and motivation suggests.

Level 2
1. Demonstrate now two spoons/ladles and two buckets/boxes, the latter placed upside-down on the floor, their bottom flat surfaces facing upwards towards baby.
2. Clearly showing how to use the two spoons/ladles (one in each hand) to knock against the surface of each of the barrels/buckets to sound a rhythm.
3. Present to baby now the same two spoons/ladles and buckets, inviting baby to follow your rhythm to knock on each bucket (in turn, or together at the same time).

4. Knocking the buckets in time to your rhythm, request baby to also "Stop" (upon your saying so), as baby stops knocking on their buckets when you say this.
5 Repeat steps 3-4-3-4.... with increasing variation and complexity of rhythm(s) as baby's interest and motivation affords.

Variations:
- Conduct any/all of the activities using two sets of percussion 'instruments' – one for you, one for baby, as you play together, or take it in turns to copy each other's rhythms each time.
- Consider to use ladles/beaters of different material quality, ..likewise for the vessels, e.g., pyrex bowl, plastic bowl, tin, wooden bowl, and so forth,
- Ditto, placing them on the floor, free standing, raised on cushions, held by yourself for baby to 'play', etc,..
- Consider to add complexity by requiring different spoons/ladles or vessels to be used to hit the different rhythms (either individually or 'in concert' with any/all others who may also be present at the time).

Additional Thoughts/Game-Activity Preparation/Lesson Planning Tips:
- As/when baby is using their spoon/ladle to strike the bucket, encourage them to strike their box/bucket about its outer surface when holding it (preferably using a bucket with a handled design, if it has one).
- Choose also a box of reasonably good quality, and that is unlikely to fail/break when hit too hard, or be 'fallen on', or otherwise squashed – which may cause breakage if of low material quality (and thus could also be damaging/abrasive to baby's skin).
- When leading the rhythm(s) for baby to knock the box/bucket with their spoon/ladle, change both the speed and complexity of the rhythm with increasing success, but be sure to give both instruction(s) *and* possibly a new demonstration guide each time, as appropriate for baby's attention level.

G/A 17.10 Matching My Stuff !

Task description:
- Exploring insertion and extraction of interlocking pieces, with colour matching.

Expected Milestone Achievements (EMAs)
- Explores the emptying and refilling of containers with various objects (Cog1)
- Associates simple words, sounds and smells with particular actions   (Cog5)

Materials:
- Coloured building bricks with connection parts (Legos, Duplos, or similar)

- Small containers/boxes, one for each colour of building brick pieces used.

Procedure:
Level 1
1. Show a set of differently coloured and interlocking building blocks (e.g., two large building blocks (e.g., Duplo/Legos) and two smaller blocks), arranged separately on the floor/table in one of two colour-sorted containers.
2. Demonstrate slowly and clearly how to take one of the coloured building blocks to be fit into another correspondingly coloured block, for baby to clearly see.
3. Present the same/similar materials now, inviting baby to carry out the same manipulations of like-coloured pairs according to your demonstration.
4. As/when baby succeeds to select, match and couple each correspondingly coloured building block, *and combines them together*, provide prompt praise and applause.

Level 2
1. Provide for baby this time two sets of *differently* coloured, but already combined, building block pairs (i.e., built to form two single, non-colour matched, two-block pieces).

Baby Milestones of Development (0-3 Yrs)

2. Invite baby to now first *disassemble* the combinations given, and then to repair them according to their corresponding colours (placing any unused single pieces into each of the two containers, pre-sorted by their matching colours as before).
3. As/when baby succeeds with *both decoupling* and *matching* each correspondingly coloured blocks, and then places the single building blocks in their respective colour-matched containers, provide baby prompt encouraging praise.

Variations:
- Following success with only a few pieces, consider to provide for baby 2, 3, or even 4-coloured combination building block set(s).
- Ditto, presenting assorted colour/sized sets across different rounds, for baby to later sort out and match for themselves.
- Allow baby free-play brick combining/disassembly, carefully copying baby's new creations, then showing her/him your own completed version(s) for comparison each time.

Additional Thoughts/Game-Activity Preparation/Lesson Planning Tips:
- Even if baby cannot firmly place the solid cylinders into the hollow sections, or baby 'incorrectly' pairs by colour successfully, be sure to nonetheless provide baby with praise (*the EMA goal here is 'placement' after all, and not colour-matching per se !*), though continuing to attempt guiding baby in observing the colours, and to match colour-coherent pairs together.
- At least initially, be advised that baby will likely require assistance when placing the block 'nipples' into the hollowed building block undersides, until sufficient practice and manipulation skill with such interlocking pieces has been developed.

G/A 17.11   BB Voice Trumpets !

Task description:
- Exploring the use of a cylinder as a voice enhancing 'instrument'.

Expected Milestone Achievements (EMAs):
- Makes simple two word utterances (e.g., "Baba eat", "Mumma have", "Dadda here"). (Comms3)
- Shows increased turn-taking during speech patterns, and increasingly with intonation. (Comms4)
- Proto-speech concerning familiar objects/events clearly understandable by others. (Comms6)

Materials:
- Hollow cylinders.

Procedure:
Level 1
1. Demonstrate two different sizes of cylindrical hollow tube, taking them to the outside of the (your) mouth in order to make different kinds of vocal sounds.
4. Present baby with the same/similar two differently sized cylindrical hollow tubes, leading baby to emit sound from their own mouths as per your demonstration.
5. Guide baby to next use differently sized "sound changing tubes" using a pre-arranged, differently coded glossary: E.g., "Oh let's use *Aaaahhh*" to mean making prolonged open-mouthed sounds, "and '*chirps*'" to make short 'tse-tse' sounds, and so forth.
4. Lead baby to next hold their "sound changing tubes" with one hand and to place it to/around (not *in*) their mouth, the another hand gently placed over the other end, occasionally 'opening' out the hand in order to send out a "wu – (silent) - wu - (silent)" strange sound.
5. If/as baby begins to display an intense interest in this vocal 'instrument' sound-making by themselves, encourage them to makes different vocal sounds of their own, providing much encouragement and prompt praise as they spontaneously do so each time.

Baby Milestones of Development (0-3 Yrs)

Level 2
1. Present now to baby *two equally large* hollow cylinder tubes.
2. Guide baby to use one hand to grasp one of the tubes, and to attempt 'joining' a second such cylinder to the end of the first (with their other hand, allowing for the length of baby's little arms !), in order to make one, much longer, "sound changing tube".
3. Invite baby to then use their new, much longer "sound changing tube" to make different sounds, with which to say/speak different words.
4. Present next *two equally small* cylindrical hollow tubes, inviting baby to once more carry out/explore making new sound productions as before, to practice making different variations in sound.
5. Lead in praising baby each time they succeed in producing a variety of sonorous sound productions, with warm encouragement (even if the actual sounds produced might be rather unpleasant to listen to !!).

Variations:
- Consider inviting various family members (or whomever else may be present) to each make/demonstrate their own different "sound changing tube'" noises in such a way as to carry on a dialog, and exchange of sounds in turn (or even imitate the sounds of others just heard).
- Lead baby to use their "sound changing tube" to carry out a variety of sounds for practice, e.g., to imitate car horns, train blowing a whistle, sounds of "wu -", different animal's calls, and so forth.
- If baby appears to be particularly interested in the effects caused by this kind of tool use, consider also to 'talk into' other more sound-reflective surface such as a bucket, or box.
- Ditto, using the same tools over the ears to change the way sounds be heard.

Additional Thoughts/Game-Activity Preparation/Lesson Planning Tips:
- Be sure to invite/guide baby in using the mouth 'covering' to amplify the emission of baby's sounds when using their "sound changing tube", and especially making sure that baby does NOT instead place the cylinder *into* their mouth (or otherwise bite at its edges, which they may feel tempted to do still at this age !).
- Be sure to provide only cylindrical hollow tubes which have been inspected clean, disinfected, and dried before use in this activity.
- Also prepare, and have available, wet wipes and paper tissues and so forth, for immediate use to clean-up with, as when the baby begins to emit their sounds they are also likely to produce and expel any amount of saliva (also useful for cleaning the edges of a non-paper "sound changing tube" itself !).
- Unless fascinated with their 'voice trumpets', try to minimise as far as possible the use of the same "sound changing tube" by baby and others,..... such attention can reduce any health risk, whilst also helping reduce the instance of any cross-person infection (or baby's mouth sores, and so forth).

G/A 17.12 Just Following Your Suggestion !

Task description:
- Exploring sounds, sites and actions, according to the suggestion(s) of others.

Expected Milestone Achievements (EMAs):
- Climbs onto furniture in order to obtain object out of reach (G5)
- Points to specific book images when asked, "Where is the x ?" (Comms1)
- 10-20 or more words now in common, daily usage (Comms5)
- Increasingly attentive to the causes and effects of the activities of others (SP3) (especially other babies/infants).

Materials:
- Animal chart &cards (with magnetic, felt or Velcro backing), large cushioning.

Procedure:
Level 1
1. Demonstrate an animal chart card (with removable items using a magnetic, felt, or Velcro backing), *leading baby in such a way that you can come to know whether baby 'knows' the different animals by name in turn*, then arranging each piece visibly out on the floor/table – for baby to clearly see.
2. Invite baby now, asking, "Where is the xx animal ?", baby being required to then point it out from amongst all the others on the floor (unless reliably speaking ?).
3. As/when each baby clearly demonstrates their choice/knowledge correctly, lead excitedly in providing praise for each correct response.
4. Promptly now present baby with each kind of different animal, then, calling out each of the specific animal's names in turn, inform baby (when holding that particular animal-named card), that, "It is time for this animal to go home now", e.g., "It's getting dark now, the puppy must go home to sleep".
5. Invite then baby, having selected the puppy picture card, to then act accordingly, to go towards the animal chart card containing the 'puppy kennel', and to then place their 'puppy card' onto that animal chart location, to which it belongs.

6. If/when baby 'correctly' places their card as assigned, be sure to indicate your thanks and prompt praise, as they do so.
7. Repeat steps 4-7, using the different animal image cues, as baby's interest and attention allows.

Level 2
1. Demonstrate a second animal chart card, again leading baby in such a way that you can *be sure which of the animals shown baby 'knows' by name*.
2. Using a variety of different large-scale cushioning (and/or other furnishings/props about the room), build several model 'animal homes'.
3. Place then about the room several animal chart cards/images low on the four walls/furniture of the room.
4. Invite baby to then seek out and take to the animal chart card each individual animal card/image which you assigned each time (one at a time). E.g., saying that, "It is getting towards daylight, and the small rabbit must go home now", inviting baby to then seek for the rabbit image card, and to then go place it in its 'home'.
5. As/when baby 'correctly' places their card as assigned, be sure to indicate your "Thanks", and prompt praise, as they do so.

Variations:
- Show/put out an animal chart card, asking baby, "What is this ?", inviting baby to attempt replying to your question(s). So long as baby says the animal's name, or somehow 'correctly' imitates the target animal's sound, or its movement, respond with affirmative praise and, "Thanks", thus encouraging baby to further express him/herself more verbally each time.
- Ditto (or extending level 2), require/invite baby to move towards the 'home' of each animal in the 'style of movement' of their target animal each time !
- If available materials allow, consider using clearly recognisable soft toys/models or finger puppets in place of animal picture card images (being sure to match baby's ability to identify individual models by animal name).

Additional Thoughts/Game-Activity Preparation/Lesson Planning Tips:
- Consider preparing several animal chart cards for baby (maybe with fewer different animals on each), so avoiding adaptation (and hence loss of interest) if running too many rounds using the same stimuli each time.
- The room's large-scale cushioning arrangement may prove a barrier for baby, but may also be their tool (if placed higher ?), e.g., the chart cards/hidden 'homes' laid aside them could be in more easily reachable positions, instead of being too high on the walls, or hidden near a 'hole in the ground'.

– 10 –

Baby Milestones of Development

(With 100+ Fun Activities to Help Demonstrate Them)

[Age 18 Months]

ψ

Expected Milestone Achievements
Age = 18 Months

[Key: e.g., 7 = Game No. 18.7]

Gross Motor

• Increasing controlled use of joints, rather than making stiff limbed movements	1, 2, 4, 5, 6
• Descends stairs alone, even if only in seated, 'bumping' style/position	1
• Makes deliberate forward ball kicking (rather than simply 'walking into' ball)	4
• Successfully attempts to move away from others' lap or chair (without help)	
• Imitates tool use as demonstrated by adults (other than hand-tools)	9
• Stands up in order to move to a new location, without support, when called	5, 8

Fine Motor

• Increasingly willing to imitate the manual actions of others	3, 4
• Stacks and restacks falling block towers into new configurations	7
• Attempts joint movement rather than whole-arm throwing (i.e., more bending at elbows/wrist)	4
• Will copy examples of drawing single curves/lines, by taking turns	
• Shows spontaneous scribbling/drawing (without prompting)	
• Frequently produces single-stroke line drawing	3

Cognitive

• Will stack 3-5 similar objects 'in order' (e.g., by size)	7
• Attempts various ways to 'escape' restrictions of pushchair, highchair/ car seat harnesses (including straps/buckles)	6
• Rotates/empties objects in order to obtain desired effects, and/or access to contents	7, 8, 9
• Able to drink from cup unaided, with little/no spillage	12
• Uses a variety of 'tools' for specific purposes	3, 9
• Seeks help when failing to operate mechanical or electrical toys/objects	

Communication

• Uses 40-50 (or more) words now in common, daily utterances	
• Shows adult-like use of fingers and hands when animating stories	10
• Points to object images, before object is mentioned in storyline, (especially body parts)	10
• Follows familiar single-step verbal commands/instructions, without gesture	2
• Links words representing different ideas (e.g., "Mamma have drink")	9, 12
• Knows 'when' to 'start a conversation' (filling a silence/pause in other's speech)	11

Socio-Personal

• Seeks attention of others by pulling on their hand, arm or clothing	1, 11
• Enjoys exploring/sharing some outdoor activities with other infants	
• Enjoys watching/listening to familiar TV/radio characters	
• Throws objects into boxes/baskets (as a game with others)	5
• Identifies significant others by sound alone (e.g., 'Papa' via phone/recording)	
• Actively seeks help from others when failing to achieve something	1, 2, 5, 8, 11

G/A 18.1   Take Me There !

Task description:
- Exploring the making of requests for help, and the directing of others' attention.

Expected Milestone Achievements (EMAs):
- Increasingly controlled use of joints, rather than stiff limbed movements (G1)
- Successfully attempts relocation from others' lap or chair (without help) (G4)
- Seeks attention of others via hand, arm or clothes pulling   (SP1)
- Actively seeks help from others when failing to achieve something   (SP6)

Materials:
- String, coat hangers, clothes pegs
- Animal or fruit picture cards (or corresponding clearly recognizable 3D toys).

Procedure:
Level 1
1. Demonstrate a set of animal or fruit picture cards, *your determining that baby both 'knows' and can identify them by name*, then clip each card (in turn) to a string hanging from the ceiling/clothes hanger/curtains/furnishings for baby to see.
2. Invite/carry baby (preferably on your back, tho' front facing), as you request baby to now guide you in taking them to the 'correct' location each time to enable baby to stretch out their hand to unclip a particular card. E.g., saying "Lucy, please bring me the 'Dog/Apple' card/toy" [baby then guiding you to take them to the 'dog/apple' card/toy, and to retrieve it from the ceiling/hanger/furnishing string].

NB: *TRY TO AVOID THE TEMPTATION TO INDEPENDENTLY MOVE ACCORDING TO YOUR OWN UNDERSTANDING OF BABY'S INSTRUCTIONS, BUT TO INSTEAD MOVE ONLY ACCORDING TO BABY'S INSTRUCTIONS AND INDICATIONS EACH TIME – EVEN IF NOT LEADING TO THE CORRECT TARGET !*

3. As/when baby successfully requests movements and guides you to carry them to the 'correct' card assigned to them for collection, *and* then takes down the card and presents it to you, provide prompt praise and encouragement as they do so.

Level 2

1-3 Repeat the level 1 steps, this time allowing baby to roam the floor whilst looking up to the walls/ceiling (or wherever the target cards are), in order to identify their location, thereafter requesting your help in being raised up high enough to reach each in turn.

Level 3 [If more than one adult be present in the room]
1. Invite this time a 2nd person (parent/guardian) to work in coordination with you to carry baby, each of you using both your hands to connect with the other, alternately cross-linking forearms to form a 'seat'.
2. Once so coupled, now squat down to let your baby 'passenger' extend each of his/her two legs 'inside' your elbow spaces and to then sit down.
3. Gently standing together, lifting baby in the process, invite baby to now guide you as their 'human *chair*' to move toward the target card(s) as per the assigning method of level1 (steps 2-3, above).

Variations:
- Situate baby to sit on your shoulders (or back-pack harness if referred), in order to select the requested picture card/object each time (being careful of any ceiling-based light fittings which may be low enough to collide with baby's head !!).
- Ditto, situating baby secured in their own wheeled toy, pram or buggy each time.

Additional Thoughts/Game-Activity Preparation/Lesson Planning Tips:
- When stopping for baby to unclip the target card, it is OK for you to adjust your posture a little, *only once stopped*, in order for baby to then reach out their hand to collect it (otherwise may be hard for baby to give detailed instruction to orient !)
- As/when you are carrying baby around the room/home, according to baby's instructions, *resist the temptation to move directly toward the card position which was requested* (and clearly visible to you also !), but instead to move only according to the instructions provided by baby, who will most likely be pointing at their assigned target card, or tapping on the your left/right shoulders or head ! (rather than talking' to you ?).
- Be sure to provide different target requests appropriate to your baby's vocabulary and understanding of language each time (and across rounds), so letting/facilitating baby to be realistically searching *for* and collecting the different cards over time.
- As/when baby is sitting down with you coordinating to make a chair with your arms (level 3), guide baby to use both their arms and hands to surround each of your necks, in order to increase their stability and balance (remaining especially vigilant when baby may let go of both supports, when reaching for and unclipping their target card/toy with both hands – consider to practice this manoeuvre with a soft toy before attempting to 'chair' baby !!).

G/A 18.2   Speleology 101 !

Task description:
- Exploring continuous flow of movement along a self-made pathway.

Expected Milestone Achievements (EMAs):
- Increasingly controlled use of joints, rather than stiff limbed movements   (G1)
- Follows familiar single-step verbal commands/instructions, without (Comms4) gesture.
- Actively seeks help from others when failing to achieve something   (SP6)

Materials:
- Soft cushions/furnishings, crawling tunnel (or simply make with boxes/chairs covered by sheets/blankets).

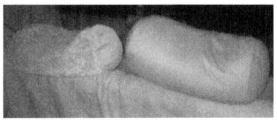

Procedure:

Level 1
1. Create and demonstrate two-three inverted U- or V-shaped cushion-builds (or use chairs and a blanket) to form a short linear crawling tunnel, situated so as to allow the easy penetration of light inside.
2. Invite baby to arrive at one end (side) of the tunnel, encouraging baby to enter and progresses through the crawling tunnel to reach out of the other side, providing baby with praise and applause as they emerge, ... repeating the activity for as long as baby's interest/motivation demands.

Level 2
1. Create now an extension to the tunnel using 3-5 inverted U-/V-shaped cushion builds (or with other materials to hand), to form a much longer linear crawling tunnel, this time placing the pieces much closer together so forming a relatively darker tunnel for baby to enter.

2   Repeat as per level 1, continuing the activity for as long as baby's interest/motivation affords.

Variations:
- Demonstrate a soft round/square column of cushions, inviting baby to climb over or around the columns to arrive at the opposite side.
- Demonstrate now two separate columns, put together, inviting baby to climb over/around the round columns as before, (if in a group or running as a fun party game, possibly organise as a baby-parent/guardian-racing teams if the builds be large enough ! ?).
- Build and demonstrate 3-5 round/square columns, separate but together, inviting baby to climb on and about them over/through the round columns as per either of the variation options suggested above.

Additional Thoughts/Game-Activity Preparation/Lesson Planning Tips:
- *Be sure to set up the initial (first) crawling tunnel configuration such that it will allow the penetration of the ambient room light (or daylight), so that baby will be more willing to crawl through it; only later when combining multiple pieces to form the larger/longer tunnel, begin to place the pieces closer together, when baby will have become less easily afraid, having adapted and enjoyed 'disappearing and re-emerging' without incident a few times, in the lighted version earlier.*
- Note that baby will likely require guidance to initially enter (especially if resistant to tunnel entry), and also may express hesitation if thinking there might a 'block'/trap, instead of a tunnel exit. Be sure to situate any other person(s) present to be a certain distance away, so better enabling baby to both see and hear you as they move towards the light and sound (where you now are,... rather than pushing baby into the tunnel from behind !).
- According to baby's abilities, comfort and confidence levels, be sure to increase/decrease the tunnel length each time, building shorter or longer piece combination tunnels only as baby comfortably adapts to the challenge each time.

Baby Milestones of Development (0-3 Yrs)

185

G/A 18.3 Copy Colour Matches !

Task description:
- Exploring the corresponding pairings of different objects and materials by colour.

Expected Milestone Achievements (EMAs):
- Increasingly willing to imitate the actions of others (F1)
- Frequently produces single-stroke line drawing (F6)
- Uses a variety of 'tools' for specific purposes (Cog5)

Materials:
- 4 differently coloured paper discs, drawing paper (each with a differently coloured line drawn across it)
- Non-toxic baby-friendly wax crayons, adhesive (tape or paste).

Procedure:
Level 1
1. Demonstrate pre-drawn papers, each showing *either* a thick red, yellow, blue, or green line on them, respectively.
2. Show next the red, yellow, blue, and green coloured discs, demonstrating how to take one of each shape, and of the corresponding colours, and to then attach the line vertex to the round disc, to create an image of a balloon or lollipop.
3. Present now to baby *one* of the line drawing papers, and all 4 different discs.
4. Invite baby to then attach their coloured line to *the* round disc of the corresponding colour.
5. As/when baby succeeds with completing their colour-matched attachments, provide baby with praise promptly, and put it on one side in order to later have created a single display of "My many balloons".
6. Repeat steps 3-5, each time offering baby a different coloured line to affix to the same colour-matched paper disc.

Level 2
1. Demonstrate four plain white drawing paper strips, using a differently coloured wax crayon to 'draw' on each one of them, either, a thick red, yellow, blue, or green line, respectively.
2. Show next the red, yellow, blue, and green coloured discs, demonstrating again how to take one of each strip of the corresponding colours, and to then attach the line vertex to the round disc, to again create an image of a balloon/lollipop.
3. Present similar materials *for baby to colour/draw, then repeat* the level 1 steps, as before.

Level 3
1. Demonstrate next some similar coloured line drawing papers, but with each line this time containing a hollow circle (in a different place of each 'bar' for each).
2. Show now various colours and sizes of discs, demonstrating how to attach the correspondingly coloured and 'correctly' sized disc *into* the line/bar's hollow circle, so completing the line to form a uniform coloured bar, for baby to clearly see.
3. Present now the same/similar set of material to baby, inviting baby to act according to the specific line colours and hollow circle size, choosing to affix the corresponding disk (from their collection) to insert each time.
4. As/when baby chooses the 'correct' disc to attach/insert each time, provide prompt praise and encouragement, adding each 'completed' bar to the baby's art gallery for all to see and enjoy.

Variations:
- To increase/decrease the level of difficulty, increases the number of colours, shapes and/or sizes for baby to select/screen during each round.
- Another, alternative stimulus, would be to introduce a central body (of some definable animal, of a given colour, and invite baby to attach the appropriate limbs (from a selection of differently coloured/shaped legs, arms, and head) to that body.
- Ditto, requiring baby to build imaginary animals using only different (i.e., NON-MATCHING) limbs !

Additional Thoughts/Game-Activity Preparation/Lesson Planning Tips:
- Upon the drawing paper, make the line/bar very thick (maybe even the entire width of the paper strip), so affording baby easier identification of its colour each time.
- It is very likely that you will need to guide baby in attaching the 'hollow circle' inserts within the bars, but do try to resist the temptation to change baby's choice of disc, if not the 'correct' one each time.
- If/when baby does not pair successfully, try not to correct baby and exchange the colour too eagerly, but instead guide baby to observe and contrast the disc and line colours, and only then encouraging baby to choose a different pair (then do the same again).

G/A 18.4   Muscle Hussle !

Task description:
- Exploring the controlled and coordinated use of lower limb joint musculature.

Expected Milestone Achievements (EMAs):
- Increasing controlled use of joints, rather than stiff limbed movements (G1)
- Makes deliberate forward ball kicking (rather than 'walking into' it) (G3)
- Increasingly willing to imitate the actions of others (F1)
- Attempts joint movement rather than whole-arm throwing (e.g., (F3)
  more bending at elbows/wrists).

Materials:
- Small-medium sized ball (soft to the touch if 'kicking' barefoot).

Procedure:
Level 1
1. Demonstrate a small-medium sized ball, slowly and gently using your foot to make the ball move in controlled actions, for baby to clearly see.
2. Present the same/similar ball, inviting baby to play 'soccer' with their foot, whilst also providing them protection from falling as they do so.
3. As/when baby succeeds with suitable agility and control to kick the ball out and about, provide prompt praise and encouragement for their efforts.
4. Repeat steps 1-3 several times with baby's different feet L=>R=>L=>R,... each time.

Level 2
1. Demonstrate a same/similar ball, this time slowly and gently using the foot to make more realistic soccer ball kicking control actions, for baby to clearly see.
2. Invite/guide baby to 'play soccer' with their foot, whilst providing protection from baby swinging the ball too high/hard enough to hit their face/head with it ! (especially if the ball be tied to the ankle/waist (see Variations+Tips1 below).

Baby Milestones of Development (0-3 Yrs)

3. As/when baby succeeds with suitable agility and control in kicking the ball out and about, provide prompt praise and encouragement.
4. Repeat several times, encouraging baby's use of their different feet L=>R=>L=>R,.... Alternating with their preferred choice of foot each time.

Variations:
- Prepare for baby a roped ball. Holding the free end of the rope yourself, guide baby to play soccer with their foot, letting the ball swing to and fro as they do so.
- Ditto, attaching the ball rope to a chair or table leg, or even another string or pole suspended from a coat hanger. [A secondary advantage of doing this is that you will not have to travel to reclaim the ball each time !]

Additional Thoughts/Game-Activity Preparation/Lesson Planning Tips:
- Using a ball with a short rope attached (or held in a string-bag), the 'free' end then tied to baby's own ankle/waist, will allow shorter waiting times (due to reduced retrieval activity), and/or prove suitable for conducting the task with baby in stationary standing/leaning/seated or prone positions. *Remember that the target EMA here is to observe/strengthen the body and muscle coordination skills required to make deliberate kicking, not to 'score a goal' or have the ball arrive at a certain destination at this time !*
- During level 1, try to keep control of the ball close to/on the floor, at least at first.
- For level 2, the ball may also be hung airborne, above the ground ~10 cm/3".
- If/when baby is holding the rope with the hand, and then using the foot to play soccer, baby will encounter certain difficulty in coordinating their hand and foot (and each with their eyes) at the same time; it may thus be necessary to recruit your help, as you carry the rope together (whilst baby concentrates upon controlling the movement of the ball with their foot).
- Consider also to allow baby flexibility in their choosing to use either/both their left and right foot to kick the ball at different times.
- Consider to use a 'soccer' ball of sufficient softness (especially if baby is developing a strong kick) so as to minimise the damage made possible by being hit with the misdirected ball flying across the room and hitting your prized ornaments [consider to conduct this activity outdoors, else hide/remove glass and other fragile objects and items from strong ball kicks leaving the 'soccer field' area !! (likewise removing baby's shoes/slippers will decrease the balls' kick power transfer).

G/A 18.5   Smoother Mover !

Task description:
- Exploring a greater flexibility of movement along, over, and around objects.

Expected Milestone Achievements (EMAs):
- Increasing controlled use of joints, rather than making stiff limbed movements. (G1)
- Stands up in order to move to a new location, without support, when called (G6)
- Throws objects into boxes/baskets (as a game with others) (SP4)
- Actively seeks help from others when failing to achieve something (SP6)

Materials:
- Large cushions large cushions, boxes, large ball, basket/box, small toys/socks.

Procedure:
Level 1
1. Design a flat surface footpath in the room, slowly and gently demonstrating how to use your hands and upper body to move the large ball along the pathway, for baby to clearly see.
2. Present now the large ball, leading baby to either a specific footpath section, or to the footpath 'start' (depending upon room size, and baby's known movement abilities).
3. Invite baby to now move/push along the large ball through the footpath to the 'end', as you carefully observe baby's increasing flexibility at the knees and ankles as they attempt redirecting the ball, while keeping it within the pathway bounds.
4. As/when baby begins to show steady impetus with moving the ball forwards in a controlled way, whilst also exercising care in maintaining their track on the footpath, provide prompt praise and enthusiastic applause following their achievements.

Level 2
1. Design now an undulating surface footpath in the room (i.e., a pathway with several direction changes, up-down, right-angles or an S-bend), and then slowly and gently demonstrate how to use the hands and upper body to move the large ball along the pathway, for baby to clearly see.
2. Repeat the level 1 steps 2-4, as baby's increasing skills allow.

Level 3
1 Repeat levels 1 &/or 2 (depending upon baby's mobility and balance control), placing several small toys (or rolled socks) along the pathway for baby to collect and/or throw into a basket/box placed visibly just outside the pathway, as they encounter them, whilst moving along the path.

Variations:
- Build undulating sloping roads (not steps) with cushioning along the pathway.
- Provide baby with different large-scale toys with success across time, e.g., introducing a peanut ball, stepping stones, playmat squares, circular cylinders, different balls, wheeled vehicles/trolleys, inviting succeeding baby to impel these different items along the increasingly complex pathway over several rounds.

Additional Thoughts/Game-Activity Preparation/Lesson Planning Tips:
- Encourage baby to control the items which they are pushing along their assigned pathway as much as possible, so preventing collisions and deviations, and thus exercising increased body muscle involvement and control.
- Be sure to remain ever vigilant as baby is pushing along their balls/cylinders/vehicles etc., ever standing by to rescue/soft land their falling.
- *When pushing 'uphill', baby will quite naturally try to use the ball as an additional body support - on the downhill runs discovering the ball will roll more directly and easily (possibly to their surprise !), and will thus require support in overcompensating their balance, and may fall.*

Baby Milestones of Development (0-3 Yrs)

G/A 18.6   Up and Over We Go !

Task description:
- Exploring and planning a route through a 3D maze of obstacles.

Expected Milestone Achievements (EMAs):
- Increasing controlled use of joints, rather than making stiff limbed movements. (G1)
- Attempts various ways to 'escape' restrictions of pushchair, highchair/ /car seat harnesses (including straps & buckles). (Cog2)

Materials:
- Obstacle course pieces (boxes, cushions), Hula hoop), baby stroller.

Procedure:

Level 1

1. Build/arrange in the room, and demonstrate, an obstacle pathway, set up with things to stand on, step over/through (even under), to be moved through, one piece at a time.
2. Slowly now demonstrate crawling on the floor along and through each of the pieces including any standing frames/hoops/tunnels, in order to arrive at the other end, without knocking any of the pieces down, or far away from their starting location (NB: *its always helpful for you to remind yourself what the world looks like from baby's height point=of-view* !!), but if too small for you, demonstrate the course to baby using a large soft toy).
3. Invite/lead now baby, to pass along and through the various pieces comprising the obstacle course/tunnel/climbing set, as per your demonstration.
4. As/when baby safely reaches the end point, greet her/him warmly as they arrive, providing prompt praise and hugs as they do so.

Level 2

1-4 Repeat the level 1 procedure, this time starting baby from a secured position in (strapped into) their baby stroller, high chair, or car seat, allowing them to aid 'escape' to the start of the obstacle course by attempting to first release themselves from their buckled safety harness, returning to the same location and 'safety' once completing the course.

NB: *although potentially 'teaching' unwanted escapology skills here, please remember that the true purpose of the clips and buckles is to help prevent injury during collision, and not to primarily serve as imprisoning devices ! E.g., Baby's caught in a building fire will more likely survive if able to free themselves from such 'restraints',....*

Variations:
- Make creative use of the various pieces/parts to be found about the room/house, in order to create the most attractive and enjoyable obstacle course available to baby. This will increase motivation, whilst enhancing your own creativity in building increasingly interesting and challenging pathways for baby to traverse each time.
- Ditto, placing/'starting' points amongst/inside any tunnels/mazes built, then putting some visible toys outside the tunnel/maze to attract baby to work towards them, requiring them to cross these barriers, as they walk/crawl forwards across the remainder of the obstacle course in order to gain their target toy each time.
- To increase the difficulty further (and without making the course more complex) consider to simply request baby to carry some item in their hands as they negotiate the obstacle course.
- Ditto, setting up several items for baby to transport from one end of the course to the other, so many that they cannot all be carried during a single trip through the course.

Additional Thoughts/Game-Activity Preparation/Lesson Planning Tips:
- When setting up any tunnels, separate each frame (whether open boxes, chairs or hoops) by about one meter/yard distance when on the floor, and possibly more if holding them up yourself, or if suspended above the floor.
- According to room' size, consider to establish more than one cave/tunnel in the room for baby to explore during their course.
- Increase the level of difficulty further by requesting baby to carry with them some object(s), either one at a time throughout, or staggered in a relay fashion.
- *Beware of using too strong an attractive target toy if baby requires motivation to continue interacting with the obstacle course – a very strong stimulus will cause baby to move directly towards the 'goal'/target toy at the end of the course by the shortest possible path – and possibly ignore (simply avoid/step over) the obstacle course items completely !!*

Baby Milestones of Development (0-3 Yrs)

G/A 18.7   Serial Order Please

Task description:
- Exploring the serial ordering of items according to shape and size.

Expected Milestone Achievements (EMAs):
- Will stack 3-5 similar objects 'in order' (e.g., by size)   (Cog1)
- Rotates/empties objects in order to obtain desired effects,   (Cog3)
  and/or access to contents.
- Stacks and restacks falling towers into new configurations   (F2

Materials:
- Stacking rings, shape sorter

- Picture puzzles (2D Jigsaw) &/or 3D blocks) [see Variation 4].

Procedure:
Level 1
1. Demonstrate a set of three to five stacking rings and a spindle, arranged at random upon the floor/table.
2. Slowly show how to arrange this set of items, each stacked one on top of another, according to their size, for baby to clearly see.
3. Present now the same complete set of (separated) pieces, inviting baby to rearrange them all to be all stacked together, one atop the other as previously demonstrated.
4. As/when baby succeeds with full set stacking, and presents their completed stack, provide prompt praise and encouragement.

Level 2
1. Demonstrate the pieces of a shape-sorting set, again arranged at random on the floor/table.
2. Slowly show how to use/arrange the items with respect to the shape-sorter block, for baby to clearly see.
3. Present the same complete set of (again now separated) shape-sorter block/item set, inviting baby to place each of the pieces into the shape-sorter block's matching holes as per your demonstration.
4. As/when baby succeeds with full set 'posting', and presents their completed/full shape-sorter block stack for you to see, provide prompt praise and encouragement.

Variations:
- If no ring-spindle set be available in the home, consider using stacking blocks, cups, or similar containers (else make some using paper, card or folded fabric/clothing).
- If standard ring completion prove too simple now, consider asking baby to stack them in reverse order (smallest at bottom), or according to some different colour/size order sequence requested (which can be changed for each round !).
- Invite baby to build replica copies of example towers, built in non-serial (random) size orders.
- Ditto, using a variety of colour and/or size ordering variations, 2D & 3D puzzles.

Additional Thoughts/Game-Activity Preparation/Lesson Planning Tips:
- Before being encouraged to attempt building stacks, guide baby to pay close attention to observing the key features of your sample/example demonstrations each time; After baby has built their stack, invite baby to contrast their own creation with the sample, observing and pointing out whether there is anything different, and if so, guiding baby to change/adjust the details to match, accordingly.
- Consider to introduce additional coloured 3D puzzle set pieces as baby's ongoing success and motivation allows.

Baby Milestones of Development (0-3 Yrs)

195

G/A 18.8   No Stone Stepping Stones II

Task description:
- Exploring and planning a route through an obstacle field to reach a goal.

Expected Milestone Achievements (EMAs):
- Stands up in order to move to a new, location, without support, when called (G6)
- Rotates/empties objects in order to obtain desired effects, and/or (Cog3) access to contents.
- Actively seeks help from others when failing to achieve something (SP6)

Materials:
- Floor Maze (various cushions, boxes/containers etc.,)

- Transparent tape (to make a 'sticky floor' maze/), musical instrument, toy fruits and vegetables, animal puppets.

Procedure:

Level 1
1. Place on the room floor some transparent tape (or ribbon) in a basic shaped labyrinth (maze) set up for the activity (sticky side facing upwards).
2. Enter the sticky labyrinth, to place in the maze' central position many toy fruits and vegetables.
3. Next invite/guide baby to go forward and collect the toys, carefully observing *how* baby moves along the floor in order to gather their targets, and in particular, whether baby realises/responds to the adhesive tape stuck to the floor, and feels uncomfortable when treading on it, and/or steps over it.

4. If baby collects the toys directly, and realises/avoids (steps over) the floor's adhesive tape, provide prompt praise and encouragement.
5. Repeat steps 2-4, this time placing animal puppets at the centre to attract baby's attention.
6. Again, be vigilant to observe whether baby shows any change in their stepping-movement behaviour, for example, might they begin to "bridge over" the adhesive tape (to avoid treading on the sticky adhesive tape) in order to gain their toy targets.
7. As/when baby does avoid the adhesive tape in the process of gaining their toy targets, provide special encouragement and praise.
8. Repeat steps 5-7 using musical instruments, (also replacing/repairing the tape maze parts as/when necessary).

Level 2
1. With level 1 success, establish now a series of 'higher' barriers (requiring a larger stepping/planning movement pattern) using cushions or small boxes placed/reaching across from one side of the room to the other.
2. Place different toys about the labyrinthine path to attract baby's attention and provide target locations, as before.
3. Invite/guide baby to move forward and collect the toys, again carefully observing *how* baby moves among the floor obstacle field in order to gather their targets, and in particular, whether baby appears uncomfortable when treading on the sticky tape, and/or instead chooses to now step over them.
4. Again, be vigilant to observe whether baby shows any change in their stepping-movement behaviour, for example, in "bridging over" the obstacle pieces in order to gain their toy targets each time now.
5. As/when baby does avoid stepping on the path obstacles in the process of gaining their toy targets, provide special encouragement and praise each time they do so.

Level 3
1-5. With level 2 success, establish additional cushions (relatively large) which are to be used as "doors" or "gates", - baby being required to now open and close them as they pass through these 'moveable barriers', in order to proceed further along their pathway(s) each time.

Variations:
- Consider to use the adhesive tape and/or small cushions arranged separately in the room to form a floor "ladder" shaped road (e.g., I..I..I..I..I..I..I..I), reaching across from one side of the room to the other.
- Ditto, using any assortment of floor-based obstacles.

Baby Milestones of Development (0-3 Yrs)

Additional Thoughts/Game-Activity Preparation/Lesson Planning Tips:
- Regardless of whether using the adhesive tape or other 3D objects for baby to "return through" obstacle sets, try to arrange at least three barriers for baby to overcome, being sure to also watch that baby cannot easily fall over on their face during their attempt to arrive at the centre toy display (which is likely, given that baby will probably have their eyes focused upon their targets, and NOT upon the floor immediately in front of them !).
- Be sure to guide baby in being able to 'feel' the floor surface changes 'differently', whilst also steering them towards their goals !
- In tackling the level 1 activity, baby may or may not be wearing socks. Be sure to determine their 'feeling' perceptions regarding the sticky surface as 'barrier' to be avoided – also making wet-wipes (or warm soapy water) available for baby's feet washing should they become tacky with adhesive residue.
- For level 3, ensure that baby remembers to 'close' their doors/gates each time passing through them, before continuing along towards their goals and visual targets.

G/A 18.9   Finding the Flow !

Task description:
- Exploring the signalling of information at a given location, in order to affect a differential response.

Expected Milestone Achievements (EMAs):
- Imitates tool use as demonstrated by adults (other than hand-tools)   (G5)
- Rotates/empties objects in order to obtain desired effects, and/or   (Cog3)
    to access contents.
- Uses a variety of 'tools' for specific purposes   (Cog5)
- Links words representing different ideas (e.g., "Mamma have drink")   (Comms5)

Materials:
- Route markers (arrowed direction indicators on floor)

- Or, 3D mounted direction markers/arrows/signs.

Procedure:
Level 1
1. Demonstrate a set of colour-, or symbol-coded 'route markers' on a footpath, ensuring that baby observes the different coded/sign indicators each time.
2. Clearly show now that the different indicators can be removed (can change location, and the directions being indicated (i.e., be turned over, and/or replaced by others), and placed about the floor to guide a walking path.
3. Present now several route indicators, inviting baby to select 3-4 different direction indicators to be used.
4. Finally, invite baby to place their newly chosen indicators to form a single directional footpath on the floor for *you* (and anyone else present) to follow/explore each time.
5. Repeat steps 3-4 as necessary, until baby is competently leading the activity.

Level 2
1. Demonstrate now a "T-shaped" path, with the possibility of different direction -coded footpaths being possible at the T-junction (i.e., turning Left, or Right, according to the signal (e.g., arrow) arranged to indicate which direction to take, each time.
2. Show now the effect of changing the arrow direction to indicate the taking of the alternative path upon reaching the T-junction.
3. Invite baby to travel from either of the three ends, stopping to change the centre (T-junction) indictor arrow to form the signal for the next journey person to follow (either yourself, or baby themselves, next time arriving at the same junction).
4. Invite baby to continue moving along the various line paths, following the 'new route' as found indicated (and change either by you, or by baby earlier, offering prompt praise as they do so.

Level 3
1-5. Continue to add complexity and variation (in distance, angle and rotation, etc) according to baby's increasing success, motivation and interest level(s).

Variations:
- Place two paths side by side, inviting baby to take one (and yourself the other), and then to move along your respective paths each (observing the direction markers shown for each), as you each do so.
- Ditto, inviting baby (and/or yourself) to change each (their own) path to show a different direction to be take at certain points along the path.
- Consider inviting baby to hold the end of a single rod/pole (that you are also holding the other end of), thus requiring you to both walk together along your paths at the same speed (whilst also offering baby additional support/balance, if needed).
- With considerable success with levels 1-3, present any number of coded direction indicators, inviting baby to then freely combine them in several different ways for the exploration (by then either following baby physically, or their 'instructions' as now laid out on the floor for all to see/use !).
- Finally, combine all available direction signs/pieces to form one single footpath for further exploration – possibly extending the pathway to lead outside the room – and changing any given piece(s) as may be appropriate to your/baby's intended purposes each time.

Additional Thoughts/Game-Activity Preparation/Lesson Planning Tips:
- Insure that each route's sign sets/direction pieces are in good repair, clean, and not dangerous to baby if trodden/fallen on, so helping minimise any risk of injury.
- Ditto, minimising infection risk, especially in preventing baby from placing any movable signs/parts into their mouths, nose and/or eyes after walking on/into them.

G/A 18.10   Expressive Selves !

Task description:
- Exploring emotional expressions and situations for display and discussion.

Expected Milestone Achievements (EMAs):
- Shows adult-like use of fingers and hands when animating stories   (Comms2)
- Points to object images, before object mentioned in storyline,   (Comms3)
  (specially of body parts).
- Increasingly attentive to the causes and effects of the different   [M18-SP4]
  behaviours of others' (especially other babies/infants).
- Imitates eye blinking and several other immediate adult facial gestures [M19-SP4]

Materials:
- Old boxes/containers, Stickable smiley (and not-so-smiley) illustrations showing different facial expressions).

Procedure:
Level 1
1. Demonstrate six plain (non-patterned) boxes/containers, leading baby to recognise the six different facial expressions (one on each), each showing a different emotional (facial) expression.
2. Slowly show how to place/stack these cubes in a pile, building them together one by one.
3 Present one of the stickers to baby, and to then identify, "talk about", imitate, or otherwise attempt to express the content as may relate to that chosen facial expression, as shown on that particular sticker/card.
4 Finally invite baby to come forward and to put their sticker/card together with a matching stickered box seen previously (during step 1), either stick onto, or in it.

5 As/when baby does this (however they may actually choose to express themselves), provide baby with encourage and prompt praise following their response(s).

Level 2
1. Present to baby now two boxes, in each of which you have placed,, respectively, three different facial expression cards/stickers, together with some other *non*-smiley face or object images.
2. Invite/guide baby to next look *for* the facial expressions and other characters to be found within their boxes, then to place them together on the floor/table, classified according to their type, then to return them to two (or more) boxes, such that each contains only one type of object (category) only.
3 With/without your guidance, as/when baby can 'correctly' choose each homologous series' members from the assorted cards/stickers provided, reward baby with prompt praise and encouragement each time.
4. Repeat steps 1-3 according to baby's individual ability and level of understanding /expressiveness – increasing the task difficulty with ongoing success.

Variations:
- As an alternative to preparing 6 boxes/containers, each with a different smiley face/facial expression, one on each (L1), consider instead to prepare a single cube/box – with a different smiley face/facial expression placed *on each of its 6 sides*.
- Ditto, matching 'pairs' of the same facial expressions as may be found on two different 6-face cubes – baby keeping one pair to play with for some (short) time.
- Explore the different emotional expressions and facial expression discs, inviting baby to imitate the different faces, and accompanying situations, according to the willingness and attention of baby to engage in such interaction.
- Ditto, using mirror-play to explore the different facial expressions with baby together.

Additional Thoughts/Game-Activity Preparation/Lesson Planning Tips:
- As/when baby appears to be looking *for* the different emotional expression cards, or appears to be wondering about the possible 'meaning of' the different facial expressions, AND displays an emotional reaction to it, be keen to observe, think about, and try to better understand your baby's behavioural responses – *(this is the real goal and rationale of the task as far as TD is concerned !).*
- Ensure the relative safety/security of ALL items that you provide for baby, especially checking for damaged or sharp edges, so avoiding scratching or otherwise damaging of baby's skin.
- Ditto, and if designing the materials for reuse again another time, assuring thorough cleanliness, with sterilisation and drying of any stickable materials, both before and after each use.

G/A 18.11   Hoop Cars !

Task description:
- Exploring shared play in the close company of others in the same space(s).

Expected Milestone Achievements (EMAs):
- Seeks attention of others by pulling on their hand, arm or clothing   (SP1)
- Actively seeks help from others when failing to achieve something   (SP6)
- Follows familiar single-step verbal command/instruction, without gesture (Comms4)
- Knows 'when' to 'start a conversation' (filling a silence/pause in   (Comms6)
  other's speech).

Materials:
- Roadway building pieces, cushions, Hula hoop.

Procedure:
Level 1
1. Establish a clear 'roadway' in the room using large cushions, then demonstrate the use of a hula hoop set about your waist position.
2. Invite baby to come to you and to be your 'passenger', baby following behind you as you (both) now stand together inside the hula hoop that you are holding (i.e., both standing inside your 'hoop-car').
3. Pretend to 'start your automobile' (by sound), leading your (baby) passenger along together as you gently rock from side to side, whilst moving slowly forward along the 'roadway' and back to your starting position (parked).
4. Invite now baby to play the role of driver, yourself now the passenger, as your baby driver leads you to pass through the same/different runway to arrive at some previously assigned location (that you had specified before your 'leaving').
5. Upon your safe arrival, be sure to express thanks to your baby driver, providing prompt praise without waiting too long to do so.

Level 2

1. Establish this time a more complex, non-straight 'roadway' in the room, again using large cushions/boxes etc.,

Baby Milestones of Development (0-3 Yrs)

2. Invite baby to prepare as driver, yourself and a favourite soft toy/doll (or some 3rd person present ?), to be baby's 'additional' passenger, the 3rd 'person' following behind yourself and baby as you (both) stand together inside the 'hula car' that the driver (baby, and yourself) are already holding.
3. Pretending to 'start your automobile' (by sound), lead baby to now play the roles of driver and passenger (in turn), as baby leads both the 1st and 2nd passengers along the now curved roadway to arrive their assigned location(s) (that you had previously specified).
4. Continue to invite increasing numbers of baby-driver/baby-passenger trips along the roadway(s) according to the passenger numbers, and roadway space(s) available (and/or as baby's interest/motivation persists).
6. Upon your safe arrival at any and all destination(s) each time, be sure to encourage all baby's passengers to express "Thank you" to their baby-driver each time (you should 'speak' for the soft toys/dolls), providing prompt praise without waiting too long after arrival to do so.

Variations:
- With increasing control, establish a crossroad junction "X" in the centre of the room (or to allow continuation into spaces outside of your chosen activity room) for baby to acknowledge stopping, and/or speeding up and slowing down as they come across a policeman (soft toy, object, traffic light, or 3rd person) stopping the traffic coming either way at different times and places !
- Ditto, introducing other obstacles, train crossing/pedestrian crossing, and so forth.
- Consider to also invite the baby's passengers to embark from different starting spots (e.g., a kitchen-based taxi rank), the baby later having free choice of stopping the "vehicles" passing, and whether even to be a 'driver' or "passenger" at different times (able to 'park' their vehicles in a designated garage area, for you to take over the driver role).

Additional Thoughts/Game-Activity Preparation/Lesson Planning Tips:
- When you are yourself the passenger, consider using a larger sized hula hoop, else you may need to stand outside the hula hoop (but still behind baby).
- Allow baby as much interaction as possible (whether passenger or driver), so increasing each other's understanding of not only their physical movement control, occasionally changing the baby pairings with any others present, to increase the amount of socialization across the different participants as possible – (like real taxi drivers in London, NY, Mumbai or Hong Kong would !!).
- Whilst attending to the core EMA foci (largely Communications and Socio-Personal in nature today), be sure to monitor/regulate baby's speed control (starting and stopping), as well as control of movement direction, object avoidance, etc.

G/A 18.12   Eating by Colours

Task description:
- Exploring food choice and preparation, to request.

Expected Milestone Achievements (EMAs):
- Able to drink from cup unaided, with little/no spillage   (Cog4)
- Links words representing different ideas (e.g.,   (Comms5)
    "Mamma have drink").
- Increasingly willing to imitate the manual actions of others   (F1)

Materials:
- Various kinds and colours of fresh fruit (seeded and sliced), fruit tray
- Plastic fork/spork, clear plastic wrap, paper cups
- Disinfection fluid or wet-wipes, small towel.

Procedure:
Level 1
1. Before the session have prepared, and now demonstrate, a fresh fruit tray (e.g., of sliced/cut orange, strawberry, grape, kiwi fruit, and so forth), securely wrapped in clear plastic wrap.
2. First, use disinfection fluid and/or a 'wet-wipe' paper as provided for baby (and yourself), to clean both your hands, before touching any food area.
3. Invite now baby to use their own plastic fork/spork to take up a piece of an assigned *colour of* fruit (but not the fruit by name !), and to then feed themselves (and/or you) to eat and enjoy.
4. As/when baby has selected the 'correct' fruit as requested each time, provide prompt praise.

Level 2
1. Invite this time a soft toy/doll (or other person if present) to select which fruit is to be taken, *again only according to its colour, not identifying the fruit by name.*

2. Having requested the selection, invite/ask baby to help them select the fruit choice according to the colour mentioned, and to then use their plastic spork/spoon to help you eat and enjoy it.
3. As/when baby chooses the correct item *and* feeds it to you, express prompt thanks and praise to baby each time.

Level 3
1. Consider to also invite baby to distribute a small cup of water to all/any participants, especially checking for spillage when drinking their own, if not doing so in passing them around.

Variations:
- Invite baby to help feed a soft toy or doll with their plastic spork (monitoring movements carefully to avoid foodstuffs moving towards the eye or nose instead !!).
- Invite baby to feed others according to assigned fruit *names*, rather than their colour. [NB: How to cope with 'Orange' ? !!]
- Present to baby a toy 'cut fruit combination' set, each time providing baby with only one segment of each kind of fruit or vegetable; e.g., if a carrot piece, invite then baby to seek for the corresponding pieces from a pile of mixed pieces, requiring baby to sort through them in order to find and then put together their 'whole' carrot (and then to also deliver it whole to their 'customer' !).

Additional Thoughts/Game-Activity Preparation/Lesson Planning Tips:
- As/when baby eats any food (or attempts to assist others with eating) with their plastic fork/spork, pay keen attention to their guidance, so helping avoid baby accidentally cutting/stabbing him/herself (or others !).
- For the 'shared feeding' rounds, prepare many plastic forks beforehand, being sure to provide baby promptly with a new/clean fork each time serving a different person (or having dropped it/placed it into their own mouth), thus attending to health concerns, and avoiding any spread of infection between different persons.
- Ditto, using paper cups for foodstuff transfer instead of a spork/fork.
- Likewise, after delivering fruit morsels to the mouth (of own or others), be sure to reclaim any empty/used forks from baby (who may otherwise play with them, or wave them about in their hand – and possibly inflict unintentional injury to themselves or others nearby).

– 11 –

Baby Milestones of Development

(With 100+ Fun Activities to Help Demonstrate Them)

[Age 19 Months]

Baby Milestones of Development (0-3 Yrs)

Expected Milestone Achievements
Age = 19 Months

[Key: e.g., 3 = Game No. 19.3]

Gross Motor
- Walks without stiff-limbed gait/action, or losing balance so often — 1, 3, 5, 6
- Walks up (and down) a few stairs unaided — 5
- Stands, and comes to new location(s) when asked to so — 6, 7
- Reaches with outstretched arm when hearing "Hold my hand, please" — [M20-19.1], 5
- Climbs on objects without prompting, in order to see things from a higher position — 7, [M20-19.5]
- Willing and able to remove clothing at appropriate times

Fine Motor
- Offers hand with appropriate finger grasp positions when reached for by another person — 3, 4, 9
- Turns single book pages unaided — 11
- Successfully stacks 5-6 blocks to make a tower
- 'Twists' screw top lids and 'pulls' lever caps of containers
- Identifies several pictures by pointing at them (from amongst others) — 11
- Makes crayon/chalk marks with tips, rather than flat surfaces in order to draw

Cognitive
- Frequently succeeds with matching shapes with sorting holes upon first attempt — 4, 8
- Will copy/reproduce simple block patterns (3-4 blocks), given examples — 11
- Spontaneously stacks 3-5 objects in order of increasing size — 11
- Rotates tools such as a spoon or cup in order to use them — 1, 2, 9, 10
- Identifies familiar objects by touch (without seeing them) — 2, [M20-19.3]
- Uses crayon to scribble several lines without lifting from paper

Communication
- Shows appropriate response to simple requests (e.g., "Close the door, please") — 2, 8
- Points to own body parts when named (especially of/around head/face)
- Imitates short sentence questions (e.g., "Where dada ?", "What is it ?") — 6
- Speaks babble 'language' in longer (yet still unintelligible) 'sentences' — 10
- Enjoys demonstrating a variety of different sounds by causing them — [M20-19.2]
- 'Talks' and laughs when exploring bath toys (especially with bubbles) — 12

Socio-Personal
- Successfully shares sorting of simple shapes, and building large 2-D picture puzzles — 3, 8
- Explores washing and drying of own hands — 10, [M20-19.11]
- Experiments with caring behaviour using doll/soft toy (e.g., feeding, washing) — 4, 10
- Imitates eye blinking and several other immediate adult facial gestures
- Spontaneously imitates adult health behaviour (tooth-brushing, hair-combing) — 12
- Increasingly engaged by water and sand play (alone or with others) if available

G/A 19.1 Menu Selectors

Task description:
- Searching and matching specific fruits and vegetables from distractor boxes.

Expected Milestone Achievements (EMAs):
- Walks without stiff-limbed gait/action, or losing balance so often (G1)
- Rotates tools such as spoon or cup in order to use them (Cog4)
- Follows familiar single-step verbal command/instruction without [M18 Comms4] gesture.

Materials:
- Toy vegetables and/or fruit, large boxes, bath towel.

Procedure:
Level 1
1. Demonstrate 5 large boxes, opened at one end, facing baby, arrange on their side.
2. Choose three fruit and/or vegetables toys, placed on the floor: e.g., an apple, a banana, and an orange, *checking to make sure baby knows these object names.*
3. Place then each of the three fruits/vegetables in one each of three of the boxes.
4. One piece at a time, present a sample of each of the three fruits and vegetables (same as those placed in the boxes, and maybe no longer visible to them ?), and then invite baby to go forward to find/retrieve it.
5. If baby successfully attains the 'correct' item, share praise even if not at first successful in attaining the target, encouraging baby to await the next round as you restock the boxes, having carefully observed the initial direction in which baby moved off (even if not then attaining any of the food/target objects).
6. Repeat steps 4-5 until baby has succeeded (increasing the level of difficulty if solving 'correctly', and relatively fast each time).

Level 2
1. Demonstrate again the 5 large boxes, opened at one end, arranged on their side, but this time in different orientations, their open sides facing away from baby.
2. Choose three fruit and/or vegetables toys, placed on the floor: e.g., a carrot, a potato, and a tomato, *checking to make sure baby knows these object names*.
3. Place each of the three fruits/vegetables inside *only one each of three* of the boxes
4. One piece at a time, present a sample of each of the three fruits and vegetables (same as those placed in the boxes, now no longer visible), and again invite baby to now go forward in order to find/retrieve the one that matches it.
5. Be sure to observe the direction in which baby initially moves in order to retrieve their assigned target each time (so indicating deliberate motor planning).
6. Repeat steps 4-5 until baby has succeeded as per level 1.

Level 3
1. Demonstrate now 7 large boxes, opened at one end, arranged upside down,
2. Choose four fruit and/or vegetables toys, placed on the floor, again using those that baby clearly knows the object names of.
3. Place each of the tour fruits/vegetables in *one each of four of the seven* boxes
4. One at a time, present a sample of each of the three fruits and vegetables (same as those placed in the boxes), inviting baby to once more go forward to find/retrieve another one like it.
5. Again observe the direction which baby initially moves off in, in order to retrieve their target each time (indicating both baby's spatial memory and motor planning).
6. Invite pretend food sharing, as baby returns to share their 'find' with you/toys (or any other persons present), as they act as if eating, tasting, and enjoying the fruits/vegetables harvested from the box-fields.
7. Repeat steps 3-6 until baby has succeeded in retrieving all the hidden targets.

Level 4
1-n. Repeat the level 3 activity, only using 5 large boxes, opened at one end, arranged on their side, at different orientations, but this time covered by towels (their open sides not visible).

Variations:
- Consider to place the boxes at different heights and/or orientations, so allowing their open end to be more OR less visible each time.
- Guide baby's search and retrieval according to verbal-only requests - i.e., without using example 3D physical objects, and possibly later, as being requested by a different person (if present) each time.

Additional Thoughts/Game-Activity Preparation/Lesson Planning Tips:
- When placing the target fruits and vegetables in the boxes, be sure to attract baby's attention to what you are doing, so strengthening their object-location associations as much as possible.
- For each round, be sure to exchange the toys promptly, so maintaining baby's curiosity, interest and motivation to continue their searches.
- *Pay special attention to observing which (if any), of the toys baby gains more often 'correctly' from the box(es) - such may indicate baby's toy/object preferences - you can then use such information to help (or hinder !) difficulty level enhancements in future (i.e., by your then knowing what kind(s) of objects baby might be prepared to work harder to obtain).*
- If baby continues to fail in succeeding to find the fruits and vegetables from the boxes, try to avoid the temptation to help too much, or to give rewards directly. Instead, reduce the level of difficulty (visible targets/reward, closer box proximity, fewer choices (hence reducing memory load), increasing the difficulty only with increasing success).

G/A 19.2 Hidden Treasure !

Task description:
- Exploring the sensory features of different identifiable objects by touch.

Expected Milestone Achievements (EMAs):
- Imitates tool use as demonstrated by adults (other than hand-tools) [M18-G4]
- Rotates tools such as spoon or cup in order to use them (Cog4)
- Identifies familiar objects by touch (without seeing them) (Cog5)
- Shows appropriate response to simple requests (e.g., "Close the (Comms1) door, please").

Materials:
- Cup, ladle, ball, apple, banana, toy vehicles, [items that baby can identify]
- Mystery bag (cloth/plastic, for baby to 'feel' into, but *not able to 'see' into*).

Procedure:

Level 1
1. Demonstrate use of the 'mystery bag', informing baby that inside it there are many toys (though maybe only one at first ?).
2. Ask baby now, "Does the mystery bag' contain a 'cup' ?". Putting out a hand to 'feel' the outside of the bag, tracing the cup's edges to show that a 'cup-shaped' object is indeed inside.
3. Continue to demonstrate, referring to each of the toys contained in turn, according to the 'correct' request/question(s) asked each time.
4. Present now toys and the same/similar 'mystery bag' to baby.
5. Invite/guide baby to feel the mystery bag containing a single, then multiple, toy(s), allowing them to explore it a while once 'correctly' identified.
6. Next, replace the toy in the bag with a new one, and then guide baby to explore each new toy by touching/feeling it through the bag.
7. If baby still 'correctly' names the toy that you have replaced in the bag, provide encouragement promptly; *If not identified correctly, encourage baby to continue attempting until successful, offering praise promptly, and as appropriate.*

Level 2

1. Demonstrate the 'mystery bag' again, informing baby that inside it there can now be many toys inside (e.g., maybe 4-5 now).
2. Ask baby, "Does the mystery bag' contain a 'Block' ?". Putting out a hand to 'feel' the outside of the bag, tracing the block's edges to show that a 'block-shaped' object is indeed inside.
3. Continue to demonstrate, referring to each of the toys contained in turn, according to the request/question(s) asked each time.
4. Present next all the toys, *this time already inside* the mystery bag, to baby.
5. Invite/guide baby to trace them one by one, the first mystery bag's toy, allowing baby to play with them as they 'correctly' identify each one.
6. Returning the toy to the bag each time, advise baby as to which toy to look/feel 'for', and identify next.
7. Each time baby matches 'correctly', promptly praise/encourage baby's efforts.

Variations:
- Prepare two identical toy sets, placing one set into the 'mystical bag' (without baby knowing what is inside), with the other set requesting baby to take up one toy each time, then encouraging baby to touch/explore the toy (like a sample to memorise the 'feel' of) which you are then about to assign them as the next target.
- Ditto, then placing baby's hand *into* the bag in order to take out the same toy (without seeing it), so allowing baby to use direct touch sensations to drive their decision-making (i.e., to determine what it is), based upon their feeling the different toys' shape and texture only.

Additional Thoughts/Game-Activity Preparation/Lesson Planning Tips:
- Throughout this activity try to reuse the same objects (touched and seen) - as far as is possible, encourage baby's to name these familiar objects each time that they 'correctly' see/feel them.(increasing the level of difficulty by increasing the *number* of objects, and hence options to choose from, each time).

G/A 19.3   Match & Dispatch !

Task description:
- Exploring colour matching across objects (e.g., a *red* box & *red* ball).

Expected Milestone Achievements (EMAs):
- Attempts to imitate organised patterns/arrays of objects (e.g., by   [M21-Cog4]
  colour, size).
- Walks without stiff-limbed gaits/action, or losing balance so often   (G1)
- Offers hand with appropriate finger grasp positions when reached for   (F1)
  by another person.
- Successfully shares sorting of simple shapes, and building large 2-D   (SP1)
  picture puzzles.

Materials:
- Red coloured box, red-coloured ball, other coloured balls, basket/bag.

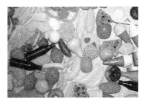

Procedure:
Level 1
1. Demonstrate a basket/box as container, inside of which may be placed a ball.
2. Arrange the ball now on the floor, with the box, showing how the ball may be taken up and placed into the box.
3. Present coloured balls, in a basket, to baby.
4. Place a red ball into the correspondingly coloured (red) box, inviting baby to select the same-coloured ball from their set, and to then put it to the appropriate box.
5. Provide prompt encouragement/praise with increasing success.

Level 2
1. Demonstrate the basket as container, inside of which may be placed this time several differently coloured balls.
2. Arrange one ball now on the floor, with a box of the same colour, showing how the ball may be taken up and placed into that 'matching-colour' box.

3. Place now a green ball into the correspondingly-coloured (green, or green-stickered/coded) box, inviting baby to select the same coloured ball from their set, and placing it also into the appropriately-coloured box.
4. Change the choice of coloured materials and instructions each time, providing prompt encouragement/praise with increasing success.

Level 3
1. Demonstrate again the basket as initial ball container, inside of which may now be found various non-ball objects, but each of the same colours as those of the ball sets previously used in levels 1-2 (e.g., toy fruits & vegetables, cars, soft toys).
2. Arrange a ball now on the floor, with the box, showing how the ball may be taken up and placed into the box as before.
3. Present baby with only a coloured ball set in their basket, as before.
4. Next take up and place a *red non-ball* object into the correspondingly coloured box, inviting baby to select the same coloured ball from their set, and to then carry it over to the appropriate box.
5. Provide prompt encouragement/praise with increasing success.

Variations:
- Consider to distribute boxes of different colours about the room, inviting baby to act according to the instructions given, with regards the corresponding objects and/or coloured box placements/locations, after seeking out their coloured object targets and relocating their chosen matching toys each time.
- Mix and match object selection and relocation, by alternating your and baby's following each other's selections made each time - 'follow-the-leader' style.
- Invite a different person (if someone else be present) to make the requests/instructions each time (with increasing success only !).

Additional Thoughts/Game-Activity Preparation/Lesson Planning Tips:
- Increase the level of difficulty by making the colours (to be distinguished) more similar to each other (e.g., using light green and dark green, or bi-coloured).
- Consider coding each kind of colour to also indicate a different performance, for example have 'dark red' require baby's selecting/placing of the ball 'in' the box, but 'light red/pink' indicating placing the object 'on' the box.
- With complex objects, be aware that baby may 'correctly' act according to component features of the whole object only when colour pairing (e.g., selecting a white car having red headlights or a red stripe pattern on it, when matching for a 'red' object).

G/A 19.4   Stringing them all Together

Task description:
- Using a tool to thread a flexible substrate through holes.

Expected Milestone Achievements (EMAs):
- Offers hand with appropriate finger grasp positions when reached for by   (F1) another person.
- Places plug into water sink and/or threads large-holed beads onto string   [M22-F2]
- Frequently succeeds to match shapes with sorting holes upon   (Cog1) first attempt.
- Experiments with caring behaviour using doll/soft toy (e.g., feeding,   (SP3) washing).

Materials:
- Model round disk (with at least a central eyelet hole) + shoelace
- Model round disk (with outer eyelet holes, and two other eyelet holes symmetrically mid radius) [Can easily make if no retail version(s) available in the home]

- Straws (thick & thin), dish, string, Baby doll/soft animal toy (shoe-sized 'feet' !)

Procedure:
Level 1
1. Demonstrate the small card/disk with holes, sharing with baby to observe, especially the hole in its the centre.
2. Next taking out a straw, demonstrate piercing of the hole with it, then 'sewing' a string/lace through it, and letting the disk then rotate about the string through its centre.
3. Continue to use the straw to now complete the outside threading of other holes, or demonstrating very quickly, to pretend that the red "candied fruit" on the string is very good to drink (detail here depending upon your material being used, see example 'melon piece' illustration above).
4. Present now with three short straws, inviting baby to complete the round disk and string via the straw, for them to then pretend to enjoy the "candied fruit" taste.

Level 2
1. Demonstrate a second (multi-holed) disk/card, and share with baby to observe, pointing to two mid-radii symmetrically placed holes (drawn like a real shoe, or can actually use a shoe !).
2. Show again the string threading using the straw, but this time threading through the two adjacent holes at the same time, with the disk folded, the round disk becoming semi circle-shaped (thread all the paired holes if baby's skill allows).
3. Continue to use the straw to thread other holes, using a real lace (and even a real shoe) as preferred, as baby's motivation and developing fine motor skills allow.

Variations:
- Consider to continue with active 'sewing' practice using large wooden beads and string.
- If not succeeding well, offer a longer straw or solid (open) rod, for baby to thread objects onto.
- Try threading onto shoelaces, or having baby place wooden clothes pegs onto it.
- Present both thick and thinner straws, with large and small eyelet's on the round disks, to then assess baby's choice of sewing straws each time, respectively.
- If reasonably competent with the task levels proposed, consider inviting baby to place real laces (or relatively thin and flexible straws) through real shoe eyelets [which may/may not have been placed upon a toy doll or soft toy 'feet'].

Additional Thoughts/Game-Activity Preparation/Lesson Planning Tips
- If no threading eyelet templates be available in the home, use a real shoe, or make a simple kit using relatively stiff cardboard with holes made to allow easy threading of string diameter(s) to be used
- Be sure to use short straw lengths, so helping avoid self/stabbing into baby's eyes.
- If using coloured shoelaces, consider to use those with intact aglets, as the less manually-controlled baby will find these pre-formed (ended) 'strings' relatively easy to work with as threading tools (as TD still does, even now !).
- *Be careful also to determine exactly how much baby is personally achieving in the construction task here – try to avoid the temptation to keep demonstrating, or otherwise remaining keen to 'do it for them' rather than your simply assisting baby in completing this task by themselves (else baby will become a spectator, as 'mummy/daddy do it' !).*

G/A 19.5   River Crossings

Task description:
- Exploring adventurous 'stepping stone' planning to reach a target location.

Expected Milestone Achievements (EMAs):
- Walks without stiff-limbed gaits/action, or losing balance so often   (G1)
- Walks up (and down) a few stairs unaided   (G2)
- Successfully attempts relocation from others' lap or chair (without help)(M18-G4)
- Reaches with outstretched arm when hearing, "Hold my hand, please" (G4)

Materials:
- Floor mats/marked areas, stepping-stones (stiff boxes/containers/cushions).

Procedure:
Level 1
1. Create an alley/path in the room using floor mats, separated by a visible gap.
2. Demonstrate using the feet to step on the floor mats from one end of the room path to the other end, allowing neither foot to step outside the floor mat coverage areas.
3. Invite baby to now 'line up' behind you, and one by one, to "cross the river" (gaps) with you, together.

Level 2
1. Create a new alley/path in the room, again using the floor mats, this time separated by a much/slightly larger visible gap, and now with one 'stepping stone' placed in a much larger gap between the floor mats *at one point*.
2. Invite baby to again follow behind you, to "cross the river" once more, now also using the 'stepping stone' (a hard raised surface, box/container/cushion) as per your demonstration.
3. Be sure to provide baby with continuous protective support, as needed (even though there be no real risk of 'getting wet'; baby could easily twist an ankle or miss-step about obstacles, and fall.

Level 3
1. As baby continues to walk more smoothly in level 2, adjust the gap distance between the 'stepping-stone' and the mats, and/or vary its height (with baby's increasing success) - even introducing a 2nd stepping stone if ability allows (?).
2. Be sure to again provide baby with continuous protective support with 'step' walking, as needed.

Variations:
- Increase the range and style of pathway decoration, obstacles & stepping stones with success, so enhancing baby's movement with interest and challenge.
- Consider using differently sized boxes to build the road, so allowing baby to explore walking at a higher level above the ground (as baby's performance and increasing stability allows).

Additional Thoughts/Game-Activity Preparation/Lesson Planning Tips
- As baby attempts to use the stepping-stone(s) for the first time, lead baby to walk held with a single-handed only, so encouraging familiarity with the task/activity, whilst also increasing their self-confidence.
- *If using firm cushions rather than a more solid 'stepping stone' material, choose cushioning which is relatively stable (chair seat or back) rather than a soft pillow-like cushion which will cause baby considerable instability and balance difficulty once stood upon.* [Plastic bowls/food boxes, or wooden structures/solid cases would be better for this purpose].
- When using alternately higher and lower 'stepping-stones', be sure to assist only for as long as baby really needs it, and only in order to help them maintain balance whilst moving.
- *As you may also wish at his stage to encourage baby to walk more (and to perhaps crawl less), make sure that increasing levels of praise are offered to baby when doing so.*
- Be careful to ensure that during any walking and/or balance training of this sort, the pathway design avoids crowded spaces (cluttered either with hard objects, room furnishings or even other people for baby to collide with), especially at this critical time of walking skill acquisition, sensory-motor coordination, integration and practice.

Baby Milestones of Development (0-3 Yrs)

219

G/A 19.6   Time for Football

Task description:
- Developing increased muscle strength, coordination and senses of balance, by manipulating objects with the feet.

Expected Milestone Achievements (EMAs):
- Deliberate forward ball kicking (rather than simply 'walking into' ball)   [M18-G3]
- Walks without stiff-limbed gaits/action, or losing balance so often   (G1)
- Stands, and come to, new location(s) when asked to so   (G3)
- Imitates short sentence questions (e.g., "Where dada ?", "What is it ?")(Comms3)

Materials:
- Soft soccer ball (with attached rope if preferred), open box/cushion-built 'goal'.

Procedure:

Level 1

1. Demonstrate use and movement of a soft soccer ball, (with attached rope if needed/preferred – tying one end to baby's leg or waist to reduce distance or damage !)
2. Using either foot, make an effort to show (using the foot only) how to make the ball rock back and forth.
3. Invite baby to now attempt 'one time play' soccer, presenting them a ball.
4. If tied, later untie the string, fixing the ball in place on the ground, encouraging baby to at first kick it without moving their whole body position.
5 Pay careful attention in following baby if then mobile, so giving protection as needed, and especially in *avoiding baby colliding with furnishings/walls/others (as they are likely to be looking at the ball, and not looking fwd towards where they are moving/going to !!)*

Level 2
1. Demonstrate use and movement of the soft soccer ball, (without attached string, even if available), towards the cushion-built (or open-sided box) 'goal'.
2. Invite baby to next demonstrate scoring a 'goal' by aiming to kick the ball between the upright supports of your 'cushion-built/box' goal as per your demonstration.
3. If/when each time baby scores a 'goal', be sure to encourage such action with praise promptly.

Variations:
- As baby interacts successfully to 'play soccer', encourage baby to then kick the ball towards you, for you to then 'catch' the ball (making exaggerated movements each time, in order to enhance/keep baby's interest and motivation).
- Consider also using both hands to hold baby's hand, leading baby to pursue the ball to 'play soccer', so strengthening not only their levels of interest, but also strengthening their leg muscles, sensory motor integration ability, and sense of dynamic balance control.

Additional Thoughts/Game-Activity Preparation/Lesson Planning Tips
- Paying careful attention to baby's thigh and lower limb strength, adjust the ball and (baby) distance from the cushion/box 'goal' with increasing success.
- Initially using a ball with a short rope attached, the 'free' end then tied to baby's ankle/waist, will allow shorter times (due to reduced ball retrieval time/activity), and/or also prove suitable for conducting tasks with baby in stationary standing/leaning/seated or prone positions..
- If beginning to move faster when playing 'soccer' here, keep aware to avoid baby's colliding with furnishings and other room features, paying especial concern to immediately assess any injury to baby's head if bumped.

G/A 19.7   More Houdini Feats

Task description:
- Exploring exit routes from within a simple maze matrix.

Expected Milestone Achievements (EMAs):
- Attempts various ways to 'escape' restrictions of pushchair,   [M18-Cog2]
  highchair/car seat harnesses (including straps/buckles).
- Stands, and come to, new location(s) when asked to so   (G3)
- Climbs on objects without prompting, in order to see from higher position (G5)

Materials:
- Coloured boxes (quite firm/solid), small toys.

Procedure:

Level 1
1. Arrange 5-10 boxes (not too high-sided) to form a square matrix on the floor
2. Invite/place baby somewhere inside the "maze" of boxes, preferably close to the centre.
3. Remaining yourself *outside* the matrix/web on the periphery, encourage/attract baby with a preferred toy, in an attempt to have baby try to navigate a path through the different boxes, walking towards their newly found 'exit', and to gain the toy that you are holding, and to then play with it/them for a while.
4. As baby succeeds to find their way out of "the Houdini Maze" (box matrix) and "escapes" each time, encourage with prompt reward/praise.

Level 2+
1-4. With success, repeat level 1 procedures, using slightly larger boxes
    (so as to require baby to lift their legs higher, and/or increase balance control).

Level 3+
1. Continue to build increasingly higher "Houdini Mazes"/matrices of boxes with success.

2. Again placing baby in a central location to begin, pay close attention to observing baby's chosen routes of 'escape' each time.

Variations:
- Consider to 'release' baby from their initial position (at the centre) from their high chair/stroller each time.
- If sturdier materials be available, consider to invite baby to try similar escapes by stepping ON the boxes/containers each time (positioned upside-down on the floor – open face to the ground).
- Likewise, with the boxes faced open-side up – requiring baby to step INTO then out of the different boxes as they move outwards each time.

Additional Thoughts/Game-Activity Preparation/Lesson Planning Tips:
- This task affords a great opportunity to see exactly what 'baby's world' might look like from the "baby's point of view". *I encourage you to frequently get down upon your hands and knees to 'look around' (moving your head & eyes only) as you also then 'see' the world initially from a few-to-30 cms above the ground only !! – and, … sore, heavy neck looking around, yes ?,….*
- As baby walks/climbs/spiders toward their 'exit' in escaping, ensure that you remain available to provide suitable protection, *but not route-planning assistance*, in maintaining baby's safe 'escape'. As far as possible (some box packing ballast may also be helpful), prevent baby from simply pushing them out of their way in reaching their chosen exit path(s) each time !).
- Pay special attention to observing the route(s) chosen when negotiating boxes of differing sizes and heights from the ground, and remember this information for future activity planning !

Baby Milestones of Development (0-3 Yrs)

223

G/A 19.8　　Shaping Up !

Task description:
- Identifying and exploring circles, triangles, and squares.

Expected Milestone Achievements (EMAs):
- Frequently succeeds to match shapes with sorting holes upon first attempt (Cog1)
- Successfully shares sorting of simple shapes, and building large 2-D (SP1) picture puzzles.
- Shows appropriate response to simple requests (e.g., "Close the door, (Comms1) please").

Materials:
- Shape *Picture-Cards* (or self-drawn circles, triangles, squares, stars, each on a separate paper), boxes.

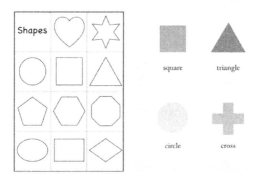

Procedure:

Level 1
1. Demonstrate different shape *picture-cards* in turn, a triangle, and a square, arranging examples of each on the floor for baby to clearly see.
2. Lead baby about the floor to know, in turn, the names of these different shapes.
3. Present next the set of shape *picture-cards*, together with two boxes on the floor.
4. Invite baby to now place the appropriate shape *picture-card*, in turn, as you request each by name, baby to act according to the information given each time, to, e.g., "Please find a square *picture-card*, and go to place it in the blue box".
5. Encourage prompt praise for all 'correct' responses.

Level 2
1. Demonstrate again the same two different shaped *picture-cards* in turn, the triangle, the square, and this time also the circle, and the star, again arranging examples of each on the floor.
2. Lead baby about the floor to know, in turn, the names of these shapes.
3. Add now close to the new shape *picture-card* set, four boxes on the floor.
4. Invite baby to next place the appropriate shape picture-card, in turn, as you request each by name, baby to act according to the information given each time, e.g., "Please find the star *picture-card*, and go to place it in the yellow box".
5 Provide prompt praise for all 'correct' responses, as and when they occur.

Variations:
- Increase the level of difficulty by adding circles, other coloured shapes, ellipses, rectangles, etc., for baby to identify.
- Invite baby to gather different sizes or colours of the same shape together in one place.
- Increase the difficulty further, by encouraging baby to verbally name the shapes which you show them on a group of shape cards.
- Instead of using paper/card, consider using 3-D coloured block shapes, and/or a shape-sorter toy set parts for item categorisations each time.

Additional Thoughts/Game-Activity Preparation/Lesson Planning Tips:
- Be sure to check the condition of all the *picture-cards* before use in the activity, cleaning or replacing/laminating them as appropriate (and especially so, if dirty, or having developed any jagged edges).
- If preferring to make your own, simply draw your shapes with thickly outlined edges, and with an ink offering maximum/clear contrast with the paper colour(s) being used.
- Consider to pin/peg such cards/papers to the wall/furnishings/hangers, if not wishing to play the activity on the floor.

Baby Milestones of Development (0-3 Yrs)

G/A 19.9   Helping to Serve the Soup !

Task description:
- Exploring the use of tools to retrieve otherwise 'out of reach' objects.

Expected Milestone Achievements (EMAs):
- Rotates tools such as spoon or cup in order to use them   (Cog4)
- Offers hand with appropriate finger grasp positions when reached for   (F1)
  by another person.

Materials:
- Basket with hole, long handled plastic/wooden ladle, small soft ball
- Preferred toy, toy vehicle, toy fruits and vegetables.

Procedure:
Level 1
1. Demonstrate a basket/bag, inside of which are differently sized and shaped small toys, and above which is a hole in the basket through which a ladle may be inserted in order to acquire them [or use attached paper with hole).
2. Demonstrate clearly how to put out a hand and to use the ladle to acquire 1-2 toys, ensuring that baby is directly looking at what you are doing (else will find this a very difficult skill to imitate !).
3. Present the basket and toy set, inviting baby to try and find the solution to taking out the toys from the basket by themselves (using the same ladle tool).
4. Pay close attention to observing *how* baby acquires their toys each time (if at all), praising both attempts and successes promptly, as/when they do so.

Level 2
1. Pile a selection of small toy's above the hole on the outside of the basket (or a small box with hole), placed randomly at different orientations (lying this way and that, close to the hole).

2. Encourage baby to now use the ladle (and not their hands) to move/rotate the toys *into* the basket/box (through the hole), without simply pushing them in.
3. Again, pay careful attention to observing how baby attempts to reposition the toys each time, praising success promptly when they achieve their goal of getting the toys into the basket/box each time.

Variations:
- Consider to use wide, coloured ribbons to be put through basket holes using clothes pegs or straws as tools.
- Invite baby to attempt to gain toys with the use of a 'stick' placed in a suitable gap containing them (e.g., between two boxes), and which are otherwise beyond their reach, even at an arm's-length.

Additional Thoughts/Game-Activity Preparation/Lesson Planning Tips:
- Consider choosing a ladle size/shape that will fit relatively tight/loosely into the basket/box hole, such that it is difficult for baby to use it to make the basket fall easily down/over.
- You will find that you do not need to prompt baby to action (if the target toys are attractive). Instead, simply encourage baby to use their own strategy(ies) in thinking/exploring any means to gain the toys, but *without* using their hands.
- *Baby's natural solution will obviously be to use their fingers to acquire the toys, putting them through the hole to take the toys - making an effort to keep the basket beyond arm's length will help eliminate this tendency.*

G/A 19.10 Waiting and Dining Services

Task description:
- Exploring the use of a small tool to share food with others.

Expected Milestone Achievements (EMAs):
- Speaks babble 'language' in longer (yet still unintelligible) 'sentences' (Comms4)
- Rotates tools such as spoon or cup in order to use them (Cog4)
- Experiments with caring behaviour using doll/soft toy (e.g., feeding) (SP3)
- Exploring washing and drying of own hands (SP2)

Materials:
- Ladle/spoon, small bowl, fresh raisins*, Hand cleaning/washing/drying materials
- Face mask, or fun mask made from decorated paper plate with 'open mouth'.

* = see also Activity Preparation Tips below !

Procedure:
Level 1 [Following hand washing/drying procedures]
1. Demonstrate the use of a bowl, inside of which is a raisin.
2. Next demonstrate the use of a ladle to scoop up the raisin, and to use it to then bring the food (raisin) towards the mouth to eat.
3. Present the same/similar materials to baby, encouraging/inviting baby to feed him/herself, and to eat the raisin (or other preferred food stuff of similar size) in the manner just demonstrated.

Level 2
1. Show the "paper mask", informing baby that the face owner's belly is empty, and thus that they are quite hungry.
2. Demonstrate use of the ladle to again scoop up the raisin, but to now feed the mask by placing the raisin between *its* lips (i.e., through the hole, the raisin then caught by your hand, or dropping into a second bowl behind it).
3. Present the same/similar mask to the baby, inviting them to do the same.
4. Encourage the action with prompt praise for baby to have the compassion to feed another, informing baby that the paper mask person has now become very happy.

Variations:
- Consider inviting baby to feed you, with fresh grapes (directly with the fingers at first, then with the tool afterwards).
- If others be present at the time, consider organising two (maybe more ?) persons in a group, inviting baby to then attempt feeding others, and to then eat together.
- If no suitable ladle be available in the home, consider to use an unusual spoon, spatula, or similar "non-spork-like" tool/object).

Additional Thoughts/Game-Activity Preparation/Lesson Planning Tips:
- When choosing small food items for this activity, do so long BEFORE you plan to start the task with baby, and so have available your food item choice(s) close to hand (whether or not wishing to have baby consume fresh raisins or grapes), so that baby is not left alone waiting for you to go prepare something.
- Allow baby to attempt feeding with the ladle as far as possible, even if continually sprinkling the dry food onto the ground. You might also later invite/guide baby to help clean up the spillage with you together (at a later time).
- Pay special attention to preventing baby picking up and eating food items which have fallen to the ground, for both health and safety reasons.
- All tableware prepared should be thoroughly disinfected before use, the raisins checked to avoid any hairs having stuck to them during manipulation.
- You may also take this opportunity to guide baby in grasping the bowl 'correctly'.

G/A 19.11 You and I Together

Task description:
- Exploring sharing together, with "You" and "I".

Expected Milestone Achievements (EMAs):
- Turns single book pages unaided (F2)
- Identifies several pictures by pointing at them (from amongst others) (F5)
- Will copy/reproduce simple block patterns (3-4 blocks), given example (Cog2)
- Spontaneously stacks 3-5 objects in order of increasing size (Cog3)
- Follows familiar single-step verbal command/instruction without gesture. [M18-Comms4]
- Knows 'when' to 'start a conversation' (fill silence in group) [M18-Comms6]

Materials:
- Bells, trays, bowls, plastic bottle, stiff-paged books, building bricks.

Procedure:

Level 1
1. Invite baby to come and sit face-to-face with you, in front of each of you a small bowl, a tray and a bell.
2. Demonstrate pronoun naming allocations by lifting a bell from the tray, and placing it into baby's bowl, whilst at the same time saying "You (have one)".
3. Next, place the bell in your own bowl, whilst at the same time saying "I (have one)"
4. Invite baby to repeat your action(s), as you accompany the actions with the same words, each time.
5. Finally, after baby has assigned all of the remaining bells, lead baby to load each bell into different plastic bottles, to make musical instruments, and play together.

Levels 2-3
1. Invite baby to come and sit face-to-face with you again, this time following your verbal instructions to identify book pages/pictures, and/or construct simple brick stacks.

Variations:
- Run the same task replacing the "You" and "I", with "Yours" and "Mine".
- With baby's increasingly stable sociability, and if others be present in the room, consider to combine two or more persons to join with baby as one single group, requesting cooperation between the various persons present to carry out the "You" and "I" assignment(s) each time.
- To further encourage extended turn taking with advanced speakers, play the converse "reply' game with baby, e.g., having said to baby in a questioning tone of voice, "I am called Mummy/Daddy/x ?", baby 'correctly responds by placing the bell in the bowl in front of you/x. If, "I am 19 months old", placing the bell in his/her own bowl, etc.,...
- Ditto likewise, with increasingly complex statements (and thus increasing levels of difficulty),... "You are the little baby male/boy or the female/girl ?", "Whose hand is this ?", ... "This is a part of whose hair ?", and so forth, inviting baby to use "me" and "you", or "You" and "I" in turn, *as answers* to the questions as most relevant each time.

Additional Thoughts/Game-Activity Preparation/Lesson Planning Tips:
- Although designed for use by primarily English language speakers, simple modification of the instructions/suggested sentence pronouns (and use/non-use of personal pronouns in general) will allow for the activity's employ for any language/culture of choice.
- When providing guidance/praise to, or otherwise 'correcting' baby in this task, try as best as you can to determine that the "You", 'Your", "I", "Mine" (etc.) concepts, are being perceived as being 'correct' from baby's point of view (i.e., *baby's "I", "Me"*).

G/A 19.12   Catch It If you Can !

Task description:
- Exploring interactions by throwing and catching a ball.

Expected Milestone Achievements (EMAs):
- Throws objects into boxes/baskets (as a game with others)   [M18-SP4]
- 'Talks' and laughs when exploring bath toys (especially with bubbles) (Comms6)
- Spontaneously imitates adult health behaviour (here tossing laundry)   (SP5)
- Likes to play 'catch' and similar thrown-object games with others   [M20-SP2]

Materials:
- Soft rubber ball, used clothing (ready for washing), laundry box.

Procedure:

Level 1
1. Demonstrate a soft rubber ball, inviting baby to share/help you with a coordinated action, for both to enjoy.
2. Invite baby to first hold the ball in both hands, and to then attempt to throw the ball.
3. With both your hands attempting to catch baby's thrown ball, rolling the ball back to baby, gently along the floor, for him/her to throw back to you once more.
4. Provide praise to baby for good control, promptly.

Level 2a
1. Invite/guide baby to next use both their hands (with small opening), in preparation to catch the soft rubber ball (as gently thrown by you, towards baby).
2. Gently throw the ball towards 'prepared' baby's arm position, encouraging baby to then use both their hands in a coordinated way, so hugging in a curving movement toward the chest, in order to catch the ball.
3. Render baby suitable assistance, and encouragement, as this is a VERY difficult eye-hand and arm-head-trunk coordination *and* timing skill for baby to at first learn, then mastering only after much perseverance and practice !!

4. In whatever way baby actually receives the ball (or simply goes to pick it up from its eventual resting place), encourage baby to continue making a return throw of the ball to you, so facilitating turn-taking (even if not throwing/catching well at this time).

Level 2b
[especially useful if baby does not/cannot adequately catch mid-air objects in flight]
1. Invite baby to simply toss clothing into a box/bin, making the opening progressively smaller, or further away to increase the level(s) of difficulty with increasing success.

Variations:
- With developing expertise, consider to combine two (or more if present) persons in the room into a single group, then instructing each other (including baby), to play "Throw 'n Catch, If you Can" with each other, in triangular/square formations.
- Ditto, seated around the floor as a single group, throw a plush puppet to each person (in turn), having instructed each to invite baby to 'meet and greet' the plush puppet when s/he arrives (or is thrown towards baby), and to then throw the puppet back to you, who then continues to throw the plush puppet to other persons in turn.
- If not wishing to use/toss soiled clothing (to simulate laundry duties), consider to use the soft ball (and other similar balls) as missiles to then be gently thrown into various boxes/ins/containers placed about the floor of the room.

Additional Thoughts/Game-Activity Preparation/Lesson Planning Tips:
- According to baby's arm muscle strength, carefully monitor and adjust the distance and throw speeds with which baby may best be expected to be able to successfully catch a ball (at each point in time).
- Ditto, with baby realistically being able to reach a certain bin distance, via their 'throwing'.
- In the face of continual difficulty in baby's catching skill, consider to gently drop-throw the ball into baby's forearm-hand-elbow position, so letting baby experience some success by hugging the ball as, and when, it arrives.

ψ

Baby Milestones of Development (0-3 Yrs)

– 12 –

Baby Milestones of Development

(With 100+ Fun Activities to Help Demonstrate Them)

[Age 20 Months]

ψ

Expected Milestone Achievements
Age = 20 Months

[Key: e.g., 2 = Game No. 20.2]

Gross Motor

• Walks fast, (even runs ?), without stumbling or bumping into objects	1
• Walks several stairs spontaneously, and unaided	5, 7
• Changes direction when avoiding objects in path of movement	12
• Carries own weight (with balance) when running, unsupported	12
• Climbs upon a chair to see on table when asked "What's on the table ?"	5
• Throws a ball with over-arm movement	12

Fine Motor

• Changes palm grip according to size and shape of object being offered	2, 3, 7
• Grips jars or tubs appropriate to turning/levering their lids open	4
• Uses a spoon to self-feed without turning it upside-down and spilling	9
• Shifts orientation of a held spoon or fork when scooping for use	9
• Identifies 6-10 pictures by pointing at them (amongst others)	6, 10
• Draws without changing hand/crayon tip holding posture mid-stroke	

Cognitive

• Selects correct shapes for visible sorting-box holes	8
• Successfully stacks 7-9 blocks in a tower	
• Starting to correctly predict unseen object motion (balls moving in tubes, behind objects, etc.)	
• Picks up and rotates bottle in order to drink from it	9
• Imitates sequences of adult facial expression changes	3, 8
• Explores more challenging toys/activities with increasing interest	2, 6, 7, 12

Communication

• Shows appropriate response to action requests (e.g., "Bring the teddy-bear here, please")	1, 8,10,11
• Knows and uses as many as 50+ single words	
• Attentive to different verbal instructions, without directly looking at the person speaking to them	3, 6
• Imitates 3-5 words sentences of others (even if not understanding their meaning)	4, 12
• Occasionally sings repetitive rhymes and canons for self-amusement	
• Offers objects with 'speech', and facial expressions to self in mirror	10, 11

Socio-Personal

• Imitates body part touching whilst watching an adult do the same (especially parts of the face, chin, ears and neck)	10,11
• Likes to play 'catch' and similar thrown-object games with others	[M19-18.12]
• Copies adult's drawing single lines, in any direction	
• Enjoys 'putting dolls/toys to bed', or enacting hygiene routines with soft toys/animals	4, 11
• Imitates household chore behaviours (e.g., cleaning, sweeping, wiping spills)	9
• Self-stimulated by interacting with mechanical/electronic toys with curiosity	2, 8

G/A 20.1   Hiking the Hike

Task description:
- Exploring and planning an uneven path adventure.

Expected Milestone Achievements (EMAs):
- Walks fast, (even runs ?), without stumbling or bumping into objects   (G1)
- Reaches with outstretched arm when hearing "Hold my hand, please" [M19-G4]
- Shows appropriate response to action requests (e.g., "Bring the   (Comms1) teddy-bear here, please").

Materials:
- Stepping-stone pathway (small mats/marked areas, with path lined with various cushions, boxes/containers, etc.,).

Procedure:

Level 1
1. Arrange a path using stepping stones in a regular straight line, demonstrating how to simply move from one end to the other, without touching the floor.
2. Invite baby to now come forward and attempt to travel the same path, as per your demonstration.
3. As baby continues to travel steadily along the path, and without falling, encourage baby with prompt praise and motivation.
4. Repeat according to baby's interest level(s), considering to increase the level of difficulty by changing the required movement direction from a straight path to a more complex path of twists and turns, with increasing success.

Level 2
1. With level 1 success, arrange now an identical second path next to the first, organising baby to stand on one, yourself in the other, each with your own (parallel) path to follow. (Possibly connected by each holding one end of a pole).

2. Invite baby to now come and join you at the 'start', and to attempt to travel the same path, again simply moving from one end to the other, without touching the floor.
3. As baby continues to travel steadily along the path, and without falling, encourage with prompt praise and motivation (ignoring whether you are ahead of, or behind baby, as you do so).

Level 3
1. Arrange a new path, this time introducing some direction change(s) to the line, demonstrating how to simply move from one end to the other, again without touching the floor.
2. Repeat as per levels 1-2, considering to increase the level of difficulty further by changing the required movement direction(s) with increasing success.

Variations:
- Consider increasing the level of difficulty and sensorimotor control required by making the stepping stones further apart.
- With increasing confidence crossing the stepping stones, assign different 'ranks' to baby's skill levels (colour-coding them according to design difficulty levels ?)
- Increase the significance/duty of travelling the pathway (to baby), e.g., to "Save a plush toy animal, and to bring it safely home", or to "Deliver a toy to a friend" waiting at the other end to affect baby's motivation and interest (i.e., *turning what at first may look like simply a motor task, into a combined GM/Comms/SP task*).

Additional Thoughts/Game-Activity Preparation/Lesson Planning Tips:
- As the pathways constructed for use in this activity can present a walking surface at some altitude above the floor, remain vigilant and provide protection to baby's body (possibly supporting, but without holding them all the while), so helping to break baby's fall if falling down from/between the elevated stepping stone paths, so preventing any significant injury.
- Although solo stepping may still present significant difficulty for some babies of this age, be sure to allow baby to attempt it alone, and to try walking one/two 'stones'/short sections, even if falling (supported), and to continue again if keen to do so. But remain nearby should baby require you to be initially attempting to walk the pathway whilst holding on to you, even if with one hand only.
- *Consider also inviting baby to remove their socks in order to walk upon the stepping-stones and/or obstacle path with better 'sensation' – so better exploring the materials with an increasing number of internal and external body senses [pressure and temperature sensors in the skin, but also the body muscle stretch receptors and inner ear vesicles (detecting balance offset)].*

G/A 20.2   What do I Hear ?

Task description:
- Exploring the sensations and appearance of different musical instruments and their sounds.

Expected Milestone Achievements (EMAs):
- Changes palm grip according to size and shape of object being offered   (F1)
- Explores more challenging toys/activities with increasing interest   (Cog6)
- Enjoys demonstrating a variety of different sounds by causing them   [M19-Comms5]
- Self-stimulated by interacting with mechanical/electronic toys with curiosity (SP6)

Materials:
- Musical instruments (castanets, drum, tambourine, bells, shakers/maracas, etc.,)
- Mp3 player, or similar device to broadcast to room (not using headphones).

Procedure:
Level 1
1. Demonstrate, in turn, different musical instruments and name them each time (e.g., if shaking shaker/maracas, inform baby, "This is a shaker/maracas").
2. Arrange each of the musical instruments demonstrated on the floor for baby to clearly see.
3. Invite baby to now come closer, asking them to distinguish the different musical instruments as you name them, and to cause each to then sound, e.g., if asking baby to, "Find the hand drum", the 'correct' response would be for baby to identify which one was the hand drum, and to then beat/tap it in making its sound, etc.,
4. As baby succeeds to find the musical instrument which you have named each time, provide immediate praise.
5. Finally, invite baby to now choose the musical instrument which they would like to 'play', and to follow some music broadcast to the room, or your own self-generated rhythm/singing, in order to stimulate baby's 'musical concert performance'.

Level 2
1. Demonstrate, in turn again, different musical instruments, naming them each time (e.g., if beating a small drum/tambourine, inform baby, "This is a drum/tambourine"
2. Arrange each of the musical instruments demonstrated on the floor for baby to clearly see.
3. Next, choose a musical instrument from the collection on the floor, demonstrate its use again, asking baby, 'What is the name of this instrument ?".
4. As baby names the musical instrument 'correctly', either ask baby to imitate the musical instrument's sound, rewarding baby by giving the instrument to them once they have done so (however [in]accurately !)
5. Finally, invite all present (baby/yourself, and any other person(s)) to 'play' their chosen musical instruments, this time together, in producing your very own 'Happy home concert hall musical performance'.

Variations:
- Provide baby with different musical instruments, inviting baby to follow your rhythm to play each type of musical instrument. E.g., if presenting a shaker/maracas, lead baby to play the different rhythm(s) using the shaker/castanet; Next presenting baby with a hand drum, lead baby to then carry on with their rhythm performance using the hand drum. Finally, allow baby to choose their preferred musical instrument (and/or to distribute further instruments amongst any others present), to form a home orchestra performance !
- If no musical instruments be available in the home, either make some simple percussion instruments (e.g., placing dried rice/bean inside clean, sealable bottles/jars/tins to make different shakers), or demonstrate use of any available electronic musical instrument devices, as appropriate [though not deal].

Additional Thoughts/Game-Activity Preparation/Lesson Planning Tips:
- If baby cannot answer as to the musical instrument's name, repeat the name often so as to create/deepen the impression/association between the object and its name for baby to memorise.....
- ... Indeed, encourage baby say each musical instrument's name at every opportunity, or task them to speak the corresponding name(s) of the different musical instrument(s) at different times, rewarding baby with possession/play time with the same musical instrument named each time.
- If introducing new instruments to the home for the purpose of conducting this task, be sure to prepare musical instruments of good material quality for baby to explore/play.
- Be sure to adjust/allow for the posture/seating distance baby must make between you and themselves each time, according to the size/shape/playing style of each particular instrument being handled, whilst also giving baby the guidance and protection they may require, so helping avoid collisions (especially with facial skin), or accidents with the musical instrument being moved about.

G/A 20.3   Touchy Knowledge

Task description:
- Exploring and identifying non-visible objects by touch.

Expected Milestone Achievements (EMAs):
- Identifies familiar objects by touch (without seeing them)   [M19-Cog5]
- Changes palm grip according to size and shape of object being offered (F1)
- Imitates sequences of adult facial expression changes   (Cog5)
- Attentive to different verbal instructions, without directly looking at the (Comms3) person speaking to them.

Materials:
- Ping pong ball, plastic ball, small rubber ball), box, towel
- Stylus (wax crayon, pencil, paint brush)
- Legumes (peanut, seeds, soybean), toy fruits or vegetables (apple, banana).

Procedure:
Level 1
1. Demonstrate a medium sized box, inside of which has been placed different sized toys and various material/quality balls.
2. Next, continue to demonstrate, one at a time (taking out – looking at – naming – and then returning) the different objects from inside the box, then covering it with a towel, for baby to clearly see.
3. Invite baby to now approach the box, place their hand *under* the towel and into the box, in order to 'fish out' and remove (using touch only) the type of ball which you ask for, by name, each time.
4. As baby succeeds to fish out the 'correct' ball each time, provide immediate encouragement and praise, repeating the actions with additional objects until the box is empty. [NB: *replacing previously removed objects will help keep the level of difficulty consistent – else the task becoming easier with time as other distracters be removed*].

Level 2
1. Demonstrate the same box, inside of which is now placed different sized toys and various material/quality of stylus (writing instruments, pen, crayon. pencil, brush).
2-4. Continue as per level 1 steps 2-4, using the different materials now introduced.

Level 3-4
1-4. Repeat the level 1-2 activities, each time using differently small- and larger-sized toys and various dry beans legumes, then fruits and vegetables.

Level 5
1-4. If baby's language skills allow, repeat any of activity levels 1-4, exchanging roles with baby yourself, alternately as requesters and seekers/guessers each time.

Variations:
- Consider to invite baby to place the same set of items *into* the box, and then to take the same items out again, but before removing them each time, must tell you (and anyone else in the room) which item it is, and (letting everybody look at it), to say whether baby is 'correct' or not, and clapping with encouragement promptly if 'OK'.
- Periodically replace the item set with more interesting toys with which baby is familiar (or maybe *not* so familiar ?), letting the 'next' object set for baby be preceded by clear 'identify/name object sessions' in order to further enhance baby's interest and continued motivation.
- The level of difficulty can always be increased by including objects which are more similar in size, shape and/or texture,.... Each to then be distinguished from every other by touch alone (baby's arm inside the box/bag, the items not visible).

Additional Thoughts/Game-Activity Preparation/Lesson Planning Tips:
- Provide relatively small toys or other items for this activity, paying keen attention to not letting baby admit retrieved objects into their mouths, so helping avoid risks of toxicity or choking/swallowing.
- With the small items placed in the box, baby may find the object grasping to be quite difficult at first without the aid of vision. Be sure to wait patiently, and not to make direct eye-contact with baby whilst they initially struggle to select what they are 'looking' *for*. [NB: It is TD's view that otherwise pressurising baby to produce their 'guess' quickly, will cause them to speak their 'guess' without actually using any of the tactile information otherwise available from their hand !].

G/A 20.4 Twisting Free !

Task description:
- Exploring rotary capped vessels in order to acquire their contents.

Expected Milestone Achievements (EMAs):
- Grips jars or tubs appropriate to turning/levering their lids open (F2)
- Imitates 3-5 words sentences of others (even if not understanding (Comms3) their meaning).
- Enjoys 'putting dolls/toys to bed', or enacting hygiene routines with soft (SP4) toys/animals.

Materials:
- Small soft toy animals/finger puppets
- Bottle or jar (transparent, with baby-palm sized twist-top lid), wide-mouthed jar.

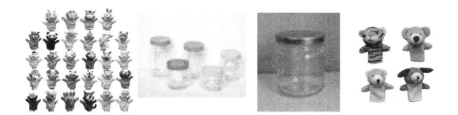

Procedure:

Level 1
1. Demonstrate a jar/bottle, inside of which is visibly placed a soft toy animal.
2. Show lid removal, then placing it directly on the floor, making reference to the toy, as you begin to reach in and directly take it out ('free' it) from the jar/bottle.
3. Present the jar/bottle with toy animal/finger puppet, inviting/guiding baby to 'save' the animal, by releasing it from its 'enclosure'.
4. As baby successfully opens/removes the bottle cap (by rotating it), and takes out the animal referred to, ensure provision of prompt praise and encouragement.

Level 2
1. Provide now a larger (wider-mouthed) bottle/jar, inside of which is again is placed a visible toy animal/finger puppet.
2. Invite/guide baby to 'save' the animal as before, by removing the lid and releasing it from its enclosure, to enjoy the fresh air once more.
3. As baby successfully opens/removes the bottle cap (by rotating it), and takes out the animal referred to, ensure provision of prompt praise and encouragement.

Variations:
- Consider to install coloured silk kerchief/scarves in the different bottles/jars for baby to retrieve.
- If available, provide a variety of differently sized and shaped jars/bottles, and/or different styles of lid/cap, for baby to seal/unseal, with animals to place in [*DO NOT, however, invite baby to explore/use medicine bottles with tamper-proof caps*].

Additional Thoughts/Game-Activity Preparation/Lesson Planning Tips:
- If/when successfully removing the bottle/jar cap, but then unable to take out the animal, encourage baby to think/struggle a while on their own, rather than either removing it for them yourself, or simply telling baby *how* to solve the problem directly.
- Be sure to choose bottles/jars made of materials that are not too brittle in quality, so helping avoid their being dropped/sat upon and breaking, or otherwise causing any significant injury or damage.

Baby Milestones of Development (0-3 Yrs)

G/A 20.5   Climbing Balloon Mountain

Task description:
- Exploring stretching and climbing in order to acquire out-of-reach objects.

Expected Milestone Achievements (EMAs):
- Climbs objects without prompting, in order to see from higher position [M19-G5]
- Walks several stairs spontaneously, and unaided   (G2)
- Climbs upon a chair to see on table when asked, "What's on the table?"   (G5)

Materials:
- Soft mats, firm cushions, sturdy boxes, balloon.

Procedure:
Level 1[If the home environs allow, use actual stairway/steps, else construct 'mountain']
1. Arrange the room with a first-level level stair using a mat/firm cushion (increasing the altitude only gradually) against the wall/sofa, for baby to climb up.
2. Reachable only from the top layer stair (higher each time), fix/attach a balloon.
3. Invite baby to now come to you by the wall/sofa, as you stand nearby the mat/cushion forming an 'open arms' protecting wall to catch an unstable baby's fall.
4. Encourage/guide baby to next attempt the first-level stair climb, in order to collect the balloon above, 'on the top of the mountain' stairway.
5. As baby succeeds in climbing up to reach/take the balloon from the top, provide baby with the most outrageous applause and encouragement for their efforts.
6. Repeat steps 2-5 with increasing success, raising the number and/or height of the steps to be climbed to enhance the difficulty level (after each success has been enjoyed a few times).

Level 2
1. Arrange the room next with a multi-level level staircase (again increasing the altitude only gradually) *this time in the centre of the room*, for baby to climb up.
2. Reachable only from the top layer stair, fix a balloon hung from the ceiling/hanger.

3. Invite baby to now come to you at the centre of the 'balloon mountain'.
4. Encourage/guide baby to now attempt the multi-level stair climb, in order to collect the balloon hanging above the top of the 'mountain'.
5. As baby succeeds in climbing up to reach/take the balloon from the summit, facilitate/provide baby with applause and encouragement.
6. Invite baby this time to then also get themselves (climb) down from the highest point that they have reached each time (likely, but ideally not by sliding down !).
7. Repeat steps 2-5 with increasing success, raising the number and/or height of the steps to be climbed, slowly over time according to baby's growing confidence.

Variations:
- Instead of using a balloon, place other (preferred) small toys at the summit, (possibly that baby cannot see from the base, but shown to have been put there) once familiar with/engaged in the activity). Invite baby to then seek and find it, once climbed/crawling around the highest peak, then crawling down again (possibly by a different 'route', only then will they be able to discover the toy, which they can then take down to show you and play with awhile.

Additional Thoughts/Game-Activity Preparation/Lesson Planning Tips:
- Ensure that any floor mat is slip free to the room floor surface, and soft but firm enough, to avoid baby's crawl scratching, whilst also providing a safe landing after any fall.
- Ditto, selecting boxes/containers and firm cushions of sufficient rigidity that they will support baby's weight without compromising strength, and/or significantly upsetting/challenging baby's balance control ability too much.
- As baby may walk alone now, s/he may pitch their soles and easily slip. Consider inviting baby to take off their shoes and socks when walking/climbing on the 'mountains'.
- If worried that the balloon may burst/explode when handled at the summit and unnerve/frighten the 'climber' (who may then momentarily lose their balance and fall), consider substituting it with a soft inflated rubber ball.
- *As baby begins to climb up above their previous 'comfort level' each time, ensure that you refuel baby with frequent encouragement as their bravery and courage increases; but without unduly urging baby to move well beyond their capabilities in too-big-a-step at once, so helping baby to balance their personal safety-consciousness and confidence at the same time.*
- As/when baby climbs (either up or down), as far as possible allow baby to do so by themselves, your only protecting/touching baby when about to fall.

G/A 20.6   Search & Match It !

Task description:
- Identifying matching pairs of images, and indicating their location by gesture.

Expected Milestone Achievements (EMAs):
- Identifies 6-10 pictures by pointing at them (among others)   (F5)
- Explores more challenging toys/activities with increasing interest   (Cog6)
- Attentive to different verbal instructions, without directly looking at the person speaking to them.   (Comms3)

Materials:
- Picture cards (fruit/animal pictures, laminated ?) each card showing a single object/image, e.g., an apple, a strawberry, melon, lion, panda, etc, (with x2 of at least some, if not all pictures).

Procedure:
Level 1
1. Present a set of fruit picture cards (each showing a different fruit) to baby.
2. Demonstrate each fruit picture card in turn (from a 2nd set), inviting baby to find the same (matching) picture card from their set, so forming a matching pair when paired together with yours.
3. As/when baby has found their matching image picture card, encourage them to present it to you, to check/contrast (also sharing the match with anyone else who may be present).
4. If baby has brought the 'correctly' matching picture card, provide praise promptly.

Level 2
1. Distribute a new set of picture cards (showing different fruits/animals, but also this time different colours of EACH fruit/animal, to baby (e.g., a purple and a green grape, red and a yellow apple, one brown and one black and white cow).
2. Demonstrate each picture card in turn, inviting baby to find the same picture card from their set, so forming an *identical* matching pair (incl. type *and* colour match).
3. As/when baby has found their matching image picture card, encourage checking and contrast, noting whether they really are identical – or only partially matching by type, and/or its colour only !).
4. If baby has brought the 'correctly' matching picture card, provide praise promptly, and in accordance with the 'degree' of match, relative to forming a truly *identical* match !

Variations:
- Placing the picture cards on/about the room's four walls (or other readily visible places), encourage baby to seek for the matching cards and to then point to them, and/or pick them up and to carry them to you.
- Ditto, hanging the different picture cards from the room ceiling/fittings (and inviting baby to either gather (if low enough), or to simply point to them.
- Provide picture card sets of two which 'look similar' to a target card (but are not truly identical, inviting baby to compare them in order to discover (and tell) in what way(s) they are actually *dis*similar [category, shape, colour, size, etc.,].

Additional Thoughts/Game-Activity Preparation/Lesson Planning Tips:
- If no pre-printed object/image cards be available, simply make your own by cutting/pasting magazine pictures on to old card, or drawing them with bold outlines on white paper (cut to A5-6 or post-card size).
- Try to avoid the temptation to either hold/sort the picture cards for baby to select from – remember that this task is primarily designed for use here as a sensory-motor and verbal skill development task/activity (and not a purely cognitive one, per se).
- If/when baby points to/presents a clearly 'non-matching' picture card compared to your sample target picture card, try not to appear to be denying/rejecting baby's response directly, E.g., "Why do you [baby] choose this one ?", or "Why do you believes that they are the same ?"; but instead, inquire of baby each time "In what way(s) are they actually *dis*similar/different ?", perhaps becoming more clear about your activity/game instruction(s) for baby as s/he prepares for the next round's pair matching.
- Be sure to have checked the condition and cleanliness of all of the picture cards to be used in this activity – cleaning (not just wiping !) drying, and replacing any which may have damaged/jagged edges of danger to baby's skin.

G/A 20.7   Reach Out & Take Me Down

Task description:
- Exploring reaching, gripping, and manipulation of small object connectors.

Expected Milestone Achievements (EMAs):
- Walks several stairs spontaneously, and unaided   (G2)
- Changes palm grip according to size &shape of object being offered (F1)
- Explores more challenging toys/activities with increasing interest (Cog6)

Materials:
- Coloured ribbons, coloured clothes pegs, stepping stones.

Procedure:
Level 1
1. Arrange the room with coloured ribbons hung from the ceiling/walls/fittings, the lowest end of which would hang *at a height close to that of baby's chest.*
2. Upon the coloured ribbon(s), place differently coloured clothes' pegs (the highest clipped so as to require baby to simply stand up, in order to reach them).
3. Demonstrate slow and gentle grasping of a coloured ribbon (to hold it stable), then one at a time clearly show how to reach, grasp, and 'unpeg' the clothes pegs in order to remove them.
4. Invite baby to now come forward to take down other coloured ribbon's pegs.
5. As/when baby succeeds in unpegging from the ribbons, and brings down their removed pegs for you to count, provide prompt encouragement and praise.

Level 2
1. Arrange the room with coloured ribbons hung about as before, the lowest end of which this time hangs at a height *close to that above* baby's forehead.
2. Upon the coloured ribbon(s) place differently coloured clothes' pegs (the highest clipped so as to require baby to stand on their tiptoes with an outstretched arm in order to reach them.
3 Invite baby to now take down the coloured ribbon's pegs once more.

4. As/when baby succeeds in unpegging from the ribbons, and brings over their removed pegs for you to count, provide prompt praise and excited applause.

Level 3
1. Arrange the room and ribbons as per level 2, now with stepping stones nearby.
2. Upon the coloured ribbon(s) place again differently coloured clothes' pegs (the highest clipped this time so as to prevent baby being able to remove them *even if* they do stand on their tiptoes with an outstretched arm in order to reach them (encouraging *baby to work out their own solution* as to how to reach them !).
3. Invite baby to now come forward and to take down the coloured ribbon' pegs.
4. As/when baby succeeds in unpegging their ribbons, and brings down their removed pegs for you to count out, provide prompt encouragement (recruiting the applause of all/any others who may be present also).

Variations:
- Consider to use different instructions when inviting peg removal - e.g., request taking down the pegs in order of height, colour, type, etc,.. one at a time.
- Ditto, assigning a specific number to be retrieved, in order to increase baby's interest and motivation to work towards acquiring them for you.
- Ditto, "Please collect 3 blue pegs for teddy-bear"; "2 Red pegs for Grandma", etc.,
- Arrange for the hung coloured ribbons to be spaced relative far apart from furnishings, so helping to avoid baby colliding with it (unless needing as support).
- Make sure that sufficient stepping stones and/or other soft cushions are both visible and accessible, for baby to collect and relocate to their ribbon hanging areas (in order for them to reach the higher pegs in the level 3 activity).

Additional Thoughts/Game-Activity Preparation/Lesson Planning Tips:
- The coloured ribbons hanging from the ceiling/door ledge/drape fittings/coat hanger must be relatively strong and secure, requiring significant effort in order to be accidentally pulled down/broken (another otherwise clever solution discovered by baby !!).
- As/when baby is standing on tiptoes to unclip the pegs from the higher positions, note that they may lean this way and that unpredictably, so be sure to provide baby with adequate protection, helping avoid baby falling suddenly to the ground (though *without supporting them all the time* !).
- Choose coloured plastic pegs (which are relatively easy to grip/open), or attractive wood clips (requiring less effort to pinch), so increasing baby's interest and motivation to work towards acquiring them.

G/A 20.8   Pick and Put !

Task description:
- Exploring object feature discrimination, sorting and placing - according to size, colour and shape.

Expected Milestone Achievements (EMAs):
- Selects correct shapes for visible sorting-box holes (Cog1)
- Imitates sequences of adult facial expression changes (Cog5)
- Shows appropriate response to action requests (e.g., "Bring the teddy-bear here, please"). (Comms1)
- Self-stimulated by interacting with mechanical/electronic toys with curiosity (SP6)

Materials:
- Shape board, shape sorter and corresponding shape pieces.

- Stickable smiley (and not-so-smiley) illustrations (showing different facial expressions), small box/container (to stick them onto).

Procedure:

Level 1

1. Demonstrate a small shape board, its surfaces, and the 'correct' shaped positions on the shape board into which one of the pieces fit.
2. Continue to now demonstrate the remaining types of corresponding shapes and shape-board arrangements.
3. Now demonstrate on the floor/table, showing baby clearly the corresponding shaped 'holes' on the shape board, for baby to explore, so discovering their corresponding shapes and locations.
4. Invite baby to now place a single piece into its paired-shape 'hole' on the shape board which 'best' corresponds to the many spaces in/on the board.
6. As/when baby completes their placement, provide prompt praise (according to how 'correct' the placement was *(NB: some shapes will easily 'fit' into the 'wrong' shaped or sized 'holes' if pressed hard enough !)*.

Level 2
1. Demonstrate now all of the pieces at once, of different sizes, and their 'correct' shaped 'hole' position targets on the shape board, into which they fit.
2. Now again demonstrate on the floor/table, showing baby clearly the corresponding shaped and sized 'holes' on the shape board, for baby to explore, whilst discovering the differently-sized pieces' 'correct' locations.
3. Invite baby to now place the different pieces into the same-sized and shaped holes onto the shape board.
4. As/when baby completes their placements, provide prompt praise (according to how 'correct' the placements were *(NB: some shapes can be 'fit' into the 'wrong' shaped or sized holes)*.

Level 3
1-4. Repeat the level 1-2 procedures, this time using 3D blocks and a shape-sorter.

Level 4
1. Demonstrate a small box/container on the floor/table, clearly showing baby that each of the box/container's six sides shows a different facial expression ("smiley") face/sticker.
2. Present to baby now a similar-looking box and stickers/papers, showing how to affix ONE of the smiley face stickers/papers to one of the box' side faces.
3. Depending upon baby's ability(ies) and interest/motivation levels, EITHER continue to demonstrate building a 'replica' of the original model (continuing to place the remaining 5 stickers onto the different box sides), OR invite baby to do so at their own pace.
4. As/when baby completes their placements, provide prompt praise and encouragement (and possibly quite independently of how 'correct' each placement was each time ?).

Variations:
- To increase the level of difficulty, provide baby with more blocks (and of increasingly similar/different types), than are actually required in order to 'correctly' complete the shape board as currently instructed !
- Provide multiple shape boards/sorters for baby to complete, requiring baby to sort more similar looking (even identical) pieces each time.

Additional Thoughts/Game-Activity Preparation/Lesson Planning Tips:
- Be sure to allow baby sufficient time to explore and discover block and hole pairings independently, *providing suitable help only* (e.g., when baby is clearly *not able* to put the block into the [otherwise 'correct'] hole, then guiding baby to rotate the block/shape's position).
- Be sure to use only materials which have been cleaned and disinfected (both before and after each activity use), checking also the plastic/wooden edges for smoothness, replacing/securing them if broken or jagged, so avoiding puncturing or scratching baby's hands and skin.

A/G 20.9   Self-Feeding Time !

Task description:
- Exploring independent drinking and feeding.

Expected Milestone Achievements (EMAs):
- Uses a spoon to self-feed without turning it upside-down and spilling (F3)
- Shifts orientation of a held spoon or fork when scooping for use (F4)
- Picks up and rotates bottle in order to drink from it (Cog4)
- Imitates household chore behaviours (e.g., cleaning, sweeping, wiping spills) (SP5)

Materials:
- Drinking glass/cup, bowl, spoon/spork,
- Raisins or biscuit, mineral water or other preferred baby drink/fruit juice, towel.

Procedure:

Level 1
1. Present a small towel for baby, together with a paper glass/cup, and water.
2. Demonstrate drinking the water from the glass/cup.
3. Invite baby to now also attempt to use the same cup, and to slowly drink their fruit juice/water, without spilling any of its contents.
4. Give prompt praise as baby succeeds with their task.

Level 2
1. Cleaning the floor (if/as necessary, following level 1 completion), now present baby a spoon and a bowl containing a few raisins/biscuit pieces.
2. Invite/guide baby to feed him/herself with the spoon/spork in order to eat the raisins. *Carefullly observe baby's willingness/resistance to using wrist rotation in preventing spillage as they bend joints at the shoulder and elbow in bringing the spoon towards the mouth.*
3. As/when baby feeds him/herself without spillage, provide prompt praise and encouragement (continue feeding/food manipulations as appropriate).

Variations:
- Invite baby to feed either the water and/or the raisins/biscuits to you, for *you* to then eat (typically requiring less use of wrist action as reaching forwards).
- Consider providing differently sized/shaped cups for baby to attempt taking the water to drink.
- Ditto, using different styles/sizes of spoon/spork for baby to attempt feeding him/herself, and/or feed others with.

Additional Thoughts/Game-Activity Preparation/Lesson Planning Tips:
- Be sure to supply baby-friendly spoons/sporks of reasonably high quality of material. If nonesuch be available in the home, try to avoid the brittle plastic quality materials which may easy splinter when crushed, or cups with scratchable edges or handles which may abrade baby's skin.
- Before conducting this activity, please ensure that you are comfortable with the chosen foodstuffs and 'table-manners' being used throughout (i.e., try not to suddenly decide to do this without preparation, hastily searching for novel foodstuffs whilst baby is waiting).
- Ditto, modifying the activity detail consistent with your particular family's taboos/preferences/customs, if any, whilst also allowing for any known food allergies when choosing foodstuffs to eat.
- Ensure that all materials to be used are thoroughly disinfected, clean (not just 'wiped'), dry, and that all presented food and water (or fruit juice) taken from fresh (or unopened) packaging, undamaged, complete, and well within expiry date(s).
- Prepare wet tissues and absorbent paper towels nearby for immediate cleaning should any spillage(s) occur.
- Consider providing a waterproof bib for baby, simultaneously paying attention each time baby is independently manipulating the fruit juice/water cups, to help avoid (any excessive) sprinkling of fluids which will dampen/soak baby's (and other's !) body, clothes, and room furnishings.

Baby Milestones of Development (0-3 Yrs)

253

G/A 20.10   Body Part Spotting !

Task description:
- Exploring, distinguishing and naming one's own, and others' body parts.

Expected Milestone Achievements (EMAs):
- Identifies 6-10 pictures by pointing at them (amongst others)   (F5)
- Shows appropriate response to action requests (e.g., "Bring the   (Comms1)
  teddy-bear here, please").
- Offers objects with 'speech', and facial expressions to self in mirror   (Comms6)
- Opens and closes mouth when asked to do so   [M21- Comms3]
- Imitates body part touching whilst watching an adult do the same   (SP1)
  (especially parts of face, chin, ears and neck).

Materials:
- A3/A4 card/paper (with image of human body clothes' rectangle body), sticky paper spots (or similar), and detachable sticky paper (?) eyes, nose, ears, etc
- Doll, large paper images of human face (without the five features).

- Scaled pictures of the five facial features (nose, ears, eyes, mouth & eye-brows)
- Ditto re paper body doll and various clothing items.

Procedure:

Level 1
1. Lead baby (in a standing position) to follow your invitations to, in turn: "Touch your nose with your finger", "Close then open your eyes", "Touch your ears", "Open then close your mouth", "Shake your head",…."Stretch out your left hand", "Stretch out your right hand", "Pat your tummy", "Kick out your left leg", "Shake your right leg", "Jump up and down with both feet",…. "Bend at the waist/knees", etc.,…
2. As/when baby provides the 'correct' feedback/movement according to your instructions each time (*this is your chance to also learn/see whether baby demonstrates knowledge of the names and locations of each of the specific body parts being named each time*).

Level 2
1. Demonstrate now the face card/paper template, showing the various body parts, with spots covering them,…. or without eyes, nose, ears, etc,….
2. Present baby the 'picture', pointing out some of the missing body parts, which would otherwise complete the image of an attractive friend.
3. Give to baby now a first body part sticker (e.g. a nose).
4. Invite baby to then place their body part sticker onto the paper template, in order to 'reveal' more of their new friend's whole appearance.
5. As/when baby 'correctly' completes the image further, present additional pieces for attachment, until completing the whole facial image with all their features.
6. Provide prompt praise and encouragement as they do so.

Level 3
1. Prepare and distribute a new card-template/body paper, showing the various whole body and parts, as per level 2, but this time without hat, shirt, trousers, skirt, etc, or other 'parts' stickers.
2. Invite/guide baby to now place their clothing item stickers onto the card/paper template manikin, in order to 'reveal' the whole dressed person, now with all their clothes on (ideally using a different set for each/some future rounds !).
3. Once completed, encourage baby to next 'present' their new 'whole person' to you, and to talk about the differences/changes, as you provide praise and encouragement all the while.

Variations:
- To increase the level of difficulty, increase the number and complexity of the body parts to be named/used in completing the whole body each time.
- Consider checking identification, naming and vocabulary skills using a mirror, with an activity involving the naming of baby's own face parts at the same time.

- Consider also to provide an additional human body picture (so forming a family or persons?), onto which may be attached various items of clothing (e.g., hats, shoes/boots, gloves, coats, trousers, skirts, etc.,), inviting baby to place the clothing onto the appropriate corresponding body parts, each time.
- Consider to encourage baby to talk about what it is they are doing (as they do it), when dressing,… e.g., getting ready for bed ?,.. to go out., ready to eat., etc.…

Additional Thoughts/Game-Activity Preparation/Lesson Planning Tips:
- Provide sticky papers which are not too small for baby to distinguish between, and allow baby to rip/restick the parts they show onto different papers or cards by him/herself.
- Try not to worry about mistakes/inaccuracies made as baby repositions the different parts each time, allowing baby to also observe the entire reconstructed character; only then encouraging baby to attempt themselves to discover any 'oddities', and to 'repair' them if they might wish to make adjustments (preferably without your assistance).
- You may, however, help to put together relatively large part locations (e.g., a whole left leg, or right arm), then only guiding baby to secure the smaller parts, so reducing the overall level of difficulty (if needed).

G/A 20.11   BB Bath Time !

Task description:
- Exploring self-hygiene and body care.

Expected Milestone Achievements (EMAs):
- Exploring washing and drying of own hands   [M19-SP2]
- Enjoys 'putting dolls/toys to bed', or enacting hygiene routines with soft   (SP4) toys/animals.
- Shows appropriate response to action requests (e.g., "Bring the   (Comms1) teddy-bear here, please").
- Offers objects with 'speech', and facial expressions to self in mirror (Comms6)
- Imitates body part touching whilst watching an adult do the same   (SP1) (especially parts of face, chin, ears and neck).

Materials:
- *Baby* toothbrush, cup, shark/dolphin/alligator mouth (card- or, 3-D model)

- Towel, bowl
- Baby doll, children's non-toxic modeling clay, wax crayon (or lipstick).

Procedure:
Level 1
1. Demonstrate a model shark/dolphin/alligator toothed-mouth toy (moistening the teeth with children's modelling clay), toothbrush, and cup.
2. Allow baby to discover that the <shark>'s teeth are dirty (with modeling clay).
3. Demonstrate next how, with the toothbrush, you can eliminate the 'dirt' from the <shark>'s teeth.
4. Invite baby to now take a turn to clean the shark's teeth, presenting the cup and brush to them for the purpose.
5. Provide baby with prompt encouragement all the while they attempt to gently clean the modelling clay away (from the model's teeth).

Level 2

1. Demonstrate next the toy baby doll, upon the face of which has been placed baby's name using wax crayon (or other easily removed material – e.g., lipstick ?)
2. Show next a bowl (shallow filled with water), and a towel.
3. Taking up the towel, slowly show baby how placing it into the bowl will cause it to become wet, then wringing it out, gently wash the face of the baby doll, wiping off <baby's' name> (in this case) from the baby doll's face.
4. Present now a newly 'dirty-faced' baby doll, bowl and towel, to baby.
5. Pour a little water into baby's bowl, inviting baby to now wash the face of their baby doll friend, as you try to simply supervise (ideally hands off !) baby's actions.
6 As/when baby finishes their washing chores, request baby to then wash their own hands, *and to dry* them with the towel provided.
7 Encourage baby to then clean up their washing area(s), and to present their freshly cleaned baby-doll friend to all/any present, promptly receiving praise as they do so.

Variations:

- Increase the level of difficulty/interest by providing baby with a comb/brush, requesting baby to brush/comb their own, and/or *your* hair themselves.
- Ditto, providing baby with a clean toothbrush, towel and a little water in a cup, letting baby clean their own teeth for themselves, before then washing their face.

Additional Thoughts/Game-Activity Preparation/Lesson Planning Tips:

- Be sure to provide new, disinfected, or at least thoroughly cleaned toothbrushes and towels for baby to use (and whilst cleaning the model, preventing placement of the brush into their own mouth at any time!).
- Provide only small hand towels, conveniently sized for baby's palmar grasping and twisting.
- Encourage/help baby to keep the bowl and/or cup stable (when containing water, so preventing baby shifting it about to much (and spilling to the floor), and/or otherwise wetting their (and your) clothes.
- As/when baby wets the towel and twists it to wring dry, be sure to guide baby in so doing, over/into the bowl (to prevent floor soiling/dripping, as *baby's wringing strength will surely be still insufficient to rid it of as much water as it actually holds*). If spillage does occur, encourage immediate use of the towel (with others if necessary) to promptly dry all affected surfaces, so helping avoid slips and falls, which may result in bumps or bruising at a later time if forgotten.

G/A 20.12   BB Fetch it for For You !

Task description:
- Exploring the collection, transport, and controlled placing of objects to order.

Expected Milestone Achievements (EMAs):
- Changes direction when avoiding objects in path of movement   (G3)
- Carries own weight (with balance) when running, unsupported   (G4)
- Explores more challenging toys/activities with increasing interest   (Cog6)
- Imitates 3-5 words sentences of others (even if not understanding   (Comms4) their meaning).
- Throws a ball with over-arm movement [tho' NOT the focus of task here !] (G6)

Materials:
- Toy bowling set (or own made version of same), small balls, large toys/objects.

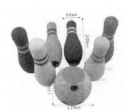  

Procedure:
Level 1
1. Demonstrate a set of bowling bottles (or similar), setting them down along a reasonable throwing distance from a 'bowling line', from which a ball/rolled socks may be thrown.
2. Clearly demonstrate to baby how to 'reset' the bowling bottles, helping to stand them up in 'formation' after being knocked down (bowled over) each time.
3. Invite/guide baby to help reset the bowling bottles after you now knock down the bottles once more.
4. As/when baby thereafter succeeds in completing the bottle resetting, lead baby to play bowling together: Striking down the bowling bottles with the ball/socks, then resetting them for the next round/person to take their turn.
   (**NB:** Remember that the focus here is upon controlled ball release timing, NOT bottle hitting per se,.. likewise over-arm throwing NOT expected, tho' it may occur !)

Level 2
1. Demonstrate next a collection of large toys/objects, in a disordered pile which lay heaped low down in a single location of the room.
2. Clearly and slowly show how you can use the same collection of objects to build an attractive display (somewhere else in the room (table/furnishing/stacked boxes), like that in a shop, which requires more items to be collected and carried across the room from the pile, in order to complete it.
3. Invite/guide baby to now go and collect items (one at time) from the pile, and to deliver it to you, either placing it carefully on the ground in a specified place, or onto an actual display being built up (depending upon baby's balancing ability).
4. As/when baby succeeds completely with their multi-step task, ensure that you (and any others present) applauds in offering immediate praise and encouragement.

Variations:
- To increase the level of difficulty, invite baby to complete the collection and delivery stages as fast as possible, and with increasingly larger/awkward objects to carry, over time.
- If wishing to see baby building and object placing (rather than simply carrying and moving), invite baby to take objects from the pile, and to return with it to their own 'building site' where they are then to build a replica structure based upon an example structure that you have provided for them to copy (and which baby can supply objects for, one at a time as you build yours also ?).
- Ditto for task (or if no 'skittle/bottles' be available/buildable in the home), use larger and smaller boxes/baskets as targets for baby to 'throw' their balls into – or matching differently coloured balls with differently coloured boxes, each colour placed at a different distance (maybe inviting baby to try doing this all at the same time as you do, but from different throwing locations !).

Additional Thoughts/Game-Activity Preparation/Lesson Planning Tips:
- Whilst baby is engaged in the collection/delivery/placing process, ensure that you can maintain much patience (compared to baby), encouraging baby to do as much as possible without help, and to thus not offer your help to baby too readily.
- Likewise, be sure to provide baby with prompt encouragement appropriate to each aspect of the task (the target reward here being given especially for the safe transport of, and object's manipulation, with control), so helping baby to feel a sense of achievement, with *their ideally also understanding what it is they are being praised 'for' !*

– 13 –

Baby Milestones of Development

(With 100+ Fun Activities to Help Demonstrate Them)

[Age 21 Months]

ψ

Expected Milestone Achievements
Age = 21 Months

[Key: e.g., 7 = Game No. 21.7]

Gross Motor	
• Maintains stable upright posture when stops running	3, 12
• Runs or walks with abrupt direction change, without bumping or falling on obstacles	3, 11, 12
• Jumps up and down (though maybe needing support of one foot on floor)	4
• Negotiates stepping/climbing obstacles whilst shifting visual focus near/far distance	7
• Attempts to kick ball with swinging leg/foot	12
• Throws a ball towards target location and/or specific direction	6, 12

Fine Motor	
• Places objects down on flat surfaces without dropping them	2, 6
• Realises *significance* and use of remote control devices	5
• Correctly points to/touches several body parts, when requested to do so	1
• Pincer grip shape made before picking up small object shapes	7, 11
• Attempts to turn book pages at appropriate times during reading	
• Rotates 'turned' blocks to match an example block array	6

Cognitive	
• Begins to ask "What's this" when finding new objects	9
• Corrects orientation of tools for immediate use after handling	1, 5, 7
• Locates and obtains correct objects when needing (or asked for) them	1, 4, 5, 8, 11
• Attempts to imitate organised patterns/arrays of objects (e.g., by colour, size)	[M19 18.3], 6, 9
• Explores use of familiar object for novel purpose (e.g., using a fork as a rake)	1, 7
• Attempts copying of complex multi-line drawings	

Communication	
• Correctly names familiar object pictures when pointed to by others	9
• Identifies familiar objects or people in complex pictures/images	
• Opens and closes mouth when asked to do so	[M20 19.10], 10
• Correctly uses 1st person possessives (e.g., mine, me)	
• Babbling with 'adult-like' speech intonation when 'talking' to dolls and/or soft toys	8
• Activates 'correct' sounds using chosen musical instruments	2

Socio-Personal	
• Spontaneously explores novel objects alone (e.g., putting empty box on head)	
• Increasingly willing/able to put on own clothing	
• Finds and presents certain objects when asked for them	2, 3, 8, 11
• Seeks/requests others to join a shared activity of interest	2, 3, 4
• Actively seeks 'playmates' when available	
• Pushes stroller/cart with *some* attention to avoiding collisions with objects/others	

G/A 21.1   Hear Here, my Body Parts !

Task description:
- Exploring the sounds, sights and feelings associated with different body parts.

Expected Milestone Achievements (EMAs):
- Correctly points to/touches several body parts, when requested to do so   (F3)
- Corrects orientation of tools for immediate use after handling   (Cog2)
- Locates and obtains correct objects when needing (or asked for) them   (Cog3)
- Explores use of familiar object for novel purpose (e.g., using a fork as   (Cog5)
    a rake).

Materials:
- Tambourine (or home-made equivalent sound maker).

Procedure:
Level 1
1. Situate baby either seated or standing alone.
2. Demonstrate the appearance, use and sound(s) of the tambourine (or similar 'tool'), presenting it as an 'instrument' to charge the human body with energy; lead by providing instructions as to how/when/where to use it, inviting baby to follow your instructions to charge their different body parts each time.
3. To begin, invite baby to follow you in holding both hands extended out evenly on both sides, with feet apart, standing, and saying, "We are now two robots, which occasionally need energy recharging".
4. Encourage baby to now explore their (own) robot's different body part locations with 'energy', leading baby to identify each (of their own) body parts, and show the most 'appropriate' electricity input response when touched. [E.g., when you might say, "Robot's head,… energy in now", gently moving/shaking the head would indicate that energy is being applied to the head (i.e., a 'correct' response as invited from baby – who will initially imitate your response).

5. Once baby appears comfortable with the task, continue to mention different body parts needing energy to be put into, until the whole body has been covered, then lead baby to rest on the floor. [E.g., "Robot's hand - energy" (both hands/arms held up above normal resting positions), "Robot's leg - energy" (leg shows straightening from original bent knee, tho' not kneeling down) and so forth, so when "out of energy", baby/robot's whole body would be laid down prone, actually on floor, as if asleep).
6. When WITHOUT energy, say to baby, "I must give the robot a new charge of energy", then, patting baby's buttocks lightly with the tambourine, let baby stand, charging each body part (as necessary, and identifiable, one part at a time), so reforming baby's posture to a straight, upright body shape once more.
7. Repeat several times, as interest and motivation allows, and/or until baby is clearly able to identify each of their own body parts (as you mention them), clearly, and without simply imitating your own movements/gestures each time.

Level 2
1-4. Repeat level 1 (steps 4-7), this time being more specific with body parts to be identified/moved (i.e., 'left leg' rather than 'leg'; 'upper arm' rather than 'arm').

Level 3
1-4. Repeat level 1 and/or 2, this time presenting the tambourine to baby, and to invite them to recharge their own body parts each time, by shaking the tambourine upon the rechargeable body part (by name, without demonstration) each time.

Variations:
- After several rounds, invite any other person present to use the same body part/energy instructions, so leading both yourself and baby to explore the robot game together.
- As a final robot recharge exercise, consider inviting baby to use the tambourine to recharge you alone, as robot !

Additional Thoughts/Game-Activity Preparation/Lesson Planning Tips:
- When initially leading baby to play 'as robot' player, remember that, on the one hand you are providing the instructions to cause focus upon individual body parts by name (maybe posturally, as well as vocally, depending upon baby's language and vocabulary levels ?); on the other hand you will need also provide a role-model for baby's response signals, as baby will follow your lead by imitation; After several rounds, try letting baby simply listen to your instructions, then making their response, as you observe baby moving each body part/spot understanding [*without being able to simply imitate your gesture(s)*].

G/A 21.2 Know and Play It Right !

Task description:
- Exploring and imitating the most commonly made sounds and rhythms producible by different musical instruments.

Expected Milestone Achievements (EMAs):
- Places objects down on flat surfaces without dropping them (F1)
- Activates 'correct' sounds using chosen musical instruments (Comms6)
- Finds and presents certain objects when asked for them (SP3)
- Seeks/requests others to join a shared activity of interest (SP4)

Materials:
- Musical instrument set I (shaker/maracas, hand drum, hand bells, castanets)

- Musical instrument set II (loudspeaker/paper megaphone, triangle, cymbals, tambourine).

- Bath towel/blanket.

Procedure:
Level 1
1. Demonstrate the musical instrument set I (shaker/maracas, hand drum, hand bells, castanets – [or home-made versions of such]).
2. Sound/play each of the musical instrument set in turn (*in its most normal way*), always allowing baby to hear/feel the shape and sound of each.

3. Next, take a large bath towel/blanket to form baby's work surface, as you now use it to cover the musical instrument set on the floor/table.
4. Now play each musical instrument's sound (without letting baby see the musical instruments, now hidden under/behind the bath towel/cover), one at a time.
5. After playing/sounding each one, lift the bath towel to let baby choose/indicate which one it was that they thought they had heard, and to then themselves recreate the same sound, using the musical instrument which they had selected.
6. As/when baby chooses the 'correct' instrument, and then offers the 'correct' imitatory performance, provide much applause and encouragement.
7. Repeat as interest/motivation allows, continuing to promptly play/operate the remaining instruments, being sure to allow baby to attempt to play/perform with each before returning them to the collection beneath the blanket/towel each time.

Level 2
1-7. Repeat level 1, this time using the instrument set II, or your version of such).

Variations:
- Consider presenting the set(s) of musical instruments to baby; demonstrating the playing and naming of each of the musical instruments of the set; Next, naming one of the musical instruments of the set, invite baby to choose from their set the one that you have named, and encourage their performance (using that instrument), in order to present a short orchestral concert !
- If multiple persons be present: Distribute a different musical instrument to each person present (including yourself). Selecting one musical instrument for performance, demonstrate a simple rhythm fragment, inviting then each person in turn (or later, all together) to then play the same rhythm that you had just demonstrated. [NB: to then up the level of difficulty – do such without the different person's being able to see your demonstration – requiring them to use a different instrument to do so each time].

Additional Thoughts/Game-Activity Preparation/Lesson Planning Tips:
- As the loudspeaker/paper megaphone will require the use the mouth close to the 'instrument', pay close attention to the health and cleanliness of its use by baby, and according to baby's ability [consider also providing one loudspeaker/paper megaphone for yourself and baby (&/or others person(s) present) to 'sing'/vocalise together].
- If few, or no pre-made instruments be available to you at this time, consider placing grains of dried rice, or small bells into different plastic bottles that you have cleaned and dried (e.g., used water bottles), sealed and covered, which may then be gently shaken/rocked.

Baby Milestones of Development (0-3 Yrs)

- Baby hand-sized tins, or small plastic jars may also work well – especially if you can produce several different sounding 'shakers', each producing a different sound when shaken [dried rice, beans, buttons, stones, dice, candies, salt, ball-bearings, bells).
- Ditto, considering to make some wind chimes of your own, by simply attaching sea-shells, bells, or metal strips to a coat-hanger, disc or cylinder with string/fishing line.
- Please ensure that all instruments are clean, wiped and dry, both before and after the task/activity session, and put away in a dry place.

G/A 21.3   Musical Dances, Stop and Go !

Task description:
- Exploring multi-sensory motivation, using specific sound-bites to guide self-controlled movement cessation.

Expected Milestone Achievements (EMAs):
- Maintains stable upright posture when stops running   (G1)
- Runs or walks with abrupt direction change, without bumping or   (G2)
  falling on obstacles.
- Finds and presents certain objects when asked for them   (SP3)
- Seeks/requests others to join a shared activity of interest   (SP4)

Materials:
- Music sample (mp3 or similar), tambourine.

Procedure:
Level
1. Demonstrate the tambourine, inviting baby to stand and do a warm up exercise.
2. Play the tambourine in a traditional way, whilst giving instructions, as you invite baby to follow your rhythm with movement, whilst also demonstrating corresponding movements for baby to imitate: (i) to walk together: "Walk, walk, walking, walk, walk, walking" (marking time); (ii) to jump together: "Jump, jump, jumping, jump, jump, jumping" (in-situ, jumping up/down in place); (iii) running together: "Run, run, running, run, run, running" (running in place, or turning small circles); stopping together: "Stop now, stop now, let's all stop, now let's stop, stopping still" (standing still immediately, after stopping whatever motion was last active).
3. After several warm-up rounds, use some 'area indicator' in the center of the room to establish a large circular runway.

4. Lead baby, now standing with you together, at the beginning of the circular runway, assuring that there is a (safe) distance between you.
5. Guide baby to now travel together (behind you) along the runway, as you both follow the tambourine rhythm, whilst using the same "keyword phrases" as used during the warm-up movement exercise to determine movement style.
6. Once you stop striking the tambourine and say, "Stop", baby is to immediately stop walking/jumping/running together with you at the same time.
7. As/when baby can immediately stop moving upon receiving the "Stop" signal each time, encourage prompt praise and applause (so reinforcing both baby's listening and instruction-following skill developments).

Level 2
1-7. Repeat level 1, this time occasionally changing the rhythm/tempo (speeding up/slowing down), as you play the tambourine with steady rhythm and sing movement code-word instructions, all the while still leading baby's movement.

Level 3
1-7. Repeat again, now also changing/adapting the circular runway's shape/route after a while, and/or the posture to be made after the walking/jumping/running stops, e.g., immediately sitting down, "Freezing" ALL motion in place, changing direction when resuming movement, etc,...

Variations:
- Present to baby a hand bell/shaker, inviting baby to again follow the motion code words of your rhythm and demonstration, whilst baby also now plays their own musical instrument whilst making the corresponding movements with you.
- Establish a straight-line (rather than curved) runway with ground mats in the middle of the room, assigning baby (and whomever else may be present) to move along the runway one at a time, as you stand facing them from one side of the room; As baby (or any other) now looks at (watches) your demonstration re what they are next to do, "Listen to the rhythm, and the code-words indicating the required movement(s)", then say, "GO", promptly encouraging and rewarding baby with motivation as they continue to move, until given the "Stop" signal – with more praise/applause when stopping immediately upon signal emission.

Additional Thoughts/Game-Activity Preparation/Lesson Planning Tips:
- Pay special attention regarding baby's position establishment and movement control, both unidirectional and/or with bidirectional rocking, ensuring baby is cleared by a certain distance from any hard furnishings, so avoiding your lively exited baby being in danger of collision and or accident with objects/obstacles.
- Be sure to emphasise baby's following the code-worded movements, and rhythm(s), so aiding baby to make increasingly faster, yet increasingly controlled adaptive changing movement behaviours; and especially so when beginning to finally "Stop" with personal control, having previously and frequently fallen down when attempting to stop whilst moving at relatively high speed !

G/A 21.4   Fruit Picking From Up High !

Task description:
- Exploring reaching and gathering objects from height, whilst standing off-balance.

Expected Milestone Achievements (EMAs):
- Jumps up and down (though maybe needing support of one foot on floor) (G3)
- Locates and obtains correct objects when needing (or asked for) them   (Cog3)
- Seeks/requests others to join a shared activity of interest   (SP4)

Materials:
- Gauze scarf, toy fruit (e.g., peach), basket, cushions/boxes.

Procedure:
Level 1
1. Establish a 'runway' path in the room using firm cushions and boxes, initially as one short and narrow obstacle construction, with a basket at the start position, and a toy peach (or other fruit) attached to the room wall/furnishing (besides the path), or hanging from the ceiling (above it).
2. Invite/lead baby to stand on a line near to the start of the 'runway', informing baby that they are to move along the runway towards the end.
3. Hold baby's hand in leading her/him to safely jump onto the runway area, and to travel along the path to the opposite end, and to then pick the fruit before returning to the start position, where baby jumps off the path, and places their fruit into the basket previously placed there.
4. As/when baby moves along with your support (helping bridge their balance as they move over the tactile path), be sure to recruit provide praise and encouragement all the while.

Level 2
1-2. Repeat as level 1, this time with the toy peach (or similar non-heavy model fruits, toys) lightly taped to the underside of a gauze/silk scarf suspended high, as a fruit covered scarf 'ceiling', from which baby may then reach up to and 'pluck' the fruits.

Variations:
- Provide baby with soft cushioning to jump up and down on (as if on their bed), letting them to jump up and pick fruits from the gauze scarf as per level 2.
- Again using the level 2 configuration, steadily increase the height/reach required to pluck fruits from the scarf (NB: *your help will be needed for baby to accurately aim a high and successful 'pick', aiding their regaining balance once landing back on the floor on two feet, whilst also increasing your shared interest and interaction throughout the activity*).

Additional Thoughts/Game-Activity Preparation/Lesson Planning Tips:
- Note that your help will typically be needed in assisting baby to jump with steady landing each time. According to baby's ability, consider to use both your hands or mixed holds, with baby occasionally being supported single-handedly.
- When doing so, encourage only with helping baby balance (i.e., avoid the temptation to 'lift'), whilst also paying attention to observing their whole body dynamics, and especially, to not make any effort to entrain baby's arm, so avoiding their loss of self-balance control exercise, and possibly arm-muscle pulling injury ! (pulling against their body weight).
- Likewise for the level 2 situation: provide baby close protection, but only in such a way as to allow baby full movement freedom from your support when jumping to 'pick the peaches'.
- Also for level 2, be sure to adjust the 'peach on scarf' height appropriately for baby (increasing the height with ongoing success) – so entraining successive jump heights to altitudes well within baby's capability to reach and move the fruits away from the scarf (yet still stretching their musculature control skill and task difficulty with increasing success).

Baby Milestones of Development (0-3 Yrs)

271

G/A 21.5   Driving Self-Control !

Task description:
- Exploring the use of a remote control device to operate vehicle motion.

Expected Milestone Achievements (EMAs):
- Realises *significance* and use of remote control devices   (F2)
- Corrects orientation of tools for immediate use after handling   (Cog2)
- Locates and obtains correct objects when needing (or asked for) them (Cog3)

Materials:
- Remote control device, remotely controlled vehicle (or similar interactive object).

Procedure:

Level 1
1. Demonstrate a remotely controlled vehicle (or similar device, hiding the remote control device at this time).
2. Manipulate the controls remotely, causing the remotely controlled vehicle (or similar interactive object) to advance, inviting baby to now approach the remotely-controlled vehicle, so allowing baby to increase their interest in it.
3. Next, clearly show the toy vehicle to baby as you also demonstrate the vehicle's remote control device, manipulating the remote control to cause the toy vehicle to now shuttle back and forth.
4. Place now across the room the same/similar remote control vehicle, and present to baby the appropriate remote control device.
5. Invite/instruct baby to now manipulate the remote control device, in order to cause 'their' toy vehicle to now move without directly touching the vehicle.
6. As/when baby successfully causes 'their' toy vehicle to move using the remote control device, provide prompt praise and encouragement (however 'uncontrolled' the vehicle movements actually are !).

Level 2
1. Provide again baby with a remote control vehicle and several kinds of remote control devices (each 'looking' as if they may be suitable to control a remote vehicle).
2. Invite/guide now baby to attempt using the different remote control devices (only one of which should actually affect the vehicle), in order to discover 'which' of them actually matches, and really controls, the remote controlled vehicle that is presently in front of them.
3. As/when baby succeeds in 'correctly' identifying the appropriate control device, encourage success by providing prompt praise.

Variations:
- Provide for baby pictures of different family-home electrical appliances, and pictures of their corresponding remote control devices, inviting baby to attempt 'correctly' pairing them together.
- Consider offering several paired remote control devices to baby, seeing whether s/he can determine which of the objects (different vehicles/lights/TV/Radio, etc) each remote device may be used to control which object.

Additional Thoughts/Game-Activity Preparation/Lesson Planning Tips:
- As/when baby begins to gain expertise with their remote control vehicle experience(s), be sure to pay close attention to observing whether/how baby starts to remember how to operate the various functions of the remote control device that they are manipulating (especially if it has more than one function !), or perhaps forgets and requires frequent reminders/assistance from you as to its different uses (i.e., *else baby is simply 'button pushing' repetitively without any clear 'intention' to make the vehicle move in any 'particular' way*).
- As/when baby begins to 'control' the remote control device, ensure that you start to then provide 'certain/more specific' instructions in order to cause *particular vehicle movements* (e.g., cornering left, or right, parking in a U-shaped space), whilst also providing targeted, positive encouragement and praise, so increasing baby's interest and motivation to continue playing with this toy *in a more purposeful, deliberate, way*.
- As/when baby is able to remotely control vehicles, be sure to have carefully chosen items appropriate to baby's individual abilities (e.g., don't expect baby to be able to control and fly a helicopter !), also paying close attention to avoiding their being able to easily damage their vehicle, or any of the room's decor/fixtures/other materials, or otherwise injuring themselves (or others).

G/A 21.6   A Place For Everything !

Task description:
- Exploring the precise placement of objects in specified orientations and positions.

Expected Milestone Achievements (EMAs):
- Places objects down on flat surfaces without dropping them   (F1)
- Rotates 'turned' blocks to match an example block array   (F6)
- Throws a ball towards target location and/or specific direction   (G6)
- Attempts to imitate organised patterns/arrays of objects (e.g., by colour, size) (Cog4)

Materials:
- Large building blocks, bowling bottles (or homemade sims)

- Labelling, skittles or plastic bottles, small ball(s)/rolled socks.

Procedure:
Level 1
1. Attach small paper/labels to mark a point/some points on the room floor.
2. Place now a bowling bottle/skittle on each label that you have fixed onto the room floor, to present a (group of) target bowling bottle(s) in one place for baby to knock down by 'bowling' a ball towards the bottles.
3. Invite/guide baby to return the bowling bottle(s) to their upright positions (if knocked down !), according to each bottle's label position on the floor.
4. As/when baby succeeds to regroup the bowling bottles into their predetermined line-up positions (as pre marking stickers), provide excited and prompt praise.
5. Present the bowling ball to baby once more, encouraging them to repeatedly attempt to 'strike' down the bottles with the ball/socks.
6. Repeat steps 3-5 until baby becomes adept and/or tired with both bowling and resetting of the bottles each time.

Level 2
1. Attach a long straight line of marked points with the labels on the floor (or some other 'marker' as preferred), each spaced at a very close distance between them.
2. Present a set of relatively large building block pieces to baby.
3. Invite/guide baby to next place each of their building blocks according to the label positions along the straight line (to form a 'domino trip line') of standing bricks as illustrated 'falling' below:

4. As/when baby succeeds to produce a long, straight line of standing building bricks according to the markings on the floor surface (even if not 'exactly' every one in place), provide immediate praise and encouragement.
5. Finally, invite baby to move (push over, forward) the 'first' building block, its falling causing each subsequent building block in turn to also fall, so producing the 'domino effect' forward to the end of the line !

Variations:
- Present to baby both some bowling bottles *and* building blocks, inviting baby to come forward and to place one or two of their items onto coded label spaces that you have marked on the floor – checking to see whether baby 'correctly' places each item according to its type, and orientation (thereafter adding/subtracting other objects as appropriate to labels, as new ability levels are attained).
- Ditto, using a variety of objects with their surface features matching different label 'shadow shapes' (like a giant, flat, shape-sorting task !).
- Ditto, using the *same* shaped blocks, but placeable in 2-3 different orientations and directions (i.e. baby being required to 'fit' the same shaped/sized (rectangular) bricks according to different labels, each matching the same rectangular brick's different surface shapes !

Additional Thoughts/Game-Activity Preparation/Lesson Planning Tips:
- When attaching the 'labels' to the floor (or other 'indicators'), be sure to use tape/adhesive that is non-toxic, and relatively stable, but also easy to clean up from the floor surface (without leaving any adhesive or paper residue).
- If no skittle/bowling set be available, create your own using cleaned/dried plastic drink bottles or similar vessels, made attractive/functional by decoration or content as required (though if adding content, do not 'fill' with so much material as to prevent them being knocked over with a lightly bowled ball by baby !).

G/A 21.7   Grasp it from Up High !

Task description:
- Exploring use of a tool to grasp an otherwise unobtainable object.

Expected Milestone Achievements (EMAs):
- Negotiates stepping/climbing obstacles whilst shifting visual focus between near/far distance. (G4)
- Pincer grip shape made before picking up small object shapes (F4)
- Corrects orientation of tools for immediate use after handling (Cog2)
- Explores use of familiar object for novel purpose (e.g., using a fork as a rake). (Cog5)

Materials:
- Coloured ribbon, animal puppet/toy(s), loop, pegs, boxes
- Firm cushions and/or cases/boxes (to form a platform/steps or stepping stones firm enough to support baby's weight/balance).

Procedure:

Level 1

1. Prepare hung coloured ribbons suspended from the ceiling/open doorway (or simply a hand-held clothes hanger), at the end of each coloured ribbon placed a clothes peg.
2. Clip an animal puppet onto each coloured ribbon, and also a loop, on the loop hanging a 2nd coloured ribbon (the 2nd coloured ribbon passing through the loop, and tied on both sides to make a knot).
3. Place the animal puppet at such a height that baby will need to stand on their tiptoes, and even if reaching out their hand will still not be able to grasp the puppet, but CAN grasp the 2nd coloured ribbon.
4. Demonstrate grasping of the 2nd string in order to 'pull down' the animal puppet.
5. As/when baby succeeds in using the 'drawing' of the 2nd coloured ribbon to gain access to the animal puppet each time, provides prompt praise and encouragement.

Level 2
1. Following level 1 success as a foundation, present next a length of coloured ribbon to hang threaded through the loop and tying a knot, baby gaining access to the toy by directly pulling the ribbon.
2. Lay a firm box nearby the hanging animal puppet, the box location deviating slightly from being placed directly below the puppet's position, so requiring baby to move it before its being used as a tool (used as a step to be climbed upon).
3. Invite baby to now attempt to reach the hanging animal puppet, and to take it down.
4. Carefully observe whether baby might be *una*ble to catch the coloured ribbon in order to pull it down, and if so, to then guide them (but not merely by 'telling them') that they may be able to climb up using a box/cushion, paying close attention to observing if baby crawl/climbs directly onto the set of boxes, or chooses to first adjust them in order to succeed in gaining a better resulting position, relative to the position/location of the animal puppet/toy's position.
5. As/when baby attains their target, be sure to provide prompt praise and encouragement (together with some time to play with their goal object once reached – rather than immediately taking it away, and thus demotivating future efforts !!).

Variations:
- Consider to arrange similar reaching/toy acquisitions, using a 'rake' or similar tool for baby to 'contact and draw' the toy back towards them. Offer the choice of using several tools (some of which would *not* perhaps be helpful in the current situation).
- Ditto, using a net to 'catch fish' (or any small floating objects) in shallow water, without using the hands directly.

Additional Thoughts/Game-Activity Preparation/Lesson Planning Tips:
- If/when baby is climbing whilst using a set of boxes stacked to gain access to the toy, *try not to be too eager in helping baby to adjust the box set position(s), thus better enabling baby to think for themselves of the solution, after undergoing failed attempts to gain much motion in achieving their reaching goal.*
- If baby attempts to acquire the animal puppet with the coloured ribbon *not* tied with a knot (i.e., ignoring the loop), they will fail each time, because baby will then only draw the coloured ribbon through the loop to an end (the long end), and therefore only taking down the loop threaded onto the coloured ribbon.
- Encourage with patience, rehanging the coloured ribbon maybe many times as necessary, so allowing baby to continue attempting to reach their goal, again and again, else baby may think from then on they only need grasp the coloured ribbon by both sides in order to take down the animal puppet.
- As/when baby is climbing up the set of boxes to gain their toy goal, ensure that you are nonetheless willing/able/ready to provide protection and support, standing at baby's side, and thus help avoid baby's falling down and injuring themselves.

G/A 21.8   I Know Where It Is !

Task description:
- Exploring and remembering knowledge of object names and their locations.

Expected Milestone Achievements (EMAs):
- Locates and obtains correct objects when needing (or asked for) them   (Cog3)
- Babbling with 'adult-like' speech intonation when 'talking' to dolls   (Comms5)
  and/or soft toys.
- Finds and presents certain objects when asked for them   (SP3)

Materials:
- Animal puppets/plush toys, toy fruits and vegetables, boxes
- Sound blocks (see also 'additional tips' section below).

Procedure:
Level 1
1. Demonstrate three same-coloured boxes, each with one open-side facing baby, arranged in a row on the floor.
2. Show next, in turn, three animal toys, referring to each clearly, by name: e.g., if a cat, say, "Cat"; dog => "Dog", rabbit, etc, putting each then into a different box, as baby clearly watches you do so.
3. Invite baby to now come forward and to take out a particular animal from its 'home' box, as specified by you each time: e.g., if the rabbit, then saying, "Please would you collect the rabbit from his box, to come and say hello to us".
4. As/when baby succeeds to choose the 'correct' animal toy from its location, and then proceeds to take out the rabbit, give baby much applause and encouragement.

5. Continue promptly to invite baby to again come forward and to take out another animal from *its* box, as specified by you each time: If this time the cat, then saying, "Please would you collect the cat from her box, to come and say hello".
6. Now only one animal remains, finally, saying "Which animal has not yet come out ?",..... Guiding baby to say "The dog" (or whichever remains).
7. Now change the position of the last remaining animal (i.e., placing it into a different box), reloading the others, and preparing for a new round.

Level 2
1. Demonstrate five same-coloured boxes, *this time each open-side facing the floor*, again arranged in a single row.
2. Slowly show five fruits and/or vegetables toys in turn (e.g., apple, peach, strawberry, banana, carrot), slowly placing each under one of the five boxes
3. Repeat the level 1 steps 3-7, according to baby's continued interest and motivation
   [NB: for an auditory version of the task, consider to use different sound boxes to be hidden each time].

Variations:
- Using five boxes, put three types of toys, one under each of three (of the five) boxes only. Invite baby to then locate a specific (named) toy, according to your request.
- Consider inviting another person who may be present to make the same/similar request(s) of baby (or possibly of you, or each other, to do so in turn ?).
- Instead of the solid boxes, consider to use partly opaque, or clear plastic bowls, asking baby to then identify 'who' is underneath/behind each of the different bowls, and to then take them out for hug.
- For an auditory version of the task, consider to use different sound boxes to be hidden each time.

Additional Thoughts/Game-Activity Preparation/Lesson Planning Tips:
- Be sure to manipulate all animal toys and boxes both slowly, and without obscuring the placement actions with your own arms or other body parts, so allowing baby to clearly see 'where' each animal is being placed (else they will not be sure which location(s) will need to remembered !).
- *Ensure that baby 'knows' the name of each animal (or at least the name of the one that you are requesting them to approach – hence the detail of steps 1-3), else baby cannot follow your instructions (even if they understand them).*
- If/when baby is *unable* to choose the correct location, and/or cannot find the animal which you have requested, guide baby to continue to locate/search until finding it, so increasing baby's perseverance and self-confidence with eventual success.

- Consider allowing adequate/sufficient time for any interaction time for play, and/or baby play time with you, if requested; *i.e., play time once animal toys have been successfully recovered (rather than immediately taking it away from them – i.e., let them enjoy the consequences of their success, and thus better realising the significance of their own actions, in learning to follow instructions)*
- If you do not have access to (or do not possess) sound boxes, substitute them with home-made shakers and simple sound-making vessels for baby to explore similarly [using, e.g., empty candy tins, (opaque) water bottles, or other vessels – each containing a different material, such as dried beans, buttons, marbles, feathers/cotton wool, etc.,].

G/A 21.9   I Can Tell You What It Is !

Task description:
- Exploring, naming and remembering single icon pictures.

Expected Milestone Achievements (EMAs):
- Correctly names familiar object pictures when pointed to by others   (Comms1)
- Begins to ask "What's this" when finding new objects   (Cog1)
- Attempts to imitate organised patterns/arrays of objects   (Cog4)

Materials:
- Animal pictures (one image per picture, blank on one side).

Procedure:
Level 1
1. Demonstrate three different animal pictures, and arrange them on the floor: e.g., one of a cat, one of a dog, another of a panda.
2. Inform baby what is the name of each animal (real animal name, not pet names !).
3. Ask baby to then call out each animal's name as you show each card again, placing each then 'face down' on the floor, once baby has 'correctly' identified it.
4. Using your finger to closely point to each (now down-facing) picture card each time, ask baby, "What animal picture was on the other side of this one ?", inviting baby to attempt making a verbal reply, indicating the name of the animal as shown in the picture (which is currently face-down, on the floor).
5. Immediately after/as baby has replied, quickly turn over the picture card to reveal which animal picture can really be seen there, for baby to see.

6. Compare now the real picture, with baby's verbal name response (correct, not correct ?), giving baby applause for their verbal achievement, and increasing praise and encouragement if also completely 'correct'.
7. Repeat steps 4-6 until all (3) pictures have been explored in this way (continuing according to the number of different cards baby can name), then arrange the same/or a different set of pictures as per step 3 above, in preparation for another round.

Level 2
1. Demonstrate this time a new set *of five* different animal pictures, and arrange them on the floor: e.g., one of a tiger, one of a frog, a chicken, rabbit and a fish.
2. Inform baby what is the name of each animal (animal type, not pet names !).
3. Ask baby to now call out each animal's name as you show each card again, placing each face down on the floor as before, after they 'correctly' do so.
4. Repeat as per level 1 steps 4-7 until all (5) pictures have been explored in this way, then arrange the same/a different 5-picture set in preparation for the next rounds.

Variations:
- With level 1-2 item success, and checking for adequate vocabulary with each new picture example (before using it with baby), consider to increase the item set size or the category of picture(s) to be used – otherwise continuing to invite baby to remember and say the name of them each time in order (for you) to be sure.
- Ditto, using black and white tone pictures (instead of full coloured ones) for baby's identification and stating of names.
- Ditto, using a wider group of images from different categories (clothing items, transport vehicles, scenes/locations, family member photos, etc).
- To create an auditory version of the task, consider to match the cards with their corresponding animal sounds – later using the animal sounds also as an initial stimulus (remembering that the goal this time is *to facilitate baby's verbal response in naming the target item* (so don't just invite them to match the sound with the 'correct' picture instead !!).

Additional Thoughts/Game-Activity Preparation/Lesson Planning Tips:
- When providing baby's with pictures, be sure that you know whether baby has had sufficient time to study any target picture, *and can clearly indicate to you that they both know, and can say, the name of each animal/object* being depicted in the picture,.. BEFORE inviting them to then say what is in the picture that you are talking about, and whether or not they can see it at that time (i.e., at this age/stage, bay may know/speak/remember more than they can express !!).
- Consider using 'off the shelf' picture cards (single-sided pictures only), or if making cards of your own, be sure to either laminate them or smoothen edges/corners, so helping avoid scratching/piercing of the baby's skin.
- Use pictures with bright, rich colours (at least at first), so providing an attractive image with which to stimulate baby's interest and motivation for the task.

G/A 21.10   Windy Movements !

Task description:
- Exploring the effects of self-generated air currents to move objects.

Expected Milestone Achievements (EMAs):
- Opens and closes mouth when asked to do so   (Comms3)

Materials:
- Feather, slips of coloured paper/tissue, ping-pong balls, boxes, mirror.

Procedure:
Level 1
1. Lead baby to open and close his/her mouth (pretending to be a fish ?) in order to practice their labial muscle movement control, *as/when asked* to do so.
2. Demonstrate next a feather, making exaggerated movements of your own external mouth parts, causing the feather to slowly, but noticeably move as you gently blow towards it, so attracting baby's interest. (can hang on a string if wishing to exaggerate the effect further)
3. Present the same/similar feather to baby, inviting/guiding baby to blow (according to the demonstration just shown) in order for them to cause the feather to fly/move once more.
4. As/when baby succeeds with blowing and causing the feather to move in this way (maybe NOT allowing baby to also hold it in their hand (preventing the feather's movement then being caused by their finger/arm/hand movements alone !), applauding baby's achievements with praise and encouragement.
   [Consider to use a mirror in demonstration, both your and baby's images clearly visible to baby, as you each purse your lips to blow each time].

Level 2

1. Demonstrate a cushion/box, with scattered coloured slips of paper/tissue on top.
2. Slowly and clearly show that, by again making exaggerated movements of your own external mouth parts, how your blowing can this time cause the coloured slips of paper to fly upwards in many directions (baby possibly becoming very excited when seeing this take place !).
3. Present to baby now the same cushion/box, and scatter coloured slips of paper in a small pile on its surface.
4. Invite/guide baby to again blow out air according to your demonstration, in order for them to this time cause the coloured paper strips fly about in all directions.
5. As/when baby succeeds in causing the paper strips to fly about using only their exhaled breath, ensure applause and praises for baby with the appropriate amount of feedback (i.e., so rewarding excitement *and* encouraging motivation).

Level 3

1. Situate a ping-pong ball on top of an upturned box (to provide a flat surface), and then slowly and clearly show that, by again making more exaggerated movements of your own external mouth parts, how your blowing can causes the ping-pong ball to roll about, and in such a way as to cause it to travel to the edge of the box surface, and to then fall off the edge and onto the floor (or into a 2nd open box "splash", if arranging one that way (or on a table)).
2. Present the same set of materials for baby to explore, inviting baby to then move the ping-pong, again using only their exhaled breath [possibly holding hands in order to prevent baby simply grabbing it ! ?].
3. As/when baby achieves making the ball's movement in this way (the fine control of the ball's direction not being so important just now !), assure applause for baby's achievements with continuous praise and encouragement.

Level 4

1. Demonstrate next a 'catch box', with its open side this time facing towards you at the end of a runway (built from cushions) laid on the floor.
2. Show now a ping-pong ball, placing it on the floor in front of you, now facing a 'catch box' at the end of the 'pathway'.
3. Getting down on all fours *(its always helpful to see the world from baby's viewpoint now and again !)* gently blow the ping-pong ball towards/and into the open-sided 'catch box' goal.
4. Repeat as per level 3 steps 2-3, allowing baby to follow the procedure as newly demonstrated.

Variations:

- Consider installing some water in a bowl (maybe also serving as the '2nd box' in level 3 ?), inviting baby to then blow on the water to see the affects of their blowing upon the floating ping-pong ball's movement.

- Cover baby's head with a fine gauze/silk scarf, inviting baby to opening their mouths and to blow an air current, in order to move the gauze scarf such they can see something, or be seen by someone else !

Additional Thoughts/Game-Activity Preparation/Lesson Planning Tips:
- Consider to hang/tie the feather to a light string/ribbon, so increasing the ability of baby to realise the fether's movement as being caused by your/their blowing towards it.
- Ditto, exploring the movement (and sound making) of a wind chime, or windmill.
- As baby's blown air pressure will be relatively light, you may need to encourage baby to practice blowing at several strengths, in order to see different objects move (think of the disappointment that some babies (and their parents) sometimes show when trying to 'blow out' their early years' birthday cake candles !!).
- Be also careful to provide feathers and slips of tissue paper which really will move when only relatively weak baby's blowing strength is used.
- *Pay close attention to NOT blowing with baby at the same time* (this can be sometimes hard for you to inhibit, as you may well enjoy sharing this game), in order to enable baby to learn the skill faster, whilst also helping avoid stimulating baby's eyes to blink, and/or inhaling your partially-toxic breath through their nose and mouth.
- To prevent other potential accidents of choking or swallowing, be sure to inspect and clean away baby's body parts/clothing which may have remaining pieces of feather or slips of paper become attached to them (likewise any stray saliva !).

G/A 21.11   Treasure Hunt !

Task description:
- Exploring choice selection from amongst distractors, selecting targets according to specific requests received.

Expected Milestone Achievements (EMAs):
- Runs or walks with abrupt direction change, without bumping or falling   (G2) on obstacles.
- Locates and obtains correct objects when needing (or asked for) them   (Cog3)
- Pincer grip shape made before picking up small object shapes   (F4)
- Finds and presents certain objects when asked for them   (SP3)

Materials:
- Stepping-stone pathway (small mats/marked areas, with path lined with various cushions, boxes/containers etc)

- Bean Bags, plush animal puppet/toys, toy fruits and vegetables

Procedure:
Level 1
1. Spread about the room large cushions to form an obstacle course.
2. Place fruit and vegetable toys around the cushion path's corners and so forth, and in other random locations.
3. Illustrate ahead of time, that "There is an animal (puppet/plush toy) that you [baby] may come to meet later, and that this animal is very hungry, and has invited you [baby] to help search about the field [room] for some fruits and vegetables for him/her [the toy animal] to eat please".
4. Invite baby to now find as many foodstuffs as they can find, and to finally present the 'gifts' of food to the animal, for him/her to eat.
5. Be sure promptly thank baby for their food 'gifts' (on the animal's behalf), and encourage baby to then continue to seek and gather more, until all have been found.

Level 2
1. Repeat the level 1 procedure several times, increasing the level of difficulty of movement, complexity and 'food' location finding amongst the obstacle course [field] arranged for baby to navigate amongst each time.

Variations:
- For level 1, consider to up the level of difficulty further by requesting baby search *for*, and only collect, fruits OR vegetables each time, or even *specific* fruits (e.g., bananas),... etc...
- [Esp if not wishing to use a room-set obstacle course] Provide baby with a box/basket, inside of which are some ping-pong balls, marbles, dried peas or beans, small balls, building blocks, spoons, and so forth, amongst a pile of torn coloured paper strips then, then invite baby to explore their box, in order to, for example, "Please find and bring to me the black soybeans from your box",....

Additional Thoughts/Game-Activity Preparation/Lesson Planning Tips:
- As/when baby is in their search process, pay close attention to observing *how* baby is pursuing their target(s), whilst always attending to baby's safety, especially when climbing up/down any obstacles in the 'field', thus helping avoid baby colliding with other room furnishings and falling down.
- Again during the searching time, encourage, but DO NOT TELL baby where the target items are (as they otherwise are about to pass their locations), so only guiding baby with regards physically balancing and following about the obstacle course pathway safely (and not to target locations, though can consider to add 'getting warmer/cooler' cues, to add interest if unsuccessful search is lasting too long !).
- If/when baby finds and presents items NOT requested to be gathered, remember to nonetheless express thanks to baby, then guiding them to continue seek for what *was* requested of them that time.
- Ensure the cleanliness and safety aspects of all items used during this task, cleaning/sterilising all of the target and distractor toys, both before and after their use.

G/A 21.12   Soccer Boxes !

Task description:
- Strengthening control required to maintain postural balance whilst swinging legs.

Expected Milestone Achievements (EMAs):
- Maintains stable upright posture when stops running   (G1)
- Runs or walks with abrupt direction change, without bumping or   (G2)
  falling on obstacles.
- Attempts to kick ball with swinging leg/foot   (G5)
- Throws a ball towards target location and/or specific direction   (G6)

Materials:
- Active obstacle course of cushions, large inflatable ball.

Procedure:

Level 1
1. Create and demonstrate the setting up of a simple 'Penalty shoot' area using several cushions, or similar soft furnishings, situating baby seated on one of the cushions, near to the 'goal' box.
2. Sitting next to baby, slowly and gently 'throw' the ball towards the goal (open sided box on the floor).
3. Invite/lead baby (*without* physical support) to attempt the same action, whilst also providing prompt praise and encouragement, saying, "Baby can score a goal now all by him/herself!", "Baby is becoming so strong and really powerful now !", or somesuch. *(The hope is that the baby will begin to integrate one or both arms forward in an attempt to propel the ball forward, using their own muscles and controlling their shifting body weight, whilst also exploring the coordinating and timing of the many actions required to release the ball appropriately).*

Level 2
1-3 Repeat level 1, this time setting up an open box laid sideways on the floor, encouraging baby to this time use the foot (both left and right, over different rounds) to propel the ball towards the newly positioned goal each time.

Variations:
- Although most babies will by now be independently standing and walking (even running) unsupported at this time – consider increasing the difficulty (and thus enhancing the different muscle co-ordinations/integrations by changing the distance from, and size of, the goal (relative to the ball) to be reached each time.
- If no soft inflatable ball be available (best for preventing room object damage !), consider using a light football or tennis ball instead.

Additional Thoughts/Game-Activity Preparation/Lesson Planning Tips:
- *These activities provide an experience similar to that of a suspended swing, but when baby is (even gently) swinging their arm/leg in order to propel the ball here, be sure to observe their head (and thus brain) movements upwards and/or downwards, providing support in case they may feel dizzy as a result of the sudden stopping movement when releasing throws/kicking the ball each time. [Be sure to observe carefully baby's limb muscle coordination and control as being exercised here, remember that the target EMAs are not focussed upon goal scoring accuracy !]*
- Be careful to remove/secure any objects in the room which may become hit/damaged by contact with the flying balls from baby's direction (which could initially be far away from their intended goal !!)
- Be sure to also use a light ball if possible, or at least of suitable size and weight each time for use by baby's hands and feet.

ψ

Baby Milestones of Development (0-3 Yrs)

- 14 -

Baby Milestones of Development

(With 100+ Fun Activities to Help Demonstrate Them)

[Age 22 Months]

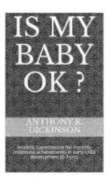

ψ

Baby Milestones of Development (0-3 Yrs)

Expected Milestone Achievements
Age = 22 Months

[Key: e.g., 2 = Game No. 22.2]

Gross Motor	
• Pursues moving object (ball) with controlled walk/running gait and speed	4, 6
• Starts and stops running freely without colliding with objects or others	4
• Actively searches for objects and takes/places them in suggested locations	1, 4
• Jumps up and down freely, without floor contact (i.e., with both feet off the ground)	9, 12
• Kicks a ball towards target location and/or specific (if general) direction	5
• Kicks ball with swinging leg and/or foot (e.g., more flexible at hip, knee, & ankle)	5, 12
Fine Motor	
• Manages large buttons/poppers on clothing	10
• Places plug into water sink and/or threads large-holed beads onto string	3, 9
• Able to correctly point to, or touch, 7-10 own body parts	2, 10
• Changes position of light switches and other binary position controls	
• Acquires small visible items from bottles by rotating/shaking them	
• Organises toys/objects into recognisable patterns and symmetries	3, 8
Cognitive	
• Transfers fluids between containers without gross spillage	7, 11
• Spontaneously explores novel objects (e.g., shakes/bangs them together)	8
• Organises objects according to simple categories (e.g., size, colour, *or* shape)	3, 5
• Requests names for new or unfamiliar 'found' objects	11
• Finds new uses for familiar objects without prompting	6
• Identifies familiar cartoon characters in novel places, magazines, TV images, etc	1
Communication	
• Demonstrates frequent use of more than 50 single words	
• Correctly uses 2nd person possessive (e.g., yours, you)	2
• Asks for names of shelf items when out shopping	
• Requests novel, visible objects out of reach, using words	5
• Correctly identifies different sounds by name	
• Asks to be told the names of new or unfamiliar objects	11
Socio-Personal	
• Attempts to clean own teeth, given equipment (and help) to do so	11
• Using words, rather than crying, in order to request help from others	4
• Sensitive to operation of "on/off" control buttons, relative to other controls	
• Play-feeds dolls or soft toys without significant spillage or smearing of face/body	10
• Keen to jump and/or move in coordination with others	9, 12
• Beginning to treat dolls/soft toys as if babies or friends	2, 10

G/A 22.1 Round About Ball !

Task description:
- Exploring image search and identification of image content(s), by request,

Expected Milestone Achievements (EMAs):
- Identifies familiar objects or people in complex pictures/images [M21-Comms2]
- Actively searches for objects and takes/places them in suggested locations. (G3)
- Identifies familiar cartoon characters in novel places, magazines, TV images, etc. (Cog6)

Materials:
- Assorted balls
- Animal pictures, character pictures (incl baby ?), pictures of fruits and vegetables.

Procedure:
Level 1
1. Demonstrate a large ball, onto the surface of which are attached a number of different pictures, each showing an image of a simple/single object, person, or animal.
2. Clearly show how to push the ball along the floor (or rotate in the hands if preferred), stopping at each picture (when facing towards baby), and leading baby to know what is shown in each of the pictures, e.g., a penguin, puppy, apple, mama, and so forth.
3. Present now the same ball, inviting baby to search for the picture image which you request each time (asking baby, e.g., "Where is the cat ?").
4. Invite baby to now gently roll the ball about the floor (or to rotate it in either your, or baby's hands), whilst looking about the ball until they find the picture of the cat, remove it from its location, and pass it to you, as you respond with much praise.
5. Continue to assign search for the other pictures, until all have been collected, repeating the task (maybe changing the pictures used each time ?), according to baby's continued interest and motivation level.

Baby Milestones of Development (0-3 Yrs)

Level 2
1. Demonstrate next a different kind of ball (or even a completely different kind of object, large soft toy, box, etc), on the surface of which, are attached a number of different pictures, this time each showing an image of a simple/single character (policeman, doctor, builder, teacher, bus driver, spacewoman, etc,..).
2. Clearly show how to manipulate the object in a controlled way, stopping to see each picture again, and checking with baby to know what is shown in each of the pictures, e.g., builder, teacher, fisherman, spacewoman, and so forth.
3. Present now the same/similar object to baby, inviting search for the picture image which you request each time (e.g., "Where is the chef/cook, driver ?").
4. Continue as per level 1 steps 4-5.

Variations:
- Consider to use photo images of different activity participants, parents/guardian, grandparents and/or other family members/friends (even cartoon characters ?) which are both familiar and recognisable (especially if also nameable) by baby at this time.
- With increasing success, introduce images showing objects/people/animals which 'look' more similar to each other, in order to increase discrimination powers, and thus the levels of differentiation difficulty, as appropriate.
- Ditto, reducing the use of colour cues, instead presented black and white, or sepia hued images, thus again increasing the level of visual acuity required to succeed in identifying the different images shown.

Additional thoughts/Game-Activity Preparation/Lesson Planning Tips:
- Be sure to provide picture images of a size suitable for manipulation according to baby's current palmar/pincer grasping abilities.
- Attach the pictures reliably (yet easy for baby to detach) on/from the ball/object to be manipulated, so helping avoid baby either falling as the ball is made to turn, or from simply using the ball's rotational energy to cause the pictures to 'fall off' (without baby then being able to first look at/select them !!). [Maybe a box will serve this purpose rather than too small a ball, for baby just now ? – best to experiment with possible materials yourself awhile, before starting this activity with baby].

G/A 22.2 You Name It, I Can Touch It

Task description:
- Exploring by touch the location and identification of named body parts.

Expected Milestone Achievements (EMAs):
- Able to correctly point to, or touch, 7-10 own body parts (F3)
- Correctly uses 2nd person possessive (e.g., you, yours) (Comms2)
- Beginning to treat dolls/soft toys as if babies or friends (SP6)

Materials:
- Small stickers.

Procedure:
Level 1
1. Begin the task by inviting baby to shake hands in greeting you (and/or each other, a grandparent/nanny, or whomever else might be present at the time).
2. Next, holding hands together (in a circle, if with others): - sing the nursery song: "Blowing, bubbles, blowing bubbles", and when reaching, "I blew a really big bubble that hit my hand', open up one of your hands (as if holding and stuck together by a large imaginary bubble), as it then "pops" when 'touched' !
3. Separating your hands (after being "stuck together" each time), then resume the song, with dancing movements whilst you start to sing once more.
4. Repeat steps 2-3 several times, each time changing the identified body part to be 'stuck' together !! (i.e., instead of "hand", say "foot", "nose", elbow, knee, and so forth).

Level 2
1. Invite/guide baby to now play "Stickers Stick !".
2. At the baby's own initiative, encourage them to place one small sticker on to a named place on their own body, thereafter making contact with same area upon/with your own body.

Baby Milestones of Development (0-3 Yrs)

3 Facilitate encouragement with much prompt praise and applause as baby achieves increasing identifications and cooperative movements according to each new body part suggestion made.

Variations:
- Consider to play the same game/activity using real bubbles !!

- Another alternative is to encourage baby with dancing movements, bringing together each your 'requested' body parts (or simply touching their own ?), each time the music stops.
- If not wishing to run such an active 'touchy' task, consider remaining seated with a doll or large soft toy, using *their* 'body parts' as comparisons to then identify and label.

Additional thoughts/Game-Activity Preparation/Lesson Planning Tips:
- Be sure to pay attention to safety and possible health-consciousness when using stickers to cover body parts. For example, try to avoid overuse (even any use) of the mouth parts or eyes, when encouraging baby to come together with you (or non-parent others), so helping reduce the risks of infectious organism sharing.
- Consider carefully the choice of body parts with respect to the differences in that baby may be sometimes more or less willing, to behave 'intimately' with others, and preferring/showing comfort with certain distances of separation/closeness when touching them (or even choosing not to, which should always be respected).

G/A 22.3   Plan, Target, Grip

Task description:
- Exploring and planning grip shape and strength for handling small objects.

Expected Milestone Achievements (EMAs):
- Places plug into water sink and/or threads large-holed beads (F2)
  onto string.
- Organises toys/objects into recognisable patterns and symmetries (F6)
- Organises objects according to simple categories (e.g., size, (Cog3)
  colour, *or* shape).

Materials:
- Adhesive tape, large and small coloured bells, plastic straw/string & beads

- Cups (handled and non-handled).

Procedure:
Level 1
1. Place several adhesive tape folds horizontally on the wall/board surface/window glass, with its sticky surface facing outwards, attaching large bells to that adhesive surface.
2. Demonstrated a cup, and slowly use of your thumb and opposing index finger (of the same hand) to form a pincer grip around the large bell attached to the wall/window, and to then place it into the cup, for baby to clearly see.
3. Present now the cup, inviting baby to collect one of the bells and to place it into their cup, as per your demonstration.
4. As/when baby succeeds to use a pincer grip in order to remove/acquire their bell, provide prompt praise and encouragement.

Level 2
1. Repeat level 1 steps 1-4, using progressively smaller bells, and/or other objects – also considering to use cups with different, or no handle(s) each time.

Level 3
1. Once baby's pincer grip and hold is strong (or at least usable for manipulating progressively smaller objects held in baby's hand) – introduce the plastic straw and beads – slowly demonstrating the threading of beads on to the straw – otherwise following the same procedure as for baby in levels 1-2 above.

Level 4
1. With success in threading onto the plastic straw in the level 3 activity, consider introducing progressively less firm materials for baby to try threading the beads, finally using a flexible string or a shoelace (in order to exercise baby's increasing fine-motor dexterity and muscle-coordination control).

Variations:
- If no bells be available for the session, consider to replace materials with a quantity of small toy fruits, dried sunflower seeds or large (dried) beans.
- Ditto, using such to be taken/collected from a given location (to be manipulated and transported), and to be then placed in a bowl, for making soup !
- Alternatively, place the adhesive tape strip on the floor (or even your own clothing), for baby to then use their pincer grip to retrieve and relocate them to a collecting vessel/bowl provided for the purpose.
- If no threadable beads be available, create some by piercing holes through dried nuts, stones or sea shells, bottle tops, etc..

Additional thoughts/Game-Activity Preparation/Lesson Planning Tips:
- Be sure to pay careful attention to preventing baby from placing the bells (or any other small objects) between their lips for exploration, so helping avoid the danger of swallowing or choking.
- When setting up the locations of target objects, consider the height of baby, as they will need to select their retrieval locations accordingly (e.g., consider offering vertically-placed as well as horizontally-placed target sets), the lowest spots being relatively easy for the smaller baby to reach (or place cushioned steps/ramps nearby for their optional use or additional problem solving demonstration). *NB: This might also be a good time to also get down onto 'all fours' yourself – and to remind yourself how different the same world looks like from baby's point of view !!*
- When threading, consider pegging/knotting one end to stop beads running off !

G/A 22.4 Moving Targets !

Task description:
- Exploring controlled target throwing, with and without self-motion monitoring.

Expected Milestone Achievements (EMAs):
- Pursues moving object (ball) with controlled walk/running gait and speed. (G1)
- Starts and stops running freely without colliding with objects or others (G2)
- Actively searches for objects and takes/places them in suggested locations. (G3)
- Throws a ball towards target location and/or specific direction [M21-G6]
- Using words, rather than crying, in order to request for help from others (SP2)

Materials:
- Small balls/rolled-up socks, toy basket/bag, boxes, bean bags.

- Hula-hoop/coat hanger, tiles/mats/string/rope/ribbon (to form a 'footpath').

Procedure:
Level 1
1. Prepare two boxes at one side of the room, each containing a quantity of differently coloured, small balls (socks, or similar safely throwable objects).
2. On the other side of the room, lay four differently coloured toy baskets/containers (ideally of the same colours as those of the balls/socks/objects to be thrown), separating the boxes and basket areas by flat objects placed on the floor (tiles, ribbon, hula-hoop) to form a 'stepping-stone footpath' between them.
3. Demonstrate now the task/activity, taking up two small balls from the box (one in each hand), then run/jump over/across/through/along the 'pathway, remaining 'inside' the pathway at an 'end point' marker (closest to the box(es)), then separately throw each of the small balls/socks still held, into the basket of each ball's corresponding colour, after which returning yourself to the starting position.

4. Invite baby to now stand together with you at one side of the room (the 'starting position'), and to then collect and transport 1-2 balls, and to carry them forward along the pathway, in order to place them into their corresponding coloured baskets, as previously demonstrated.
5. As/when baby succeeds with placing/throwing their ball into the boxes each time, be sure to provide the most appropriate encouragement and prompt praise.

Level 2
1. Arrange now the collection (target) boxes to be in the centre of the room, inside of which are placed differently coloured bean-bags (bricks, or something other than balls/socks).
2. Around the room spread 2-3 footpaths, each footpath' terminal ending with a hanging hula hoop/held coat hanger, situated slightly above baby's head position, and at a distance from the footpaths end (maybe with a 'catch pool'/box immediately behind/below it ?).
3. Demonstrate next the task/activity, running along the pathway up to the terminal, having gathered 1-2 beanbags/objects along the way; stopping before the hanging hula-hoop/hanger, and then throwing the beanbag through the hoop/hanger (and into the 'catch pool' behind/below it).
4. As/when baby succeeds with throwing their beanbag through the hoop/hanger, quickly provide prompt encouragement and praise for their efforts.

Variations:
- Consider laying a ring of cushions (circular form) in the room, inside of which are many differently coloured small balls/rolled socks, inviting baby to stand inside of it also (with the balls/socks), then to find and throw particular balls/socks of a requested colour out of the 'pool', for you (outside the pool) to catch each time.
- Ditto, rotating the requesting catcher each time (if other persons be present) moving around in a circle, with one person inside the pool at any given time !).
- With increasing abilities, consider to run the task as a 'race' with baby competing with you (or as a two teams if others also present), waiting in turn to run the pathways, one at a time.

Additional thoughts/Game Preparation/Lesson Planning Tips:
- If no/insufficient quantity of balls be available, simply use rolled up (clean) socks !).
- Choose throwing distances carefully (for baby, according to their increasing strength, accuracy and motor coordination ability).
- For level 2, be sure to offer praise for baby succeeding with simply throwing their ball/bag through the hula hoop/hanger – it is not so important *where* it lands just now ! (though do consider to increase the difficulty (height/distance) with practice and success).
- Create a number of footpaths for level 2, and consider using two suspended hoops/hangers, the different footpaths converging upon them both.

G/A 22.5   Flexible Hurdling

Task description:
- Leg reaching and power kicking with increased limb motion and flexibility.

Expected Milestone Achievements (EMAs):
- Kicks ball with swinging leg and/or foot (e.g., more flexible at hip, knee, & ankle).   (G6)
- Kicks a ball towards target location and/or specific (if general) direction   (G5)
- Organises objects according to simple categories (e.g., size, colour, *or* shape).   (Cog3)
- Requests novel, visible objects out of reach, using words   (Comms4)

Materials:
- Floor marking material (to form a flat ladder/step set on the floor)
- Inflatable (or soft) ball.

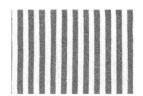

Procedure:

Level 1
1. Arrange and demonstrate either a drawn, or 3D row of supported 15 centimeter/3 inch high obstacles (or floor markings like a flat ladder ?), to provide a "111111111111"- looking structure suitably spaced to allow baby to step over each obstacle/drawn black rung.
2. Invite/lead baby to bridge/step over each obstacle (or rung of the ladder), possibly holding just *one of baby's hands* until they arrive at the other end of the obstacle row.
3. Pay special attention to whether, and how, baby chooses to use their lower limb muscle and joints when stepping over each time, encouraging knee bending, as well as (previously preferred) rotation/swinging at the hip joint, in supporting the strength and balance required to make this movement.
4. As/when baby succeeds with stepping over/bridge(s) the obstacle set, facilitate appropriate encouragement and prompt praise each time.

Level 2
1. Arrange and demonstrate now a more complex row of supported 15+ centimeter high obstacles (using soft wood/branches or building bricks according to baby's now known obstacle negotiation abilities), to provide a less evenly, and more widely spaced "1. . . 1. . . 1. . . 1"-looking structure for baby to now try and overcome.
2. Invite/lead baby to again bridge/step over each of the obstacles, as before.
3. As/when baby succeeds to step over/bridge(s) each time, facilitate with the most appropriate encouragement and prompt praise each time.

Level 3
1. Set up a next a series of 'targets' about the floor of the room, using the same equipment reorganised and spread amongst other cushioning pieces.
2. Demonstrate a 'centre spot' from which a soft inflatable ball is to be kicked towards one of the set targets as requested (by you) each time, each target having a different 'goal score' value if hit accurately.
3. Again, facilitate baby to encourage their use of increased knee bending, as well as the (previously preferred) rotation/swinging at the hip joint when preparing and then executing their kicking movement, in guiding the ball towards their target with the foot each time.

Variations:
- Arrange a number of small balls about the room, and/or some interesting toys scattered about; Invite baby to then take on the responsibility to collect and carry the various objects, and to then jump/overcome several hurdles erected in front of 'home boxes' that the balls/toys then need to be placed into.
- Similarly, consider using individual obstacles, pieces of cushioning, low furniture, sturdy boxes, then requiring baby to step over the different pieces (the 'hurdles', each piece with a target object attached to the back of it), before collecting them together to then place them in a basket (or if using bricks, to later use them in order to set about building a tower of great height, to then knock down, yeah !).

Additional thoughts/Game-Activity Preparation/Lesson Planning Tips:
- Be sure to allow for the most suitable adjustments to obstacle heights according to baby's growing ability and motivation for task (without shifting the level of difficulty *every* time, thus affording baby time to enjoy each new success before receiving a new challenge to be overcome).
- Encourage baby to attempt as many types of different obstacle hurdling/ball kicking as possible, all the while providing baby with the most appropriate encouragement and prompt praise each time.

Baby Milestones of Development (0-3 Yrs)

G/A 22.6   Politely Put !

Task description:
- Exploring large object lifting and its subsequent deliberate placement.

Expected Milestone Achievements (EMAs):
- Places objects down on flat surfaces without dropping them   [M21-F1]
- Pursues moving object (ball) with controlled walk/running gait and speed.   (G1)
- Finds new uses for familiar objects without prompting   (Cog5)

Materials:
- Boxes, bean bags/small balls, plastic troughs/boxes.

Procedure:

Level 1
1. Construct a set of boxes/cushions in a line to form a room barrier/wall, in the centre of which is a two-level stacked box-set inserted to form a 'gate', also laying about other cushions/furniture pieces around the room.
2. Demonstrate now some other boxes, placing each on different cushions for baby to clearly see (located elsewhere in the same room).
3. Demonstrate now how to 'open' the gate [by lifting the top box off to the left, the lower box to the right], 'enter' to the other side, then replacing the two (now 2nd layer boxes) back to their 'closed gate' postions); then to retrieve each of the other (non-wall) boxes, placing each upon the other, in order to build their own stack (one on top of the other to create a new chosen wall of boxes elsewhere).
4. As/when baby succeeds in stacking their boxes (without assistance) *and*, they do not fall down, provide baby prompt praise and encouragement for their efforts.

Level 2
1. With level 1 as a foundation activity, place now many beanbags (balls, or similar interesting objects) and plastic troughs/bins on one side of the room.

2. Invite baby to now take up a plastic trough, and to find and place as many balls/ bean-bags as they can, into their trough; and to then ship it though the 'gate' into the room (as before), and to put to it onto one of the flat-topped cushions.
3. As/when baby succeeds with loading their plastic troughs, transports it through the 'gate' to place it on the cushion (*and* without dropping any of the contents), provide prompt and appropriate praise and encouragement.

Level 3
1. Repeat level 1 again, this time using any sizes of boxes/containers, with and without baby also, either: (a) carrying increasing numbers of stackable objects (e.g., small pillows/beanbags) on their heads, and/or (b) slowly 'walking' a football with their feet, as they do so [possibly requiring a cushion-walled pathway, so as to not lose the ball to far away after kicking each time ?).

Variations:
- Consider arranging sets of boxes and various cushions to form multi-layered racks, initially laying different toys/objects about the room; inviting baby to then gather specific pieces or toys, and to then place them, according to specific colour sequences and arrangements that you then specify.
- Ditto, with lower difficulty levels using real 3-D models pieces that you then use to build something, inviting baby to gather the parts over time, with which to then build their own copies of.

Additional thoughts/Game-Activity Preparation/Lesson Planning Tips:
- Initial rack/tower building/object placements may be helpful (for at least some babies) if placing their pieces against a wall, so as to avoid baby achieving 'failing' build experiments, otherwise resulting in the collapsing of their structures and hurting themselves (or others), or their stumbling forward and falling over their boxes !
- Provide for baby only relatively soft quality materials to work with during this task/activity, so helping avoid careless scratching/wounding of baby's skin whilst manipulating the various pieces made available for stacking.

G/A 22.7   I'm a Little Artist

Task description:
- Exploring the use of writing/drawing implements, in response to copy models.

Expected Milestone Achievements (EMAs):
- Attempts copying of complex multi-line drawings   [M21 Cog6]
- Transfers fluids between containers without gross spillage   (Cog1)

Materials:
- Paint pigment(s), & palette, thick & thin brushes (or can use vegetables !)

- Tooth brush cup, water, clothing protective bib
- White paper, lined A4 paper (and/or similar art/craft materials)

Procedure:
Level 1
1. Demonstrate a pigment palette, upon which are several kinds of beautiful colours; a brush cup inside of which is some water (or place on box-lid), and a brush.
2. Show now a blank white paper, and demonstrate the use of a thick brush, dipping firstly into one kind of coloured pigment, transferring it with the brush to the paper via a single horizontal stroke, then returning the brush to the cup in order to gently wash it; dipping it then again into a second coloured pigment from the palette to create a second painted line stroke; holding up the work for baby to clearly see.
3. Present now a protective bib for baby to wear, and the same/similar material set, offering help in dressing for painting, and to then hold/use the brush, and attempt painting strokes as per your previous demonstration.
4. Once completed each drawing/painting, invite baby to clean and return their brushes (and dirty water) to you, providing much praise and encouragement as they do so, then laying aside their work in a safe place to dry in the air.
   [NB: *Towards the end of the session, arrange for baby to present their work for the home's very own "Baby art gallery", to present and describe their new piece(s], and to also be available for interview/photography for lasting memory !!]*.

Level 2
1. Present now to baby a picture with hatched grid lines drawn on an A4 paper, and a (thinner) pen/brush.
2. Slowly demonstrate the drawing of a 'scaled' line image, using the grid lines as guides to length and relative position of each outline stroke of the object to be drawn – showing your result for baby to clearly see.
3. Invite baby to now attempt to draw/brush with the thin pen, dipping into the pigment, and then drawing/painting with it along the lined grids in order to imitate/replicate the drawn image/object, as just demonstrated.
4. Be sure to observe whether and how baby is able to freely draw/paint, praising baby all the while, and especially promptly when 'correctly' moving across the grid lines in an appropriate way, according the their own individual drawing ability level.
   [NB: Remember that the goal here is holding/manipulating the writing instrument, and imitation of writing/drawing activity – and NOT the artistic image quality that is of importance to determine here !].

Variations:
- Consider to provide images (as per level 2, step 2) for baby to place 'underneath' their own grid line papers, and to then 'trace' (rather than free-draw) a copy of that image onto their own paper (now on top of the sample drawing to copy trace), for baby's practice in mastering the handling of their writing/drawing implements, and in producing stroke lengths.
- Alternatively, provide baby with plain white cloth (which they may turn around, when affixed (by clothes pegs) to a board), inviting baby to then draw onto the plain white cloth (or even maybe to make a new T-shirt of their own unique design, though need fabric-washable paint!), rather than onto paper.

Additional thoughts/Activity Preparation/Lesson Planning Tips:
- Be sure to make use of old clothing/a protective bib (of whatever sort), and/or over-sleeves for baby to wear, which you may accept paint being spilt upon.
- *Especially observe baby's preferred/natural hand signals/postures used when handling/using the pens or brushes, the grasping and the drawing/painting articulation will likely be the same at first, and will need to change in their dexterity with increasing attention to drawing in a more detailed way*
- Encourage/help to guide baby in drawing only within the edges of the paper's surface, and along the grid lines (if any) [so preventing unwanted table-painting !]
- In order not to waste an entire paint-bottle's contents in a single session (if not using dry pigment), place a small portion of the pigment onto a plate, so allowing baby only to dip from the pigment plate, each different colour in a different 'pallette' location of the same plate
- Select only paint pigment which is certified child-safe, non-toxic and water-based, whenever possible.

G/A 22.8   A Place For Everything II"

Task description:
- Exploring the repositioning of a disordered array to replicate an example set.

Expected Milestone Achievements (EMAs):
- Organises toys/objects into recognisable patterns and symmetries   (F6)
- Spontaneously explores objects (e.g., shakes/bangs them together) (Cog2)
- Demonstrates frequent use of more than 50 single words   (Comms1)

Materials:
- Sound blocks, 6-picture-face 'cube puzzle' set.

Procedure:

Level 1
1. Demonstrate a sound block box, showing how that sound block may be placed together with others in an arrangement to form a 9/12/16-item sound block box set
2. Show and give to baby one block at a time, inviting them to them place it back into the set tray, one piece at a time, each time.
3. Present next 2-4+ boxes each time, placing the increasingly empty box set tray on the floor each time.
4. Invite baby to now help you to complete the tray with all its sound blocks once more, arranged so that no contents are visible when viewed from above.
5. Repeat step 4 such that ALL blocks now have their contents visible once placed back onto the tray.
6 As/when baby successfully contributes to the completion of the tray set, provide prompt praise and encouragement.

Level 2
1. Demonstrate now a tray of picture blocks (which need be placed in a certain order to form a single picture when viewed across all sides)
2-4 Repeat the level 1 procedure several times, using different picture completion requests and conformations each time.

Variations:
- Consider providing baby with x number of different sound block boxes or bricks, on each block's surface to which you have attach a different design/picture. Invite baby to now arrange the different sound block boxes, according to a particular pattern that you assign to each round (e.g., to show different trees, birds, people's faces, transport vehicles, stickers or toys, one on each side of each box).
- Ditto, upping the difficulty level by assigning different categories to each row of bricks to form the 9-block cube, or increasing the similarity of items belonging to the different categories.
- Ditto, *reducing* the difficulty level by using fewer blocks each time, or using simpler categories such as shape and colour alone (rather than complex pictures).

Additional thoughts/Game-Activity Preparation/Lesson Planning Tips:
- If no sound blocks or picture blocks be available in the home, simple 6-picture block sets may be built by sticking a different part of the picture to each of the 6 sides made up of a nine-cubes (of a building brick set), and simply cutting and affixing the paper's six pieces onto the different sides of the blocks, accordingly.
- Ditto, to create a picture of baby, once fully assembled the 'correct' way!
- *When attempting to rotate the blocks already placed upon the tray, note that for baby, the peripheral block box will be relatively easy for them to turn over, but the inner pieces will offer them much difficulty (at least initially). Provide baby sufficient time and encouragement, avoiding the temptation to assist, but instead waiting-out their frustrations, and observe the way(s) in which baby persists in attempting to solve this problem for themselves.*
- *If/when insisting upon giving baby guidance, and wishing to interact with baby during problem solving, simply use a pointing finger to assign a particular block for baby's attention and manipulation, inviting baby to carry out all of the manual manipulations, turning of blocks over and around, by themselves.*
- Pay close attention to baby's exposure to the sound block corners that they are holding, so helping avoid bumping of these corners into their own (or other's) face or glasses.
- Ditto, also preventing baby from throwing the blocks that they are holding – either down to the floor, or away from them, or as directed at a third person (for whatever reason).

Baby Milestones of Development (0-3 Yrs)

G/A 22.9   Fruit & Veggie Fishin'

Task description:
- Exploring the acquisition of objects by extending body position and manipulating tools.

Expected Milestone Achievements (EMAs):
- Negotiates stepping/climbing obstacles whilst shifting visual focus near/far distance.   [M21-G4]
- Jumps up and down freely, without floor contact (i.e., with both feet off the ground.   (G4)
- Places plug into water sink and/or threads large-holed beads onto string.   (F2)
- Keen to jump and/or move in coordination with others   (SP5)

Materials:
- Toy fruits and vegetables (tied/connected with stiff paper/wire loops)

- Smooth stick/ladle, large curved coat hanger, stepping stones (pathway).

Procedure:
Level 1
1. Demonstrate a river stepping stone pathway, inviting baby to come forward, and to sit somewhere inside the 'river', as if in/on a 'boat/rock'.
2. Show now a ladle/long-handled spoon, placed alongside the 'boat' in the river, and a variety of several (large-ish) paper-looped toy fruits and vegetables.
3. Demonstrate now the grasping of the ladle, and its use in inserting its long end through the loop attached to each toy fruit or vegetable, using it as a 'hook' to gather the target fruit back into the 'boat' like a 'freshly caught fruit fish' !
4. Present to baby now the ladle/long-handle spoon, having dispersed various toy fruits and vegetables around baby's boat (preferably beyond their arm's reach !).

5. Invite/guide baby to try inserting their ladle handle through the loops attached to the each of the 'fruits and vegetables fishes', and to thus draw their 'catch' into the 'boat' that they are seated in/on.
6. As/when baby succeeds in 'landing' their fishy fruits and vegetables via their ladle fishing rods, be sure to provide prompt praise and encouragements for their efforts each time.

Level 2
1. Repeat level 1, this time replacing the ladle with a large, round-edged plastic coat hangers, using the hanger hook, as a 'hook' to catch the 'fishy food' string loops.

Level 3
1. Increase the level of difficult further (if successful with levels 1-2), by using smaller loops and/or more flexible loops (of string/ribbon) which might require more motor skill in 'catching' a hold of them with the tool.

Variations:
- If baby is not so comfortable with 'catching' their 'fish' with loops (for whatever reason) consider using magnetic materials.
- Ditto, attaching adhesive tape (sticky-side facing outwards) to increase the likelihood of successful purchase in acquiring their 'fishy fruits' (if not too heavy, and especially helpful for the less coordinated baby, at least at first).

Additional thoughts/Game-Activity Preparation/Lesson Planning Tips:
- Provide for baby only such ladles as have thick, clear plastic/wooden handles, preferably one which is also clean, and brightly coloured, so attracting interest in its use.
- Ditto, the tool being used to have relatively smooth surfaces, without any edges likely to scratch baby's skin.
- As/when baby prepares to sit in their 'boat' fishing for fruits and vegetables, ensure that you remain nearby, so being available to aid in providing protection when negotiating the river's stepping stones in reaching their 'boat/rock', and helping prevent any injury which may otherwise have resulted from overbalancing due to any sudden changes in baby's center of gravity, and causing them to then topple over.

Baby Milestones of Development (0-3 Yrs)

G/A 22.10   Feed Me, Clothe Me, Please

Task description:
- Exploring the willingness and ability to self-dress/feed, and assist others in need.

Expected Milestone Achievements (EMAs):
- Manages large buttons/poppers on clothing (F1)
- Able to correctly point to, or touch, 7-10 own body parts (F3)
- Play feeds dolls or soft toys without significant spillage or smearing of face/body (SP4)
- Beginning to treat dolls/soft toys as if babies or friends (SP6)

Materials:
- Baby doll (already wearing clothes with buttons), another garment with buttons.

- Toy 'food plate', toy 'food', stickers.

Procedure:

Level 1
1. Place the toy 'food' within the sight of baby, as visible from a comfortable distance.
2. Invite baby to join with you, sitting face to face with each other.
3. Ask baby to hold the baby doll (or teddy bear) whose name might be <XXX> (where XXX is named) and to explore/play with it for a while. Next have the doll 'cry' in front of baby, informing baby that "'XXX' (baby doll) is hungry, so what might we do/what can we do to help ?"
4. Guide baby to next look around the room, and to find some 'toy food' with which to feed the 'toy' doll.
5. As/when baby succeeds with (pretend) feeding the baby doll, encourage the action by providing prompt praise and encouragement.

Level 2
1. Guide/invite baby to now 'go out and play', together with the baby doll/teddy.
2. Present a sticker for baby and provide exploration time. After some time, possibly detecting a pause in play interaction, imitate the sound of the baby doll saying, "Could you please help me place the sticker onto my nose…?"
3. Invite baby to next place stickers onto the corresponding body parts of the baby doll as per your instructions, saying, "…on nose", …"ears", …"belly", "…shoulders"…,' etc.,… each time.
4. As/when baby succeeds in placing the stickers onto the 'correct' body parts, provide encouragement with prompt praise and applause.

Level 3
1. Place the clothed baby doll/teddy on the floor, just short of baby's reach.
2. Demonstrate 'undoing' 1-2 buttons on a garment, the whole process being conducted clearly and slowly such that baby can (and does) easily observe the detailed actions of your finger and button movements.
3. Present now the baby doll to baby, inviting baby to 'undo' the buttons in the same way as you had just demonstrated.
4. As/when baby succeeds undoing all the buttons, provide prompt praise and encouragement as they do so.

Level 4
1. Present another (different) garment, also with buttons.
2. Place the new clothing on to the doll/teddy bear.
3. Demonstrate this time how to 'do-up' 1-2 buttons in a manner which allows baby to clearly and slowly observe all the detailed actions required in completing the task
4. Present now the baby doll to baby, asking baby to do-up the buttons as per your previous demonstration.
5. As/when baby succeed dealing with all the buttons, lead in providing baby with much prompt praise and encouragement.

Variations:
- L1: Consider increasing the level(s) of difficulty by enriching the kinds of toy food or even using real food (especially noting that better success may involve use of baby's own favourite or preferred foods.
- L1: With baby's increasing ability with handling the stickers, consider adjusting the difficulty by changing the verbal instructions used each time, e.g. "Please pass the watermelon to me, and then give the banana to the doll".
- L1: The distance between baby and the toy food could be increased further, but should at no time be placed outwith baby's immediate line of sight. … Unless, considering to deliberately hide/cover the toy foods in front of baby, for baby to reveal/find at a later time !
- L3-4: Instead of using the baby doll/teddy bear (and doll clothing), consider to use your own or baby's own clothing – if made with relatively large fitting buttons and eyes/holes/loops for baby to be able to manipulate relatively easily.

Additional Thoughts/Game-Activity Preparation/Lesson Planning Tips:
- *Be sure to carefully observe baby's performance, throughout the activity, the goal being the manual manipulation and dexterity skill in coordinating the finger muscles, and not necessarily the successful securing/release of all the clothing button's per se !*
- As baby does-up/undoes buttons during the process, be sure to provide enough time, waiting patiently without interrupting baby as they struggle with their (possibly) new manual task(s), each time (and especially so, at first).
- *As baby succeeds with doing something new/difficult, it is important to share their success by providing prompt praise and encouragement.*
- With increasing success, continue to adjust the level(s) of difficulty of the activity according to baby's increasing abilities.

G/A 22.11   I Know What's In My Mouth !

Task description:
- Exploring and talking about the mouth (and its contents !).

Expected Milestone Achievements (EMAs):
- Opens and closes mouth when asked to do so   [M21-Comms3]
- Attempts to clean own teeth, given equipment (and help) to do so   (SP1)
- Transfers fluids between containers without gross spillage   (Cog1)
- Requests names for new or unfamiliar 'found' objects   (Cog4)
- Asks to be told the names of new or unfamiliar objects   (Comms6)

Materials:
- Hand mirror, soft tissue paper, tray

- Familiar candy, or preferred *real* fruit/vegetable foods.

Procedure:
Level 1
1. Demonstrate a mirror, then, slowly opening your own mouth, breath gently onto the mirror's surface, send out an "Haaaaaaarh" sound, as your breath condenses on the mirror surface, for baby to clearly see.
2. Demonstrate the effect again, wiping the condensation away with soft tissue paper, this time closely showing baby how you (or they) may then also use a finger to draw a doodle on the mirror when condensing your breath each time on its surface !
3. Invite baby to now come closer and to open their mouth in order to breathe out and 'steam up' the mirror as per your demonstration, allowing them to closely observe the moist breath (steam) condensing effect.
4. Present now the mirror and tissue paper for baby to explore, inviting baby to again try causing the same effect for themselves.
5. As/when baby succeeds to achieve this, provide prompt praise, and encouragement with laughter and curiosity each time.

Level 2

1. Present again now the (cleaned) mirror and fresh tissue paper (to wipe away any condensed breath each time during this activity), together with small pieces of different food stuffs on a tray.
2. Invite baby to attempt feeding him/herself the fruit/candy (taking off any wrapper as necessary), and to then place it into their mouth to eat.
3. After a short while (and before swallowing), invite baby to look at their reflection in the mirror, to open their mouth, and to observe the position/state of the partially-chewed/sucked candy inside the buccal cavity.
4. Guide baby to now close their mouths once more, and to continue chewing/sucking until it has all gone/or is swallowed – then to look once more into their mouths to see if it is still there (or what else they may notice to be different (colour change, more/less moisture, dirty teeth !, etc.).
5. Continue to provide baby with different foodstuffs (e.g., small biscuit, fruit, vegetable), once more repeating steps 2-4 in exploring the effects of their processes of chewing and sucking the different foods, using the mirror each time.

Level 3

1. If unwilling to eat/chew at this time, continue explorations by inviting the simple counting of dentures (teeth) and/or inviting baby to name the contents of their mouth: their teeth, tongue, gums, tonsils, etc (or whatever baby believes they may be able to see 'in there' !!).
2. Enhance any discussions by doing the same yourself, then sharing your own observations and verbal descriptions of what 'you' can see in your own mouth also !

Level 4

1. Complete the session(s) with baby attempting to clean their own teeth after last eating – providing a familiar (or new !) brush designed for baby to use – then taking a final look into their now-sparkly-cleaned mouth ! (?).

Variations:

- Invite baby to imitate/follow example lip/mouth shapes in order to make certain sound productions, for practice.
- Ditto, closing the mouth tight to blow up the cheeks, then deflating them slowly, making a "breaking wind" whoosh sound.
- *Consider to frequently 'clean your teeth' together with baby, so instilling a regular habit of cleaning and personal care/hygiene management.*

Additional thoughts/Game-Activity Preparation/Lesson Planning Tips:

- Be sure to initiate frequent cleaning and disinfection of baby's mirror, whilst discouraging baby from licking or 'kissing' the mirror surface, providing tissue paper to promptly wipe away any exhaled breath and/or saliva.
- Be careful to also observe baby's health status before offering food stuffs, avoiding any know materials which may produce any allergenic effect for baby.

G/A 21.12   Passing the Ball with Me

Task description:
- Exploring the movement of toys, through cooperative play.

Expected Milestone Achievements (EMAs):
- Jumps up and down freely, without floor contact (i.e., with both feet off the ground).   (G4)
- Kicks ball with swinging leg and/or foot (e.g., more flexible at hip, knee, & ankle).   (G6)
- Keen to jump and/or move in coordination with others   (SP5)

Materials:
- Small balls, inflatable balloon (inside of which is a bell)

- Bath towel, lightweight bed sheet.

Procedure:
Level 1
1. Demonstrate a bath towel placed flat on the floor, placing upon it an inflated balloon, inside of which you have placed a small bell.
2. Holding one side of the bath towel each (one hand each taking a different corner of one end), the other end secured to solid surface, slowly raise the arms high and low in order to rock the balloon to-and-fro (and more aggressively to cause it to be thrown into the air), for baby to clearly see.
3. Invite/guide next baby to gently rock the bath towel with you together (each of you now holding the two corners of each end), in order to cause the balloon to bounce, the bell ringing softly as it does so [NB: Be sure to allow for the difference in your & baby's different arm lengths - *baby will likely use whole body jumping movements to make the suspended objects move – rather than simply lowering/raising their arms – at least at first ?*].

Level 2
1. Demonstrate now a lightweight bed sheet, inviting baby to grab and hold onto the sides of the sheet (standing along its two side lengths), and to gently rock the sheet up and down together with you.
2. Throw now an inflated balloon onto the sheet's surface (as previously with the towel), to then be bounced up and down upon the sheet, as it follows your and baby's combined waving energy, causing it to bounce and jingle about.
3. Introduce now additional small balls (a few at a time), as they continue to also bounce up and down as they fall upon the sheet surface, as baby becomes increasingly excited, and continues to rock the sheet up and down.
4. Repeat steps 1-3 several times, increasing the size of the sheet held each time (by gradually unfolding it, and/or inviting others if such be present in the home at the time) to participate in waving the sheet up and down each time.
5. Pay close attention to observing whether baby draws the sheet up or down upon their own initiative/rhythm, and/or invites you (or other person) to also draw the sheet in any particular way(s) [either verbally or according to some gesture/facial expression/eye contact they may be making from time to time].

Variations:
- Holding the sheet/towel between yourself and baby him/herself, encourage by demonstration/turn-taking how to cause the balloon/balls to move up and down on the sheet by gently swinging the leg forward, and using a kicking action against the underside of the towel/sheet, to make the bell(s) jingle as you do so.

Additional thoughts/Game-Activity Preparation/Lesson Planning Tips:
- As baby may become very excited when rocking the bath towel, *take care in observing whether they do indeed even notice the ball or attempt to continue causing the ball to deliberately move after a while ! [Baby may instead be simply enjoying the process of rocking the towel/sheet up and down together with you/others, and not actually notice their own effects upon the balloon/balls' movement !].*
- Be sure to also remember that, when rocking the towel/sheet together with baby, there will be some considerable effect caused solely by the height difference between you as 'large' adult and little baby, and thus possibly cause injury to baby's arms if being stretched by the much stronger adult's (also excited) play actions !!
- After several warm-up trials, both yourself and baby may wish to take a break and cool down a while. If so doing, wait for baby's clear signal/ request (invitation) to continue on their own initiative in order to resume playing together once more; You may also consider to guide baby in inviting others (if present) to join in with their playing together (but do not push a clearly tired baby to continue if showing fatigue and/or resistance to extending their participation and fun time engaged in this activity.

ψ

– 15 –

Baby Milestones of Development

(With 100+ Fun Activities to Help Demonstrate Them)

[Age 23 Months]

ψ

Baby Milestones of Development (0-3 Yrs)

Expected Milestone Achievements
Age = 23 Months

[Key: e.g., 5 = Game No. 23.5]

Gross Motor

• Balances own weight whilst walking along a narrow path/line	1, 4, 8, 10
• Walks/runs along uneven textured surface/path without stumbling/falling	1, 4
• Stands on 'tip-toe' when look up to see what is outside a window, or on a table	6
• Jumps freely (but still with a skip-like gait ?)	5, 6
• Ascends and descends stairs, in novel places, and without help	1, 3, 5
• Throws or kicks a ball at a target with appropriate force	

Fine Motor

• Catches or makes contact with a moving balloon in the air	4, 6
• Enjoys playing with buttons and control knobs	
• Appropriately grasps/holds parts of wheeled toys when pushing/pulling them along	8
• Pencil/pen grip becoming increasingly stereotyped (same grip each time used)	9
• Imitates drawing of multiple-line images	
• Draws with increasingly fluent strokes/movement	9

Cognitive

• Plays with familiar objects in unfamiliar ways (stacking food)	9, 12, [M24.23.7]
• Sorts familiar items by colour, shape *and* size	2, 7, 8, 9, 12
• Gathers objects together according to their similarities (other than colour & size)	2, 7, 11, 12
• Spontaneously turns novel containers, to release contents	8, 11
• Increasingly interested to manipulate/catch moving objects	4, 5, 6
• Seeks/finds small chair or box to stand on in order to obtain object out of reach	6

Communication

• Increasingly sensitive to different vowel sounds, and their meanings	
• Responds correctly when asked "Where is xxx ?" in pictures	
• Understands references being made to unseen objects	3, 5, 10
• Frequently makes multiple syllable responses to questions (e.g., "It is here, mama")	7
• Produces reliably interpretable multi-word utterances	2
• Uses 1st and 2nd person pronouns (I, me, yours, mine)	11

Socio-Personal

• Reaches for someone's hand when 'ready' or about to initiate walking	4, 10
• Predicts location of non-visible object moving behind a screen (or other obstruction)	
• Increasingly willing to explore interactions with novel toy(s)	8, 12
• Excited to repeat (predictable) turn-taking games with others	1, 7
• Plays in front of a mirror with more subtle facial expressions and sounds	
• Enjoys recognition in/of familiar playmates	10

G/A 23.1 Moving Along, Rough or Smooth !

Task description:
- Exploring and maintaining balance when negotiating a path with uneven surface.

Expected Milestone Achievements (EMAs):
- Balances own weight whilst walking along a narrow path/line (G1)
- Walks/runs along uneven textured surface/path without stumbling/falling (G2)
- Ascends and descends stairs, in novel places, and without help (G5)
- Reaches for someone's hand when 'ready' or about to initiate walking (SP1)
- Excited to repeat (predictable) turn-taking games with others (SP4)

Materials:
- Steppingstones, cushions/floor markings (to form pathway).

Procedure:
Level 1
1. Establish a path across the length of the room to include the 'river stepping stones' (using available objects, or by marking the floor), demonstrating how to negotiate the river stones in order to arrive at the far side of the room, 'without touching the water' (floor), for baby to clearly see.
2. Invite baby to come forward to join you (and anyone else who might be present, and to form a single line, one behind the other), and to then take their turn in walking along the 'river's stones', from one side of the 'river' to the other side, with baby using you as support, as/when necessary.
3. As/when baby smoothly travel across the river 'stones', WITHOUT falling down, be sure to provide prompt praise and encouragement, as they to do so.

Level 2
1. Establish an undulating or/wavy line path across the length of the room using similar materials (i.e., not a straight-line path, clearly demonstrating how to negotiate the new path in order to arrive at the far side of the room, but again, 'without touching the water (floor)', for baby to clearly see.
2. Repeat the level 1 steps 2-3, until baby is confident with their achievement(s).

Level 3
1. Following success with levels 1-2, establish now a novel path across the length of the room, this time using a variety of large cushioned materials, clearly demonstrating how to negotiate the path in order to arrive at the far side of the room, again 'without touching the floor'.
2. Continue as before, allowing baby to make use of your physical support only as really necessary, in order to maintain their upright posture and balance each time, adding complexity and variation of materials being used, with increasing success across multiple rounds according to baby's interest and increasing ability level(s).

Variations:
- With success and increasing expertise, consider to combine the 'river stones', and other cushioned pieces, in order to establish a single, longer winding path (possibly double back several times or with box steps up and down ?).
- Ditto, inviting baby to deliver a toy(s) from one side of the room to some other location, thus occupying their hands/arms, and requiring/exercising increasing balancing skills as they do so.
- Use a wider variety of large-scale cushioning shapes and balance-posture-change opportunities, so building a larger range of increasingly steeper walkways and obstacles as available furnishings, introducing 'found objects' for baby to collect, as imagination allows,

Additional thoughts/Game-Activity Preparation/Lesson Planning Tips:
- During baby's uneven surface walking, ensure that you avoid the temptation to support baby's weight by the arm (in aiding their balance), but instead merely encourage baby to walk along alone, even if baby shows poor grasp of the balancing required to remain upright; NB: *it is critical that baby must learn how to cope independently when imbalanced, and understand the need, and* how *to protect him/herself, without falling down to the floor whilst negotiating an uneven surface.*
- When baby succeeds to negotiate their way across increasingly longer, and relatively more rugged pathways, provide especial encouragement, so allowing baby to feel/enjoy their success with pleasure, thus fiercely competing with their earlier selves, as they successfully compete with increasing confidence (for the same reason). However, *do try to resist the temptation to up the difficulty levels too soon after each new achievement success, or in too larger increments each time).*

G/A 23.2   Colour-Me Petals

Task description:
- Exploring item categorisations according to their surface colours.

Expected Milestone Achievements (EMAs):
- Sorts familiar items by colour, shape *and* size   (Cog2)
- Gathers objects together according to their similarities (*other than*   (Cog3)
  by colour and size).
- Produces reliably interpretable multi-word utterances   (Comms5)

Materials:
[Produce pictures/images via magazine cutouts, or simple marker-pen drawings of your own]
- Coloured flower pictures [on an A4 paper, arrange four rows of different kinds of flowers (to show at least two types of flower)].
- Flower pot picture [on an A4 paper - in six different colours, with a stem, *but which do not have any flowers/petals attached*].
- Flower pot picture [on an A4 paper – as all black/brown, with a stem of a different colour, which do not have any flowers/petals attached, *but DOES match the colour of at least one of the flower examples to be used*].
- Adhesive tape/non-toxic baby-friendly glue or paste.

Procedure:
Level 1
1. Demonstrate the A4 paper showing four rows of flowers, presenting baby with two flowers, e.g., the first row may contain two chrysanthemums, the second row roses, the third row sunflowers, a fourth row just green foliage (leaves).
2. Demonstrate now the same multiple-flower collection, placed on the floor or table, and choose the differently coloured flowers to paste on to the correspondingly coloured pot, with black stem to form now a pretty flowering branch.
3. Present the same/similar A4 paper pots & stems to baby, thus also making a particular colour to be assigned to them for the round.
4. Invite baby to next select, and then use the differently coloured flowers to paste each according to the given flower colour information (as previously assigned), each successively added as correspond to each matching pot and flower's colour.
5. As/when baby creates their new patterns according to the colours assigned to be matched, and pastes the flowers to make a newly flowering branch, provide prompt praise and encouragement (considering also to mount a display/gallery of baby's pictures somewhere uncluttered in the room/home, for all to later see).

Level 2
1. Demonstrate the initial same four rows of flowers, baby again to be presented with two flowers, as before.
2. Repeat the level 1 steps, again choosing different coloured flowers for baby to paste/stick on to the corresponding pots, but this time also with the selection of matching-coloured stems to form the flowering branch, but in otherwise identical pots (then adding these new pictures to baby's display/gallery of new pictures).
3. Whilst engaged in the task, encourage baby to talk about what they are doing, request items out of reach, show/display their progress, etc, providing prompt expressions of interest, praise and encouragement every time they do so.

Variations:
- Provide for baby A4 paper, showing multiple-potted flower sets (having trunks. stems and branches, but no flowers), each potted flower's trunk/stem and branches' colour NOT the same. Present to baby the coloured flowers, inviting baby to select flowers and paste them on each time matching with the colours according to the trunk/stem/branch' colouration, to form a beautiful garden (the final paper garden when completed will appear to be filled with differently coloured flowers to add to your display gallery !).

Additional thoughts/Activity Preparation/Lesson Planning Tips:
- When providing baby with corresponding twig or trunk and branch colour choices, be sure to offer twigs, trunks and branches of sufficient thickness, with colours appropriately clear, for baby to be able to easily distinguish between them.
- Ensure that the flowers and A4 paper carry easily reusable adhesive fixing, such that baby may easily repaste/refix, or to remove (to make corrections), and may thus use them again as necessary (use of large post-it stickers might be another option).
- Likewise ensure that the trunk, branch or twig colours do indeed correspond to the flower colours issued, so avoiding the colour deviations being too different, and thus confusing/frustrating baby.

G/A 23.3   Up & Down We Go

Task description:
- Exploring ascending and descending staircases with minimal assistance.

Expected Milestone Achievements (EMAs):
- Ascends and descends stairs, in novel places, and without help   (G5)
- Understands references being made to unseen objects   [cf Var3] (Comms3)

Materials:
- Real staircase (as home environment allows), ...OR...

- ... use large cushions, cases/boxes (to build one !)....

Procedure:
Level 1 [Use a real staircase if available in/close to/immediately outside the home]
1. Situate large-scale cushioning with ascending and descending ramps/steps, placed in the centre/side of the room, BUT *not resting against the wall/furniture*.
5. Shadowing, but not supporting baby by the arm(s), gently encourage baby to attempt making both the uphill (from the floor) and downhill portions (back to the floor) of the setup, paying special attention to working towards maintaining independence (with increasing comfort and confidence) with the descending parts.
6. As/when baby is able to climb alone, and especially turn/descend alone, provide prompt praise and encouragement as they do so – adding additional steps with baby's increasing success and confidence.

Level 2
1. Repeat level 1, this time encouraging baby to descend backwards (this may require offering additional arm support ?) – ideally by placing the stairway besides the wall, rather than baby relying upon your help/support.

Variations:
- Be sure to set up the stairs for level 2 very close to/right up against the wall (when using constructed firm cushions/cases/box sets), to build 'longer' stairways in the room.
- If struggling to maintain an upright posture for very long when either ascending of descending, *be 'on hand' at all times as baby is climbing up or down the 'stairs', holding baby by one hand only* (if at all), offering support *only* as baby is imminently about to take a fall (and not guiding them forwards/backwards at any time) – *else baby will NOT learn the increasingly coordinated muscle and postural adaptation skills required to maintain their independent balance control.*
- Consider to make creative/adventurous use of any real staircase(s) situated either within, or nearby/outside the home – so enhancing baby's learning opportunities and developing interest/expertise with independent sensory-motor control (e.g., inviting baby to "go see what is at the top" [having hidden a toy on the highest stair, perhaps later not visible from below]).

Additional thoughts/Activity Preparation/Lesson Planning Tips:
- When NOT really needing you to support them by the arm (in order to maintain their balance), merely stand by baby's side, providing only safekeeping and security (and *especially so when reversing down* "the stairs").
- For level 2 especially, situate yourself with outstretched arms ready to provide baby protection, and also a heightened sense of security, whilst avoiding the temptation to take the initiative in making body contact with baby unless falling, or to do so only if/when baby is obviously "stuck", and unable to climb back down his/herself independently, and thus requiring you to render support and assistance in order to continue at all.
- If the latter is the only problem, consider installing some visible rewards at the place where baby will arrive following their successful stairs descent (a preferred toy ?). This will increase the stimulation and motivation for baby to make their way back down the stairs to the floor once more, whilst simultaneously providing a clear signal of achievement, reward and encouragement.

G/A 23.4   Walking the Walk !

Task description:
- Exploring coordinated balance whilst traversing a narrow path.

Expected Milestone Achievements (EMAs):
- Balances own weight whilst walking along a narrow path/line   (G1)
- Walks/runs along uneven textured surface/path without stumbling/falling   (G2)
- Catches or makes contact with a moving balloon in the air   (F1)
- Increasingly interested to manipulate/catch moving objects   (Cog5)
- Reaches for someone's hand when 'ready' or about to initiate walking   (SP1)

Materials:
- Uneven raised pathway on the floor (marked or physical object(s)), balloon.

Procedure:

Level 1
1. Build a relatively narrow parallel track pathway (like a railroad) along the floor, between each track a distance suitable for baby's feet/leg size, when standing with one foot on each 'track'.
2. Demonstrate the use of both feet (one on each track), walking in this manner (with each foot stepping on the same roadway each pace), from the beginning of the roadway until arriving at the end point.
3. Invite baby to now walk (one at a time on the tracks behind/in front of you), according to your request, from the beginning to the end point.
4. As/when baby can use both of their feet to successfully generate a coordinated walk, and also maintains their balance without falling down, provide prompt praise and rewards (possibly using a preferred/attractive toy at the end to provide added motivation).

Level 2
1. Following some success with L1, introduce the novelty of baby coordinating their timing of arrival at certain point(s) along the pathway by encouraging them to catch/touch a balloon that you have released in the air at some point along the baby's pathway towards the end point.

Variations:
- Consider to increase the distance between the roadway tracks with increasing success and ability level achievement.
- Ditto their height above the ground, though be sure to do so only for the most competent of babies at this age/stage !

Baby Milestones of Development (0-3 Yrs)

Additional thoughts/Game-Activity Preparation/Lesson Planning Tips:
- Most babies at this age/stage should NOT really need you to support them physically (solely in order to maintain their balance), but it is OK for you to stand at their side (but not in front or behind as this would distract their visual attention from observing their feet/roadway surfaces !), so helping provide a safer/softer landing if tending to fall down.
- If baby is resistant to traversing the tracks, consider placing some visible reward(s) at the end of the roadway(say, a preferred food/toy), so increasing the stimulation and motivation for baby to make their way to the very end of the roadway/track each time.

G/A 23.5   Aerial Targets

Task description:
- Exploring the throwing of objects towards a given target location.

Expected Milestone Achievements (EMAs):
- Throws or kicks a ball at a target with appropriate force   (G6)
- Jumps freely (but still with a skip like gait ?)   (C4)
- Increasingly interested to manipulate/catch moving objects   (Cog5)
- Understands references being made to unseen objects   (Comms3)

Materials:
- Flying saucer/Frisbee, card or thin plastic plate/large coaster or square foam block floor mat, hula hoops/large boxes/containers (as thrown-object targets).

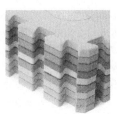

Procedure:

Level 1
1. Demonstrate a flying saucer/paper plate, standing on one side of the room, and gently throw/toss the flying saucer/plate, in order to glide it low across the room for baby to clearly see.
2. Present now the same/similar flying saucer/plate to baby, assigning baby the task of standing, and then throwing their flying saucers/plates from a specially region marked on the floor (can use as standing in a hula hoop, in a safety-conscious way).
3. Invite/guide baby to throw the flying saucer/plate in a suitable way, and with the strength required to reach a region/box/basket setup at some distance in the room (or perhaps marked in some other way as a target area on the floor ?).
4. Invite baby to stand next in the hula hoop, facing the room at one side, and to then throw their flying saucer plate, observing/recording how far it travels each time (being cautious to have first removed/displaced any damageable objects/ornaments should they be accidentally hit/knocked down !).

Baby Milestones of Development (0-3 Yrs)

5. As/when baby is able to launch their flying saucer/plate beyond a certain distance, be sure to provide prompt praise and encouraging applause *[in some circumstances/housing spaces, it may be preferable to conduct this task in a hallway, of even outside the home ?]*

Level 2
1. With baby showing good release and throwing (at least launching their Flying Saucers in their intended direction ?), arrange now a second area (hula hoop 2) standing in the centre of the floor, held upright or leaning against a furniture.
2. Starting in a standing position at a distance corresponding to baby's ability, demonstrate standing in the 'throwing position' area (hula hoop 1), gently throw/launch the flying saucer plate in a direction causing it to 'fly' *through* the open set upright hula hoop circle, to the other side (if no hoop be available, use something constructed from/suspended from a coat hanger, or use a sheet over two chairs to make a tennis net OVER which their IFO is to be sent/flown each time ?).
3. Assign baby to stand facing you, opposite the same vertical hula hoop/'net' that you passed your flight through/over, standing in turn in their own hula hoop on the floor, in turn to throw their flying saucer/plate back to you, encouraging baby to throw their flying saucer/plate through the vertical hula hoop circle also (for you to then collect and pass back each time).
4. As/when baby succeeds to pass it through/over the hoop/net each time (or at least releases it to fly in the appropriate direction, with appropriate force), provide prompt praise and applause together.
5. Replace yourself in the activity (if another person be present), by later inviting them to now continue flying the UFO back and forth to baby, for as long as baby's motivation and interest allows.

Variations:
- If more than 2-3 persons be present in the home at the time of this activity, invite them to throw/pass their flying saucer/plate between each other, possibly with baby at a central location amongst 2-3 other participants.
- Ditto, considering to apply the same equipment to hold a 'Home-Baby World Cup' Hoop Penalty throw-off ! (using multiple paper plates as UFO/frisbies) – the hoop circle serving as the 'goal' as it passes through or using a large box/container to collect them as they fall, changing the distance/location of the goal with baby's increasing throwing accuracy with time.
- Ditto, (using a soft inflatable ball) – the hoop circle serving as the 'goal' as baby takes turns with you to kick the ball through it.

Additional thoughts/Game-Activity Preparation/Lesson Planning Tips:
- Be sure to make an effort to arrange baby's throwing of their flying saucer/plate's launching positions and directions so as to avoid the hitting of other persons, and/or valuable/breakable objects – so avoiding sustaining of any injuries, or accidents (as far as it may be possible to predict them !).
- Ditto, including the closure/blockage of any open windows, if located on an upper floor/storey of a high-rise building !
- Make sure that you are always providing [a], realistic goal(s) for baby to establish and will attempt each time, adjusting the distance(s) according to baby's developing ability each time, so ensuring that baby remains motivated to participate, whilst engaging with continuing hope and confidence, with an enhancing sense of achievement.
- *If still struggling with saucer/plate release timing, throwing of the flying saucer and its aerial movement will also be uncontrolled, so be sure to offer baby special attention and additional guidance* (with patience).

G/A 23.6   Out of the Air !

Task description:
- Exploring the manual grasping of airborne movable objects.

Expected Milestone Achievements (EMAs):
- Jumps freely (but still with a skip-like gait ?)   (G4
- Stands on 'tip-toe' when looks up to see what is outside a window   (G3)
  or on a table
- Catches or makes contact with a moving balloon in the air   (F1)
- Increasingly interested to manipulate/catch moving objects   (Cog5)
- Seeks/finds small chair or box to stand on and obtain object out of reach (Cog6)

Materials:
- Inflated Helium (He) balloon, coloured ribbons, soft animal toys (or similarly attractive light-weighted objects), light inflatable ball, small chair/step.

Procedure:
Level 1
1. Attach to a prepared Helium-filled balloon a coloured ribbon, to the other end of which is attached a soft animal toy, sufficiently light to allow the balloon to continue to float in the air (at a height/position which requires baby to jump up into the air in order to catch it).
2. Position the balloon to be loose in the room at a central location.
3. Invite now baby go come forward and to attempt to grasp the fluttering balloon, in order to gain the animal toy, when specifically referred to, each time.
4. As/when baby succeeds in attaining the animal toy, provide prompt praise and encouragement as they have done so.

Level 2
1. Attach this time to the same Helium balloon a much longer coloured ribbon, the balloon reaching to a height placing them against the ceiling, the coloured ribbon hanging in the air just above baby's head (a small chair/step nearby).
2. Invite baby to now attempt to bring down the balloon.

3. Encourage baby to jump up and to catch the coloured ribbon, then to begin gathering it around their hand(s), so causing the balloon to come closer and closer to them, until they may finally grasp it with both their hands.
4 As/when baby retrieves the balloon in this way, encourage/provide prompt praise taking back the balloon for further rounds (after allowing some time for baby to 'play' with their rewarding acquisitions, after 'working' so hard to achieve it !).

Variations:
- Present to baby a light inflatable ball, inviting baby to be separated by a certain distance (according to baby's strength/ability), and to carry out 'to-and-fro' throwing and catching of the ball between you, as baby stretches out their arms in order to catch the ball each time, then throwing it back to you.
- Consider blowing bubbles in the room, inviting baby to attempt grasping the bubbles as they pass over their heads (you may wish this to be done only over/inside the bath, or even outside the home, so avoiding greasy blobs forming on the room furnishings).

Additional thoughts/Game-Activity Preparation/Lesson Planning Tips:
- As/when baby successfully selects and retrieves the toy animal referred to, help baby to remove the ribbon from the animal toy once taken down, so as to prevent baby grasping and bursting the balloon with their finger nails (which will cause them sudden surprise, and possibly a fearful/tearful reaction).
- Likewise choose only a high quality strength cartoon balloon from the market for baby to attempt capturing; do not use ordinary air-filled balloons for this task, so better avoiding balloon bursting, and baby's possible injury.
- Once the activities have ended for your planned session, present the balloon to baby, allowing them to keep the balloon in the family home for free play (or if also entertaining other visiting babies, to present it as a gift to be taken away with them [if this be welcome, and wishing to do so]).

G/A 23.7   Back Where It Was Before

Task description:
- Exploring the reassembly of given arrays of separate object pieces.

Expected Milestone Achievements (EMAs):
- Sorts familiar items by colour, shape *and* size   (Cog2)
- Gathers objects together according to their similarities (*other than*   (Cog3)
  colour and size)
- Frequently makes multiple syllable responses to questions (e.g.,   (Comms4)
  "It is here, mama")
- Excited to repeat (predictable) turn-taking games with others   (SP4)

Materials:
- Animal cards and mosaic backing (magnetic/felt/Velcro)
- Block picture puzzles, animal/object shape sorting board.

Procedure:

Level 1
1. Slowly demonstrate the piecing together of a disassembled animal mosaic plate/shape-picture sorting set, or simple puzzle.
2. Place together at first, e.g., an animal/shape' piece (onto the board), for baby to clearly see and explore, as all mounted in their 'correct' positions.
3. Present now the same disassembled materials, for baby to replicate your demonstration.
4. Invite baby to reassemble the complete set according to the material set's pieces as chosen (one piece at a time), baby given pieces which correspond to the remaining 'correct' spaces for placing additional pieces each time.
5. As/when baby succeeds with 'correctly' placing their given new piece into its appropriate position each time, provide prompt praise and encouragement.

Level 2
1. Present now the empty template to baby, together with 2-3 of the accompanying separated pieces (e.g., two animals/shapes).
2. Invite baby to now reassemble their set pieces according to the template's cut-out shaped spaces, their choices to correspond with the 'correct' spaces for placing each of the pieces given.
3. As/when baby succeeds with 'correctly' placing their given pieces into their positions into the template, provide prompt praise and applause.
4. Repeat steps 1-3, presenting baby with increasing numbers and kinds of matching pieces each time (until finally 'handling'/receiving/sorting *all* pieces at once).

Level 3
1-4. With increasing success, repeat level 2, this time presenting baby with increasing numbers and kinds of matching *and non-matching* distractor pieces to select from each time for reassembly. [NB: using pieces from other puzzles as distractors].

Variations:
- Provide baby with a pile of several kinds of model toy, then invite baby to select one of them according to a (maybe unique ?) characteristic feature which describes one/some of them, requesting baby to then seek for the corresponding match from the array given. E.g., request of baby, "Please give to me the yellow toy", "…the soft toy", "… A toy which has eye's, please", "… One that is made of wood, please", and so forth. As/when baby selects their 'instruction-matching' toy, encourage baby to point out also any others which may have the same feature(s), providing prompt enthusiastic praise for baby if simultaneously able to demonstrate this also.
- Ditto, with baby taking turns with you to sort ONE item from the SAME toy set, into one of a number of baskets labelled/arranged to hold differently sized, shaped or coloured materials, different kinds of toy, etc,… on different rounds.

Additional thoughts/Game-Activity Preparation/Lesson Planning Tips:
- Be sure to provides a good mix of animal/object picture pieces for baby, so arranging more/less obvious discrimination difficulty by shape/colour differences, according to baby's current and developing ability level(s).
- NB: Even when baby has chosen the 'correct' piece/block to put into the template/array, sometimes they will resist the need to rotate/adjust their orientation in order to be well fit into their 'correct' physical spaces, and thus baby may be very quick to determine that they have 'incorrectly' selected the 'wrong piece' – and to then continue to search for a new match (actually rejecting the 'correctly' chosen one, because it 'doesn't seem to fit with other pieces'); Be ready to guide baby in exploring the rotation of any/all chosen pieces in an attempt to assemble them using a variety of different positions (and especially so when selecting the 'correct' pieces first time !).

G/A 23.8 Transfer Vessels

Task description:
- Exploring the need to use different methods to handle different vessels in order to transfer the same materials between them.

Expected Milestone Achievements (EMAs):
- Balances own weight whilst walking along a narrow path/line (G1)
- Sorts familiar items by colour, shape *and* size (Cog2)
- Spontaneously turns novel containers, to release contents (Cog4)
- Appropriately grasps/holds parts of wheeled toys when pushing/pulling them along (F3)
- Increasingly willing to explore interactions with novel toy(s) (SP3)

Materials:
- Handled buckets (to have handles for baby to carry/manipulate them)/bags
- Boxes, small balls (or rolled-up socks), toy fruits or vegetables

- Wheeled vehicle (baby-buggy/walker/stroller).

Procedure:
Level 1
1. Set up a 'pool' of many small balls at one side of the room, at the other arranging a baby stroller, buggy (or similar wheeled vehicle suitable for transporting the balls), between which is a clearly defined pathway for baby to travel along.
2. Introduce baby to the footpath, presenting also to baby an empty box.
3. Invite baby to now stand at the 'pool side' and to begin manually loading small balls into their box, and to then carry it (now with its loaded balls) along the footpath to the wheeled vehicle, and then to load their balls onto the wheeled vehicle (either as a box, or by pouring their balls from their box, and into some other vessel on/in the wheeled vehicle awaiting them.

3   Carefully observe *how* baby elects to then handle their box/hold their box whilst pouring its balls into another/vehicle.
4   As/when baby successfully transfers many small balls into their vehicle, without spilling too many of them onto the floor each time, invite baby to then sit inside/on/push their wheeled vehicle along the pathway back to their starting position, in order to play with their successfully shipped small balls as a reward.

Level 2
1-6 Repeat level 1, this time requiring baby to carry their balls/fruits/vegetables from the 'pool' to the vehicle using a small handled bucket/basket/bag of different kinds each time.

Variations:
- With level 2 success, consider providing baby with two handled-buckets/bags to load and carry (not too large !), inviting baby to simultaneously use their two different hands to carry their two buckets (one in each hand) along their pathway, and to then again pour their balls into their vehicles.
- For level 1 consider to add the dimension of colour – e.g., *requiring* baby to use ONLY the same coloured/colour-marked boxes to select/convey balls/socks of the same colour along the pathway each time.

Additional thoughts/Game-Activity Preparation/Lesson Planning Tips:
- As different babies will move along the pathway with their box/bag of balls in rather different (possibly idiosyncratic) ways, be sure to pay close attention to observing how baby especially does this (and *there is NO standard or 'correct' way)*: E.g., they may appear more/less concerned about ball spillage, or not, or maybe it will be more important perhaps for them to be more concerned with *how* to travel the pathway without falling over, keen to reach their vehicle without hitting it before releasing their balls, and so forth.
- *Likewise, different babies will choose to carry their bucket(s) of balls in possibly very different ways, some will use a single-handed grip, some using both hands in a coordinated way, others simply (at least at first) demanding that "Mummy do it !", etc,..... Regardless of this, they will certainly have to use quite a different technique to pour their balls from the bucket (if still holding it by its handle), relative to the box pouring technique that they had most likely used earlier.*

Baby Milestones of Development (0-3 Yrs)

G/A 23.9   Animal Dress Up !

Task description:
- Exploring the use of unfamiliar materials to construct familiar object features.

Expected Milestone Achievements (EMAs):
- Pencil/pen grip becoming increasingly stereotyped (same grip each   (F4)
  time used)
- Draws with increasingly fluent strokes/movement   (F6)
- Plays with familiar objects in unfamiliar ways (stacking food)   (Cog1)
- Sorts familiar items by colour, shape *and* size   (Cog2)

Materials:
- Coloured clothes pegs
- Cat (animal) head image (without whiskers), cat (animal) head image (with whiskers); hedgehog images (one with prickles, one without).

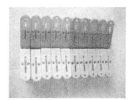

Procedure:

Level 1
1. Demonstrate the two hedgehog images (one with prickles, one without).
2. Clearly show now several different coloured clothes pegs arranged on the floor, slowly demonstrating how you can use your right middle finger and thumb to pinch the clothes peg to clamp/unclamp it, finally pegging it to the hedgehog's back (on the image without prickles), so turning the hedgehog into a 'peg-prickled' one !! Continue to demonstrate for baby, as they begin to see "The hedgehog growing prickles !".
3. Present now the same/similar (non-prickled) hedgehog image and 6 clothes pegs to baby, inviting baby to give their own hedgehog some fine prickles.
4. As/when baby provides their hedgehog with clamped clothes pegs (as previously demonstrated), provide prompt praise and encouragement.

Level 2
1. Demonstrate next the two cat head images (one with whiskers, one without).

2. Again clearly show several different coloured clothes pegs arranged on the floor, slowly demonstrating how you can this time use your *left* middle finger and thumb to pinch the clothes peg to clamp/unclamp it, finally pegging it to the cat's cheeks (image without whiskers), so turning the cat into a 'peg-whiskered' one !! Continue to demonstrate for baby, as they begin to see "the cat growing its whiskers !".
3 Present now the same/similar (non-whiskered) cat's head image and clothes pegs to baby, inviting baby to give the cat some splendid whiskers too.
4 As/when baby provides their cat with clamped clothes pegs (as previously demonstrated), provide prompt praise and encouragement as they do so.

Variations:
- Consider presenting to baby differently coloured hedgehog and cat-head images, inviting baby to then also choose the correspondingly coloured clothes pegs to clamp for the hedgehog and/or cats prickles and whiskers, respectively.
- Ditto for human hair styling – given human face images (without head hair).
- Ditto for crocodile teeth, dragon or dinosaur's back !,...etc.,...

Additional thoughts/Game-Activity Preparation/Lesson Planning Tips:
- When choosing clothes pegs to provide for baby, use preferably a coloured plastic material of reasonable quality, so allowing baby to operate them relatively easily, yet also safely; *if baby needs to use some very large amount of strength to be able to let open the peg 'mouth' open, such uncertainty with success may provide physical difficulty, and thus decrease baby's motivation to participate (however 'funny' they may feel this activity to be !).*
- To encourage ambidextrous hand control, guide and encourage baby to pursue attempting clamping at least the left cheeks' whiskers with their left hand (or the right with their right, if showing a left-handed use preference) for the kitty cat, so letting their baby practice using their less praticed hand for this fine motor-integration task.

G/A 23.10   Postal Deliveries

Task description:
- Exploring the delivery of requested items to assigned locations/others, having invited company.

Expected Milestone Achievements (EMAs):
- Balances own weight whilst walking along a narrow path/line   (G1)
- Understands references being made to unseen objects   (Comms3)
- Reaches for someone's hand when 'ready' or about to initiate walking   (SP1)
- Enjoys recognition in/of familiar playmates   (SP6)

Materials:
- Large cushions, cases/boxes (to build an obstacle pathway !).

Procedure:

Level 1

1. Situate about the room(s) a complex pathway using a variety of obstacles, arranging also a variety of 'end point' cushions where different members of the family present might be invited to sit (or other caregivers/friends, soft animal toys).
2. For each round, assign each to a different cushion 'end point' seating location.
3. Invite/lead now baby to cooperatively carry together with you a cushion or box along the pathway to a specified location, naming the person/toy to be found at that location, and to present their 'cushion gift' to them once arriving there (*baby should be encouraged to lead the way, and to determine how to get there each time*).
4. As/when baby succeeds in coordinating with you to ship their cushion/box along the obstacled pathway to the 'correct' destination together, present baby with a large hug and praise.
5. Continue to invite further 'gift presenting' trips in making additional recipient-targeted deliveries, as baby continues to take additional cushions/boxes to their assigned next recipients/locations, repeating steps 3-4 as necessary/appropriate.

Level 2

1. Place about the room(s) a number of different boxes (without specific pathway), placing other persons present/soft toys/dolls in each of the boxes.
2. Invite baby (or baby pairs if such be present, to cooperate mutually) in order to carry a relatively large cushion/box (this time without help, all by themselves) from a pile of such located at one side of one of the rooms (or in the hallway/by the front door), in order to present it to a particular place/person (other parent, person/soft toy), as you have specified, requesting that baby places their carried/retrieved objects besides that person/toy as they remain standing inside their different boxes !
3. With increasing success, encourage baby to continue transporting their loads, requiring increased coordination between/along small-to-gradually-longer pathways (and maybe involving several steps/stairs if readily available ?).
4. As/when baby succeeds in coordinating targeted cushion/object delivery, *be sure to encourage recipients to say 'Thank you' to baby upon receiving their gifts each time, whilst also facilitating enjoyment in giving, via large hugs and praise.*

Variations:

- To increase the level of difficulty further, consider to change the obstacles to be avoided whilst baby is carrying objects (both when partnered/assisted, and when struggling alone), adding corners, slopes, etc., as readily creatable in the room.
- Ditto, changing the weight, and or awkwardness of the object(s) to be carried.
- Ditto, using simple boxes, but having required baby to also collect/gather specific items to put into the boxes, *as requested by the receiving person, each time* [the baby thus needing to remember a small list of items, when out of sight of the items being referred to, at the time !]

Additional thoughts/Game-Activity Preparation/Lesson Planning Tips:

- As/when 'you and baby' as a team moves along together in transporting your deliveries, guide baby to remain also steady with their grip/balancing of the cushion, so as to not to drop them to the floor.
- Be ready to intervene/help (without doing the task for them !), at all times during baby's delivery schedule.
- *NB: when carrying relatively large boxes, baby will likely block their own line of sight of their target direction/recipient (this they will not at first realise !!), and will thus find it relatively difficult to remain balanced, but will likely continue anyway (?), especially when transporting in a not-so-well-coordinated way with another person.*
- *Most babies at this age should, however, NOT really need their parent/guardian to support them physically (in order to maintain their balance), but it is OK for you (or another) to stand at baby's side, as they move along (but not in front of, or behind them, as this would distract baby's visual attention from observing their feet/pathway surfaces !).*
- Ditto, providing help only when providing a safer/softer landing if looking tired, or seeming as if as they are about to fall over.

G/A 23.11   I Know Who's is Who's

Task description:
- Exploring and describing ownership and possession of item allocations, according to request.

Expected Milestone Achievements (EMAs):
- Uses 1st and 2nd person pronouns (I, me, yours, mine)   (Comms6)
- Gathers objects together according to their similarities (other   (Cog3)
  than colour and size)
- Spontaneously turns novel containers, to release contents   (Cog4)

Materials:
- Personal baby and parent/caregiver's possessions, soft animal toys,
- Small toy fruits and vegetables, boxes.

Procedure:
Level 1
1. Prepare two different kinds/sets of toys (e.g., animals and small toy fruits/vegetables or cars.
2. *If another adult be present:* Invite that person to come forward with a set of boxes, and to perform the following demonstration together with you, for baby to observe: firstly, inform them that, "The animal items will all belong to you (yours = the other person's) for a short time",.. "The toy fruits and vegetables will be mine (yours) for a short time". Next, take up a toy and place it in your right hand for baby to clearly see, asking the other person: "Can you guess who's this is, is it yours, or mine ?" The other person should then point to your hand and say either "Yours" or "Mine", then take the item from that hand (if an animal), the person having guessed correctly that it was for them, the taking of the animal as a reward; if guessing incorrectly, look to baby for advice, then continue.

3. Present now the same/similar sets of items to baby, inviting/leading baby in play guessing the category possessor (by name) for each of the toys in turn, requesting baby to say "Yours" or "Mine" each time (according to its type/category).

Level 2
1. Having reclaimed the toy collections used in level 1, lay the same items now inside a different box (each later to be referred to as now containing either 'Your toys", or "My toys" from before, when asked)
2. Invite baby to now come forward and to select a box set from their initial (new) locations, in order for each to be returned to their previous 'owner' [baby saying out loud "This is mine", or "This one is yours, belongs to you/other"].
3. With success, consider also to invite baby to empty both boxes into a single pile on the floor/table, telling for each item of the pile in turn, which toy belongs to them, or to you (e.g., "Mummy's", "Daddy's", "Yours", "Mine"), before 'correctly' giving it to them in turn, saying upon delivery, E.g., "This one is yours/mine" as appropriate.
4. As/when baby correctly assigns and restores the 'correct' possession/boxes to their last assigned 'owners', provide appropriate praise and encouragement.

Variations:
- For level 2, consider to mix up the boxes asking/, "This is not mine,... who's is it ?"; the owner then claiming "That one is mine/belongs to me", then going forward to collect it from you.
- Likewise using personal possessions (clothing/glasses/cellphone/books/bag) gathered into a pile, then distributed following a set of similar verbal questions and answer sets, each receiving their possessions back once identified verbally by baby.
- Ditto, running a 'lost property' office scenario, in which baby needs to again verbally claim the ownership (without simply pointing/nodding in agreement with another's suggestion).

Additional thoughts/Game-Activity Preparation/Lesson Planning Tips:
- As/when baby takes any item(s) to their true owner each time, encourage/guide baby to again say "Who's is it ?" or "To whom does it belong ?". Encouraging baby to engage with, and produce, increasingly sophisticated adult-like language performance (e.g.,, to say, "This is my mother's", rather than simply "Mama" in response to possessive questioning).

G/A 23.12   Baby Sous Chef' Chopping Board

Task description:
- Exploring the use of a tool to change the character features of a given object's appearance.

Expected Milestone Achievements (EMAs):
- Plays with familiar objects in unfamiliar ways (stacking food)   (Cog1)
- Sorts familiar items by colour, shape *and* size   (Cog2)
- Gathers objects together according to their similarities (*other than* colour and size)   (Cog3)
- Increasingly willing to explore interactions with novel toy(s)   (SP3)

Materials:
- Toy food preparation/chopping board set (non-connecting building blocks), tray.

Procedure:
Level 1
1. Demonstrate first the separate identically-coloured pieces of a long, 'pre-chopped' item from the set (carrot or bread ?, or even use rounded building blocks for this purpose just now), allowing baby to observe that the longer 'complete' item and the separate pieces are actually the 'same thing(s)' in some very essential way.
2. Show next two such sets at the same time, side by side, e.g., a carrot (one as 'complete'/together, the other as separate (not-too-close) pieces.
3. Present to baby now just one kind of fruit or vegetable blocks, inviting baby to explore the pieces for themselves, and to 'restore' them to show completed 'fruit'- or 'vegetable'-looking familiar appearances.
4. Finally, invite baby to prepare their best fruit or vegetable to then give to you (or present to another person present) to try, and pretend to taste/enjoy the offering, with much thanks to baby, so enhancing their motivation, praise and encouragement.

Level 2
1. Demonstrate a complete carrot model, then clearly show how to 'cut' the carrot using the toy set's 'knife' cutting along the 'slits', removing the cut piece for baby to clearly see, sharing the subsequent loaded 'cut' pieces on the tray, for you and baby to then pretend to taste and enjoy (before gathering them back once again).
2. Present the same/similar set of items/tools for baby to now explore, together with several different kinds of toy fruits and vegetables.
3. Ask now baby saying, "I would like to try a piece of <x> for myself (where <x> is piece of an assigned fruit or vegetable) to eat, inviting baby to select and 'cut' such a piece using their chopping blocks to provide the requested slice(s) to you each time.
4. As/when baby serves you 'correctly', encourage baby by saying, "Thank you", and then pretend to eat/enjoy the results.

Variations:
- Provide baby with a pile of differently-coloured and/or shaped toy fruits and vegetables on a chopping block, inviting baby to assemble their choice pairings, arranging them in the same places on a serving tray, restored to present them as complete fruits and/or vegetables in appearance, provide then a pretend tasting and choice session for you to engage in.
- Ditto, providing such for others (whomever else may be present in the home at the time).

Additional thoughts/Game-Activity Preparation/Lesson Planning Tips:
- If no toy cutting set be available in the home, prepare a simple home-made kit from modelling clay or flour & water (food colouring could create additional realism if needed, or even a real pre-cut carrot), using a blunt wooden stick or spatula as a 'knife'.
- Encourage/guide baby to touch two kinds of different quality materials for comparison, so letting baby be advised of/express their feeling(s) of the differences between them.
- Continuously guide baby in use of the toy knife when initially 'cutting' things, using one hand to hold the toy food, another hand to grasp/hold the knife hilt to make the 'cut' (*remembering that baby may not realize that they cannot put their finger 'back together' if it is sliced !!*).
- Especially when baby has cut the fruit or vegetable and then returned the pieces to their original state (whole) fruit model shape, provide prompt praise and encouragement.

- 16 -

Baby Milestones of Development

(With 100+ Fun Activities to Help Demonstrate Them)

[Age 24 Months]

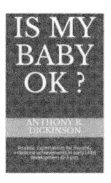

ψ

Baby Milestones of Development (0-3 Yrs)

Expected Milestone Achievements
Age = 24 Months

[Key: e.g., 7 = Game No. 24.7]

Gross Motor

• Balances own weight whilst walking along a single, narrow path (< 30 cm/ 12 Inches)	3, 6
• Carries objects whilst walking	1, 3, 4, 6
• Climbs easily up/down stairs (given the choice !)	6
• Jumps with both feet simultaneously off the ground	8
• Throws and kicks a ball at target with appropriate force	6, 8
• Will attempt to ride a tricycle with assistance	

Fine Motor

• Picks up and arranges coins/discs to produce 'same-side' patterns	8
• Copies simple brick, block or similar item construction sequences	2, 7, 9
• Makes definable model shapes from clay, plasteceine or Blu-Tak	5
• Takes apart (and refits) toys with component parts	5, 7, 9
• Imitates drawing of multi-directional lines	
• Folds paper in particular ways (by example)	5

Cognitive

• Sorts a variety of different objects by their type, size, shape *and* colour	1, 3, 11
• Sorts the *same set of objects* according to EITHER their sizes, shapes OR colour	2, 7, 11
• Successfully searches for objects hidden under covers	10
• Plays with keyboard and/or other musical instrument with discerning/differential effect(s) for sounds heard	
• Enjoys 'putting things away' and 'getting them out' again	9
• Follows simple instructions without visual aid or gesture	1, 3, 8

Communication

• Responds 'Yes'/'No' when asked "Is xxx in the picture ?"	
• Will search for, and collect, unseen objects when asked for them	1, 9, 10
• Appropriately uses 1st and 2nd person possessives (mine, yours, Mama's)	10, 11
• Answers questions with more than one (appropriate) word	3, 10
• Frequently uttering multi-syllable phrases (e.g., "Teddy eat banana now")	10
• Repeats words and/or actions of others (especially if novel)	4, 8

Socio-Personal

• Reliably monodextrous with hand preference for certain tasks	2, 7, 11
• Increasingly aware of self as being distinct/different from others	11
• Begins to show significant amounts of make-believe play	5
• Responds more enthusiastically when in the company of other children	
• Speaks/points to pictures/object to express interest to others ("Look, there's a boat")	10
• Acts/plays out imaginary stories/adventures (either alone, or with others)	5

G/A 24.1   Stepping to the Colours

Task description:
Exploring route following according to explicit verbal requests.

Expected Milestone Achievements (EMAs):
- Carries objects whilst walking   (G2)
- Sorts a variety of different objects by their size, shape *and* colour   (Cog1)
- Follows simple instructions without visual aid or gesture   (Cog6)
- Will search for, and collect, unseen objects when asked for them   (Comms2)

Materials:
- Stepping stone pathway (*using objects or marked flooring space, either coloured or colour-labelled*).
- Relatively large single-coloured objects (*or at least matching/associable with each of 3-4 colour-assigned runways*).

Procedure:
Level 1
1. Set up in the room several coloured runways (e.g., red, yellow, blue and green).
2. In the centre of the room set up a 'pool' of differently coloured objects to later be selected from, and carried by, baby (each kind of colour and quantity matching the number of coloured runways set up).
3. Lead baby to stand, and to move forward (together with you if/as necessary), in a clockwise direction along the open floor.
4. At some point whilst moving forward, call out, for example, "Yellow", requiring baby to then stop all movement, and to then go stand on/in the yellow stone/area.
5. As/when baby succeeds to stand on the 'correct' coloured stone/area each time, provide prompt encouragement and praise.
6. Continue to then promptly repeat steps 3-5 according to baby's continued interest and motivation, requesting them to respond to the different verbal colour cues and stepping stones, for each round.

Level 2
1. Following success with the level 1 activity as a foundation, place now differently coloured stepping stones in the centre of the room.
2. Invite baby to stop moving according to your requests as before, but this time requiring them to first move towards the centre object pool to search for an assigned (e.g., 'yellow') object from the centre object 'pool', before going on to stand upon the appropriately (same) coloured ('yellow') stepping stone according to your request, whilst still also holding their yellow object.

3. As/when baby succeeds in reaching and standing upon the correspondingly coloured stepping stone, with their 'correctly' coloured object, *and* remains there without falling down, provide immediate praise and encouragement.
4. Continue to then promptly repeat steps 2-3 according to baby's continuing interest and motivation, requesting baby to continue responding to the different verbal colour cues, objects, and locations each time.

Variations:
- Following level 1 success, consider increasing the number of colours (and coloured objects) to look *for*, search from, and stand on, so requiring baby to increase their specific cognitive search and selection skills.
- Ditto using different *shapes*, *sizes* of objects, and stepping stones/areas (independent of colour).
- Ditto, now combining BOTH colour AND size *or* shape in search requirements.

Additional thoughts/Game-Activity Preparation/Lesson Planning Tips:
- If no obvious 'stepping stones' be available in the home (baby weight-baring firm cushions, cases/containers/large blocks/boxes), consider to create 2D versions using existing floor tiles, string/paper or small play mats (colour-coded with stickers if not coloured as required); or simply assign different 'areas' of the room to be reached, as marked by something on the floor close to the wall(s).
- Be sure to place the stepping stones in positions which are relatively well separated from each other, so providing baby adequate movement space.
- Pay close attention to baby's safety, so helping avoid baby's colliding with furnishings, or not stopping with control, and falling down.
- If baby is unable to follow the verbal instructions alone (*ref target EMA here Cog6*), consider to offer additional help by holding up an appropriately coloured cue card to indicate the assigned colour to be used/followed at the beginning of any given round (reducing its use with increasing success).

G/A 24.2 Babacus Builders

Task description:
- Exploring the creation of a serially-ordered sequences according to request.

Expected Milestone Achievements (EMAs):
- Copies simple brick, block or similar item construction sequences (F2)
- Sorts the *same set of objects* according to EITHER their sizes, shapes OR colour (Cog2)
- Reliably monodextrous with hand preference for certain tasks (SP1)

Materials:
- Plastic straw/string & beads.

Procedure:

Level 1
1. Demonstrate a straw and 10 differently coloured hollow beads, slowly and gently showing how to thread (link) several beads onto them, one by one, to form a single long 'bead chain' for baby to clearly see.
2. Present a similar looking set of 10 differently coloured hollow beads to baby.
3. Invite baby to then thread these hollow beads together to form one, single, bead chain as previously demonstrated.
4. Once completed, invite baby to demonstrate the result(s) of their creativity, providing much applause and praise after doing so.

Level 2
1. Present to baby three differently coloured straws and beads, but this time of only 3 different colours of each, and more beads.
2. Invite baby to now thread only hollow beads of the *same* colours together, to form 3 different colour-specific straw-threaded creations.
3. As/when baby succeeds in both colour-classification of the different materials, *and* then 'correctly' combines each class of coloured beads together to form three different colour-based models, provide prompt praise (and consider displaying/comparing the various baby-made models for all to see).

Variations:
- From a single (or even 2-3) piles/tins/trays of differently coloured materials, invite baby to sort and collect only a particular colour, size and/or shape of threadable materials (each time), and to then connect them together to form a single bead array.
- Ditto, assigning alternating colour patterned arrays (e.g., Blue, White, Blue, White, Blue,....; or Red, Green, Blue, Red, Green, Blue,......), increasing the complexity with increasing success.
- Ditto, introducing different material size and/or shape use requests (with or without demonstrating models for baby to 'copy' each time).

Additional thoughts/Activity Preparation/Lesson Planning Tips:
- If no hollow beads be available, consider to bore holes in cleaned & dried nuts, small stones, bottle tops, etc.,
- If baby's manipulation skills do not allow threading without previously threaded beads falling off (as they attempt to place new ones on to the straw), block one end by pacing a small clothes peg or small clip on one end to hold threaded beads in place.
- As baby gathers together their hollow beads, and whether different or not, if they are simultaneously arranging them together each time; note that the growing structure of the developing 'bead necklace' orientation will be changing (and thus increasingly more difficult for baby to hold each time they add new beads) - regardless of the order baby is threading them together. If so, offer continued encouragement to baby, but do resist the temptation to interfere with baby as you do so (*the primary goal here, remember, is the colour/shape sorting ability development, not the construction of attractive jewelry or craftwork per se !*).
- Once baby has strung together their beads well, consider asking 'What' baby sorted, before making their model tube object, inviting baby to display their imagination and continued interest in 'planning' their new model creation(s) each time.
- As baby's manipulation skills improve, consider to use decreasingly firm materials for baby to thread their beads on to (straw => coat hanger wire => unused electrical wire => shoelace =>string).

Baby Milestones of Development (0-3 Yrs)

349

G/A 24.3   Marking the Way Forward

Task description:
- Exploring the use of different location indicators (verbal/auditory and visual), in order to effect different locomotion responses.

Expected Milestone Achievements (EMAs):
- Balances own weight whilst walking along a single, narrow path   (G1)
    (< 30 cm/ 12 Inches)
- Carries objects whilst walking   (G2)
- Sorts a variety of different objects by their size, shape *and* colour   (Cog1)
- Able to follow simple instructions without visual aid or gesture   (Cog6)
- Answers questions with more than one (appropriate) word   (Comms4)

Materials:
- Route markers (arrowed direction indicators on floor)

- Or, 3D mounted direction markers/signs

- Boxes (with and/or without various content(s)), target/reward toys.

Procedure:
Level 1
1 Demonstrate a set of colour-(or symbol)-coded 'route markers' on an "T-shaped" footpath, ensuring that baby observes the different coded/sign indicators each time.

2 Clearly show that the different indicators can be removed (can change location, and directions being indicated (i.e., be turned over, around, and/or replaced by others), and placed about the floor, to guide a particular walking path.
3 Invite baby now to now go forward, and to attempt walking the same path as per your demonstration, as you point out and follow the path lines according to the different direction indicators each time.
4 As/when baby succeeds with walking along the marked path, provide prompt praise and encouragement as they do so.

Level 2
1-4. Change the marking direction indicators, so establishing different footpaths, with/without demonstrations for each following round, also requiring baby to carry boxes in front of them to increase the level of difficulty (of viewing the lines/direction indicators), according to baby's increasing abilities and skill levels.
5 As/when baby succeeds to move along the path according to the indicators, and does so independently, provide prompt praise and reward for their efforts.

Level 3
1. Establish a long single pathway using four differently coloured direction markers /pieces in the centre of the room(s), at the end of which is a bifurcated junction, in the font of which then lays two or more roads, each branching out either to the left with a red and yellow, or to the right with blue and green coloured indicator pieces only, respectively.
2. At the 'end' of each of the two branches place a target toy flat on the floor/hidden in a box.
3. Invite baby to now go forward, and to follow EITHER the green, blue, yellow or red direction indicators each time, in order to arrive at their target destination (they may be surprised to end up where they do, and what they might find there !!).
4. As/when baby 'correctly' walks along according to the colour-direction request(s) given, *and* succeeds to finally arrive at the corresponding target/reward expected, provide prompt praise and encouragement for their achievement in following instructions.

Variations:
- Vary the level of difficulty by using a variety of different words/signs to indicate the direction or choice of pathway indicator(s).
- Ditto, increasing the complexity of the pathway(s) used each time (more turns, multiple rooms/spaces).
- Ditto, adding more difficult (larger, but not heavy) objects to be carried along as baby also observes the floor direction indicators beneath them.
- Consider to also use parallel pathways, as well as simple "T", "L", and "X" configurations, possibly introducing additional cushioning and/or similar obstructions to be overcome in some places. [A roundabout ?].
- For any of the level 1-3 activities, consider to also establish the road as a double track, in the gap between placing additional colour indicator points for baby to follow, possibly mixed with other colours (or similarly marked direction indicators) as distractors.

Additional thoughts/Game-Activity Preparation/Lesson Planning Tips:

- *Be sure to determine that baby really is following the direction indicator marks in order to walk where they do, and does not simply follow the/a path's direction each time (neglecting the markers !). It is essential that baby be encouraged to thus formulate a movement plan – which may involve simultaneously establishing multiple, different roads and pathways in the room/home that will help draw attention to the need for planning.*
- As baby 'correctly' steps to their assigned colour marks only in the level 3 activity, consider interrupting baby in making continuous prompts, so ensuring that baby understands the rule of the task OK.
- Insure that the route's sign sets/direction pieces are in good repair, clean, and not dangerous to baby if trodden/fallen on, so helping minimise any risk of injury.
- Ditto, minimising infection risk, especially in preventing baby from placing any movable signs/parts into their mouths, nose and/or eyes after walking on/into them.

G/A 24.4   Narrow Paths !

Task description:
- Exploring coordinated movement along a narrow ledge.

Expected Milestone Achievements (EMAs):
- Balances own weight whilst walking along a single, narrow path   (G1)
  (< 30 cm/ 12 Inches)
- Carries objects whilst walking   (G2)
- Repeats words and/or actions of others (especially if novel)   (Comms6)

Materials:
- Floor-marking tape/string/tiles (to form a 'narrow' marked pathway) or wooden beam, large brick row to form a raised platform for baby to safely walk along)

- Boxes, firm containers, bricks.

Procedure:
Level 1
1. Construct a single channel raised ledge/path in the centre of the room/hallway using whatever materials be easily available in the home.
2. Slowly demonstrate how to move along the path, without touching the floor, as you carefully maintain your balance to arrive at the other end.
3. Invite now baby to become a construction worker/ballet dancer, and to step onto one end of the pathway/beam, and to wend their way along the top of the narrow road to reach the other end along its length.
4. As/when baby arrives at the far end of the pathway, and has not touched the floor (or otherwise stepped out of the marked thin path/fallen down), provide prompt praise and encouragement.

Level 2
1-4 Repeat level 1, this time requiring baby to collect and carry/deliver parcels like a postman needing to cross a river without getting wet feet !!

Variations:
- Extending the level 1 activity, consider using additional 2-3 stepping stones dispersed between separate sections of their narrow path/beam/bricks, to add variety and difficulty with baby coordinating their various muscles.
- For level 2, consider to later arrange the ledge/path either as a continuous straight/jagged line, or as an "X" cross beam shape.
- Ditto, and only for baby's succeeding well with the floor version(s), increasing the walking height above the floor, by using additional containers, boxes, blocks, planks, etc,...

Additional thoughts/Game-Activity Preparation/Lesson Planning Tips:
- If baby has only just started to attempt walking above ground, you will need render baby considerable assistance, whilst also letting baby experience their attempt(s) following your demonstrations, rather than trying to surmount the platform independently, at least at first.
- Even if walking well and unaided, whenever losing balance, you will still need to provide support (and a sense of comfort and security) by remaining at baby's side as they travel along any narrow ridge/pathway, and especially so if raised above the floor beyond a few cms).
- Be sure to consider adjusting the pathway design according to baby's changing ability, strength and confidence, possibly creating more than one pathway if wishing to afford baby a choice of pathway (and hence level of difficulty) as confidence level may vary greatly within the session with increasing success and motivation.
- When designing/building the walkway for baby, be sure to separate it appropriately from room furnishings (maybe away from, but possibly close to, depending upon baby's balancing skills), starting by placing it a certain safe distance, so helping avoid collisions with those furnishings if falling over/from it.

G/A 24.5   Little Sous Chef

Task description:
- Exploring the deliberate manipulation and moulding of soft materials.

Expected Milestone Achievements (EMAs):
- Makes definable model shapes from clay or Blu-Tak   (F3)
- Takes apart (and refits) toys with component parts   (F4)
- Folds paper in particular ways (by example)   (F6)
- Begins to show significant amounts of make-believe play   (SP3)
- Acts/plays out imaginary stories/adventures (either alone, or   (SP6)
  with others).

Materials:
- Children's (baby-safe, non-toxic) modelling clay, bowl
- Clean plain white paper, drawing paper (upon which is a simple picture of a coloured bowl/plate), baby-friendly non-toxic glue stick.

Procedure:
Level 1
1. Demonstrate a bowl of children's modelling clay (or home-made version of same – see Activity Preparation Tips below), slowly showing how to use the clay to form shapes by pinching it with one hand, for baby to clearly see.
2. Bring the clay now closer for you and baby to explore together, placing the bowl on the floor/table, and taking up small portion of the clay to rub between both hands, forming it into a sphere, showing to baby, and then placing it back into the bowl.
3. Present next to baby a smaller bowl of modelling clay, inviting baby to imitate your last demonstration, as they roll the clay to make many small sweet dumplings, and place them into their bowl for the master chef to cook !
4. As/when baby completes rubbing their clay to form many small dumplings, invite baby to then give their bowl of sweet dumplings to you.
5. Provide much applause and praise to baby as they do so, whilst also receiving expressions of thanks from you, as they present their dumplings to you.

Level 2
1. Demonstrate next a drawing paper, upon which is drawn an open bowl or plate.
2. Show now some plain white paper, slowly showing how to use both hands to tear the paper into small strips, then rubbing/rolling/pinching together each strip to form small paper ball agglomerate (rice grains), attaching it then with the glue stick to the drawn bowl/plate on the paper for baby to see.

3. Present for baby now a similar picture, plain paper and glue stick.

4. Invite baby to affix their rolled paper strips to create a number of cooked rice grains, placed in/on their paper bowls.
5. Finally, once baby has completed preparing their rice dishes, invite baby to then fold a clean sheet of paper as a menu, then present their bowl of rice to another person (you, other parent/care-giver) to pretend to eat with pleasure.
6. Provide much applause and praise to baby as they do so, whilst also ensuring that they receive expressions of thanks from their 'customers/guests' each time.

Variations:
- Invite baby to rub/roll their clay to create noodles, sausages, or even snowmen (or snow-women), add small sesame seed husks to create Pandas !!
- With increasing dexterity and interest, allow baby to create any variety of shapes/objects of their own choosing – either from single of multiple pieces (of clay or paper), joining several together to form a single object.
- Ditto, baby drawing their chef logo and recipe results on the folded 'menu' paper.

Additional thoughts/Activity Preparation/Lesson Planning Tips:
- Be sure to provide baby only with children's modelling clay which has been certified as being both a baby-friendly and non-toxic material.
- If no 'off-the-shelf' modelling clay be available in the home, mix normal cornflour/starch with warm water for a safe alternative.
- Be sure to maintain vigilance in supervising/paying constant attention to preventing baby's eating children's modelling clay, or otherwise placing their clay-soiled hands into their mouth, nose or eyes (or anyone else's). Ensure baby promptly cleans both their hands, including nail slits, after manipulating the clay and/or other similar materials.

G/A 24.6   Stagger Alley !

Task description:
- Exercising balance and coordination when traversing an uneven surface.

Expected Milestone Achievements (EMAs):
- Balances own weight whilst walking along a single, narrow path   (G1)
  (< 30 cm/ 12 Inches)
- Carries objects whilst walking   (G2)
- Climbs easily up/down stairs (given the choice !)   (G3)
- Throws and kicks a ball at target with appropriate force   (G5)

Materials:
- Stepping-stones, cushions/floor markings (to form pathway)
- Staircase (or cushions, cases/boxes (to build one !)

- Soft ball(s).

Procedure:
Level 1 [Use a real staircase for (G3) if available in/close to/immediately outside the home]
1. Arrange a variety of large (firm) cushioning, to create/build a series of three-dimensional arches/tunnels (placing a sheet over two chairs can also suffice).
2. Slowly demonstrate moving through the tunnel(s) by crawling through the tunnel(s) yourself, whilst baby watches you, then continuing along the pathway, towards the final 'piece' to arrive at the exit.
3. Invite now baby to pass along the same pathway, as you stand nearby each tunnel end each time.
4. As/when baby steadily crawls through the tunnel from one end to the other, and does so without changing the shape/structure of the tunnel, provide prompt praise and encouragement following their efforts.

Baby Milestones of Development (0-3 Yrs)

Level 2

1-4. Repeat the level 1 activity, with the added requirement that baby carries a ball (maybe several ?) with them as they traverse the obstacle course, midway through which is set up a 'shooting area' within which baby is required to throw (or kick) their ball(s) towards a target bucket/box situated at an appropriate distance away from the path/course [If using a real staircase for (G3), situate the target either lower on the stairs, higher up, somewhere distant from the top (once reached)].

Variations:
- With increasing success, consider to up the level of difficulty by inviting baby to carry successively larger/more awkward (but not necessarily heavier) items along the tunnel/pathways each time.
- Ditto, slowly increasing the complexity and/or unevenness of the pathway to be travelled, over time.

Additional thoughts/Game-Activity Preparation/Lesson Planning Tips:
- Stand nearby (but never inside) the tunnel's cushioning/sheeting as baby crawls or walks along it, *as the tunnel may become unstable with baby's size and weight pressing upon its structure alone; the tunnel can easily be destroyed or made loose as/when baby collides with the structure supports. Your prompt help to readjust the tunnel here in order to keep its original shape and 'closed' position may well be critical to baby's learning and success.*
- According to baby's size, consider building more than one three-dimensional tunnel and obstacles in/across room(s) if available, so increasing baby's interest and motivation to engage within the pathway(s) to completion.
- As baby crawls/walks along the tunnel(s) each time, be sure to maintain *minimal gaps* from developing between each piece of cushioning, so helping avoid baby's losing 'track' of the 'course', colliding with standard furnishings/fittings, and falling down, or otherwise becoming injured.
- If the stairs are still causing baby concern and anxiety, consider installing some visible rewards at the place where baby will arrive following their successful stairs descent, or ascent (a preferred toy ?). This can be especially useful in increasing the stimulation and motivation for baby to make their way *back down* the stairs to the floor once more, whilst simultaneously providing them a clear signal of achievement, reward and encouragement.

G/A 23.7 Creative Plants

Task description:
- Exploring the creation of ornamental objects using common materials.

Expected Milestone Achievements (EMAs):
- Copies simple brick, block or similar item construction sequences (F2)
- Takes apart (and refits) toys with component parts (F4)
- Sorts the same set of objects according to EITHER their sizes, (Cog2)
  shapes OR colour
- Plays with familiar objects in unfamiliar ways (stacking food) [M23-Cog1]
- Reliably monodextrous with hand preference for certain tasks (SP1)

Materials:
- Holed basket, polyfoam tray, paper flowers/petals on toothpicks (or similar)

- Coloured straws.

Procedure:
Level 1
1. Demonstrate a holed basket, drawing attention to the small holes in its sides.
2. On the floor/table, next explore several coloured (artificial) flowers on sticks.
3. Demonstrate now how to place the stick/flowers into/through the small holes in the (upside-down) basket, turning it into a "trough to grow flowers" for baby to see.
4. Invite baby to now come forward and place/arrange their flowers in the basket, one at a time.
5. As/when baby succeeds to place/distribute their flowers crisscrossed about the basket's sides, provide prompt praise and applause each time.

Level 2
1. Demonstrate next a small polyfoam tray/block (cup, or similar penetrable object) placed on the floor/table.
2. Slowly show baby how to take up a straw, and insert it into the surface of the small polystyrene block to make a grass sod, with protruding flower stem.

3. Present now a small polystyrene block and several coloured straws, inviting baby to insert their straws into the polystyrene block (possibly using small holes that you have already made ?).
4. As baby succeeds to independently insert all their straws (flowers) into their small polystyrene tray/block/upturned cup, provide prompt praise and encouragement.

Level 3
Repeat levels 1 and/or 2, requiring baby to imitate the creation of models (as demonstrated/presented by you each time), given similar/the same materials, varying in use of different colours and patterns each time. Consider also inviting baby to take apart their constructions, as well as to rebuild new ones (using the same and/or different materials).

Variations:
- Present to baby an empty/used (cleaned and dried) plastic mineral water bottle, prepared with many small holes, and several 'flowers' to insert into the bottle's holes, so creating an attractive coloured flower display.

Additional thoughts/Game-Activity Preparation/Lesson Planning Tips:
- If no holed basket or similar 'flower' holder be available, simply make a few tiny holes in an upturned paper cup, disposable food tray, small polystyrene (packing material) block, or egg-box, etc.
- When presenting the straws and/or sticks to baby, be sure to pay careful attention to baby's accepting/handling of them, helping prevent any scratching of their skin.
- If possible, choose a small polystyrene block style and of a strength that will not require any pre-prepared drilling of holes in order for baby to insert the straws; the baby's holding and pushing the straw's would ideally require only minimal strength to gently insert the straw into/through the polystyrene block with relative ease.
- Try to make available straws which are both thin and short, enough to penetrate the block blunt, and not sharp enough to challenge baby's safety.
- Likewise, pay careful attention to preventing baby from waving about their straws, so helping avoid contact with their (or others') eyes, facial or body skin surfaces.

Baby Milestones of Development (0-3 Yrs)

G/A 23.8 Baby Olympiad

Task description:
- Exploring and planning sequential movements for action, according to request.

Expected Milestone Achievements (EMAs):
- Jumps with both feet simultaneously off the ground (G4)
- Throws and kicks a ball at target with appropriate force (G5)
- Picks up coins/discs to produce 'same-side' patterns (F1)
- Able to follow simple instructions without visual aid or gesture (Cog6)
- Repeats words and/or actions of others (esp. if novel) (Comms6)

Materials:
- Constructed/marked pathway, small table/tray

- Soft balls, large coins.

Procedure:
Level 1
1. Construct in the centre of the room a simple runway, in the centre of which is a small table/tray/bucket containing either a small ball, a large ball, OR a small pile of coins.
2. Clearly demonstrate moving along the runway, and stopping at the table/bucket to see what is there.
3. Pick up the object found, and then, (1) if a small ball – throw it to the end of the runway, then continue along the pathway to collect it, or (2) if a large ball – place it on the floor, and then kick it towards the end of the runway, before continuing along the pathway to collect it, or (3) if some coins, to carefully rearrange them such that the 'same face' (say the head) is facing upwards on the surface of the table/tray, and then continuing towards the end of the runway to the exit/finish line.
4. Repeat each of the three actions, ensuring that baby understands the name of each action (that you create/use), accordingly.

Level 2
1. Use the same simple runway as for level 1, the centre table/tray/bucket containing the same small ball, large ball, AND the small pile of coins.
2. Invite baby to come to the 'start line' once more, this time presenting them with a SINGLE instruction as to *which* object(s) to interact with, and in what way(s): For example, include a request to pick up a ball, and to jump whilst holding it, without throwing/kicking it), each time they reach the centre of the runway, moving along to towards the exit of the runway, once having completed the task provided at the outset.
3. With success, and in order to up the level(s) of difficulty even further, increase either the number, and/or the complexity of the steps required to be remembered and performed each time, over several different and interesting challenging rounds.

Variations:
- With increasing success, consider to provide additional objects/tasks to be manipulated along the pathway.
- Ditto, inviting the more capable baby to also collect and carry an increasing load size of objects, and do something with them as they progress along the obstacle course towards the other end.

Additional thoughts/Game-Activity Preparation/Lesson Planning Tips:
- When setting up the/each pathway, be sure to arrange any table/tray/bucket at a safe location relative to the path – which may be clearly visible to baby as they approach it – so helping avoid collision and harm to baby reaching it unexpectedly.
- According to the room' size, consider to establish more than one activity station along the pathway for baby to be invited to stop and explore at (according to instructions given to baby, *before* they enters the pathway each time).

G/A 23.9   Missing Pieces !

Task description:
- Exploring the completion of an unfinished route plan, using signs.

Expected Milestone Achievements (EMAs):
- Copies simple brick, block or similar item construction sequences   (F2)
- Takes apart (and refits) toys with component parts   (F4)
- Attempts to imitate organised patterns/arrays of objects   [M21-Cog4]
  (e.g., by colour, size)
- Enjoys 'putting things away' and 'getting them out' again   (Cog5)
- Will search for, and collect, unseen objects when asked for them   (Comms2)

Materials:
- Route markers (arrowed direction indicators on floor)

- Or, 3D mounted direction markers/signs

- Boxes (with and/or without various content(s)), target/reward toys.

Procedure:

Level 1
1. Demonstrate use of the same/similar pathway(s) as used in [M24 23.3] above, this time ensuring that baby observes that there are some parts missing, then slowly showing how to put one of the missing indicators into its place (according to the path design created).
2. Present now a 'missing indicator' piece to baby, inviting baby to then go forward and to place it in one of the 'spaces' in order to help 'complete the route' (with markers).

3. As/when baby succeeds with providing an appropriate placement, provide prompt praise and encouragement.
4. Repeat steps 2-3 until all of the 'missing pieces have been included.

Level 2
1. Put together this time a single long but curving road in/across the room(s), along which again several route markers have both missing, but also 'incorrect' indicator parts included
2. Lay also to one side, a pile of 'extra' parts for baby to choose from, as they wish.
3. Invite baby to come forward and to either pick up new pieces, then replacing or repositioning existing direction markers, in order to put together a complete and functional single direction track with a one way route direction sequence set into it.
4 As/when baby succeeds with providing an appropriate new (re)placement, provide prompt praise and encouragement.
5. Finally, invite baby to walk along their new footpath, according to their own new direction indicator sequence(s), repeating steps 1-3 as continued interest and motivation allows.

Variations:
- Present to baby a new set of footpath and direction pieces identical to a completed example set already laid out on the floor, inviting baby to assemble their set pieces so as to replicate the example set shown.
- Ditto, inviting baby now 'instruct' you to create similar/novel pathways according to baby's design (and of increasingly larger complexity each time).
- Consider encouraging baby to disassemble (even put away) all the pieces before starting any new pathway building rounds.

Additional thoughts/Game-Activity Preparation/Lesson Planning Tips:
- Ensure that any/all pathway and direction marker pieces are in good repair, and thoroughly cleaned, sterilised and dried, both before and after each session' use, so minimising injury if mishandled or tripped over.
- Ditto, minimising infection risk, especially attempting to prevent baby from placing any removable parts into their mouths, nose and/or eyes (or those of others present !).

G/A 24.10 Going Fishin' Together

Task description:
- Exploring an individual task in a shared-play space activity context.

Expected Milestone Achievements (EMAs):
- Successfully searches for objects hidden under covers   (Cog3)
- Will search for, and collect, unseen objects when asked for them   (Comms2)
- Appropriately uses 1st and 2nd person possessives (mine,   (Comms3)
  yours, mama's)
- Answers questions with more than one (appropriate) word   (Comms4)
- Frequently uttering multi-syllable phrases (e.g., "Teddy eat   (Comms5)
  banana now")
- Speaks/points to pictures/object to express interest to others   (SP5)
  ("Look, there's a boat").

Materials:
- Fishing combination set (magnetic/felt/velcro)

- Ladle (long handled spoon), small magnets, paperclips, card
- Bowl (transparent and/or opaque) versions, flat tray.

Procedure:
Level 1
1. Demonstrate a fishing combination set (or your homemade version of such, see Tips section below), slowly and gently showing how to use the 'fishing pole' to "catch" the 'fishes', for baby to clearly see.
2. Gather now with baby together, closer to the fishing pond (bowl), each of you holding a similar fishing rod to explore.
3. Invite baby to sit with you face-to-face around/across the 'pond', taking it in turns to then 'fish' together, and then presenting your 'catch' to the other, each time.
4. As/when the non-fishing person has waited patiently for their turn (and/or politely requests access to the fishing bowl after receiving a caught fish (and rod if only one 'fishing pole' be available), provide prompt praise and encouragement for their actions.

Level 2
1. Repeat the level 1 activity, but this time with attention being paid to the selective 'catching' of differently coloured/coded fishes.
2. Place the differently coloured fishes respectively into different 'holes' in the fishing (either different locations if using a flat tray/floor space, or even different bowls/buckets for the different coloured fishes ?)
3. Invite baby to again sit face-to-face across the 'pond' from you (and/or together with any other fishermen who may be present), and to 'fish' for the differently coloured fishes (each assigned a different colour, at the same time), until they have all been 'caught' (placing back to the 'pond' any of the "wrong" colour caught, or presenting them as 'gifts' to the person assigned that colour as caught !).
4. As baby succeeds to cooperate with fishing at the same time, and does so without also 'catching'/keeping any fishes of the others' colour(s), provide prompt praise for their cooperative enterprise in playing (angling) happily together.

Variations:
- Consider to use a transparent bowl at first, so that baby can truly 'see' how the fishing mechanism works each time – or use an opaque vessel/box which baby cannot see the inside of, so introducing an element of surprise when fishes may appear to have been 'caught' [*Remember, however, that this task was designed for use primarily with Communication skill-related EMAs – tho' clearly useful for fine motor and Cog-related evaluations of baby's ability level(s)*]
- Alternatively, and if baby's clear vision of the whole fishes set be necessary (rather than literally fishing for something they cannot see), provide a hula hoop or open tray/string circle (placed flat on the floor), inside of which are placed different 'fish' and/or differently coloured objects (toys/stones) of some other kind, providing each person with a fishing rod, then inviting baby to 'fish' for the different items, according to your verbal request(s) [and later those of others, and/or even of baby requesting specific fishes to be caught by others ?] each time.

Additional thoughts/Game-Activity Preparation/Lesson Planning Tips:
- If no 'off-the-shelf' materials be available, simply construct similar by using a long handled spoon/ladle/stick to which is attached a short string/ribbon with a small magnet/sticky tape or paper clip. Create 'fish' by drawing colourful fishes on separate small paper/card, each with a paper clip attached (for magnet, or to build hook loops), or string/hair grip loops.
- When baby and others present are seated face-to-face, arrange for comfortable separation distances, whilst also special paying attention to baby's fishing time (and thus waiting time for others) when sharing the activity; so helping the adults avoid impatience and/or frustrations developing as baby may appear 'relatively' incompetent/slow as their fishing skills are only just starting to develop.
- Guide baby not to lie prone upon the fish plate (pond), so helping avoid a fishing pole from poking the eyes or face of their own (or another's) body.
- Likewise during cooperative simultaneous fishing, encourage baby in accepting others' caught fish/toy gifts with expressions of thanks each time they do so.

G/A 23.11   "Scoopin' them Up !"

Task description:
- Exploring an individual task whilst managing a shared personal-space.

Expected Milestone Achievements (EMAs):
- Sorts a variety of different objects by their size, shape *and* colour   (Cog1)
- Sorts the *same set of objects* according to EITHER their sizes,   (Cog2)
  shapes OR colour
- Appropriately uses 1st and 2nd person possessives (mine,   (Comms3)
  yours, mama's)
- Reliably monodextrous with hand preference for certain tasks   (SP1)
- Increasingly aware of self as being distinct/different from others   (SP2)

Materials:
- Hula hoop, soup spoons/ladles, ping-pong balls, bean bags.

Procedure:
Level 1
1. Demonstrate a hula hoop (tray, or other clearly marked area) placed flat on the floor, inside of which are placed several beanbags (or other readily identifiable, small objects that baby 'knows' the names of).
2. Slowly show how to use the soup spoon/ladle to reach out into the interior of the hula hoop ring in order to scoops up the beanbags, one at a time, for baby to see.
3. Invite baby to now come forward in taking a 'turn', and to attempt to scoop up one of the beanbags with the soup spoon/ladle, praising success as and when it occurs.
4. Place now many beanbags (or rolled up socks), each one of only two colours at first inside the hula hoop's open centre, on the floor.
5. Assigning baby to focus upon one of the two colours only, respectively (matching one of the beanbags'/objects colours), present then a soup spoon/ladle.
6. Invite baby to now attempt reaching over the hoop's edge (without their full/part body entering it also !) and to scoop up at least one of their assigned coloured sandbags, providing much excitement and encouragement as they do so.

Level 2
1. Following the level 1 activity as a foundation (with success), replace the beanbags with ping-pong balls (of either the same or different colours, as may be available).
2. Invite baby (and any other participants) to then scoop up as many of the hula hoop's ping-pong balls as they can, providing prompt praise and a tally 'score' for each as they do so.

Variations:
- Provide an array of different objects, each requiring a different level of difficulty and/or organisational achievement in order to attain them (maybe requiring baby with you to work together to gain one object, if very large) – each 'scoring' points according to the difficulty of object acquisition each time.
- Ditto, assigning baby (and/or others) different sizes and shapes, as well as colours (for collecting from amongst the same set of objects, differently each time).

Additional thoughts/Game-Activity Preparation/Lesson Planning Tips:
- As/when baby reaches out to scoop up any objects from within the hula hoop each time, ensure that they only use one hand to grasp the spoon/ladle, and without using their other hand to make contact with the toy until outside the hoop.
- *For baby at this age, scooping up the ping-pong balls may well prove quite difficult. The ping-pong balls will roll away, requiring the baby to learn how to control the spoon/ladle's direction of movement when scooping, whilst also accommodating their position and posture relative to any other persons in the area attempting to do the same !!*
- When the hoop only contains few/one remaining object(s), baby will/may appear to 'fight over it' with you. Especially in the case of the last remaining ping-pong ball, baby may even attempt to fight for space to scoop it up when rolling around; so long as baby does not violate any 'regulations/rules' that you have set, or presents a direct attack upon another, or engages in any other risky behaviour, *resist the temptation to physically stop baby continuing to reach their goal - instead requesting of baby to modestly decline, otherwise encouraging baby to strive to scoop up the last remaining item successfully.*

G/A 24.12 "Our Sand Table !"

Task description:
- Exploring engagements in cooperative play, using the same materials, in the same space.

Expected Milestone Achievements (EMAs):
- Copies simple brick, block or similar item construction sequences (F2)
- Makes definable model shapes from clay or Blu-Tak (F3)
- Able to follow simple instructions without visual aid or gesture (Cog6)
- Answers questions with more than one (appropriate) word (Comms4)
- Repeats words and/or actions of others (esp. if novel) (Comms6)

Materials:
- Baby friendly (non-toxic) modelling clay/sand, tray/bowl
- Moulds/small containers (or cookie cutter shapes, jar lids, hollow bricks).

Procedure:
Level 1
1. Demonstrate a shallow tray or bowl, inside of which is placed some modelling clay/sand, on the floor or table.
2. Slowly show how to use your hands to build the clay into a small mountain, for baby to see.
3. Invite baby to now come closer to the sand/clay tray, reaching in with their hands to construct a clay/sand mountain of their own (or together with you).
4. As baby's mountain grows to becoming completed, provide prompt praise. *and discuss* their achievement(s).

Level 2
1-4 Repeat level 1 (steps 2-3), this time demonstrating and then presenting to baby some clay/sand moulds/shape-cutters to explore and use.
5. As/when baby is willing to share their own work and materials, provide prompt praise and encouragement for their effort each time.

Variations:
- Consider demonstrating the construction of simple shapes/models for baby to copy, using/reusing the same/similar materials each time.
- Ditto, requiring baby and yourself (or whomever else may be present) to work together cooperatively in achieving same result.

Baby Milestones of Development (0-3 Yrs)

Additional thoughts/Activity Preparation/Lesson Planning Tips:
- Be sure to provide baby only with children's modelling clay which has been certified as being both a baby-friendly and non-toxic material.
- If no pre-packaged clay be available in the home, prepare a simple home-made kit from flour & water (food colouring could create additional realism, if needed !).
- Set up the 'moulding area' on/in a shallow tray/bowl if possible, as a larger sided vessel will be more easily tipped over/spilt by baby's arms when reaching into it.
- Pay constant attention to preventing baby from eating children's modelling clay, or otherwise placing their clay-soiled hands into their mouth, nose or eyes.
- Consider using a baby bib throughout the sand/clay manipulation phases of the activity, and ensure baby promptly cleans both their hands, including nail slits, after manipulating the clay and other materials.

– 17 –

Baby Milestones of Development

Complete Milestone Set Listings by Age

Ages 12 - 24 Months

[1–2 Yrs]

Expected Milestone Achievements
Age = 12 Months (52 Wks)

Gross Motor
- Makes independent stepping experiments (even short walking)
- Shows increasing confidence with balance, and wishing to be mobile
- Moves around the room holding onto a variety of objects
- Climbs stairs and on to low furniture independently (though not always climbing down again successfully !)
- Attempts pushing along/riding on wheeled toys, without help
- Turns whole body (rather than just head) to see things behind self

Fine Motor
- Maintains grip whilst rotating wrist (e.g., as when attempting to bring a spoon to the mouth)
- More skilled/selective in manipulating shape sorter, buttons or rotary knobs
- Stacks objects to form low towers (to then knock down !)
- Assembles large, simple insertion puzzle pieces together
- Twists/turns small objects and their parts
- Draws continuous lines with crayon/pencil (not just scribbling)

Cognitive
- Shows simple groupings of classes/categories of objects, puts together in one place
- Enjoys exploring object properties (e.g., sinking/floating them in water)
- Shows increasingly selective hand use (left or right, though still quite ambidextrous)
- Appears to 'read' and turn pages of books, especially if designed with interactive features (e,g., opens/closes flaps, raises pop-ups)
- Willing and able to reassemble simple objects when taken apart
- Produces discrete lines and scribbles with drawing materials

Communication
- Changes behaviour in appropriate ways according to sounds and spoken language heard from others (independent of vision)
- Points to images of objects/events being described
- Showing more appropriate use/imitation of adult language in context (though maybe still without any clear understanding of its meaning ?)
- Vocabulary sensitivity significantly increasing (though generates no fluent speech)
- Beginning to name objects pointed to by others ("What is x ?","Where is your/my nose ?")
- Increasing length of utterances (especially if not interrupted)

Socio-Personal
- Leads adults (by the hand) towards objects/events of interest
- Willing and interested to create and act in fictional 'plays'
- Imitates adults, possibly with toy tools, *as they are occurring* (e.g., cleaning, cooking)
- Enjoys swinging, and attempts to self-propel using feet when on wheeled toy
- Handles/explores objects inside containers, to discover what is inside them
- Invites other(s) to engage in shared creative/play activity

Expected Milestone Achievements
Age = 13 Months

Gross Motor
- Bearing own weight unsupported, feet flat on ground most of time
- Attempts bending down to pick up dropped items, whilst standing

- Attempts walking with less dragging and/or tripping over own toes
- If walking, will try walking self-supported with only one hand

- Retrieves and returns a ball rolled towards them
- Successfully negotiates small obstacle courses set up on the floor

Fine Motor
- Uses pincer grip to hold objects, even if not looking at them
- Picks up, holds, and repositions toys/other objects without dropping them
- Uses opposing finger/thumb to pick up (1cm) object on flat surface
- Perseveres/continues trying to pick up string/paper after failing to do
- Explores page-turning of books and magazines/paper
- Points to wanted objects beyond immediate reach

Cognitive
- Retrieves items from small containers by shaking or poking at them
- Retrieves visibly-hidden objects without prompting
- Recognises self and familiar others in photo/video images
- Enjoys generating sound by banging a variety of different objects together
- Deliberately places multiple objects *into* the same container
- Imitates the efforts of others to write, scribble or draw lines

Communication
- Follows simple verbal requests, without accompanying gestures
- Tries to join in 'singing' simple nursery rhyme actions without imitation (following a verbal request/suggestion to do so)
- Uses the same double syllable sounds to refer to fewer objects (e.g., bottles, teddy bears and father are no longer *all* referred to as being "dada")
- Acquires attention and/or objects in ways other than by simply crying
- Shows appropriately controlled head nodding (e.g., to indicate yes/no responses)
- Recognises a wider variety of faces and facial expressions

Socio-Personal
- Attentive to distant objects which are being pointed at/to, by others
- Helps with dressing once clothing is in contact with the body
- Predicts participation in an increasing number of daily routines
- Cleanly releases held objects being passed/handed to another person
- Enjoys experimenting with own image in mirror (and with others, if present)
- Looks at objects (if present) that are being referred to by others

Baby Milestones of Development (0-3 Yrs)

Expected Milestone Achievements
Age = 14 Months

Gross Motor
- If standing unsupported, will try walking with only one hand held by another person
- Tries to stand up independently and take steps without support
- Pro-actively walking rather than crawling across distances
- Walks many consecutive steps before stumbling, or sitting
- Attempts to climb up onto furniture unaided
- Squats down in order to pick up an object from standing position

Fine Motor
- Successfully stacks 2 stable blocks on top of each other
- Touches, grasps and/or reaches towards unfamiliar objects
- Attempts to imitate action of throwing a ball (though may not release it at all !)
- Pincer grip used to hold/control a cup, crayon or pencil
- Makes marks on paper unaided, as if attempting to draw
- Tries to 'appropriately' turn the pages of a book

Cognitive
- Successfully avoids large object collisions when walking
- Stacks multiple objects, placing larger items below smaller ones
- Removes visible objects from bottles by turning them over
- Obtains distant objects by grasping parts, or uses tools to do so
- Imitates simple object representations drawn by others
- Focuses upon more details, including parts/components of images in pictures/books

Communication
- Imitates multi-word statements
- Begins simple nursery rhyme/game/actions without imitation (following a verbal request/suggestion to do so)
- Utterances include four or more sounds in addition to intentional use of "Mama" or "Baba"
- Produces multiple syllable sound sequences (e.g., "da-ba-boo-ba-ma")
- Generates and imitates a variety of noises (both vocally and instrumentally) for oneself, and orients towards novel sounds
- Spontaneously waves hand(s) to indicate "Hello" and/or "Bye-bye" unprompted

Socio-Personal
- Brings cup directly to mouth in order to self-feed or drink
- Enjoys exploring nesting and/or stacking toy interactions (alone or with others)
- Enjoys a variety of sounds and/or 'playing' simple musical instrument opportunities
- Excited to play on swings and watch others (though may be passive)
- Assists with dressing by pushing arms and legs through presented clothing
- Begins to undo buttons of own clothing/undress once returned home

Expected Milestone Achievements
Age = 15 Months

Gross Motor
- Walks many steps without stumbling, or sitting down
- Chooses to walk rather than crawl between rooms
- Stands up independently and take steps without support from either another person, or furniture
- Successfully climbs up onto low furniture items unaided
- Squats down to pick up an object, then resumes standing
- Smoothly stops walking, and stoops down to pick up a dropped object, arises and walks again, all in a single action

Fine Motor
- Appropriately alters/prepares grip according to different object's size and shape
- Keen to try (but often still unable) to pick up very small, flat objects
- Successfully stacks 2-3 blocks/toys on top of one another
- Imitates action of throwing a ball (with/without release)
- Independently turns a few pages of a book at one time
- Makes multiple marks on paper in an attempt to draw lines

Cognitive
- Keen to explore moving fluids in/out of containers (especially in bath)
- Reaches for dropped/distant items using a retrieving tool
- Recognises specific sounds as being the name of an object, person or event
- Developing fine control with selective grasping of one object from amongst a pile/collection
- Enjoys interacting with mobile objects, trolleys and/or rolling balls
- Attempts to imitate multiple drawn object representations

Communication
- Shows interest in body parts, and pointing to them when named
- Responds to non-visible (including deliberately hidden) sound sources
- Appears to recognise significance of facial expressions as they change
- Utterances include 6-8 or more sounds in addition to "Mama"
- Makes vocal sounds which resemble particular 'words'
- Increased production of multiple syllable sounds ('doo-doo-wah')

Socio-Personal
- Deliberately grasps food objects and raises them to the mouth using a tool (such as a cup, spork, or spoon)
- Selectively/accurately points towards desired/referenced objects
- Enjoys exploring singing and other musical games with others
- Attempts to 'look *for*' an object located in a different place (possibly outside the immediate room) when asked "Where is x ?"
- Enjoys to produce sounds and play percussive toys with others
- Holds and manipulates a spoon or fork in order to self-feed

Baby Milestones of Development (0-3 Yrs)

Expected Milestone Achievements
Age = 16 Months

Gross Motor
• Walks many steps without stumbling, whist carrying object(s)
• Prefers walking rather than crawling across large distances
• Kicks a ball with more flexible and coordinated limb joints
• Throws a ball (with release), though with little/no directional control
• Reaches down in order to pick up an object whilst moving
• Shows increased co-ordination of different body parts when climbing
Fine Motor
• Successfully stacks 3 or more blocks/toys in a stable pile
• Pulls strings and presses buttons in order to produce object movement/sounds
• Uses controlled finger grips when climbing up onto, and off of, furniture
• Scribbled patterns becoming more stable/stereotyped
• Makes longer, and increasing numbers of marks when drawing on paper
• Attempts multiple strokes/lines in order to draw a single image
Cognitive
• Spontaneously changes seating/kneeling position on a chair (in order to see/reach more distant objects)
• Remembers to pull strings and press buttons in order to produce object movement and/or sounds
• Reaches for distant items using a retrieval tool (without prompting)
• Shows more differential responses to (or curiosity about) unfamiliar objects
• Independently fills containers with small (< 1cm) objects
• Explores tearing and crumpling actions with paper, tissues and similar objects
Communication
• Looks for' and retrieves an object from a different place (even from outside room) when asked "Where is x ?"
• Becoming more attentive to adults' use of books as 'reading' and story content source (rather than being simply an object to tear/chew)
• Utterances now including the use of 3-6 reliably understandable words
• Appears to begin questioning ('What dat ?", at least in gesture, if not verbally)
• Enjoys repetitive and 'favourite' story telling/singing time
• Points and requests more accurately in order to acquire distant objects
Socio-Personal
• Shows teeth brushing attempts with increased coordination
• Responding to, and experimenting with, images in mirror
• Invites others to 'join' *their* activity by calling out loud
• Keen to invent/discover creative climbing adventures !
• Shows fear responses to particular sound sources (e.g., dog barks, loud machines)
• Show overt 'suspicion' or fear of strangers

Baby Milestones of Development (0-3 Yrs)

Expected Milestone Achievements
Age = 17 Months

Gross Motor
- Will attempt *descent* of stairs if held by the hand
- Spontaneously stands up in order to move to a new location, (without support, and without being asked to do so)
- Prefers to walk rather than to crawl, even short distances
- Seeks holding hands of others in order to secure balance
- Climbs onto furniture in order to obtain object out of reach
- Successfully throws objects (such as a ball), though with poor control of direction/distance

Fine Motor
- Freely grasps and drinks from cup without being given it
- Makes appropriate grasping and release of objects, to/from others
- Attempts two-handed ball catching (albeit unsuccessfully !)
- Attempts bent overarm ball throwing (or similarly of other objects)
- Removes whole articles of (most) own clothing, without help
- Plays with percussion toys more deliberately, and with more refined movements

Cognitive
- Explores the emptying and refilling of containers with various objects
- Identifies (some) familiar picture contents without prompting
- Opens and explores contents of cupboards (including refridgerator !)
- Keen to explore transfer of fluids between containers (especially in bath play)
- Associates simple words, sounds and smells with particular actions
- Shows consistency in use of drawing tools

Communication
- Points correctly to specific book images when asked, "Where is the x ?"
- Initiates activities (rather than passively waiting for adult prompting)
- Makes simple two word utterances (e.g., "Baba eat", "Mama have")
- Shows increased turn-taking during speech patterns, and increasingly with intonation
- 10-20 or more words now in common, daily usage
- Proto-speech concerning familiar objects/events clearly understandable by others

Socio-Personal
- Increasingly willing to explore surroundings with other infants
- Very likely to repeat behaviours which make others (especially adults) laugh
- Increasingly attentive to details of the activities of others' (especially other babies/infants)
- Increasingly attentive to the causes and effects of the different behaviours of others (especially siblings/other babies)
- Utters proto-speech concerning shared perceptions, objects & events understandable to significant others (e.g., close family)
- Assists with self-dressing (and almost ALL *un*dressing !)

Expected Milestone Achievements
Age = 18 Months

Gross Motor
- Increasing controlled use of joints, rather than making stiff limbed movements
- Descends stairs alone, even if only in seated, 'bumping' style/position
- Makes deliberate forward ball kicking (rather than simply 'walking into' ball)
- Successfully attempts to move away from others' lap or chair (without help)
- Imitates tool use as demonstrated by adults (other than hand-tools)
- Stands up in order to move to a new location, without support, when called

Fine Motor
- Increasingly willing to imitate the manual actions of others
- Stacks and restacks falling block towers into new configurations
- Attempts joint movement rather than whole-arm throwing (i.e., more bending at elbows/wrist)
- Will copy examples of drawing single curves/lines, by taking turns
- Shows spontaneous scribbling/drawing (without prompting)
- Frequently produces single-stroke line drawing

Cognitive
- Will stack 3-5 similar objects 'in order' (e.g., by size)
- Attempts various ways to 'escape' restrictions of pushchair, highchair/ car seat harnesses (including straps/buckles)
- Rotates/empties objects in order to obtain desired effects, and/or access to contents
- Able to drink from cup unaided, with little/no spillage
- Uses a variety of 'tools' for specific purposes
- Seeks help when failing to operate mechanical or electrical toys/objects

Communication
- Uses 40-50 (or more) words now in common, daily utterances
- Shows adult-like use of fingers and hands when animating stories
- Points to object images, before object is mentioned in storyline, (especially body parts)
- Follows familiar single-step verbal commands/instructions, without gesture
- Links words representing different ideas (e.g., "Mamma have drink")
- Knows 'when' to 'start a conversation' (filling a silence/pause in other's speech)

Socio-Personal
- Seeks attention of others by pulling on their hand, arm or clothing
- Enjoys exploring/sharing some outdoor activities with other infants
- Enjoys watching/listening to familiar TV/radio characters
- Throws objects into boxes/baskets (as a game with others)
- Identifies significant others by sound alone (e.g., 'Papa' via phone/recording)
- Actively seeks help from others when failing to achieve something

Baby Milestones of Development (0-3 Yrs)

Expected Milestone Achievements
Age = 19 Months

Gross Motor
- Walks without stiff-limbed gait/action, or losing balance so often
- Walks up (and down) a few stairs unaided
- Stands, and comes to new location(s) when asked to so
- Reaches with outstretched arm when hearing "Hold my hand, please"
- Climbs on objects without prompting, in order to see things from a higher position
- Willing and able to remove clothing at appropriate times

Fine Motor
- Offers hand with appropriate finger grasp positions when reached for by another person
- Turns single book pages unaided
- Successfully stacks 5-6 blocks to make a tower
- 'Twists' screw top lids and 'pulls' lever caps of containers
- Identifies several pictures by pointing at them (from amongst others)
- Makes crayon/chalk marks with tips, rather than flat surfaces in order to draw

Cognitive
- Frequently succeeds with matching shapes with sorting holes upon first attempt
- Will copy/reproduce simple block patterns (3-4 blocks), given examples
- Spontaneously stacks 3-5 objects in order of increasing size
- Rotates tools such as a spoon or cup in order to use them
- Identifies familiar objects by touch (without seeing them)
- Uses crayon to scribble several lines without lifting from paper

Communication
- Shows appropriate response to simple requests (e.g., "Close the door, please")
- Points to own body parts when named (especially of/around head/face)
- Imitates short sentence questions (e.g., "Where dada ?", "What is it ?")
- Speaks babble 'language' in longer (yet still unintelligible) 'sentences'
- Enjoys demonstrating a variety of different sounds by causing them
- 'Talks' and laughs when exploring bath toys (especially with bubbles)

Socio-Personal
- Successfully shares sorting of simple shapes, and building large 2-D picture puzzles
- Explores washing and drying of own hands
- Experiments with caring behaviour using doll/soft toy (e.g., feeding, washing)
- Imitates eye blinking and several other immediate adult facial gestures
- Spontaneously imitates adult health behaviour (tooth-brushing, hair-combing)
- Increasingly engaged by water and sand play (alone or with others) if available

Expected Milestone Achievements
Age = 20 Months

Gross Motor
• Walks fast, (even runs ?), without stumbling or bumping into objects
• Walks several stairs spontaneously, and unaided
• Changes direction when avoiding objects in path of movement
• Carries own weight (with balance) when running, unsupported
• Climbs upon a chair to see on table when asked "What's on the table ?"
• Throws a ball with over-arm movement
Fine Motor
• Changes palm grip according to size and shape of object being offered
• Grips jars or tubs appropriate to turning/levering their lids open
• Uses a spoon to self-feed without turning it upside-down and spilling
• Shifts orientation of a held spoon or fork when scooping for use
• Identifies 6-10 pictures by pointing at them (amongst others)
• Draws without changing hand/crayon tip holding posture mid-stroke
Cognitive
• Selects correct shapes for visible sorting-box holes
• Successfully stacks 7-9 blocks in a tower
• Starting to correctly predict unseen object motion (balls moving in tubes, behind objects, etc.)
• Picks up and rotates bottle in order to drink from it
• Imitates sequences of adult facial expression changes
• Explores more challenging toys/activities with increasing interest
Communication
• Shows appropriate response to action requests (e.g., "Bring the teddy-bear here, please")
• Knows and uses as many as 50+ single words
• Attentive to different verbal instructions, without directly looking at the person speaking to them
• Imitates 3-5 words sentences of others (even if not understanding their meaning)
• Occasionally sings repetitive rhymes and canons for self-amusement
• Offers objects with 'speech', and facial expressions to self in mirror
Socio-Personal
• Imitates body part touching whilst watching an adult do the same (especially parts of the face, chin, ears and neck)
• Likes to play 'catch' and similar thrown-object games with others
• Copies adult's drawing single lines, in any direction
• Enjoys 'putting dolls/toys to bed', or enacting hygiene routines with soft toys/animals
• Imitates household chore behaviours (e.g., cleaning, sweeping, wiping spills)
• Self-stimulated by interacting with mechanical/electronic toys with curiosity

Expected Milestone Achievements
Age = 21 Months

Gross Motor
- Maintains stable upright posture when stops running
- Runs or walks with abrupt direction change, without bumping or falling on obstacles
- Jumps up and down (though maybe needing support of one foot on floor)
- Negotiates stepping/climbing obstacles whilst shifting visual focus near/far distance
- Attempts to kick ball with swinging leg/foot
- Throws a ball towards target location and/or specific direction

Fine Motor
- Places objects down on flat surfaces without dropping them
- Realises *significance* and use of remote control devices
- Correctly points to/touches several body parts, when requested to do so
- Pincer grip shape made before picking up small object shapes
- Attempts to turn book pages at appropriate times during reading
- Rotates 'turned' blocks to match an example block array

Cognitive
- Begins to ask "What's this" when finding new objects
- Corrects orientation of tools for immediate use after handling
- Locates and obtains correct objects when needing (or asked for) them
- Attempts to imitate organised patterns/arrays of objects (e.g., by colour, size)
- Explores use of familiar object for novel purpose (e.g., using a fork as a rake)
- Attempts copying of complex multi-line drawings

Communication
- Correctly names familiar object pictures when pointed to by others
- Identifies familiar objects or people in complex pictures/images
- Opens and closes mouth when asked to do so
- Correctly uses 1st person possessives (e.g., mine, me)
- Babbling with 'adult-like' speech intonation when 'talking' to dolls and/or soft toys
- Activates 'correct' sounds using chosen musical instruments

Socio-Personal
- Spontaneously explores novel objects alone (e.g., putting empty box on head)
- Increasingly willing/able to put on own clothing
- Finds and presents certain objects when asked for them
- Seeks/requests others to join a shared activity of interest
- Actively seeks 'playmates' when available
- Pushes stroller/cart with *some* attention to avoiding collisions with objects/others

Expected Milestone Achievements
Age = 22 Months

Gross Motor
- Pursues moving object (ball) with controlled walk/running gait and speed
- Starts and stops running freely without colliding with objects or others
- Actively searches for objects and takes/places them in suggested locations
- Jumps up and down freely, without floor contact (i.e., with both feet off the ground)
- Kicks a ball towards target location and/or specific (if general) direction
- Kicks ball with swinging leg and/or foot (e.g., more flexible at hip, knee, & ankle)

Fine Motor
- Manages large buttons/poppers on clothing
- Places plug into water sink and/or threads large-holed beads onto string
- Able to correctly point to, or touch, 7-10 own body parts
- Changes position of light switches and other binary position controls
- Acquires small visible items from bottles by rotating/shaking them
- Organises toys/objects into recognisable patterns and symmetries

Cognitive
- Transfers fluids between containers without gross spillage
- Spontaneously explores novel objects (e.g., shakes/bangs them together)
- Organises objects according to simple categories (e.g., size, colour, or shape)
- Requests names for new or unfamiliar 'found' objects
- Finds new uses for familiar objects without prompting
- Identifies familiar cartoon characters in novel places, magazines, TV images, etc

Communication
- Demonstrates frequent use of more than 50 single words
- Correctly uses 2nd person possessive (e.g., yours, you)
- Asks for names of shelf items when out shopping
- Requests novel, visible objects out of reach, using words
- Correctly identifies different sounds by name
- Asks to be told the names of new or unfamiliar objects

Socio-Personal
- Attempts to clean own teeth, given equipment (and help) to do so
- Using words, rather than crying, in order to request help from others
- Sensitive to operation of "on/off" control buttons, relative to other controls
- Play-feeds dolls or soft toys without significant spillage or smearing of face/body
- Keen to jump and/or move in coordination with others
- Beginning to treat dolls/soft toys as if babies or friends

Expected Milestone Achievements
Age = 23 Months

Gross Motor
- Balances own weight whilst walking along a narrow path/line
- Walks/runs along uneven textured surface/path without stumbling/falling
- Stands on 'tip-toe' when look up to see what is outside a window, or on a table
- Jumps freely (but still with a skip-like gait ?)
- Ascends and descends stairs, in novel places, and without help
- Throws or kicks a ball at a target with appropriate force

Fine Motor
- Catches or makes contact with a moving balloon in the air
- Enjoys playing with buttons and control knobs
- Appropriately grasps/holds parts of wheeled toys when pushing/pulling them along
- Pencil/pen grip becoming increasingly stereotyped (same grip each time used)
- Imitates drawing of multiple-line images
- Draws with increasingly fluent strokes/movement

Cognitive
- Plays with familiar objects in unfamiliar ways (stacking food)
- Sorts familiar items by colour, shape *and* size
- Gathers objects together according to their similarities (other than colour & size)
- Spontaneously turns novel containers, to release contents
- Increasingly interested to manipulate/catch moving objects
- Seeks/finds small chair or box to stand on in order to obtain object out of reach

Communication
- Increasingly sensitive to different vowel sounds, and their meanings
- Responds correctly when asked "Where is xxx ?" in pictures
- Understands references being made to unseen objects
- Frequently makes multiple syllable responses to questions (e.g., "It is here, mama")
- Produces reliably interpretable multi-word utterances
- Uses 1st and 2nd person pronouns (I, me, yours, mine)

Socio-Personal
- Reaches for someone's hand when 'ready' or about to initiate walking
- Predicts location of non-visible object moving behind a screen (or other obstruction)
- Increasingly willing to explore interactions with novel toy(s)
- Excited to repeat (predictable) turn-taking games with others
- Plays in front of a mirror with more subtle facial expressions and sounds
- Enjoys recognition in/of familiar playmates

Expected Milestone Achievements
Age = 24 Months

Gross Motor
- Balances own weight whilst walking along a single, narrow path (< 30 cm/ 12 Inches)
- Carries objects whilst walking
- Climbs easily up/down stairs (given the choice !)
- Jumps with both feet simultaneously off the ground
- Throws and kicks a ball at target with appropriate force
- Will attempt to ride a tricycle with assistance

Fine Motor
- Picks up and arranges coins/discs to produce 'same-side' patterns
- Copies simple brick, block or similar item construction sequences
- Makes definable model shapes from clay, plasteceine or Blu-Tak
- Takes apart (and refits) toys with component parts
- Imitates drawing of multi-directional lines
- Folds paper in particular ways (by example)

Cognitive
- Sorts a variety of different objects by their type, size, shape *and* colour
- Sorts the *same set of objects* according to EITHER their sizes, shapes OR colour
- Successfully searches for objects hidden under covers
- Plays with keyboard and/or other musical instrument with discerning/differential effect(s) for sounds heard
- Enjoys 'putting things away' and 'getting them out' again
- Follows simple instructions without visual aid or gesture

Communication
- Responds 'Yes'/'No' when asked "Is xxx in the picture ?"
- Will search for, and collect, unseen objects when asked for them
- Appropriately uses 1st and 2nd person possessives (mine, yours, Mama's)
- Answers questions with more than one (appropriate) word
- Frequently uttering multi-syllable phrases (e.g., "Teddy eat banana now")
- Repeats words and/or actions of others (especially if novel)

Socio-Personal
- Reliably monodextrous with hand preference for certain tasks
- Increasingly aware of self as being distinct/different from others
- Begins to show significant amounts of make-believe play
- Responds more enthusiastically when in the company of other children
- Speaks/points to pictures/object to express interest to others ("Look, there's a boat")
- Acts/plays out imaginary stories/adventures (either alone, or with others)

- 18 -

Baby Milestones of Development

An Afterword

Now that I have presented the more comprehensive 12-24 month ages' milestone sets and fun games/activities for your exploration and enjoyment with your baby in this book, it is my sincerest hope that we have also made bold strides towards helping you more adequately answer the question "Is my baby OK ?", with respect to this particular age-range, this time in a single focussed volume. Now sharing so many increasingly varying interactions with baby since the end of your first relatively quiet 12-month period of post-natal development, I hope that you are also continuing to enjoy a much reduced anxiety with regards what so often turns out to be many parents' unnecessary concerns for their growing babies, now young infant's development, especially now that baby has become so much more mobile,…. and increasingly vocal !!

That said, I continue to welcome all reader's comments and findings (both regular and perhaps surprising !), concerning your personal use of the milestone sets and activity suggestions provided for you here, and, as before, I look forward to updating future editions according to such feedback received. Such might also include pictures of your own creative play situations and equipments, should you wish me to consider including them, plus the addition of any new regional 'norm tables' built from the pooling of new results sent to me by the various user's EMA scores, from a variety of different cities and countries around the world. Such results may be sent to me directly from a baby's individual parents, or via parent-permitted data-sharing pre-clinical and ECE centres, and academic research labs). For those wishing to me send (anonymously) their monthly/periodic results of IMBO-EMA for collation, or simply provide comments for my attention, please feel free to do so via the following email address:

td2202@hotmail.com

and please, in order to maintain your privacy, include **only** the following information:

1. *Baby's age month being responded to* (e.g., 9 months)
2. *A single figure score for each of the 5 domains* (GM-FM-Cog-Comms-SP)
3. *Baby's gender* (Male/Female)
4. *The name of your city/country of residence* (Bath, England; Bangalore, India).

The only use made of this information will be in the construction of new IMBO-EMA regional 'norm-tables' (Average scores & +/- 2SD listings) for new/updated geographical location comparisons, to be published in the same format as shown earlier volumes. This will appear in future editions of that book only, once a sufficiently sized data set be acquired for each new country/city.

NB: such information as you may provide for this purpose, will not be made available to any additional third party, nor will it be used for ANY other purpose.

- 19 -

Baby Milestones of Development

Tips to bear in mind when making the Best of your Expected Milestone Achievement (EMA) Assessments

For each of the 30 items of each month range's IMBO-EMA-sets listed, the parent or care-giver needs respond in only one of three ways each time, to each EMA item, and consistently the same way with increasing age over time. Each assessment is best completed in the presence of baby, when you are both well rested and fed, with the purpose of helping baby to demonstrate most, if not all, of the EMA behaviours listed for her/his current full month-completed age as indicated, For example, if baby is now 18 months of age (i.e., has completed 18 full months of development since birth, but is not yet 19 Mths), go through the EMAs listed in the "18 Months" EMA-set, and for each item in each of the 5 domains, check *either* YES, SOMETIMES, *or* NOT YET, according to the following definitions, each time:

YES - If baby is repeatedly capable of doing the described activity right now
SOMETIMES - If baby is just beginning to do the activity
NOT YET - If baby has not started to do the activity, or has never been seen doing it

If unsure as to the best answer to any EMA item at a given time, it is always preferable to facilitate baby's actual demonstration of the behaviour in question, at the time of addressing that item, each time, whenever possible. This will provide not only a quick reality check for you if you're a little uncertain, but will afford yet another valuable opportunity for you and baby to explore some fun variation(s) in your daily routine together, whilst also engaging in some novel, interesting interactions, even if only for a short while !

A full item scoring system has been developed, and is described in earlier volumes of this series wishing to make use of that, but for the relatively simple purposes of checking baby's monthly milestone achievement here, simply note the number of YES/NO/NOT YET that you observe for each of the five domains' milestones for the current month (Gross Motor, Fine Motor, Cognitive Ability, Communication, and Socio-Personal). Then, simply note the numbers indicating any of the relative strengths and weaknesses visible in baby's ongoing development, across the five domains, whilst also noting the most significant changes that are taking place over time.

In cases where baby is consistently failing to achieve more than 2-3 of the milestones within the same domain across consecutive months, there may be some value in considering seeking an additional professional evaluation of baby's developmental progress, outside the home environment. Alternatively, it may be that such a result is instead merely indicating a developmental delay (see also the earlier section above regarding Expectation Variations) and remember that "NOT YET" in context here does *not* equate to "Will NEVER").

As each child progressively reaches each month's milestone set (total = 36 Mths = 3 yrs+), less attention will need to be paid towards differentiating 'from birth' age in months, as opposed to calendar months. Likewise, you should expect to observe fewer 'large step' developments within a shorter period of time as baby grows older and more competent with practice interacting with their environment, and moving through it with increased self-confidence and excitement for your shared eduventures together !

In answer to the question as to 'when' to conduct each monthly milestone assessment, and in contrast to the use of formal IQ testing (which is not very useful below ages of 3-4 years, and wasted money in my view), there is no problem with assessing developmental achievements as often as you might wish. There are no 'correct' answers to learn, or cheating possible with repeated use of the same (or even different) monthly milestone sets. Indeed, there is some value to your conducting frequent, repeated, milestone evaluations and activities with baby at home, and at no financial cost to you ! As you become increasingly familiar with the most realistic expectations for your baby's development, you will also be more willing to interact with baby in such a way as to learn for yourselves that, "My baby *is* OK !", and also in what ways they may otherwise be showing some delayed, or more advanced behaviours, given baby's current age*.

*NB: for parents caring for very-low birth weight and/or premature born babies, simply 'adjust' for the most appropriate gestational-age-related milestone set as has been advised you, at your regular baby clinic visit(s) or as previously advised by your post-natal nurse/family practitioner.

I am suggesting that milestone observations can be made every day, possibly weekly, but at least monthly. This will provide you not only increase the number of unique opportunities for focussed play engagements, but also your paying attention to baby's growth, and of especially the early period when relatively quiet and less mobile. Whereas it used to seem that there was only the 'sleep-feed-poop-wash-sleep' cycle for baby in their first months following birth, remember that, baby is always busy with growth and development. For example, whilst increasing their flexibility in responding to various stimuli, baby is also enhancing the efficiency of their intellectual, postural and emotional reactivity, self-control and motivational states. The significance of distinguishing between baby's different crying episodes (e.g., as expressed during baby's hunger vs wet/cold discomfort vs pain), is often one of the more memorable, if not first noticeable learning episodes for both baby and their parents. But remember also that only *some* of baby's behavioural repertoire is at times either clearly visible or audible. Once knowing what baby behaviours to look *for*, whilst also increasing baby's interaction levels with each other's increased attention *to* those behaviours, you will continue to develop not only a better knowledge and understanding of, but also a closer bonding with baby.

Indeed, the very worse thing that can happen in using these milestone sets with your baby, is that you will also learn something about yourself !... All the while, remember that the more *invisible* processes of enhanced brain growth density and complexity for self-control, sensory and motor systems, are constantly taking place, whether we are 1 month, 1 year, or indeed 100 years, old.

- 20 -

Baby Milestones of Development

Use of milestone observations as discussion/consultancy material

For those wishing to use the EMA/milestone/fun baby games and activity results and recommendations as a part of a service to client parents in a pre-clinical assessment or early child education (ECE) resource setting, commercial or community-centred play/activity sessions*, milestone observations readily lend themselves to providing both an instructional and stimulating focus for consultancy discussions with regards a specific baby's behavioural development (or lack thereof). The IMBO/EMA milestone set may be used for any particular day/class' session can always provide a short (reminder) series of ideas with which the ECE consultant may engage parents (both during and after the session that they *both* just witnessed/enjoyed). So doing will help a parent to interpret their own observational experiences following interactions with particular game/task/activity' materials *(and* to those of any other attending babies/parents engaged in the same class, at the same time), together with those of their own baby's everyday learning and developmental experience(s).

When discussing baby 'performance' with parents and care-givers alike, specific reference should always be made to the *explicit behaviours*, as they were actually exhibited/*demonstrated, BY the baby/infant* as they are developing, as individuals, and *as they have just performed during the last task activity, during the activity/session just jointly observed*. Most importantly, it does one well to try focussing upon the demonstrated behaviour(s) per se (and in particular to any positive behaviour changes/developments observed), and to place little/no emphasis concerning the baby/parent being 'good/poor' themselves, merely because baby cannot perhaps 'can/cannot do xxx *just now'*. It is, after all, only 'good' or 'poor' quality *behaviour* which is being made visible during supervised play, not the revealing of 'good' or 'poor' babies/parents !

* There are no special licence(s) required for the community or commercial use of the activities included in this, or other companion books by this author, of this IMBO/EMA baby milestone series.

ψ

- 21 -

Baby Milestones of Development

IMBO-EMA (Baby Milestone) Design-disclaimer

PLEASE NOTE THAT, ALTHOUGH THE *"Is My Baby OK ?" (IMBO)-EMA* ASSESSMEMT LISTS AND CONTENT ARE ENTIRELY CONSISTENT WITH OTHER STANDARDISED DEVELOPMENT MEASURING TOOLS (e.g., BAYLEY-III), IT WAS NOT DESIGNED TO ASSIST IN THE SPECIFIC DIAGNOSIS OR REHABILITATION OF THE COGNITIVELY IMPAIRED, BRAIN-DAMAGED OR CLINICALLY-PRESENTING BABY-INFANT CHILD UNDERGOING ANY COURSE(S) OF PHYSICAL OR PSYCHIATRIC MEDICATION. IN THE CASE OF ANY KNOWN, OR SUSPECTED, CLINICAL CONDITIONS APPLYING TO ANY INFANT CHILD, COURSES OF TREATMENT SHOULD ONLY BE DELIVERED UNDER THE ADDITIONAL SUPERVISORY GUIDANCE OF A CONSULTING PHYSICIAN, MEDICAL DOCTOR, OR CERTIFIED DEVELOPMENTAL, CLINICAL, OR OTHERWISE REFERRING PROFESSIONAL EDUCATIONAL PSYCHOLOGIST.

In addition, such milestone ability achievements as recorded from use of the monthly IMBO-EMA sets as listed here, should *not* be used exclusively in determining *healthy* development. Close attention needs remain with regards to possible alternative baby behaviour change indicators suggesting need for a clinic or hospital visit. For example, if baby 'looks different' from her/his normal self (in general appearance), or is 'acting differently' in some noticeable and unexpected way, consider to consult your regular family clinician. Such differences might include unusual skin paleness or lightening of colour, unusual tiredness or drowsiness, lack of interest, unusual irritability, anxiousness, temperature fluctuations, restlessness, prostration, or feeding irregularities. More specific condition behaviours deserving of immediate consultation with a hospital doctor might include unusual vomiting episodes, hoarseness of voice, persistent fresh blood loss or eye inflammations.

ψ

Appendix A

A Comparison of the Milestone Sets of *"Is My Baby OK ?"* (IMBO-EMAs), with other Commonly used Baby Assessment Tools

Although not perhaps always consciously focused on assessment matters, upon meeting their newly born baby for the first time, most parents will immediately look at their baby with great curiosity, checking that they are breathing/crying, and then proceed to count the number of fingers and toes they have ! This behaviour shows that right from the get-go, most parents are already interested in making physiological evaluations, and psychometric measurement of comparisons, whilst also addressing a variety of 'norm-based' comparative developmental concerns.

Within seconds if not minutes of delivery in the maternity ward, or even at home with a midwife, many modern birthing situations will see a newborn baby undergo an immediate *APGAR* evaluation. The *APGAR* test formally assesses the condition of newborn infants and identifies those that might require any life-sustaining medical assistance, such as resuscitation. The test items provide a measure of a newly born baby's appearance, pulse, responsiveness, muscle activity and breathing (think of the letters in the surname name of the test's initiator, in 1952, Virginia Apgar: **A**ctivity, **P**ulse, **G**rimace, **A**ppearance, **R**espiration). The *APGAR* score provides a qualitative measure of the newborn's success in adapting to its environment immediately post-partum. The assessment is made within the first 1-5 minutes, only takes seconds to complete, and is not repeated unless a score of below 7 of a total maximum = 10 is attained. If, after a further 5 minutes, their score is 6 or below, medical assistance is recommended, thereafter continuing to assess again at 15 minute intervals for improvement (or if a later lower score = 3 or less, neurological damage is likely suspected). The *APGAR* test has proven to be a valuable baby assessment tool for use at the time of birth, a life-saver even, but has little value for parents beyond the 1st hour or two of a baby's life.

Extending further into a baby's development, and including a wider range of behaviours, is the *Neonatal Behavioral Assessment Scale* (NBAS) of T. Berry Brazelton, first published in 1973. Rather than viewing the infant baby as simply a mechanical stimulus-responsive organism, Brazelton's NBAS administration provides for an interactive assessment, in which the examiner plays an important role in facilitating the performance and organisational skills of the individual baby. The NBAS items cover a total four domains of neurobehavioural functioning:

1. Autonomic/Physiological Regulation: Baby's homeostatic adjustments of their central nervous system as reflected in colour change, tremor, and startles.
2. Motor Organisation: Baby's quality of movement and tone, activity level, and general level of integrated motor movements.

3. State Organisation and Regulation: Baby's arousal and state liability, and the infant's ability to regulate their state in the face of increasing levels of stimulation.
4. Attention/Social Interaction: Baby's ability to attend to visual or auditory stimuli, and the quality of overall alertness.

The most recent version of the NBAS that I knew of, assessed the newborn baby's behavioural repertoire with some 28 behavioural items, each scored on a 9-point scale (plus a 20-item neurological reflex-status indicator, scored on a 4-point scale). However, the assessment was still only appropriate for use with babies aged 0-2 months of age, and although no specialist equipment is necessary, it requires extensive training on the part of the test administrator in providing reliable data and clear interpretation of the results.

The third baby assessment tool worthy of mention here is the more user-friendly series presented in the form of the *Ages & Stages Questionnaire* (ASQ, now available in its 3rd Ed, as ASQ-III). This form of assessment can be readily conducted within the home, by any literate person capable of reading and answering a few questions with sustained attention for a period of about 20-30 minutes. There are a total 20 questionnaires for the parent to complete over 5 years, one for each two-monthly period from 4 - 24 months of age, and thereafter at increasing intervals from 3 - 6 months apart from ages 27 - 60 months. Each of the 20 questionnaires presents the parent/care-giver with 30 developmental items to consider, the majority of which will also appear in the item set assessment designed for both the previous and subsequent age ranges. Each of the 30 statements of each questionnaire require a 3-way forced-choice response from the parent or care-giver, and scored according to the response-types thus made for each of five domain totals. Each age-stated developmental item set is divided into 5 behavioural domains (consistent with those used for the IMBO-EMA sets, only differing in one category's nomenclature): Communication, Gross Motor, Fine Motor, Personal-social, and Problem-solving. The results of each ASQ-x test may be easily self-administered by the parent without specialist guidance, though perhaps with less certainty as to how to interpret the results being achieved over time. This is especially true given that a key design feature of each month's items of the ASQ-x' assessment includes the repeating of so many of the previous (and following) month's items, and thus confusing many parent's expectations with regards their own baby's additional development each time, in contrast to normative others of comparable age.

The fourth and final example baby assessment tool introduced here for comparison is the *Bayley Scale of Infant Development* (BSID) developed by Nancy Bayley, and currently in its 3rd Edition (2006, BSID-III). The Bayley tests are individually administered examinations that assess the developmental functioning of infants aged from 1-42 Months. The Bayley-III is both a direct (actual test of behaviour) and indirect (questionnaire) child assessment, useful for identifying developmental norm levels, delay, and intervention planning. The direct testing is a professional psychometric test and requires use of a specialised item kit and specified equipment, only made available for sale from a single supplier, to qualified professional psychologists, doctors, and clinically-certified persons. There are again 5 assessment domains: Three scales resulting from the direct testing of the baby's abilities - Cognitive, Motor & Language skills, and two scales resulting from caregiver/parent questionnaire completions - Socio-emotional, and Adaptive Behaviours. The Bayley tests have seen their significant and extensive use in the Educational, Clinical, Medical and Research literature for many years, and remain the assessment of choice that I have used for both pre-clinical and neurological diagnosis, but require extensive professional training under extended supervision, and hence lay beyond access for most parents, ECE centre teachers, or non-clinical personnel.

The core purpose of my creating the "Is My Baby OK ?" (IMBO) EMA-based baby-infant development tool (the version printed here in this volume, c.2019-2020), is to make it available to all parents for their own use, within your own homes, or within supervised early child education (ECE) centres. With its content consistent with the professional *Bayley-III* behavioural test items used as indicators of baby development age-rankings for 0-3 years, the IMBO-EMA sets have replaced the ASQ-x series of parent-completed baby development questionnaire sets previously used in many baby/parent education centres and ongoing research programs that I have recently visited. The IMBO-EMA item sets were designed by this author to identify a finer set of incremental achievements as may be readily visible to parents, for each and *every* month of their baby/infant's development, at least for ages 0-24 months (in contrast, the ASQ-x offering different milestone sets as far as 1-3 months apart). A further challenge was to do this *without* any repeated items being presented across any two month's item sets (the ASQ-x item repetition rates across adjacent months was often as much as 70-80% identical). Using data from years of observation, and as published in the clinical and pre-clinical research findings (from my own labs, and those of participating colleagues and students), standard paediatric teaching texts, and a plethora of medical observations, the ASQ-x's milestone 'gaps' have been gradually closed, to now provide the final IMBO-EMA item sets which cover some 29 distinct and unique monthly-based age grouping lists of clearly identifiable developmental Expected Milestone Achievement sets (EMAs).

Indeed, in its currently available format here, the complete IMBO-EMA item set is the largest and most comprehensive such assessment tool of its kind, yet its use remains within the grasp of any literate parent of young babies and infants, without need for any specialist equipment, attending physician, or other professional practitioner. The IMBO fully covers the 5 key domains of human behavioural developments (Gross Motor, Fine Motor, Cognitive, Communication, and Socio-personal abilities), at a depth greater than that ever before made available in a single assessment tool. The IMBO assists parents in identifying a total of almost 900 individual milestones of achievement for their easy observation, as may normally be revealed each month within 10-15 minutes of careful observation, covering 30 items each month, from birth to 3 yrs of age.

ψ

Other books of the current author.

1. *"Baby Milestones of Development"* (UK) series I:

   - *Baby Milestones of Development (0-12 Months): With 100+ Fun Activities to help demonstrate them.*

   - *Baby Milestones of Development (12-24 Months): With 100+ Fun Activities to help demonstrate them.*

   - *Baby Milestones of Development (24-36 Months): With 100+ Fun Activities to help demonstrate them.*

2. *"Is My Baby OK ?"* (13 Volume set, East Asia ECE) series:

   " Is My Baby OK ?: Realistic Expectations for monthly milestone achievements in early child development (0-3 Yrs)" (2019-20).

3. *"Baby Milestones of Development"* (UK) series II (Forthcoming):

A further 5-part series is also being prepared, by reader request, each volume covering *all* of the age ranges (0-3 years), but arranged solely according to each of the five individual ability domains, each in a single volume: *(Gross Motor Skill Development, Fine Motor Development, Cognitive Abilities, Communication Skills,* and *Socio-Personal Skills,* respectively).

ψ

Brief Author Biography and IMBO-EMA Milestone Related Publications:

Dr. Anthony R. Dickinson

Chartered Psychologist (BPS, UK), Reg. Clin. Psy (HKSCP), AFBPsS,
FHKSCP, AFHKPS, C.Sci., C.Psychol., Dip.Neurosci., PhD.

President, Hong Kong Society of Counselling and Psychology
Senior Academic & Clinical Consultant, Jabez Counseling.

- Dean of Academic Research/Program Director, EduChina, Beijing (2015-19).
- Science Advisor, Beijing Genomics Institute (GZ), China (2012-2015).
- Visiting Professor, Institute of Neuroscience (Chinese Academy of Sciences), Shanghai (2010-2011).
- Teaching professor & Visiting Research Fellow, Pre-clinical Neuroscience & Biological Psychology, McDonnell Centre for Higher Brain Research, Washington University School of Medicine, StL, MO, USA (1999-2006).
- Lecturer in Psychology (Comparative Neuroscience and Child Development), University of Edinburgh, UK (1991-1999).
- Attache de Recherche, WHO-CIRMF, Gabon, W. Africa (1989-90).
- Res. Asst., MRC Reproduction Unit, University of Edinburgh, UK (1988-89).

Dickinson, A. R. (2019). *Is My Baby OK ? - Realistic Expectations for monthly milestone achievements in early child development*. Professional & Technical Kindle-Amazon. USA.

Dickinson, A.R. (2018). How a knowledge of *Expected Milestones of Achievement* (EMA) Inventory Can Decrease Parental Anxiety: Answering the Question 'Is My Baby OK ?". [Invited Plenary Speaker]: *4th International Conference on Depression, Anxiety & Stress Management*, Frankfurt, Germany. May 10-11, 2018.

Dickinson, A.R. & Zheng, SL-E (2017). 'Is My Baby OK ?": The Expected Milestone Achievement (EMA) inventory. [Invited Keynote Address]: *XIXth Global Congress on Pediatricians & Child Psychiatry*. Chicago, Il USA. July 12-13.

Dickinson, A.R. (2016) A Primer on Developmental Expectations for infants born premature and Caesaerian birth. *CPD Teaching Practice, Series IV* EduChina Beijing-Shanghai Joint Seminar Series. Shanghai, China.

Dickinson, A. R. & Zheng, E (2013). Comparative Early Infant Milestone Development: Measuring Babies and Engaging Parents, East and West. *International Journal of Education and Psychology in the Community*. **3(2)**: 11-21.

Dickinson, A.R. & Zheng E. (2012). Gifted Babies ?: Asian infants show earlier milestone developments compared to those born in North America. *Proceedings of the XIIth Asia Pacific Conference on Giftedness - July 14-18, 2012*, Dubai, U.A.E.

Printed in Great Britain
by Amazon

27067465R00218